Showing Like a Queen

Showing Like a Queen

Female Authority and Literary Experiment in Spenser, Shakespeare, and Milton

KATHERINE EGGERT

PENN

University of Pennsylvania Press

Philadelphia

10 9 8 7 6 5 4 3 2 1

Published by
University of Pennsylvania Press
Philadelphia, Pennsylvania 19104-4011

Library of Congress Cataloging-in-Publication Data

Eggert, Katherine.
Showing like a queen : female authority and literary experiment in Spenser,
Shakespeare, and Milton / Katherine Eggert.
p.   cm.
Includes bibliographical references and index.
ISBN 0-8122-3532-0 (alk. paper)
1. English literature—Early modern, 1500–1700—History and criticism.   2. Feminism
and literature—Great Britain—History—16th century.   3. Feminism and literature—
Great Britain—History—17th century.   4. Literature, Experimental—Great Britain—
History and criticism.   5. English literature—Male authors—History and criticism.
6. Spenser, Edmund, 1552?–1599—Characters—Queens.   7. Shakespeare, William,
1564–1616—Characters—Queens.   8. Milton, John, 1608–1674—Characters—Queens.
9. Elizabeth I, Queen of England, 1533–1603—Influence.   10. Authority in literature.
11. Queens in literature.   12. Women in literature.   I. Title.
PR428.F45   E44   2000
820.9′00082—dc21   99-046815

In memory of
Elizabeth Bredthauer Eggert

Contents

Note on Texts and Editions

I have retained the original spelling of quotations, modernizing only i/j and u/v, with the exception of quotations from Spenser, where the original i/j and u/v spellings were retained since these sometimes call attention to particular pronunciations, etymologies, and puns.

Quotations from Spenser, Shakespeare, and Milton are, unless otherwise indicated, to the following editions, which are cited parenthetically in the text. Full publication information on these editions is in the bibliography.

For *The Faerie Queene*, I use the Longman edition, edited by A. C. Hamilton. The poem is cited by book, canto, and verse numbers, and Hamilton's editorial matter is cited by page number.

For Shakespeare, I use the New (second) Arden editions, citing the plays by act, scene, and line numbers, and editorial matter by page number.

For Milton's prose, I use the Yale edition of *The Complete Prose Works*, abbreviated *CPW* and cited by volume and page numbers. For Milton's poetry, I use *Complete Poems and Major Prose*, edited by Merritt Y. Hughes. All poems are cited by line number, or by book and line numbers in the case of *Paradise Lost*. The Arguments to *Paradise Lost*, as well as Hughes's editorial matter, are cited by page number.

I

Forms of Queenship

Female Rule and Literary Structure
in the English Renaissance

IF NEARLY TWENTY YEARS of new-historicist studies of early modern England have taught us anything, it is that England's literature from 1558 to 1603 was preoccupied with the anomalous gender of the country's monarch, Elizabeth Tudor. In other words, Elizabethan literature must be regarded as just that, Elizabethan, in ways that earlier critics did not take into account. Stephen Greenblatt's *Renaissance Self-Fashioning* (1980) set the pattern by juxtaposing Elizabethan queenly and literary style, paralleling "Elizabeth's conscious sense of her identity as at least in part a *persona ficta* and her world as a theater" with Edmund Spenser's conscious and unconscious fashionings of his fictive faery realm.[1] Greenblatt's point is that the queen and the poet capitalize upon, even while both help create, a pervasive culture of strategic self-representation. But Louis Montrose's influential work on *A Midsummer Night's Dream*, published in its first version in 1983, goes further than Greenblatt's placement of Elizabeth and Elizabethan literature in the same cultural pool. In Montrose's view—first articulated in his study of Spenser's praise of Elizabeth in *The Shepheardes Calender*'s "Aprill" eclogue[2]—the queen has a uniquely reciprocal and interdependent relationship with the literary productions of her subjects. "[T]he pervasive cultural presence of the Queen," writes Montrose, "was a condition of [*A Midsummer Night's Dream*'s] imaginative possibility. And, in the sense that the royal presence was itself represented within the play, the play appropriated and extended the imaginative possibilities of the queen."[3] More than simply adopting similar representational strategies for similar ends, the queen and the poet-playwright meet within the fictional text, a venue in which each redesigns the representational configurations of the other.

In developing his theory of queenly and literary symbiosis Montrose takes the crucial step of focusing on the queen not only as a model of improvisatorial skill but also as a galvanizing force for a pervasive Elizabethan anxiety about female power, what John Knox in 1558 called "the monstrous regiment of women." Montrose's discussion of *A Midsummer Night's Dream* as a tool for airing and managing this anxiety thus enables critics who follow him to find the queen everywhere, in every figure of either rampaging or squelched female authority: in *Titus Andronicus*'s raped Lavinia, in *1 Henry VI*'s demonic Joan of Arc, and in nearly every female character in *The Faerie Queene* from the victimized Amoret to the Amazon Radigund (to name just a few examples).[4] Moreover, the queen is found manifested in the work of outwardly concentric circles of literary aspirants: from courtly habitues and queenly intimates like Philip Sidney and Walter Ralegh; to writers desirous of courtly recognition and advancement like John Lyly and Edmund Spenser; to playwrights who depended only institutionally on the monarchy, either as an agency of censorship or, conversely, as a benign sponsor and bulwark against theaterphobic church or local government officials. In all these studies, the underlying critical assumption is a vastly enlarged version of Montrose's: sooner or later, in either overt or subtextual form, writers in all literary venues must get around to taking a position vis-à-vis the woman monarch—either obsequious flattery, or misogynistic opposition, or an ambivalent stance somewhere between the two. What Greenblatt would posit, therefore, as a "circulation of social energy" between queen and author gets rechanneled, so to speak, into a different dynamic, one that consists entirely of queenly influence and either authorial resistance or authorial capitulation. This line of thinking also posits that the queen's authority, insofar as it is a specifically *feminine* authority, is represented in this way because it provides an occasion for measuring male authors' scope of influence against hers. (Female authors are generally left out of the equation.) Either by celebrating or by challenging the power of a queen—including challenging her through ironic celebration—a male writer constructs his place somewhere along the spectrum between anxious failed patriarch and unacknowledged legislator of the world.

So far, then, it is clear that critics have thoroughly taken up the first half of Montrose's axiom, that "the pervasive cultural presence of the Queen" conditioned the horizons of "imaginative possibility" not only for the drama, but for all forms of English Renaissance literature. But despite Montrose's emphasis in the second half of his formulation upon literature's reciprocal capacity not only to comment upon but also to *extend* the horizons of queenly power, critics including Montrose himself have not yet adequately addressed the motivations behind Elizabethan literature's ongoing reformulations of female authority. Instead, queenship's relationship to literary production is figured as one of compulsion. In Leonard Tennenhouse's succinct phrasing, "during the Renaissance, political imperatives were also aesthetic imperatives."[5] The phenomenon of a female monarch simply requires male authors to take up the topic of female authority, an issue that although diffusely worrisome throughout the whole of medieval and early modern culture, as numerous historians and literary critics have recently described, might not have acquired such urgency without the focusing impetus of some fifty years of women's rule. I would call this the Mount Everest theory of authorial motivation. Why write about the queen? Because she's there. Further, even the literary medium or mode in which the queen is represented is determined by Elizabeth's own customary modes of self-presentation. The queen throughout her long reign displayed herself to her realm in a theatrical and visually striking fashion; further, she was prone either to use or to disclaim her sex as need be in order to exert her will. As a result, Elizabeth's image has been most often examined in terms of those literary productions that are themselves theatrical, visually striking, and manipulative of sex and gender roles. I am thinking of course not only of the drama, particularly Shakespeare's, but also of the work of Spenser, with its elaborate use of dumb shows, tableaus, processions, paintings, statuary, and other dramatic and visual motifs, and with its speculative and shifty depictions of gender and sexuality.

The kinds of critical work I have been describing have crucially and fundamentally altered what we look for in Elizabethan literature, and I cannot overstate my own debt to and dependence on their insights. But it is time to go further. To posit female authority as *solely* directive, even circumscribing, in this way is in a sense uncritically to reproduce the misogynistic notion, common in the early modern era as well as beyond, that femininity is fundamentally debilitating. "I have the body of a weak and feeble woman," Queen Elizabeth is famously reported to have said to her troops at Tilbury as they prepared for the anticipated invasion of Spain's Armada, "but the heart and stomach of a king." In the prevailing critical mindset an early modern author might paraphrase this statement, "I know I am the subject, and therefore necessarily the depictor, of a queen, but

in my writing I do my best to have the heart and stomach of a man—
even if a man anxious about his being subjected to a woman."[6] Relying,
even unconsciously, on this point of view causes critics to beg the question I posed above: why write about the queen? To look at it somewhat
differently, if a queen's male subject necessarily shapes his own intellectual
productions solely in response to this misogynistic anxiety, then why are
the records of other venues of Elizabethan intellectual accomplishment—
law, music, geography, science, and so on—not similarly deformed by this
anxiety? After all, jurists, composers, mapmakers, and alchemists were just
as likely as poets and dramatists to depend either directly or indirectly on
the queen's approval or patronage for their livelihoods; and one does not
have to go far to demonstrate that their work similarly was concerned
with crown policies.[7] But it is difficult to argue that the influence of the
monarch's gender upon these kinds of efforts was purely a deformative,
hobbling one.

In fact, the opposite may be the case. Take, for example, Elizabethan jurisprudence's most celebrated theory pertaining to queenship, the
doctrine of "the king's two bodies," which can be read as a response to
the debilitating and even destructive effect on the realm of its monarchy's being lodged in an unpredictable and uncontrollable female body.
The sum effect of this legal fiction is that the monarch's body politic not
only subsumes, but also cures, the weaknesses of his or her physical body,
including weakness imparted by female sex. As Edmund Plowden wrote
in his *Reports* of the actions of the crown courts under Elizabeth: "[The
king's] Body politic, which is annexed to his Body natural, takes away the
Imbecility of his Body natural, and draws the Body natural, which is the
lesser, and all the Effects thereof to itself, which is the greater, *quia magis
dignum trahit ad se minus dignum*."[8] Both Elizabeth herself and some of the
anxious males of her realm made use of this paradigm in order to deflect
attention away from her unfortunate femininity and toward the essentially
masculine nature of the monarchical persona—serene, wise, and everlasting. The king's two bodies can, in other words, clear at least a temporary
space for an untrammeled masculinity.[9]

But several considerations force us to revise any notion that the king's
two bodies successfully preserve a masculine monarchy. First, as Susan
Frye points out, Elizabeth herself tended to blur the distinctions between
feminine and masculine, body natural and body politic, with the result
that she invents a new conception of monarchy, "a female body politic."[10]
Hence even for Elizabeth, femininity becomes a source of a creative re-

envisioning of the very nature of rule. Second, this re-envisioning might extend well past the monarchy, going so far as to clear a space for the assertion of extramonarchical will. As Marie Axton details in her book *The Queen's Two Bodies*, the theory of the king's two bodies was in fact used in the courts as a way of frustrating the queen's decisions, not of augmenting a transhistorically masculine monarchical authority. As Axton explains, Plowden—who was the first to articulate this legal principle fully in writing, even though it had been under development since the Middle Ages—was in fact a Roman Catholic and a supporter of Mary, Queen of Scots's claim to the English throne. His intent when he argued in 1561 that "what the King does in his Body politic, cannot be invalidated or frustrated by any Disability in his natural Body" was partly to forestall any attempts Elizabeth might make to exclude the Scots queen from the English succession; such efforts he defined as purely expedient decisions of the body natural, which ought not interfere with the unbroken, sacred line of the body politic.[11] What Plowden undertook, then, was not only a warning to the recently crowned Elizabeth, but also a repudiation of politically motivated decisions by both Henry VIII and Edward VI to exclude certain blood relatives from the succession to the crown.[12] Plowden's seemingly monarchophantic argument in fact clears a space for English courts, not England's ruler, to determine the future of national government. Indeed, it can easily be argued that it was the sixteenth-century debate over the right of women to rule that enabled the suggestion that juridical or Parliamentary or religious leaders should have a say in both royal succession and the exercise of royal power. The Marian exile Christopher Goodman asserted in 1558—the year of Elizabeth I's accession to the throne—that Deuteronomy 17:15, which instructs the Israelites to choose a ruler only from among their "brethren," allows a country to pass over female candidates for the throne in order to find a man more suitable to the job, and hence "to avoyde that monster in nature, and disordre amongest men, whiche is the Empire and governement of a woman."[13] And even a supporter of women's rule like one of the authors of the 1563 edition of *A Mirror for Magistrates* could, at best, only gamely propose that if God saw fit to ordain an innately inept woman as monarch, she would be likely to cede authority to auxiliary, male governmental figures who could step in and set things right: "And as for wysedome and pollicie, seing it consisteth in folowing the counsayl of many godly, learned, & long experienced heades, it were better to have a woman, who consideringe her owne weakenes and inabilitye, shoulde be ruled thereby, than a man which presuming upon his owne fond brayne, wil heare no advise save his owne."[14] Or as Elizabethan clergyman John Aylmer, even while he defends women's rule against John Knox's blast, puts it, "It is not she [i.e., the queen] that ruleth, but the laws."[15] In a very real sense, then, the doctrine of the king's two bodies served not so much to shore up monarchical power by de-sexing it, as to pave the way for the ascent of Parliamentary government.

My point is that Plowden's end run around the queen, though at first it seems debilitating, eventually turns out to be enabling: although legal and political institutions and their personnel must go through extraordinary contortions to accommodate the unfortunate historical fact of women monarchs, the consequence is an unforeseen avenue of liberation for precisely those institutions. In a new study of Shakespeare's early history plays, Nina S. Levine makes a similar argument about Shakespeare and his contemporaries: "The presence of a woman on England's throne . . . proved liberating, allowing them to challenge, and even to reimagine—and to rewrite—traditional dynastic and national myths."[16] These reimaginings ultimately had a very real political effect. By the time of its deposition of Charles I in 1642, Parliament took the extraordinary step of declaring itself the instrument of the king's body politic, so that "what [Parliament does] herein hath the stamp of Royal Authority, although His Majesty . . . do in his own Person oppose or interrupt the same."[17] In short, the development and use of the king's two bodies theory, both in the Elizabethan age and beyond, has an extremely complex history of gender allegiance. Plowden's support for Mary, Queen of Scots, an alternative queen to Elizabeth, ultimately contributes to eroding the legitimacy of monarchy, no matter what its sex. To make matters more complicated, the resulting ascendancy of quasi-republican government marks, in a certain way, a turn toward feminized rule, given that in the view of some, parliamentary governance itself is marked by multiplicity, unruliness, and ever-shifting grounds of authority.

In this book I argue that the same kinds of multiple reformations that queenship induces in political theory and practice can also take shape in literature. Like Falstaff, who in *2 Henry IV* turns his diseases to commodity, Elizabethan and post-Elizabethan writers seize upon the specter of female monarchy not only because it warps the circumstances of their literary moment, but also because such warping—changing accustomed patterns of thought as it does—might become an occasion for an author to restructure that literary moment. In other words, my account takes very seriously Montrose's seminal notion of the "shaping fantasies" of queenship; but I will be taking up the reverse side of previous critical descriptions of how queenship impresses itself upon the form and content of literature concerned with female authority. These "shaping fantasies" also become, in authorial practice, fantasies of literary shape. My contention is that the topic of queenship does not provoke only authorial anxiety; rather, the writers that I consider in this book turn the political "problem" of queenship, either current or remembered, to their advantage by reconstituting it in terms of new poetic and dramatic genres. As opposed to the Mount Everest theory of literary motivation, I propose the Willie Sutton theory. Why write about the queen? Because that is, figuratively, where the money is.[18]

Let me give a brief, condensed example of what I mean. The title of my study is coopted from the order Shakespeare's Cleopatra gives to her ladies-in-waiting as she prepares for death: "Show me, my women, like a queen" (5.2.226). In a clear instance of the reciprocal representational shaping Montrose discusses, the Egyptian queen commands her servants' actions, directing them to clothe her in proper monarchical attire, while at the same time the grandeur of her self-presentation depends upon their success. Indeed, it is her attendant Charmian who has the last word on the dead Cleopatra's carefully crafted persona: she declares to the consternated Roman guard that Cleopatra's suicide was "well done, and fitting for a princess / Descended of so many royal kings" (5.2.325–26). Charmian's final address to her mistress in fact rounds off Cleopatra's life by completing the queen's unfinished last words:

Cleopatra.   What should I stay—[*Dies.*]
Charmian.   In this vile world? So fare thee well.

                                                                    (5.2.313)

We may read Charmian's filling in of Cleopatra's truncated lines as a kind of authorial representation of the queen in either the obsequious flattery mode or the competitive mode outlined above. On the one hand, Charmian shows Cleopatra to the entering Romans as the queen would like to be remembered. On the other hand, Charmian's gesture constitutes one-upmanship of the sort that Susan Frye has so well outlined in Elizabethan courtiers' literary competitions with their own female monarch. But there is a third hand. For a moment, Charmian takes charge of a new form of feminized authority, one that, though inspired by the queen's, is now her own. Its newness is signalled by the Roman guard's confused response to what he sees but does not yet recognize: "What work is here, Charmian? Is this well done?" (5.2.324). Of course, Charmian's appropriation and extension of Cleopatra's scene-making does not last long. As my discussion of *Antony and Cleopatra* in Chapter 5 will detail, it devolves upon the far less imaginative Caesar to assign order and meaning to the deaths of Egyptian women, both queen and servants. But Charmian's "work" adumbrates a strategy for piggybacking on the preconditions set by queenship in order to launch a new, or at least a newly revised, literary enterprise. This book is concerned with just such innovative ventures in Tudor-Stuart England: not so much innovative venues of publishing or presenting literary work, such as the public theater, but rather modes and genres of literary form new to England, and perhaps new anywhere.

This inventiveness of form is closely related to the mixed feelings about England's literary past that marks sixteenth- and seventeenth-century literature. Obsessed as this period was with imitating classical models, English writers nevertheless understood themselves, with both dread and exhilaration, as venturing into uncharted territory. Hence, for example, Philip Sidney's inquiry into "why England, the mother of excellent minds, should be grown so hard a stepmother to poets, who certainly in wit ought to pass all other, since all only proceedeth from their wit, being indeed makers of themselves, not takers of others."[19] We can discern an analogy between literary and monarchical forms in this regard: having no praiseworthy native predecessors save the hopelessly "antique" Chaucer, English writers were forced to make their own way, just as England, alone among its major European rival nations, was forced to conduct its great experiment in female rule. But "being indeed makers of themselves, not takers of others" has its advantages, in literary as well as political terms. As Richard Helgerson has described it, even while writers like Spenser, Jonson, and Milton were engaged in raising their literary vocations to the level occupied by the deific classical authors, their peculiar historical situation found no antecedent match in classical forms: "Virgil had known nothing of Renaissance courtiership or of courtly love; Horace had never written for the public theaters; Demodocus was no literary latecomer in a generation of cavalier poets."[20] Relatively innocent of the postlapsarian "anxiety of influence" that Harold Bloom has attributed to writers who followed Milton, Tudor-Stuart authors could invent new literary forms or combine old ones as the moment suited, up to the point where the familiar labels no longer pertained—or, if applied, sounded as inappropriate as Polonius's "tragical-comical-historical-pastoral."[21] This rethinking of literary form corresponded to a rethinking of when literary history began. As Raphael Falco has detailed in a fascinating study, English writers late in Elizabeth's reign proceeded to "forge" a genealogy that began somewhere around 1580, with Sidney himself posthumously refashioned by his elegists from courtier-soldier into paterfamilias of English literature.[22] From that point dated experiments in genres and modes heretofore untried in England, and undreamt of in ancient Greek and Roman literary philosophy: the history play, the romantic tragedy, the epic-romance.

But my argument concerns more than just analogizing the way two disesteemed necessities, political and literary—queenship and the English language—became mothers of Tudor-Stuart invention. Recent studies in genre criticism assert that new literary forms come about as ways of managing (or, conversely, repressing) historical circumstance.[23] In part, I want to reaffirm this view by similarly asserting that, at significant moments in the trajectory of literature with which I am concerned, *female authority itself* is the leitmotif around which issues of experimentation in literary form emerge and cluster. This contention has to do partly with the widespread Renaissance perception that writing fiction of any sort was an effeminate occupation, and that publishing one's work either on stage or in print particularly lent itself to a destabilized gender and class identity: the writer as prostitute.[24] (I will return to this topic shortly.) But some kinds of fiction are more dangerous in this regard than others. Anticipating Hélène Cixous's and Luce Irigaray's postmodern visions of a feminine language, Renaissance poets and playwrights had definite ideas of which modes of fiction writing especially promoted effeminacy, both of the text itself and, by extension, of its reader. Central to this classification is the notion that femininity was a matter not so much of inhabiting a certain variety of body, as it was an essential state of disorderly being. Even in terms of their physiques, of course, women were thought of as as more unstable than men—colder and wetter in bodily humours, and even likely to suffer their reproductive organs' shifting position inside their bodies.[25] Such corporeal unruliness, however, was not exclusive to women; it could also be communicated across the sexes. It was commonly believed, in accordance with Galenic medical theory, that individual human bodies occupy positions along a continuum from super-masculine to super-feminine, so that a woman might ascend the scale to resemble or even become a man, whereas a man might equally slide downward into femaleness.[26] But more important, in my view—and more productive for literary analysis than attending exclusively to literature's portrayal of human reproductive equipment—

is the fact that femininity, for the Renaissance, is a state of mind: a mind that is similarly disorderly, unstable, unwilling to remain within acceptable bounds or to focus upon acceptable aims.[27]

Modes of literature that promoted this unstable state of mind were thus entirely suspect. Lyric poetry, an unmanly "toy" viewed as at best an exercise for adolescents, threatened to distract its readers from more active, useful pursuits by enrapturing them in lyric loveliness. The romance mode as well was subject to such charges. Not only did it share with much of lyric poetry a concern with heterosexual love, and hence a concern with men in danger of being overcome by women, it also embodied in its very form a kind of triviality and inconclusiveness, qualities that do not lend themselves to masculine ambition.[28] Patricia Parker notes that Sir John Harington, as translator of Ariosto's romance *Orlando Furioso*, worried "that, in becoming 'a translator of Italian toys,' he was wasting his education."[29] Drama as a medium and a form of literary work was also under particular suspicion. Theater's collapsing of genders (men in women's clothing) and of self-identity in general struck critics as a tool for "effeminizing the mind."[30] Responding to such charges, Thomas Nashe proposed the dramatic genre of the history play—an English invention—as a salutary means of reviving male heroes and hence reforming "these degenerate effeminate days of ours." A masculine form grows up around what Nashe calls "our forefathers' valiant acts," pursuits that evidently preclude the influence of the women of lyric or romance—Laura, or Stella, or Angelica.[31]

Lyric, romance, and drama are seen as so dangerous only because their charms are undeniable. Far from successfully reforming feminine into masculine literary form, in fact, the authors with which this book is concerned take, at least on occasion, the opposite tack: they rework masculine forms so that those forms both accommodate femity, and are reshaped by it as an overwhelming force. In the end, these reformations of form turn to positive or at least to startlingly inventive uses the suspicion of an effeminizing fiction. In a recent study, Catherine Gallagher has outlined how women writers of the Restoration seized upon notions of the feminine self as a commodified body—always alienated, dispossessed, indebted to others—as a way of reconceiving authorial labor itself as a process of *exchange*, rather than of *production*. Turning feminine disability into literary strategy, these writers altered prevalent notions of what a fictional self consists of, as well as of what it means to be an author.[32] My sense is that such an inversion is made possible because it is explored in advance, however tentatively and covertly, by the authors I address in this book, each of whom indulges in fantasies of an unmitigatedly feminized literary form.

It may seem strange and even patronizingly sexist to suggest that male authors, and especially the three authors who epitomize the Renaissance literary canon, shape femininity for the future cadre of female writers who are the objects of Gallagher's attention. A book on "female authority and literary experiment" might logically be expected to contain quite a different set of writers, beginning with queens who were themselves writers or literary patrons. And indeed, the literary writings of Queen Elizabeth, along with those of the French queen Marguerite de Navarre, have made their way into the canon in recent years, if inclusion in standard classroom texts like *The Norton Anthology of English Literature* is any indication. The literary efforts of nonroyal women, both aristocrats and others, have also finally begun receiving some richly deserved attention, though some other royal women writers—particularly, in my view, Mary, Queen of Scots, who was a very talented poet—still await serious consideration.[33] But these authors are not the object of my study; nor do I consider, except briefly at the conclusion of this book, the ways in which women writers of the Tudor-Stuart period either did or did not derive literary confidence from the example of women who held political power. My reasons for focusing on Spenser, Shakespeare, and Milton, to the exclusion of other authors in general and women authors in particular, are twofold. First, since my topic is literary innovation, women writers of this period would tend not to fit the bill. For reasons that are too complex to enumerate here but that would richly repay a study of their own, women of the sixteenth and early seventeenth centuries tend to write in literary veins that have already been well worked: Queen Elizabeth, for example, composes relatively predictable Petrarchan love lyrics thirty or forty years after Wyatt and Surrey; Mary Wroth writes a prose romance modeled after her uncle Philip Sidney's *Arcadia*, composed some four decades earlier; and Elizabeth Cary designs her tragedy *Mariam, The Fair Queen of Jewry* along Senecan lines, even while alluding to contemporaries such as Shakespeare who had left such well-worn models behind years before. I do not mean to belittle the literary quality of these pieces; indeed, their very belatedness is an extremely interesting feature, one that can amount to an inventiveness of a very different kind. And it is also the case that the male authors I discuss in this study are also interested in retro forms—Spenser in Chaucerian tales, Shakespeare in revenge tragedy, and Milton in all things Elizabethan.

But they are also on the vanguard, creating new literary modes that in turn will be imitated by others.

Imitation and influence constitute the second reason I have chosen Spenser, Shakespeare, and Milton for this study, rather than other authors (including women authors). Because their influence on other authors—including, in succession, each other—was so immediate and so profound, these writers' experiments in form are central to any study of how authors take up and challenge their predecessors' literary patterns. It is partly because Spenser's extraordinarily influential poem centers national history upon queenship, for example, that Shakespeare's histories, in their attempt to adapt and even supercede *The Faerie Queene* in the medium of drama, also feature authoritative women as makers and breakers of national destiny. Milton, even more ambitious, is engaged in both absorbing and rewriting the entire oeuvres of both Spenser and Shakespeare, even while he attempts topics that these titanic predecessors never dared. If the feminine authorial voice becomes important to English literary history, then, it is in part because these authors, in particular, take it up as a way of making their own way into that literary history.

Because these three writers, unlike the female authors in Gallagher's study of the Restoration and eighteenth century, are working in an era in which the idea of the self as commodity had not yet been consolidated, they imagine the feminized authorial voice along a different axis for constructing the self: the axis of monarch-subject. Along this axis the dialectic of presence and lack that Gallagher notices in the authorial voices of Restoration writers takes shape not as a dialectic between monetary value and worthlessness, or between credit and debt, but rather between command and obedience, in this case the command of a queen over her male subjects. I do not mean to suggest, of course, that Spenser, Shakespeare, or Milton portrays the authorial self as existing *only* in relation to monarchy; this proposition, insofar as it was made (or taken to be made) by early new-historicist studies of Spenser and Shakespeare, has been challenged and revised in recent years, and it would be patently absurd in the case of Milton.[34] Nevertheless, in terms of my topic the nature of the relation between sovereign and subject remains a crucial issue. It is arguably the case that, in a post–Roman Catholic era, English Renaissance writers had little place else to look but to queens—living, historical, or fictional—if they wished to find exempla for how femininity and authority might be conjoined. But as Timothy Hampton points out, the Renaissance use of the exemplum often brings about a kind of productive crisis, given that the exemplary figure often features, along with his or her virtues, qualities that are not so worthy of praise or imitation. For Hampton, this crisis of imitability becomes productive when an author questions the wisdom of modeling present action upon past heroism.[35] In the case of queenship, however, the use of the exemplum becomes radical when an author wholeheartedly *endorses* an identification with the female model because of the very fact of her femininity. Specifically, the conjunction of femininity and authority becomes a site for reconfiguring the hierarchical monarch-subject relation itself. For the authorial voice can escape the very conditions of hierarchy if it imagines itself not solely as *reversing* the circumstances of queenly rule over men, so that a masculine authorial voice might master a formerly feminine literary form, but rather as *inhabiting* the circumstances of queenly rule, so that the authorial voice dwells within and embraces the feminized form, becoming itself a master-mistress of authorial presence.[36]

My argument, then, is that queenship is proposed so often as a model and occasion for English Renaissance literary innovation because feminized authority proves an enabling strategy for negotiating otherwise unmanageable authorial straits—that is, for stretching literary shape in the direction of effeminized form. I am building here on Diana Henderson's study of lyricism in Elizabethan theater, which brilliantly argues that the presence of a female monarch not only encouraged lyric encomia toward the queen herself, but also catalyzed a reformation in lyric form. Once it became associated with a queen, Petrarchan love lyric could be converted into a vehicle for working out extended permutations of the possible associations and/or contradictions between lyric poetry and female power. Concomitantly, lyric becomes a venue for discussing the most serious of political, social, and religious issues, as well as a mode in which female subjectivity may be voiced on the English stage. "Elizabeth," says Henderson, "because of her political power, provided a unique incentive within her culture for reevaluating the feminine."[37] But I am also interested in what happens when this incentive for boosting the eminence of a literary form no longer exists. *Showing Like a Queen* is thus partly an exercise precisely in not engaging the "local readings" of early modern authors that Leah Marcus urges.[38] Whereas one of the "locales" with which Marcus is concerned is the phenomenon of English queenship under Elizabeth, my attention is directed toward the golden world authors attempt to create as an alternative to the brazen world of local circumstance. To test my thesis, the scope of this book extends past the era in which English authors had to contend with the living presence of a female monarch. Spenser died while

Elizabeth Tudor was still queen; Shakespeare's career straddled the reigns
of both Elizabeth and James I; and Milton—though troubled by the influence upon Charles I of his Roman Catholic queen, Henrietta Maria—saw
only male rulers, both kings and Protectors. Nonetheless, the unhinging
of the feminized authorial mode from the actual historical circumstance
of female rule is itself, in large part, the *raison d'être* of my study. For the
work of inhabiting feminized literary form is for the most part an exercise
in fantasy—the fantasy (at times, the nightmare) of a counterpatriarchal
literary world.

Part of that fantasy or nightmare involves nostalgia, a ready and easy
means of conceiving of alternatives to the present moment. Not coinci-
dentally, as I address in Chapter 5, nostalgia is an ailment of early modern
inception; only in the Renaissance can people begin to imagine such a radical, heartrending disjunction between their present circumstances and the
Heimat they have left behind. For both Elizabethan and post-Elizabethan
authors, the disjunction between female and male monarchy—one present,
the other gone by—can provide an especially powerful occasion and model
for reinventing literary form in the way that I have just described. Whether
queenship constitutes the horrible, degraded innovation of the present
moment or the sweetly remembered security of the past, it establishes
through counterposition the possibility of another mode of shaping the
basic conditions of existence. Depending on their specific moments of
production, the literary works I address in this book engage in nostalgia
either for a king or a queen; but in either case, the political "problem" of
queenship, either current or remembered, is turned to literary advantage.
In Chapters 2 through 5 of this book I trace a historical and literary micro-
history of two decades, 1590–1613, in which Spenser and Shakespeare mull
over the politics of female rule in the waning and aftermath of Elizabeth's
reign, devising literary stratagems around representing—or recollecting—
those historically anomalous political arrangements. My leap forward in
Chapter 6 to Milton, then, is intended to test my thesis by establishing that Spenser's and Shakespeare's seventeenth-century legacy remained
intertwined with the fortunes of feminine authority. Even after more than
sixty years of restored male rule, Milton experiments with deriving literary
form from the formulae of queenship.

Spenser's *Faerie Queene*, generally treated as the culmination of literary treatments of the cult of Elizabeth, thus becomes here a precursory
and foundational text. In *The Faerie Queene* Spenser tests strategies for
being not only troubled but also gratified by the prospect of hanging an

ambitious and innovative literary project upon techniques associated with effeminized writing. As the long process of its composition and publication proceeds through the last two decades of the sixteenth century and the first decade of the seventeenth, *The Faerie Queene* poses with increasing insistence the question of how new modes of literary design can be accomplished in response to feminine authority. It will be clear how indebted I am to Montrose's seminal studies of Spenser's *Shepheardes Calender*, mentioned above, and their treatment of Spenser's anxiety-ridden fashioning of his queen into an appropriate object for poetry.[39] My sense, though, is that in *The Faerie Queene* Spenser's gender-inflected anxiety about writing an epic to and about a queen bears fruit not only in fulsome praise and/or savage recriminations toward figures of feminine authority in the poem, but also in stunning revisions of and departures from Spenser's primary poetic models, the classical epic and the Italian romance. Even as *The Faerie Queene* seeds the careers of its most prominent heroines and antiheroines with allusions to Elizabeth Tudor and to Scotland's Mary Stuart, the poem continuously renegotiates its alliances to "feminine" modes of poetic writing as it alternatively embraces and abandons those characters. In Book 3, for example, the poem diverges from heroic epic into a more digressive genre, the epic-romance, even as it begins to associate poetic power with the feminine power of Elizabeth's many doubles in the poem, including Britomart and Gloriana. Spenser's link is "ravishment," a quality he ascribes both to seductive poetry and to powerful female characters who seize men's senses and suspend epic action. My study of *The Faerie Queene* traces how the poem's celebration of queenly and poetic ravishment in Books 3 and 4 prompts other, more reactionary generic experiments as the poem progresses—including historical allegory (Book 5), courtly pastoral (Book 6), and mythopoetics (the Mutability Cantos). All of these post-ravishment flights into new poetic modes, I contend, are designed to close off the feminine poetics Spenser himself had earlier proposed.

In some ways, Spenser's magnum opus raises as a matter of literary form the same proposition advanced by the execution of Mary, Queen of Scots in 1587, an incident much on England's mind in the 1590s, and one thinly allegorized in Book 5 of *The Faerie Queene*. The Queen of Scots's demise, the first legally enacted trial and sentencing to death of a European monarch, came about in part because of what was seen as her particularly feminine waywardness; Mary's political machinations to acquire the English throne, like her conduct before she was deposed in 1567 from the throne of Scotland, generally involved her plans to marry a prominent lord of her own choosing.[40] Ridding England of the threat of the "Scottish whore" proved a politically tricky business, then, since its precedent might justify deposing Elizabeth, herself called a whore by her detractors.[41] Furthermore, in the same way that Plowden's doctrine of the king's two bodies distinguished the will of the courts from the will of the queen, Mary's trial and execution disjoined the authority of the law, as well as the authority of Elizabeth's own advisors, from the authority of a divinely ordained monarch—a station from which Mary was never demoted in either Scotland or England, even while the English authorities were branding her an adulteress, murderess, and traitor.[42] Killing the queen, even if not their own queen, thus put England in something of a quandary. The queen's rule, as it turned out, might indeed be not only altered, but ended by force of law: that is, by a form of rule finally superior to that of the monarchy. But what would that nascent form of rule look like, once given free rein? The solution to that problem was, of course, to occupy English Parliamentary politics for much of the next century after Elizabeth's death. Similarly, Spenser's epic, I argue, ostentatiously repeals feminine rule in its closing books by successively dethroning the Amazon queen Radigund, the female knight Britomart, the titaness Mutabilitie, and even Queen Elizabeth herself. But what kind of poetry comes to fill this void left by departed queenship? How might poetic authority be conceived as something other than feminized? Spenser's breathtakingly swift transformations of poetic modes in the second half of *The Faerie Queene* play like a number of musical variations upon this question.

In the central chapters of this book I turn to Shakespeare, who, even more attuned to historical specifics than Spenser, either invents or transforms dramatic genres to accommodate and reshape topical issues uniquely associated with a feminine monarchy. First staged in the same decade, the 1590s, in which Books 1 through 6 of *The Faerie Queene* were published, Shakespeare's two tetralogies of history plays—the *Henry VI* plays and *Richard III*; and *Richard II*, *1* and *2 Henry IV*, and *Henry V*—were experiments in crafting and refining a new English dramatic genre. The range of these plays becomes a venue in which Shakespeare works out, even to the point of literary exhaustion, the possibilities for this genre. In particular, the fledgling playwright employs the history form to probe whether and how the stage might wish to attach its fortunes to the fortunes of the monarchy—necessarily, a feminine monarchy. National desire for heroic action in these two tetralogies repeatedly confronts the obstacle of a feminine or feminized authority: the witch, Joan of Arc, in *1 Henry VI*; the effeminate French in *Henry V*; even the slippery, smooth-tongued Machiavel, Richard III. Shakespeare's reiteration of this theme reflects several national dilemmas surrounding England's queen in the 1590s, in particular, whether her feminine weakness was inhibiting potential military triumph in Ireland and on the Continent, and whether her failure to produce or name an heir had hopelessly blocked English hopes for a glorious national future. But my concern is also to investigate how these feminine obstacles enable an inquiry into the gendered nature of dramatic genre. As the history plays progress, they increasingly imagine a heroic world untrammeled by femininity. But can masculine heroism give shape to a compelling and versatile dramatic form? Should the stage adopt a solely masculine authority for its own?

The history plays eventually follow the pattern of the second half of *The Faerie Queene* in hinging literary innovation upon the exclusion of feminine rule. My sense, though, is that by the close of the second tetralogy in *Henry V* (1599), Shakespeare's theater deems this experiment unwise, a kind of dead end of limited dramatic action and affect. For proof I turn to a play that followed hard upon *Henry V*: *Hamlet*, itself a revision of the hoary genre of the revenge tragedy. Though most obviously a rumination on how and why male authority figures, kings and fathers, meet their ends, *Hamlet* in my view is also a rumination on the impending death of a queen. In this case, the historic problem of the queen's participation in royal succession—a question particularly at issue at the time of the play's writing, just two or three years before Elizabeth's death in 1603—is redesigned into not only a meditation on troubled psychic relations between mother and son, but also an innovative revision of conventional dramatic revenge. For it is the existence of queenly will, Gertrude's voluntary transfer of affection from Hamlet's father to Hamlet's uncle Claudius, that sets the conditions for *Hamlet*'s peculiar form: an ostensible revenge tragedy in which a woman's wayward actions seem to impel heroic male retaliation, but at the same time distract and enervate it. *Hamlet*'s most celebrated dramatic innovation, the transformation of the revenger's mindless murderousness into Hamlet's fraught, psychologized delay, is thus predicated upon a queen's rule over Hamlet as subject. And, if recent critics are correct in positing *Hamlet* as a pivotal depiction of the formation of modern subjectivity, then that subjectivity too can come into being only under the authority of a queen.

As it does with so many other issues, therefore, *Hamlet* pulls two ways in regard to queenship. On the one hand, feminine authority has enabled, if not instigated, all of Hamlet's sociopolitical dilemmas and psychic pain; but on the other hand, those dilemmas and that pain become the stuff of a bold and influential experiment in dramatic form. Though one would never identify Prince Hamlet himself as nostalgic for queenship, the dramatic piece *Hamlet* derives its power in part from Hamlet's being forced to live under the conditions of female rule against which he protests. From *Hamlet* I thus turn to two post-Elizabethan Shakespearean experiments in dramatic form: *Antony and Cleopatra* (ca. 1607) and *The Winter's Tale* (1611), each of which stretches the equation between the rule of women and innovative play-crafting into an audacious and ultimately haunting metaphysics of the theater itself. After Queen Elizabeth died in 1603, Shakespeare reversed the history plays' nostalgia for unimpeded masculine authority into an appropriately Jacobean nostalgia for female rule—nostalgia that corresponds to the passing of a dramatic age, as well. *Antony and Cleopatra*, an experiment in "feminine" tragedy, not only proposes that queenly eroticism and instability constitute theatricality itself, but also compels an audience to desire the belated queen rather than the incoming Caesar. And as if commenting upon the power of the theater of queenship that *Antony and Cleopatra* sustains, *The Winter's Tale* elevates nostalgia for female rule to the level of magic, of raising the dead, memorialized queen from stone into life.

At the same time, however, *The Winter's Tale* reveals the potential masculine bad faith behind mourning the queen. Even while this late Shakespearean play, like *Antony and Cleopatra*, laments the fact that feminized theatricality, in all its vast potential, must be closed off, *The Winter's Tale* also reveals such circumscription to be normative in a post-gynecocratic age. Indeed, *The Winter's Tale*, in Shakespeare's variation upon the new Jacobean genre of tragicomedy and its intermingling of recovery and loss, makes the survival of masculine governance contingent upon its indulging in nostalgia for a departed queen. That masculine governance, I shall argue, turns out to be dramatic as well as monarchical and dynastic, as the very conclusion of the play deposes the remarkable feminine dramaturgy of the dead queen Hermione's vocal female mourner, Paulina, in favor of King Leontes's capacity to order tale-telling and narrative renewal.

This masculine capacity to narrate past and even future action in the absence of a willful woman is one of the cornerstones of *Paradise Lost*'s strategies for controlling, while coopting, that woman's will. The last chapter of this book turns to Milton as a way of exploring both the historical and the literary repercussions of Spenser's and Shakespeare's experiments with feminine authority. Elizabethan and Jacobean responses to queenship recirculate, in the 1630s through the 1670s, in the terms of Milton's inter-related polemics over the fate of monarchy and the ideal form of poetry. As I noted above in connection with the execution of Mary, Queen of Scots, the sixteenth-century debate over feminine rule's legitimacy becomes, in the seventeenth century, a radical questioning of monarchy's very existence; this questioning, in turn, resurfaces in Milton's own depictions of feminine authority. Taken together, Milton's divorce tracts (1643–45) and antimonarchical pamphlets (1640s and 1650s) parallel discarding an unsuitable wife with dethroning an unfit monarch—a monarch who, though a king, is described in feminized terms. As a result, while *Paradise Lost*'s unsavory misogyny toward Eve is in part a matter of controlling women in the domestic arena, it also has to do with the decades-old question of how to control a queen, and how to erect, in the place of a feminine monarchy, a Miltonic government of men privileged by their talent, education, and religion, rather than by their blood.

Simultaneously, however, Milton derives a certain kind of virtue from remembering the era of queenship: the virtue of virginity, which in the *Mask Presented at Ludlow Castle* signifies the capacity to resist unjust authority by means of inviolable self-rule. Hence, *Paradise Lost*'s engagements with the nature of human will, I argue, also are engaged with Milton's reminiscences of female monarchy—in this case, reminiscences of the advantages the model of female monarchy might suggest. Further, *Paradise Lost* is a literary experiment that derives from feminine authority in that it not only revives, in Eve, the perceived dangers of Elizabeth Tudor's or Mary, Queen of Scots's self-willed rule, but also revisits Spenser's and Shakespeare's enabling associations of feminine authority with the genres of romance, of tragedy, and of tragicomedy, genres with which Milton's epic both disputes and colludes. In many ways, Eve's willfulness is also the will of the poem, the engine of open-ended action that replaces both the deluded, self-defeating heroism of Satan's reworkings of epic, and the foregone tragic conclusions of God's oddly crabbed divine dispensation. Insofar as Adam follows rather than leads Eve, he participates simultaneously in a Spenserian willingness to be ravished by the queen and by lush poetry; in a Hamletesque capacity for suspending action in favor of self-examination; in a Cleopatran ability to spin out endless scenarios for alternative realities; and in a Leontes-like real, if brief, desire to hear his revived queen speak what she will. In this way, the literary shape of Milton's poem runs against the grain of his prose tracts' politics, which amalgamate a supposedly enlightened republicanism with the subjection of a queen into, as Shakespeare's Cleopatra puts it, "no more but e'en a woman."

It is this tension between historical circumstance and literary form with which this book is, finally, most concerned. My sense is that reviving "old" questions of when and how literary genres are invented can usefully broaden, as well as challenge, recent work on the relation between English Renaissance literature and the monarchy. Whereas my predecessor critics have *noticed* that literary works puzzle out the ambiguities of feminine authority, I wish to *explain* what literary advantages might accrue from such a focus. I do so, however, not to reconstruct in retrograde fashion the old-historicist image of the author supremely in command of the "historical background" his or her times provide to the writing of literature. Rather, I want to extend Montrose's insight regarding the reciprocal relation between culture and the literary work it informs, in order to articulate the reciprocal relation between culture and the very form of that literary work. The author, in this case, is neither entirely the product of his or her culture nor entirely the producer of new literary modes; rather, he or she exists as the mediator between the two, as that intelligence that employs each to test, protest, stretch, and/or revel in the accepted boundaries of the other. The disruptions of social and political hierarchy initiated by queenship become the occasion for major literary innovations, which in turn set new limits for what might be attempted in drama and poetry.

In a broad sense, then, my aim in this book is to marry a new-historicist account of literature as a cultural form to a literary-historical account of the succession of texts. More particularly, my intent is to account for the microcosmic shifts in attitudes toward feminine authority within a literary work, or within a series of works like Shakespeare's history plays. While such shifts are explicable partly in terms of the complex array of responses toward queenship that are always available in Elizabethan and post-Elizabethan England, they also come about as spur-of-the-moment strategies for handling the shaping of any number of transitory but tricky literary moments. To the new–historicist description of the Renaissance author as engaging in as well as submitting to improvisations of power, I thus want to add my description of the Renaissance text itself as improvisatory, shape-shifting, and in flux. As Nancy Armstrong and Leonard Tennenhouse put it, the course of any narrative is an important object of study because narrative itself consists of "the traces of the labor that went into organizing various materials, representations, representations of representations, into a reproducible and consumable body of knowledge that [can] be converted into speech."[43] I am interested in those narrative moments in which the labor of representing female authority manifests itself, not just in anxiety and bitter toil, but also in stunning craft. In this way, issues surrounding feminine authority are most enabling for Renaissance writers precisely when they are not fully articulated and delimited within the literary text either as predictable characterizations of queens or as pressing, extraliterary historical events. Rather, the historical circumstance undergoes, as in Ariel's song, a kind of sea-change within the text, becoming something "rich and strange" as the text absorbs it and reconfigures itself in response. I have in mind a version of what Harry Berger describes as the dialectical relation between "page and stage" in Shakespeare's plays. Appropriating Berger's terms regarding Shakespeare's treatment of theatricality, I would argue that the literary works with which this book is concerned "textualize" both the anxiety-producing and the liberating circumstances of feminine authority that surround or precede them. It is only when those circumstances are "*de*textualized"—that is, "[d]isplac[ed] . . . to the local habitation of theatrical and narrative circumstances"—that they "impos[e] a kind of ideological closure on the semiotic power of the text."[44] Displacing all the possibilities and contingencies of feminine authority merely onto the prosaic activities of female characters, as Spenser, Shakespeare, and Milton at times do, "detextualizes" and hence closes off the alternative strategy of these texts, which is to retain femininity, in all its frightening open-endedness, as a strategy of literary endeavor.

Female authority counts so strongly as a touchstone for such improvisations because Renaissance culture viewed women, usually with great suspicion, as inherently changeable and hence unreliable.[45] As the anonymous 1560 tract entitled *The deceyte of women, to the instruction and ensample of all men, yonge and old* puts it, "Now beholde, what myschyefe, what marvayles and what folyshnes that the false and subtil women can brynge to passe, yea that semeth unpossyble for to be, that can they doo and brynge to passe."[46] That mischief, those marvels, and that foolishness—all "that semeth unpossyble for to be"—translates into Spenser's, Shakespeare's, and Milton's examinations of their own capacities for marvelous, unanticipated literary innovation.

2

Genre and the Repeal of Queenship in Spenser's *Faerie Queene*

TO BEGIN HIS DISCUSSION of the allegory of *The Faerie Queene*'s Book 5, the great Spenser scholar A. C. Hamilton voices the private opinion of even the most enthusiastic of Spenser admirers. "Spenser's fiction seems to break down in Book 5," says Hamilton. "Probably for this reason the book is the least popular." A few pages later, however, Hamilton slightly revises his assessment of what happens to the poem's fiction in Spenser's Legend of Justice. It is not that the fiction has broken down, like some neglected machine in the garden, but that the fiction has been suppressed and restricted by Book 5's adherence to a nonfictional point of reference: "Throughout Book 5 the reader is aware of fact pressing down upon the fiction."[1] As it turns out, "fact" for Hamilton, as for most readers, exerts its greatest pressure not on the whole of Book 5, but rather on the last five cantos, where the poem turns for the first time into a series of barely allegorized events in English history of the 1580s and 1590s: the defeat of the Souldan (read England's defeat of Spain's Philip II and his Armada); the trial of Duessa (Mary, Queen of Scots); Arthur's liberation of Belge (England's liberation of Belgium from Spain); Burbon's fight for Flourdelis (Henri of Navarre's fight for the French crown); and Artegall's rescue of Irena and subsequent slander by the Blatant Beast (the adventures of Spenser's patron in Ireland, Lord Grey). One of the most difficult tasks for critics attempting a traditional explication of Book 5's allegory has been to prove Hamilton wrong, and to demonstrate that even if fact seems to subsume fiction in these episodes, the reverse is actually the case, and history remains in the service of mythmaking and idealization.[2] The trouble comes in contradicting centuries of readers' first and even second impressions to argue that what looks like mere fact is not mere fact, that history does not press down on fiction, but liberates it.

Of course "fact" in Spenser has, since Hamilton's complaint, enjoyed something of a critical renaissance. Insofar as Cantos 8 through 12 of Book 5 engage recent events, and especially in their interplay with the repressive and violent colonialist policies advocated in Spenser's *View of the Present State of Ireland*, they have recently attracted historicist commentary.[3] At the same time, the episode of Book 5 featured just before the poem's turn to fact has increasingly drawn the attention of feminist critics—not because fiction is repressed, but because feminine authority is repressed. In this episode Britomart, the female knight who has been the intermittent focus of *The Faerie Queene* since the beginning of Book 3, rescues her fiancé Artegall by decapitating his captor, the Amazon queen Radigund. Britomart then rules Radigund's city-state for a time only to turn sovereignty over to Artegall.[4] But little work has been done in either the new-historicist or the feminist mode to bridge the gap between the central and final sections of Book 5, to describe the killing of the Amazon queen and the turn to historical allegory as parts or versions of the same process or impulse.[5] The discontinuous structure of Book 5—its sudden, unexplained, and unsatisfying shift in mode from fiction to fact—is replicated by a criticism that takes up Book 5 only in piecemeal fashion.

In my view, neither the traditionalist desire to paper over Book 5's structural shift nor the current tendency to treat Book 5 merely episodically does justice to a Book whose concern is, from the beginning, transformations of *kind*. In fact, this portion of *The Faerie Queene* uniquely meditates upon what kinds of form are appropriate to latter-day poetry. The Proem to Book 5 not only dolefully announces that "the world . . . being once amisse growes daily wourse and wourse" (5.Pr.1), but also thinks of that decay in terms of materials once, but no longer, put to use:

> And men themselues, the which at first were framed
> Of earthly mould, and form'd of flesh and bone,
> Are now transformed into hardest stone:
> Such as behind their backs (so backward bred)
> Were throwne by *Pyrrha* and *Deucalione*:
> And if then those may any worse be red,
> They into that ere long will be degendered.

(5.Pr.2)

Breeding backward is the problem, but it is also the solution. If humans have degenerated rather than evolved in kind, then a heroic poem must look backward for models and materials of literary types: "I doe not forme them to the common line / Of present dayes, which are corrupted sore" (5.Pr.3). But Spenser's chronology deserves some examination here. In the second installment of *The Faerie Queene*—Books 4–6, first published in 1596—the "present day" of the poem, the moment in which "form" has become so corrupt, has already been identified as the present *in which the poem is invented*, and in which the poem is therefore complicit. In the Proem to Book 4, a disapproving figure named only as the "rugged forehead" but usually identified as Queen Elizabeth's Secretary, Lord Burghley, rebukes the poetic mode of the 1590 installment of the poem, Books 1–3. "My looser rimes (I wote) [he] doth sharply wite, / For praising loue, as *I haue done of late*" (4.Pr.1, my emphasis). In light of the rugged forehead's attack, Book 5's notoriously "tight" structure—especially, and especially in its last five cantos, its dispensing with the lush or knotty language, the odd twists of plot and identity beloved of Spenserians—seems a response to the "looseness" that *The Faerie Queene* has continued to perpetuate throughout its immediate precursor Books 3 and 4. Book 5 begins with the degeneration of form through history, but that history turns out to be the history not only of humankind, but of the poem's production.

In this chapter I wish to analyze the structure of *The Faerie Queene* in light of the unpopular form to which Book 5 turns. By using the word "degendered" rather than "degenerated" to describe the sorry pass to which form has and will come, Book 5's Proem again casts the problem of form into the terms that were previously provoked by the languorous verse of the witch Acrasia's bower in Book 2: the problem of feminine authority.[6] At the same time, the stony men of Book 5's Proem look forward to Artegall's subjection to Radigund, hinting that the knights of Book 5, like Acrasia's thralls, might demonstrate Freud's Medusa effect, where men are no longer men because they are "degendered" stones, castrated by the phallic woman.[7] By the 1611 folio of Spenser's complete works, "degendered" in this stanza becomes the more purely francophonic "degenered," a substitution that encourages us to make a more explicit connection between the end of feminine rule showcased in Book 5 and the shift in literary form that immediately follows. To reverse the effect of men becoming "degendered," enthralled by the witch, the Medusa, or the Amazon, *The Faerie Queene* must confront the perception that the poem itself has become "degenered," debased in literary kind from its purportedly original epic intent. Book 5's repeal of feminine authority becomes both the motivation and the prerequisite for its turn toward the bleak new genre of historical allegory. If, as Fredric Jameson has contended, innovations in literary genre come about to address potentially discomfiting changes in politics and socioeconomics, then we should not be surprised that, in this most self-conscious of poems, a shift in genre is baldly signalled by a shift in the gender of political regime.[8] Britomart's returning the Amazons "to mens subiection" in the middle of Book 5 is an accomplishment labelled as "changing all that forme of common weale" (5.7.42); immediately thereafter, *The Faerie Queene* itself "changes all that form."

The genre in question for Jameson is romance, which he argues expresses a nostalgia for "an organic social order in the process of penetration and subversion, reorganization and rationalization, by nascent capitalism."[9] But as Harry Berger reminds us, with *The Faerie Queene* matters of form are more complicated. If Spenser's poem expresses nostalgia for an earlier order, it does so with a canny awareness of the uses to which nostalgia can be put.[10] As it turns out, romance in the poem is not itself a nostalgic mode, but rather an experimental mode that *induces* nostalgia—the poem's own display of nostalgia for a genre it occupied before, and other than, romance. In *The Faerie Queene*, the "penetration and subversion" of order are laid explicitly at the feet not of Jameson's nascent capitalism, but rather of authoritative women.[11] And implicitly, as Patricia Parker has demonstrated, order's penetration and subversion are laid at the feet of the genre of romance, which in Books 3 through 5 of the poem is intimately associated with those authoritative female figures and their characteristic modes of thought and action. Parker identifies romance and its failure to close off narrative as the foremost source of tension in *The Faerie Queene*;[12] more recently, in a reading of Book 2 of the poem, she has identified that failure of closure with the enchantress Acrasia's (and by extension any powerful woman's) ability to "suspend male instruments," holding men in thrall. Guyon's destruction of Acrasia's Bower of Bliss at the end of Book 2, then, has the effect of restoring narrative progress: "In Spenser, the 'suspended instruments' of Acrasia's male captives are recovered as the Bower itself is overcome, and as Guyon and his Mosaic guide move forward to the narrative 'point' or end of a Book of the Governor in which both a threatening female ruler and her suspect lyricism are finally mastered and surpassed."[13] The genre of romance, the beauty of lush poetry, the power of a queen: all three elements that make the Bower so dangerously seductive are cancelled in Guyon's immoderate rampage

toward conclusions.[14] But, as many critics have noticed and as I shall reiterate below, all three of these elements reemerge in Book 3, hold sway
in Book 4, and linger stubbornly into the central cantos of Book 5. It is
therefore Book 5's turn toward history, not romance, that carries the force
of nostalgia: nostalgia for Guyon's antiromantic narrative thrust, which
managed in its "rigour pittilesse" to conquer the effeminacy induced by
both a desiring queen and an arrested, uncloseable poetics (2.12.83).

What I mean to illuminate in this chapter is one reason for the range
and malleability of *The Faerie Queene*'s literary strategies. No one can say
what genre, if any, Spenser originally intended his long poem most to resemble; the "Letter to Ralegh" appended to the 1590 edition of Books 1–3
of the poem employs only the terms "allegory" and "history" by way of explanation of the work. And it is certainly the case that Spenser is engaged
in synthesizing, in encyclopedic fashion, any number of literary forms
inherited from the classical, Christian, continental, and native English traditions. But the Letter's invocations of Homer, Virgil, Ariosto, and Tasso
place *The Faerie Queene* in the midst of Renaissance debates over the epic
versus the romance—as does the use of the term "allegory" itself, as John
Watkins points out by quoting Sir Richard Blackmore, a seventeenth-
century reader of the poem who uses "allegory" in place of the term
"romance" to describe *The Faerie Queene*'s erratic narrative motions: "But
Ariosto and *Spencer* . . . are hurried on with a *boundless, impetuous* Fancy over
Hill and Dale, till they are both lost in a Wood of Allegories,—Allegories
so *wild, unnatural*, and *extravagant*, as greatly displease the Reader."[15] Despite Richard Helgerson's undoubtedly true contention that *The Faerie
Queene*—both on the face of it and in its rejecting Tasso's ultimate preference of public virtue over private love pursuits—entirely adheres to the
genre of "Gothic" romance, within Spenser's poem we may discern a certain guilt about poetic overreliance on this unmasculine form.[16] David
Quint demonstrates that the opposition of epic to romance is one that,
beginning with Virgil, is one generated internally from the perspective
of epic itself: "To the victors [in the *Aeneid*] belongs epic, with its linear teleology; to the losers belongs romance, with its random or circular
wandering."[17] Hence each western epic subsequent to Virgil carries on a
debate concerning which perspective—the winners' or the losers' perspective, epic or romance—the poem is going to embrace most fully.

For "winners" and "losers" we might easily substitute, at least in the
normative terms of Renaissance ideology, "masculine" and "feminine."[18]
Watkins's analysis of the 1590 *Faerie Queene* suggests that the *topos* of the

abandoned woman is key to understanding how Spenser, from moment to moment and canto to canto in the poem, is either stigmatizing or recuperating Ariostan romance, signified by its associations with femininity. Concluding as he does with Book 3 of the poem, Watkins is able to establish that Spenser by that point in the poem "transcends the debate over the compatibility of romance and epic conventions by defining epic as a genre foregrounding confrontations between antithetical influences."[19] My concern, however, is with what happens as *The Faerie Queene*, appearing in further installments in 1596 and 1609, is forced to reconsider this syncretism, as the poem fully faces up to what it would mean for epic poetry not to abandon femininity, but rather, like the ideal chivalric romance hero, to champion it.

Female Will and Feminine Poetics in the Legends of Chastity and of Friendship

My first task, then, is to track the history of the alliances between poetry and femininity proposed in Books 3 and 4, alliances that eventually necessitate Book 5's generic shifts. Because Book 5's attachment to history arises just as soon as its attachment to Britomart ends, it is worth remembering that Britomart's entry into *The Faerie Queene* came hard upon the heels of a gap in history. Near the end of Book 2, Arthur in the castle of Alma finds himself reading a chronicle of Britain, a chronicle that ends just after the entry of Uther Pendragon, Arthur's father (2.10.68). Of course Arthur's name cannot be added to the chronicle because, in the time scheme of *The Faerie Queene*, he has not yet embarked upon the sequence of events that will lead him to the throne. Nevertheless, as Elizabeth Bellamy has pointed out, the chronicle's abrupt ending reveals that Arthur himself exists in an arrested moment, in a state of history that is not yet.[20] Britomart's adventures, which commence as Book 2 ends and which inaugurate the poem's fullest experiment with the genre of Ariostan romance, therefore come to occupy two contradictory pauses in narrative as Book 2 draws to its close. Guyon's successful netting of Acrasia, which closes off Book 2, seems, as I asserted above, also to foreclose upon the feminine poetics that Acrasia promulgated. But Arthur's hesitation on the brink of his future has the opposite effect: it suspends the teleology of certain ends that the telling of history might afford, and hence encourages a digression into the romantic mode.

Furthermore, Book 3 of the poem begins by taking the radical step of associating poetic power with feminine power—no matter how emasculating that power might be, no matter how it may dismay, rather than fashion, a gentleman. This extraordinary proposition is first voiced in Book 3's Proem. At first, this Proem worries that the feminine nature of its queenly subject, Elizabeth, might dissolve artistic achievement. After the narrative voice issues a caveat that "liuing art may not least part [of Elizabeth's chastity] expresse," it goes on to phrase these protestations of artistic failure in terms of sexual impotence. Even Zeuxis or Praxiteles would fall short of bringing this portrait to climax: "His daedale hand would faile, and greatly faint, / And her perfections with his error taint" (3.Pr.2). At this point the narrative voice attempts to recuperate potency for a masculine poetic enterprise by enacting certain revisions in this gendered scenario. Initially, the painter's hand "tainting" the perfections of his chaste model suggests a leading tangent that is developed further in succeeding lines:

> Ne Poets wit, that passeth Painter farre
> In picturing the parts of beautie daint,
> So hard a workmanship aduenture darre,
> For fear through want of words her excellence to marre.
>
> (3.Pr.2)

If "marring" the queen, like "tainting" her, amounts to ruining her, then these disclaimers actually advance an author's ability to overpower the queen through rapine misrepresentation. This language becomes even stronger a few cantos later in Book 3, when the narrative voice proclaims his desire to "Endite [the queen] . . . as dewtie doth excite; / But ah my rimes too rude and rugged arre, / . . . And striuing, fit to make, I feare do marre" (3.2.3). Even *not* portraying the queen adequately promises a certain masculine authorial power. "Excited" by "dewtie" (suggestively spelled to imply a kind of sexual moistness), the harsh consonants of the narrator's "rude and rugged rimes" culminate in the reiterated "marring" of his high object. In short, aesthetic failure is posed as phallic success.

Obviously, though, it is more to poetry's advantage to seduce its royal reader's sensibilities than to offend them. And shortly Book 3's Proem moves to rescind this rather improbable notion of triumphant poetic failure, when it describes the "ravishing" power of Walter Ralegh's poetic expression of unrequited desire for his queen's favors, "The Ocean to Cynthia":

But if in liuing colours, and right hew,
    Your selfe you couet to see pictured,
    Who can it doe more liuely, or more trew,
    Then that sweet verse, with *Nectar* sprinckeled,
    In which a gracious seruant pictured
    His *Cynthia*, his heauens fairest light?
    That with his melting sweetnesse rauished,
    And with the wonder of her beames bright,
My senses lulled are in slomber of delight.

(3.Pr.4)

The dangling "that" clause of this stanza's line 7—"That which his melting
sweetness rauished"—initially makes it possible that Cynthia of line 6, and
not the reader of line 9, is the one ravished by the poem. Yet Ralegh's verse
ravishes by means of its "melting sweetnesse," a phrase that makes poetry
a liquid and hence potentially feminized medium. The ravished receptor
of that sweetness turns out to be not Cynthia at all, but instead the presumably male possessor of the "senses" in line 9 that "lulled are in slomber
of delight." Feminized by a poetry that itself is feminine, Ralegh's reader
rests passively in delightful "slomber."

Book 3 here seems willingly to model itself after those moments in
Books 1 and 2 that are most dangerous to the masculine integrity of both
the knights within the poem and the male reader of the poem: those moments at which poetry becomes its most lush and enchanting exactly when
it depicts an authoritative, seductive female and her hapless victim. If
Spenser's poem is ravishing in this way—if it charms, but does not rightly
move—then it will have failed in the poetic purpose Spenser outlined in
the "Letter to Ralegh": to "fashion a gentleman or noble person in vertuous and gentle discipline" (p. 737). But Books 1 and 2 periodically veer
toward precisely this association between bewitching poetry and emasculating female power during their various scenes of seduction—Acrasia
unmanning Verdant in her bower (2.12.76–80), Duessa pleasuring and en-
feebling Redcrosse at the fountain (1.7.3–7), false Una seducing Redcrosse
in his dream (1.1.47–48). Book 3's substantial investment of both moral
virtue and poetic narrative in its female knight, Britomart, hence raises
the stakes of assigning gender to poetic success. At first glance, Britomart
seems to endanger masculine poetics as much as do the enchantresses of
Books 1 and 2. She derails the progress of male knights, including heroes

like Guyon, both by literally disarming them and by astounding and mes-
merizing those who look on her visage—a castratingly Medusan sight that
"discomfits" onlookers in Malecasta's castle (3.1.43) and "fixes" eyes in
Malbecco's (3.9.24). Chaste as she is, Britomart is nevertheless as skilled as
Acrasia in suspending knightly instruments.

   With Britomart, however, Spenser's narrative at first displays some
easiness with the associations between feminine and poetic authority,
partly because Britomart's ultimate fate is indeed a progressive one, to ac-
complish Spenser's aim of revivifying masculine epic in the modern world.
As Merlin tells her when she seeks his advice regarding her future course
of action, her role in future history is to produce "a famous Progenie . . . /
out of the auncient *Troian* blood, / Which shall reuiue the sleeping memo-
rie / Of those same antique Peres" (3.3.22). Moreover, Britomart's quest
in Book 3 is prompted, not by a desire to dominate or incapacitate men,
but rather by a vision in a magic glass—her father's glass, no less—of her
intended spouse, a vision that takes the form of a mental pregnancy: "To
her reuealed in a mirrhour plaine, / Whereof did grow her first engraffed
paine / . . . That but the fruit more sweetnesse did containe, / Her wretched
days in dolour she mote wast" (3.2.17). With this visionary lying-in Britomart is allied with Spenser himself, who in the "Letter to Ralegh" writes
of having "laboured" to "conceiue" the person of Arthur and the shape
of his adventures throughout *The Faerie Queene*. Since "Renowmed kings,
and sacred Emperours" are to be Britomart's "fruitfull Ofspring" (3.3.23),
her fate is also Spenser's project: to produce a succession of heroes, which
when complete will end in Elizabeth—*The Faerie Queene*. This epic product remains with her after her husband Artegall is gone:

> With thee yet shall he leaue for memory
>   Of his late puissance, his Image dead,
>   That liuing him in all actiuity
>   To thee shall represent.
>
> (3.3.29)

In this account of her future, it is unclear whether Britomart's reproduction of epic takes the form of her children, or of her more authorially
pertinent capacity for remembrance. In either case, her role is to "represent" and hence to revive the "Image" of the dead hero.

   This version of authorial conception and birth, however, is altered by
the abrupt end of Merlin's narrative, which halts as Arthur's history does,

with no end in sight. Merlin's tracing of Britomart's descendants ends at last in Elizabeth, whose appearance in this recitation enacts another arrestive moment, both for the pedigree and for the wizard who delivers it. "But yet the end is not," says Merlin, and "[t]here . . . stayd, / As ouercomen of the spirites powre, / Or other ghastly spectacle dismayd" (3.3.50). Merlin is as nonplussed as the knights whom Britomart defeats, and his abrupt cutoff marks the suspension of future male enterprise, which "yet . . . is *not*." Elizabeth, punningly denoted here (as Jon Quitslund has remarked) in the form of her virgin *knot*, is barren, producing *naught* and ending the Tudor line.[21] But this end also marks the beginning of Britomart's adventures, which immediately take the form of narrative digression, not lineal progression. She and her nurse/squire Glauce proceed with anything but straightforward authorial intent, as they "diuerse *plots* did frame, to maske in strange disguise" (3.3.51, my emphasis).[22] From this moment, then, Spenser's metaphor of authorial pregnancy expands so that the feminine gives form to poetic narrative. As Britomart rides along she forges her own idea of her lover, one that departs from Merlin's prophecies: "A thousand thoughts she fashioned in her mind, / And in her feigning fancie did pourtray / Him such, as fittest she for loue could find" (3.4.5). Britomart's "image" of her goal becomes one that she authorially invents not as a singular heroic purpose, but as a set of multiple and interchangeably pleasurable possibilities. And from this moment, Book 3's narration itself begins its digressive turns, as if it too wished to fashion "a thousand thoughts." Unlike the severed genealogies of both Arthur's ancestors and Britomart's descendants, the romance adventures of Book 3 invest their energies not in the hope for a singular conclusion, but rather in potentially endless revisions of chase, discovery, reverie, and flight. By taking full advantage of Merlin's "but yet the end is not," Book 3 fully exploits as poetic form the feminized qualities attributed to Ralegh's verse. On the level not only of lyric but also of narrative structure, poetry in Book 3 becomes liquid, shifting, and diffuse, and these are the qualities meant to afford readerly delight.[23]

Such poetry is best displayed in Book 3's Garden of Adonis, where the curt uncertainty of Merlin's closing sentence, "but yet the end is not," is transformed into a positive principle of "endlesse progenie" (3.6.30), so that even the arrestive power at the center of the Garden confers endlessness in the form of reanimation. The rumor that the slain Adonis still lives in Venus's Garden acquires truth over the course of a few stanzas, as the narrator shifts from the suppositional—"There yet, some say, in secret he does ly"; to the probable—"And sooth it seemes they say: for he may not / For euer die"; to the certain—"There now he liueth in eternall blis" (3.6.46–48). And Adonis's central resting place, upon the mons veneris, appropriates the epic place of beginning, in medias res, for the feminine place of beginnings, plural and indeterminate. Poetic activity itself is granted origins coinciding with this venereal center, whence spring Ovidian tales of those who have been converted into flowers, "To whom sweet Poets verse hath giuen endlesse date" (3.6.45).

Whether such a feminized poetic form is allowed much free play in *The Faerie Queene* is quite another question, however, one that has recently engaged several Spenser critics in their evaluations of fulfillment and loss in Books 3 and 4. Maureen Quilligan and Lauren Silberman both read Book 3's Garden of Adonis, despite its elements of chaos, decay, and lamentation, as a privileged site of feminine production—of earthly forms, of chaste love and marital fecundity, and of a female reader's access to understanding.[24] For them, Book 3's center celebrates a satisfying feminine poetic power. Jonathan Goldberg, in contrast, contends that the poetic pleasure offered by Books 3 and 4 is not the pleasure of fulfillment, but rather a writerly delight in castration and loss, in an excess of always-unfinished, unproductive production. Nevertheless, Goldberg shares with Quilligan and Silberman a focus on the delight afforded by feminized (or at least effeminized) constructions made available in this portion of the poem. As Goldberg describes it, Book 3's revised 1596 ending—which departs from the 1590 ending in omitting the reunion of husband and wife, Amoret and Scudamour, and thus emphasizes Britomart's unconcluded quest for her own mate—acts as a template for the continued deferrals of Book 4. For Goldberg, the pleasure of the writerly text of the entire *Faerie Queene*, but particularly of Book 4, arises from its failure to engage in unitary poetic or narrative endings. It is instead "an 'endlesse worke' of substitution, sequences of names in place of other names, structures of difference, deferred identities. It plays upon a void; it occupies the place of loss—where Britomart's wound is extended to Amoret, where Amoret is 'perfect hole.'"[25]

My own view is quite different. Beginning with its exit from the Garden of Adonis (and perhaps even within the Garden itself, as Berger has pointed out),[26] *The Faerie Queene* starts to expose its own feminized poetics as eminently unsatisfying, whether those poetics produce a full harvest of invention or whether they disjunctively cut those inventions off. And once again, that dissatisfaction is bound up with the fortunes of the poem's authoritative women. From the midpoint of Book 3 in the Garden of Adonis this feminine center will not hold; rather, the narrative embarks upon a sea of digressions that, like the sea at whose edge the habitually pursued Florimell makes yet another near escape (3.7.27), offers no assurance of fruitful outcome. Canto 7 of Book 3 is particularly dizzying in its multitudinous meanderings. Within fifty-eight stanzas the narrative turns from Florimell encountering the malevolent hag and her besotted son; to Florimell fleeing the monster the hag sends; to Florimell escaping into the fisherman's boat; to Satyrane finding Florimell's dropped girdle and subduing the monster; to the Giantess Argante fleeing a knight while bearing on her lap the "doleful Squire" of Dames; to Argante defeating Satyrane and being further pursued by the knight; to the Squire of Dames, who's been tossed aside by Argante, telling Satyrane of his unlucky quest for a virtuous woman. If Canto 7 has an anchor at all, it is the decidedly unvirtuous Argante, who as a parodic counterpart to Venus and her sexual sway over Adonis in her garden motivates not creative plenitude, but confused narration and disrupted natural hierarchy. This episode features a plethora of indefinite masculine pronouns remarkable even for Spenserian verse, as if Satyrane and the unnamed knight and the Squire are all, by virtue of their sex, equally to be picked up, dropped down, and knocked senseless by the lustful Giantess. (We do not learn until the episode is over that the unnamed knight is in fact a woman, the "faire virgin" Palladine [3.7.52].) Argante's thralldom is the evident wage of personally and poetically going astray.[27]

The second half of Book 3 continues to evince uneasiness about the Garden of Adonis's feminized conjunctions of productivity and desire, traits that reemerge (like Argante's domination) not as affirmation but as parody. For artistic creation we are given Proteus's shapeshifting and the hag's creation of the false Florimell; for feminine desire, Hellenore humped by satyrs; for male passivity, the childish Scudamour, who spends his time "beat[ing] and bounse[ing] his head and brest full sore" while Britomart engages in rescuing his bride (3.11.27). At the same time, as Berger points out, "[t]he repeated pattern of male behavior in these cantos is the shift from weaker to more aggressive forms of violence, and from victimization to tyranny: the shift, for example, from the hapless witch's son to the hyena-like monster that feeds on women's flesh; from the Squire of Dames and Argante's other victims to Ollyphant; from the fisherman to Proteus, Malbecco to Paridell, and Scudamour to Busirane."[28] However, the increased level of masculine tyranny does not correspond to an increase in poetic power. The poetic model proposed by Book 3's most obvious poet, Busirane, proves to be remarkably ineffective, an only slightly more sophisticated version of the rapine "rude and rugged" rhymes earlier invoked by the narrator. Neither Amoret nor Britomart herself is much moved by what Maureen Quilligan calls Busirane's "sadistic sonneteering,"[29] indicating that trying to convert the feminine lyricism of Acrasia's Bower and elsewhere in the poem into some new breed of masculine lyricism will not prove a successful experiment. Even though Busirane aggressively composes his charms out of Amoret's very blood, "Yet thousand charmes could not her stedfast heart remoue" (3.12.31).

And yet, the conclusion of Book 3 does not resolve itself in favor of a feminine mode of narrative progress, either. Despite the poem's continued associations between femininity and inconclusiveness, we must remember that most of the primary female characters of Books 3 and 4 *are* in fact driving toward a particular conclusion: marriage. But as Books 3 and 4 progress, both the desirability and the conclusiveness of marriage become deeply compromised, and weddings are generally either delayed or evaded. The narrative hence finds itself in a double bind. In order fully to exploit the female knighthood that, beginning with Britomart, the poem has delineated, marriage must be acknowledged as a legitimate ending to a heroic story. But in the view of the male characters who are the necessary partners in this enterprise, marriage seems largely to replicate the dangers to heroism embodied in Acrasia's bower, where knightly instruments are not sharpened, but suspended. Hence, aside from some marginal or deflected weddings (the curiously quadrangular union of Cambell to Cambina, and Triamond to Canacee; the morally suspect Poeana's wedding to the Squire of Low Degree; and the unnarrated vows of purely allegorical rivers), Book 4's narrative effort is spent eluding rather than concluding wedlock.[30] This avoidance is jumpstarted, as Goldberg points out, by the 1596 revision of the ending to Book 3, which assigns not only Britomart but also Amoret to the category of frustrated brides. The abortion of Amoret's "conceiued" hope (3.12.44) to find her husband rewrites her as a duplicate of the unhappy Britomart, who in the 1590 ending to Book 3 witnessed Scudamour's embrace of Amoret only to be reminded of her own incompletion: "In vaine she wisht, that fate n'ould let her yet possesse" (3.12.46a).

Considering that Britomart's quest was prompted by her conception of an envisioned Artegall, the 1590 ending's disjuncture of the "fate" of narrative from Britomart's wishful thinking signals the imminent demise of the feminine poetics that Britomart initially embodied.[31] This demise comes to pass in the 1596 *Faerie Queene*, in Books 4 and 5. Although the 1596 ending to Book 3 leaves both Amoret and Britomart to "wend at will" while the narrator takes his breather, the female wanderings of Book 4 have little to do with women exercising will. Rather, women's thought and desires in Book 4 seem largely to be displaced by happenstance and mistake. Britomart carelessly misplaces Amoret and untowardly jousts for the false Florimell; the virgin huntress Belphoebe, a double for Queen Elizabeth, "misdeems" Timias's attentions to Amoret.[32] And more significantly, the long-awaited encounter of Britomart with her intended, Artegall, in Book 4's "middest"—the analogue point to Book 3's superproductive, female-ruled Garden—seems pointedly to cancel Britomart's desired fulfillment. Instead, their encounter in the central Canto 6 evades a permanent union of heroine and hero, evidently because of its emasculating potential. Artegall initially fights Britomart with the rapine intent typical of a Spenserian knight in battle, but once he unhelms her he is unmanned: "trembling horrour did his sense assayle, / And made ech member quake, and manly hart to quayle" (4.6.22). Even though Britomart is in the end similarly subdued, narration remains in the grip of feminine digressiveness and masculine failure. We learn immediately after these lovers' mutual recognition that Amoret, once again failing to join her husband Scudamour's company, has "wandred . . . or gone astray" (4.6.36). As if to countervail this unpredictable feminine derailment of narrative conclusions, or as if to countervail a woman's effect upon himself, Artegall immediately sues to leave upon his initial quest, "To follow that, which he did long propound" (4.6.42).

Artegall's ability to "propound," from *proponere* ("to put forward"), establishes him as the opponent of *post*ponement and delay, even though it is he who is postponing their marriage. But in the prevailing opinion of *The Faerie Queene*'s second half, marriage itself postpones rather than embodies masculine endings. For Artegall, what is a "conceiued" hope for Amoret or Britomart would amount to a return to Acrasia's bower. From the bridegroom's point of view, marital union constitutes a kind of suspended animation. A male hero's safe response to marriage in Book 4 is either to flee it (as in Canto 6's comic argument, where "Both Scudamour and Arthegall / Doe fight with Britomart, / He sees her face; doth fall in loue, / and soone from her depart") or to contemplate it only from several heavily mediated removes, as is signified in the Temple of Venus, which hides its hermaphroditic goddess from view precisely *because*—as with man and wife become one flesh—she unites both sexes in one being:

> The cause why she was couered with a vele,
>   Was hard to know, for that her Priests the same
>   From peoples knowledge labour'd to concele.
>   .   .   .   .
>   But for, they say, she hath both kinds in one,
>   Both male and female, both vnder one name.
>
> (4.10.41)

What must be covered up (and oddly so, in the Book that contains *The Faerie Queene*'s most famous union, the rivers' wedding) is the very definition of marriage: "Both male and female, both vnder one name." Wedlock and its results are threatening enough that Venus is thrice removed from direct experience: not only by her veil, but also by the pains her priests take to mystify the truth of her form, and finally by the narrative's revealing her only indirectly, through Scudamour's tale of finding Amoret at Venus's feet.[33] Meanwhile, as I noted above, Amoret herself has mysteriously disappeared from the scene, as if the allegory of marriage can be recounted only when actual marriage has once again become impossible.

It is this revulsion from the feminine endings imagined by female authority, in my view, that accounts for the inconclusive structure of Book 4—its turns and returns, engagements and disengagements. Having devolved so much of its action upon anticipated wedlock, Book 4's ultimate evasions of marriage leave the poem confronting its own heroic void. Notoriously lacking a unitary hero, a Guyon to break the Bower of Bliss's thrall, Book 4 is seeded with ever-increasing narrative guilt for not properly ending things. The kinds of conclusions that Book 4 does feature are necessarily strained because they are not naturally arrived at, but arbitrarily imposed by the narrative voice. Canto 10, for example, reaches for completion by flatfootedly ending both Scudamour's tale and the canto that contains it with the word *end* ("So ended he this tale, where I this Canto end" [4.10.58]). Elsewhere, Book 4 begins to ask forgiveness for the cliffhanger technique that *The Faerie Queene* has employed with confidence since Book 1. Canto 11 opens by apologizing for Florimell's having been left "languishing in payne" since Canto 8 of Book 3 (4.11.1). Book 4 itself ends on a hasty promissory note, a one-line uncompleted completion like the one Artegall effects by leaving Britomart: the marriage of Marinell and Florimell, "Which," says the narrative voice, "to another place I leaue to be perfected" (4.12.35).

Repealing Queenship in the Legend of Justice

That "other place"—that place of perfection—is Book 5, which in fact begins by once again shunting aside Florimell's and Marinell's wedding in favor of Artegall's mission to rescue Irena. Hence Book 5's narrative asserts openly what Book 4's indirections implied: that marriage is not perfection at all, but rather at best a mere footnote to the glories of the heroic quest. Artegall attends the promised nuptials only as a brief stopover on his way to "his first aduenture" (5.3.40). The "firstness," the originality, of that quest, as well as Artegall's often-repeated intent to continue upon that first quest despite minor skirmishes and potential diversions along the way, is a new emphasis for a knight of *The Faerie Queene*, and one that leads us to examine what is (literally) being prioritized in Book 5. What is the first intent to which both Artegall and the narrative must insistently refer? Ostensibly, Artegall's task is to restore originary justice. But in the reiterated word that describes Artegall's judiciary pronouncements, *doome*, we hear how that "first aduenture" is dependent for its achievement of this restoration on a sense of ending, of final, irrevocable closure.[34] And as we will see, the opening pretexts of Book 5 firmly disenfranchise feminine authority from this return to finality.

　　Of all the proems in *The Faerie Queene*, the Proem to Book 5 features the most cursory and oblique reference to Spenser's queen. After declaring that God's justice, delegated to earthly rulers, allows princes "To sit in his owne seate, his cause to end" (5.Pr.10), the Proem addresses Elizabeth in only one stanza, as the "Dread Souerayne Goddesse" who initially seems to have the apocalyptic power of bringing about that doomsday:

> Dread Souerayne Goddesse, that doest highest sit
> 　In seate of iudgement, in th'Almighties stead,
> 　And with magnificke might and wondrous wit
> 　Doest to thy people righteous doome aread, . . .

(5.Pr.11)

It is difficult, given Spenser's cunning hubris throughout *The Faerie Queene*, not to read *aread* punningly: Elizabeth *areads* "righteous doome" not by discerning or pronouncing it herself, but by her act of a-reading Spenser's poem, which dispenses its own inspired judgments. The main action of Book 5 similarly weaves into its narrative structure a determination to achieve ending by substituting male for female authority. Just as the Proem addresses Elizabeth in the person of a goddess who has not appeared, and cannot appear, in the poem—Astraea, whose naming here is prefaced on her absence from the world—so too does Canto 1 go on to delineate Astraea's departure as the precondition for heroic action. It is not until she is reft from earthly sight that her foster child Artegall can begin his career. Her removal from the poem therefore at last delivers narrative into the safe keeping of the masculine. As a substitute for herself Astraea leaves Artegall the iron man Talus, "And willed him with *Artegall* to wend, / And doe what euer thing he did intend" (5.1.12). This absolute fulfillment of "what euer thing" a man intends seems a dream of narrative progress, considering the feminine postponements and beguilements of Books 3 and 4. Talus is never delayed or diverted on his way to a goal. Once he sets out after Sir Sanglier, for instance, he requires only three stanzas to find and bind his prey (5.1.20–22)—a remarkable contrast to the pursuits in Books 3 and 4, some of which are never concluded at all. Talus acts as an external manifestation of *doome*, with its connotations of finality as well as of certain judgment. In Cantos 1–4 Artegall's *doome* extends even to narrative itself, as with the end of each canto an episode in his travels is firmly and finally concluded.

That conclusiveness, however, itself comes to an end as Book 5 approaches its center, a center we have learned in Books 3 and 4 to associate with realized or potential feminine arrestiveness, with marriage and feminine (re)production. Cantos 5–7 of Book 5 in fact stage in miniature the extensive, interwoven problematics of marriage and of a feminine poetics mounted at length through Books 3 and 4. The Amazon queen Radigund's capture of Artegall externalizes what might be Artegall's nightmare of marriage to Britomart: not only do Radigund and Britomart resemble each other in looks and actions, as many critics have noticed, but Artegall crucially consents to his bondage, "to [Radigund] yeelded of his owne accord" (5.5.17).[35] Moreover, Radigund catalyzes at the precise moment of Artegall's quasi-marital oath a regression to Book 3's literary model, in which a feminine poem equally effeminizes its reader. We witness this regression in a complex moment of reader-response that goes beyond the

earlier instances of feminine ravishment it resembles, as Artegall unhelms
Radigund and sees her features for the first time:

> But when as he discouered had her face,
>   He saw his senses straunge astonishment,
>   A miracle of natures goodly grace,
>   In her faire visage.
>
> (5.5.12)

When he looks at her, what he sees is himself—and more than himself, his
arrested self: "He saw his senses straunge astonishment." It is that reading
of his own plight, himself as Verdant in Acrasia's bower, that causes him
further to be emasculated, and finally further to emasculate himself by disarming: "At sight thereof his cruell minded hart / Empierced was with pitti-
full regard, / That his sharpe sword he threw from him apart" (5.5.13). At
this point the *doome*—the finality—that he has wielded up to now returns
upon himself, enforcing not masculine completion but effeminized thrall:

> So was he ouercome, not ouercome,
>   But to her yeelded of his owne accord;
>   Yet was he iustly damned by the doome
>   Of his owne mouth, that spake so warelesse word,
>   To be her thrall, and seruice her afford.
>
> (5.5.17)

The effeminization of the knightly reader is accompanied by a similar regression to the effeminized narrative of Books 3 and 4. Unlike Cantos
1–4 of Book 5, Canto 5 ends with no ending. This time Artegall remains
in bondage, and his release is postponed till another place, "Which in an
other Canto will be best contayned" (5.5.57). Worse yet, Canto 6 in fact
fails to free Artegall, and he remains with knightly instruments suspended
while Britomart makes her way to him. Thus, like Books 3 and 4, Book 5
has feminine authority at its heart. Significantly, Britomart in Book 5's
"middest" canto, Canto 6, herself rearms.

The dilemma of the arrested text begins to be resolved as Book 5
works its way out of this feminine center, a process encapsulated in Britomart's stay in the Temple of Isis in Canto 7. The Isis Church episode has
proved especially troubling for critics trying to assert a unity of purpose

in Book 5. As Clare Kinney has put it, the episode is one of those "exemplary union[s] of Justice and Mercy" that "seems oddly irrelevant to the actual narrative progress of Arthegall and his automaton-slave Talus from one victory of force majeure to another."[36] T. K. Dunseath, in contrast, has identified Isis Church as a necessary passageway to Britomart's restoration of Artegall's progress: "Once Britomart submits herself to Divine Providence in the Church of Isis, she discovers the true nature of her mission and is able to free her lover from woman's slavery."[37] Chafing though Dunseath's condemnation of "woman's slavery" may now be, it is a condemnation shared by the poem at this point, and Isis Church becomes the site of the reiteration and recuperation of Artegall's stasis. This episode at first recalls and extends the state of overwhelming feminine power in which Artegall still lies languishing: Isis, as goddess of the moon, reminds us not only of Radigund, whose face was revealed "Like as the Moone in foggie winters night" (5.5.12), but also of Britomart herself, whose own visage has borne the same comparison and whose chastity allies her with the moon-goddess. Moreover, the dream that comes to Britomart as she sleeps at Isis's feet consistently confuses her with Isis, using only "she" and "her," not a proper name, to describe the marvelous queen that subdues the crocodile. But unlike the close of Book 3, where Britomart's state of feminine dismay and incompletion bled over into the state of the narrative, this moment of feminine governance and of feminine conception is safely framed. At first Britomart's dream seems to rediscover her former authorial mode: whereas in Book 3 she set out fashioning "a thousand thoughts" of her lover, here as she awakens "long while she musing lay, / With thousand thoughts feeding her fantasie" (5.7.17). The dream's aftermath of interpretation, however, reduces those thousand thoughts to orthodoxy. First of all, the ambiguous or oscillating gender identities inherent in the temple sort themselves out. Not only do the priests, initially of uncertain gender, now become in the person of their spokesman an unambiguous "he" (5.7.19), but the crocodile of Britomart's dreaming—which had been given both feminine and masculine pronouns, as well as variously hermaphroditic powers of tumescence, pregnancy, engulfment, and impregnation—is now unquestionably male, a figure of both Osiris and Artegall himself. And even though in the dream Isis/Britomart exerts phallic authority over that crocodile, "turning all his pride to humblesse meeke" (5.7.16), Isis's priest re-reads this episode for her as pointing not toward Britomart's subjection of men, but toward her eventual marriage and male offspring (5.7.23), reincorporating feminine power into masculine heroics as Merlin did by tracing the careers of

Britomart's male descendants. Signally unlike Merlin's vision, the priest's explication runs without interruption, "vnto the end" (5.7.24). From this point Britomart will step, not into a maze of digressive, self-made visions, but toward a certain closure of masculine heroics that she must internalize and enforce. As critics have often noticed, in Britomart's subsequent defeat of Radigund the two women warriors are scarcely distinguishable: the fray is described as a challenge between a tigress and a lioness (5.7.30). Britomart's task is, evidently, to subdue herself.

We can see in Britomart's subsequent reconstitution of Radigund's city-state the full consequences of Spenser's reading of Plutarch's "Of Isis and Osiris," a text to which the Isis Church episode alludes, although Book 5 does not explicitly refer to Isis's piecing together of her dismembered husband. Unable to find Osiris's penis, Plutarch's Isis replaces it with a consecrated replica; and so too does Britomart reerect her husband's phallic power.[38] She not only rearms him and restores the Amazons "to mens subiection" (5.7.42), she also establishes Artegall's thralldom as but a holiday aberration: "Ah my deare Lord, what sight is this (quoth she) / What May-game hath misfortune made of you?" (5.7.40). All of a sudden, and quite improbably, Artegall metamorphoses from an embarrassed, foolish Hercules to an epic Odysseus returning to his patient, waiting wife: "Not so great wonder and astonishment / Did the most chast *Penelope* possesse, / To see her Lord, that was reported drent" (5.7.39). With Artegall's promotion to head of state, Book 5's curious catalogue of ways to abuse the human head—its elaborately grisly panoply of hangings, beheadings, scalpings, and even bad haircuts—begins to make sense. All these illegitimate mishandlings of the head are cancelled in one stroke, Britomart's decapitation of Radigund.[39] From this moment, too, the narrative itself seems to know where it's heading. Artegall ventures forth once again with purpose upon his hitherto delayed quest: "He purposd to proceed, what so be fall, / Vppon his *first* aduenture, which him forth did call" (5.7.43, my emphasis). And he leaves Britomart behind.

We have heard Artegall's rededication to his "first adventure" before the end of Canto 7. Significantly, this resolution had been repeated thrice in quick succession in the brief interval between his attendance at Florimell's and Marinell's marriage, and his encounter with Radigund's crew.[40] If first intent prevails only in the respite between weddings and Amazons, how could it hold up if Artegall stayed to marry his own Amazon-like fiancée? Artegall's second separation from Britomart in fact becomes an extended meditation upon the high stakes of avoiding feminine digression, both for Artegall and for the forward movement of narrative. After his announced departure at the end of Canto 7, Canto 8 surprisingly begins not by portraying Artegall on his way, but by worrying again at the issue of female dominance:

> Nought vnder heauen so strongly doth allure
>   The sence of man, and all his minde possesse,
>   As beauties louely baite, that doth procure
>   Great warriours oft their rigour to represse,
>   And mighty hands forget their manlinesse.
>
> (5.8.1)

A comment on Artegall's recent imprisonment, it would seem—but as it turns out, the "louely baite" in question is not Radigund, but Artegall's intended wife. Despite her recent role in suppressing female sway, Britomart still represents the "allure" that Artegall must resist, if he is to escape the fate (says the narrator) of Samson, Hercules, and Mark Antony. Feminine rule of body and mind must be cut off, beheaded, as a way of propelling Artegall back "vppon his first intent" (5.8.3)—his intent and the narrative's, the rescue of Irena that is the ostensible mission of Book 5.

As both Busirane's torturous rhymes and Artegall's earlier dismissal of Britomart in Book 4 taught us, however, rejecting one version of feminine rule is not enough to restore with certainty either masculine heroics or a masculine model of poetic effect. More drastic measures are called for. In keeping with its obsessive decapitations of illegitimate authorities, Book 5 proposes a thoroughgoing revision of literary construction that ought for good and all to sever the poem from feminine influence. Feminine rule and feminized poetics are repealed in favor of the most straightforward mode that *The Faerie Queene* will ever assume, historical allegory. That is to say, the poem at this point assumes a new literary mode as a way of galvanizing the sense of an ending, the *doome* that Artegall's adventures first promised before his digression into serving a queen.

I earlier suggested that Book 5's revision of form reaches back nostalgically for the completed heroic endeavors of Books 1 and 2. If Books 1 and 2 can legitimately (if broadly) be described as the epic segments of *The Faerie Queene*, then the nostalgia that Book 5 expresses is for epic over romance. But Book 5 in its last five cantos also audaciously construes itself as more uniformly heroic than even those earlier books of epic (not to mention the *Iliad, Odyssey*, and *Aeneid*), since it thoroughly discounts feminine *otium* as holding any allure whatsoever, either for the poem or for its hero. None of the women of these cantos poses any sensual danger for Artegall or for the late-arriving Arthur. Adicia's malfeasance is described as sexual only ex post facto, once she's been banished "farre from resort of men" (5.9.2).[41] The female monster of the Inquisition's dual appearance of foul and fair briefly recalls Duessa's ("For of a Mayd she had the outward face, / To hide the horrour, which did lurke behinde, / The better to beguile, / whom she so fond did finde" [5.11.23]), but her implied weapon of seduction is never put to use. Even Duessa's sexual transgressions are described with extreme economy, with neither the seductive nor the repulsive flourishes of Book 1. The prosecuting attorney at her trial, Zele, simply mentions "many a knight, / By her beguyled, and confounded quight" (5.9.40). As well, these cantos decline to seduce their reader. Their refusal of sensual appeal extends to their poetry, which Angus Fletcher may be alone in praising as "aesthetically lean and muscle-bound."[42] Fletcher's personification of verse as a male warrior physique draws together precisely, if unintentionally, the aim of these cantos' poetic reformation, their expurgation of what Dunseath has called the poetic "suggestibility" we expect from Spenserian poetry.[43] I would argue that these cantos do not mean to be suggestive. Instead of dense wordplay and multiple allusiveness, their verse offers only a limited field of interpretation, a tunnel vision meant to afford narrative progress. Whereas *The Faerie Queene*'s poetry typically engages its reader by withholding conclusions—or as Fletcher, quoting Hazlitt, puts it, by holding the ear "captive in the chains of suspense"[44]—these cantos eagerly draw toward singular conclusions both poetic and narrative. When Canto 11 repeats the word "shield" thirteen times, for example (as Hamilton notes with irritation),[45] not only do we get the message that a knight must never discard his shield, but we also get no other message. And when Canto 8 sketches Arthur's triumphal march upon defeating the Souldan in only seven parsimonious lines, the reader is also reminded not to wallow in celebratory glee. Arthur, Artegall, and the reader all move on to the next adventure "hauing stayd *not long*" (5.8.51, my emphasis). Book 5's last reiteration of Artegall's recall to his "first aduenture" clearly navigates where he and the poem are going: "on his first aduenture [he] *forward* forth did ride" (5.10.17, my emphasis).

What minimal figurative language and swift narrative conclusions do for these cantos in small, historical allegory does writ large; the firm attachment of these cantos to easily recognizable political and military events serves to cordon off all but the most straitened avenues of interpretation.

We might be allowed a bit of wriggle room in the form of some referents that are not merely unitary: as David Norbrook points out, for example, we must hear in the rescue of Irena a reference not only to Ireland, but also to the French philosopher of absolutism Jean Bodin, who "used the term ειρηνη (eirene) to describe the highest kind of justice."[46] Kenneth Borris strenuously argues, too, that these cantos not only depict such said-and-done events as the defeat of the Armada and the sentencing of Mary, Queen of Scots, but also voice a Protestant rewriting of history into the approach of the apocalypse. For Borris, Spenser "transforms the particulars of history into vehicles for the ostensibly prophetic revelation of cultural destiny."[47] But Norbrook goes on to remind us that for Spenser as for others with more radical religious leanings, Protestant apocalyptics (like Bodin's political theory) were also a matter of historical event and analysis. If Book 5's Battle of Belge (Canto 10) is seeded with allusions to radical Protestant apocalyptic commentary, it is because Spenser's revered Leicester sympathized with those Protestant factions, seeing his expedition in Belgium as a religious war as well as a containment of Spanish imperial ambitions. Spenser's portrayal of the battle for Belge as a resounding success runs counter to fact not because its eye is on the final victory at world's end, but (arguably) because Spenser was propagandizing in favor of continued military effort in the Low Countries, in hopes that Essex would be allowed to take up where Leicester had left off.[48] Protestant messianics, far from being suprahistorical, circle back round into realpolitik, into strategic militarism and jurisprudence.

The relentlessly optimistic depiction of Belge's fate, however, like the redemption of Irena in Canto 12, finally uncovers the pitfall of these cantos' dependence on diachronic historical allegory. For of course these two episodes do not depict accomplished historical victories at all, but rather revise past English engagements, some of them not at all successful, into future triumph. When Arthur recovers a city that looks suspiciously like Antwerp (5.10.25–38), we are asked to acquiesce in an event that in 1596 has not yet taken place, and in fact never took place. In the same way, Irena's rescue comes about as elegantly as a challenge to single combat — truly a kind of wishful thinking, on the order of Hal's flyting of Hotspur on the eve of Shrewsbury. Even in the poem (not to mention in late sixteenth-century Ireland) matters are not really so easy, for like Hal's England, Irena's realm sees considerable bloodshed before Artegall undertakes his "single fight" with Grantorto (5.12.8). Artegall's prosthetic Talus manages to massacre most of the barbaric hordes before Artegall calls him back, claiming a bit belatedly "that not for such slaughters sake / He thether came" (5.12.8).[49] These intrusive details, these shadowy reminders that current uncompleted missions are not as neatly sewn up as famous past victories, expose the danger of engaging upon a historical allegory that extends from past to future. Standing in the road between past and future is the ineluctable present, where history's certain endings give way to the muddled and inconclusive status of recent current events, events that curtail any story of *doome*. But yet, still, the end is not.

In the end, Book 5's historical episodes make the case that even when barren and driven poetry replaces seductive lyric, masculine heroism is still subject to an undirected feminine authority. The liberations of Belge and of Irena, both fantasies that expose their own frustration, are framed (and hence, in *The Faerie Queene*'s juxtapositional logic, arguably caused) by two dilatory queens and their tactics of diversion. In the first case, Queen Mercilla's waffling pity for Duessa in Canto 9 is seemingly closed off by Artegall, whose judgment is accompanied by his usual epithet of first intent ("But *Artegall* with constant firme intent, / For zeale of Iustice was against her bent" [5.9.49]). Mercilla's wavering in a certain sense nevertheless still carries the day, since the pronouncement of Duessa's final sentence is delayed until the beginning of the next canto, and even then her actual punishment is elided. Surprisingly enough in this book of beheadings, the poem remains silent on whether Duessa's means of demise doubles that of Mary, Queen of Scots, her allegorical referent. Most readers assume that Duessa is beheaded, but in fact the poem tells us only that Mercilla, having delayed judgment "Till strong constraint did her thereto enforce," then "yeeld[ed] the last honour to [Duessa's] wretched corse" (5.10.4).[50] In this light, Artegall's oddly gentle decapitation a few cantos later of Grantorto ("Whom when he saw prostrated on the plaine, / He lightly reft his head, to ease him of his paine" [5.12.23]) is better read not as a somewhat extraneous detail, but as a displaced dropping of Duessa's unenacted deathstroke, as if Artegall must carry out somehow, anyhow, what Mercilla has postponed. If he finishes off Grantorto with unwonted mercy, it is because he is momentarily usurping Mercilla's role. The point is minor enough, except that this queenly stay of execution recurs when Artegall tries to conclude his final task. His mission is the same as Britomart's in Amazonia, "How to reforme that ragged common-weale" (5.12.26). "But ere he could reforme it thoroughly" he is recalled to Gloriana's Faerie Court, "that of necessity / His course of Iustice he was forst to stay" (5.12.27). Blocked in the course of first intent, Artegall turns aside toward his queen's command with a final reiteration of straightforwardness that is by now entirely ironic: "he for nought would swerue / From his right course, but still the way did hold / To Faery Court, where what him fell shall else be told" (5.12.43). This promise of narrative closure is never kept. No doome, no end for Artegall. Instead, he returns to the demanding, static embrace of Acrasia, or Venus, or Britomart, or Radigund, or Gloriana.

Gloriana's whim further serves to highlight the difficulty of constructing historical allegory as heroic accomplishment. Although depending on current events to endow narrative closure would be futile enough in any era, late sixteenth-century events in England seemed to many observers, especially those sympathetic to militant Protestantism, particularly recalcitrant to fostering masculine endeavor and its fruition. By the mid-1590s Spenser's queen had been perceived for several years as hindering a Protestant crusade on the continent; in her canny ambivalence, Elizabeth was never willing to commit the funds or the manpower for a full-scale effort against Spain. R. B. Wernham details "a secret agreement" in the Triple Alliance between England, France, and the United Provinces that "limited the English military contribution [to the Netherlands] to 2,000 men. . . . In fact, after 1594 England practically withdrew from the continental war, except for [these] forces in the Netherlands."[51] Although Burghley was partially if not primarily responsible for this policy, the Queen herself was blamed for womanish inconstancy and lack of will. J. E. Neale reports a story that circulated about the queen's endless changes of mind: "[T]he story of the carter who, on being informed for the third time that the Queen had altered her plans and did not intend to move on that day, slapped his thigh and said, 'Now I see that the Queen is a woman as well as my wife.'"[52] Elizabeth throughout her reign had used to her advantage the figuration of herself as her country's bride, but in the 1590s certain factions within England found themselves wishing that, like Artegall upon his reunion with Britomart, they might simply ride away from the inaction their wife enforces.[53] Such was the wish expressed by the Lincolnshire rector Henry Hooke, whose short manuscript treatise of 1601 or 1602 entitled "Of the succession to the Crowne of England" digresses from praising Elizabeth into desiring her replacement by a king whose "first intent" would overgo his predecessor's feminine stasis on the question of religious reform: "so the brightnes of [Queen Elizabeth's] daye . . . shineth still: and more & more may it shine unto the perfect daye: that what corruptions in justice, what blemishes in religion, the infirmitie, and inconveniency of woemanhead, would not permitt to discover and discerne, the vigor, and conveniency of man sytting as king in the throne of aucthoritie; maye diligently search out, and speedylie reforme."[54] Hooke's remarks couple a desire for the repeal of female authority with a hope for an entirely new mode of monarchical endeavor, one that brings heretofore unenacted intents to fruition. As Christopher Highley has detailed, English officials in Ireland (such as Spenser himself) shared with particular intensity Hooke's desire for a ruler whose policies were more direct and aggressive.[55]

But as Artegall's recall to Gloriana's court demonstrates, such a hope for reform in 1596 remains suspended, both in terms of English politics, where the anticipation of a king's succession only added to the internecine wrangling of Elizabeth's court, and in terms of *The Faerie Queene*'s ambitions as an activist poem. Book 5's revision of literary form might take the poem out of the realm of romance, but it cannot repeal the rule of queens, either of Elizabeth or of Gloriana. In this way Book 5 debunks the misogynist fallacy of *The Faerie Queene*'s earlier scenes of seduction and of wedlock. Artegall's recall reveals that heroic expeditions are delayed not in the private female world—not in either the illicit bower or the sanctioned bridal chamber—but rather in the public world of political aspiration. And if the poem's opposition between romance (to which that feminized private world corresponds) and masculine heroism is shown to be a false opposition, then the nostalgia for an epic form that predated romance no longer holds any attraction.

Instead, *The Faerie Queene* passes over the uncompleted ending of Book 5 by engaging upon yet another generic experiment. Book 6's reformation into pastoral stands in contrast to Book 5 not only as a conspicuously anti-epic form, but also as a conspicuously and innovatively *masculine* anti-epic form.[56] Although Book 6 seems to accept with pleasure poetry's suspension of experience—as does the narrative voice, which in the Proem admits itself "nigh rauisht with rare thoughts delight" in Faery land's delightful ways (6.Pr.1)—it does so in a way untainted by the interruptive demands of feminine authority. Queen Elizabeth's appearance in this Book is a pointed nonappearance: Colin Clout eliminates Gloriana from his configuration of the graces' dance on the revelatory Mount Acidale, replacing her instead with "certes but a countrey lasse" (6.10.25). In contrast to *The Shepheardes Calender*'s April eclogue, where Colin confidently fashioned his queen as an appropriate object for poetry, here Spenser's poetic alter ego apologetically but firmly defines poetry as that which takes shape when female rule is out of the way.[57] Even more than splintering Elizabeth into "mirrhours more than one," displacing her entirely from consideration leaves room for poetic accomplishment.

Not that Book 6 is therefore marked by triumphant poetic closure.

The "untimely breach" of Arthur's rent chronicle not only recurs as Calidore's comically blundering "luckelesse breach" in Colin's perfect vision
(6.10.29), but also might be taken as the model for Book 6's narrative,
which is hardly famous for its seamless conclusions. The end of Book 6
is similarly not one of perfection, either promised or fulfilled. Like Artegall's recall to Gloriana's court, the Blatant Beast's present-tense rampage
at the end of Book 6 wrenches poetry from the domain of the past(oral)
to the unnatural shocks of the present day, so that conclusion once again
is disrupted by uncertainty—in this case, uncertainty imposed by readers
more willing to slander poetry than to be melted into sweetness by it.
"Ne spareth [the Beast] the gentle Poets rime, / But rends without regard
of person or of time" (6.12.40). Though drastically different experiments
in poetic form, Books 5 and 6 thus share a mode of inconclusion. Both
books play out fantasies of freeing politics and poetry from feminine rule;
both envision a newly masculine poetics. And both, in the end, acknowledge those fantasies as fantasies, enacting the futility of imagining that a
male-gendered mode, either of monarchy or of poetry, will bring about
the wished-for consummation.

I come to this conclusion (or to *The Faerie Queene*'s nonconclusion),
however, with my ear cocked to Berger's warning that what we hear
in Spenser's magnum opus as *argument*—as assertion, refutation, judgment, revelation, demonstration, or any other of those rhetorical certain-
ties which we so often attribute to Spenser's poetry—cannot be taken
as "Spenser's" or even "the poem's" settled opinion, but rather must be
viewed skeptically as one of the discourses that, like dummies at a ventrilo-
quists' contest, voice the competing desires that prompt their speaking. In
his challenge to Paul Alpers's thesis that Spenser's stanzas are "modes of
address by the poet to the reader," Berger argues that "Alpers misdescribes
the transaction as an empirical one between the author and actual readers,
whereas I take it to be a virtual or fictive transaction, one that the poem
actively represents and subtly criticizes, and therefore one that constitutes a rhetorical scene of reading from which actual readers can dissociate
themselves." Hence we can undertake "an ideological reading of *The Faerie
Queene* as a critique of the cultural discourses it represents."[58] Berger's
subtle argument describes *The Faerie Queene* as radical in ways that all its
Elizabethan source materials and cultural commonplaces, rampant as they
are in Spenser's poetic field, could never countenance. I would like to make
use of his insights to examine the radical critique ultimately disclosed by
the generic experiment of Book 5: not a critique of attempting closure

via masculinized poetic form, but rather a critique of desiring closure in poetry at all. In particular, the failures of Book 5's final cantos unsettle the impulse toward closure that is, or at least can be, the impulse toward allegory. Allegory proposes that we can metonymically replace what is troublesome and undefinable by something that looks hermetically sealed: not sexuality, but Immoral Lust or Wedded Love; not savage massacres in Ireland, but a gratefully free Irena; not Elizabeth, but Gloriana. The problem of obtaining allegorical closure, however, is akin to the difficulties critics have had in plotting out Book 5's structural, mythical, or moral unity. To create a transcendent order, one must repress the messy and conflicting nature of the facts or events that are transcended. Spenser in this clunkiest portion of *The Faerie Queene* anticipates how ballasted allegoresis of his poem can become, by showing how ballasted his own poetry can be when it succumbs to a fully allegorizing impulse. For that reason I think we should see Book 5's historical allegory not so much as a failed experiment, but as an experiment whose failure is allowed to stand for all failures to impose univocal meanings upon complicated poems. Like the nostalgia for an unsullied genre before romance, Book 5 shows us, so too is the desire for unsullied truth based on false premises. Just as the "problem" of female authority precedes and enwraps and even motivates *The Faerie Queene*—and hence is not to be "solved" by backward glances to some golden age—so too are Spenserian irresolutions not to be wished away.[59]

Book 5's demonstrated failure forewarns of the dangers of excess complacency toward what critics usually take to be the real final statement of *The Faerie Queene*, the Mutability Cantos. Most critics describe *Mutabilitie* as the consummate enactment of allegorical closure. Hamilton's edition of the poem approvingly quotes a number of these judgments, including William Blissett's that the cantos are "a detached retrospective commentary on the poem as a whole, forming as they do a satisfactory conclusion to a foreshortened draft, a stopping place at which, after a seriatim reading, can be made a pleasing analysis of all" (p. 711).[60] But as Gordon Teskey has pointed out, Blissett's essay also addresses the ways in which *Mutabilitie*, not so detached from its historical moment as it seems, in fact troubles itself again with the problematics of late Elizabethan female rule. As Teskey paraphrases Blissett, *Mutabilitie* undertakes "the shocking representation (especially shocking in the late 1590s) of Mutabilitie threatening Cynthia's chair"; and Teskey adds the comment that "[c]riticism has yet to come to grips with *Mutabilitie*'s being not only unpublished in Spenser's lifetime but unpublishable in Elizabeth's."[61] Teskey goes on to suggest that *Mutabilitie* does not transcend political struggle, but rather exposes that struggle by means of yet another Spenserian gap. In this case, the gap is not the torn page of Arthur's chronicle, but rather *Mutabilitie*'s omission of a Tudor-style myth of genealogical precedence, which we expect to be brought to bear against the titaness Mutabilitie's blood-claim to Jove's throne (7.7.16). Omitting that myth causes us to remember, rather than forget, the fact that Jove's rule, like Henry VII's inauguration of the House of Tudor, was brought about only by faction and bloodshed; and to remember, rather than forget, that the placid cycles of seasonal recurrence paraded in *Mutabilitie* were brought about only by Jove's thunderbolt.[62] Allegory's violent begetting, so easily passed over in *Mutabilitie*'s lovely pageant of times, is laid much more bare in Book 5's stark poetic reformation into historical allegory, which can be put into motion only by the "dreadfull sight" of Radigund's headless corpse.

No wonder, then, that *Mutabilitie*'s last stanzas admit a powerfully subversive reading. Most readers hear the narrator's declaration that Mutabilitie's argument "makes me loath this state of life so tickle, / And loue of things so vaine to cast away" (7.8.1) as reaching toward the transcendence that allegory seems to offer. But Berger has given these lines an alternate cast that resists the allegorical temper: "I am loath to cast away this state of life and this love of things."[63] The compounding in *Mutabilitie*'s final lines of *Sabbath* and *Sabaoth*—of peaceful rest and armed hosts—gives us reason to refuse what Susanne Wofford has called "figurative compulsion" in the poem, to evade allegorical conclusions for the "vain and tickle" present.[64] Elizabeth Bellamy has pointed out that these lines' prayer to "that great Sabbaoth God" disfigures Elizabeth's own name (Eli-sabbath, God's rest).[65] That truncation, I would add, in turn enforces the "trunkation" of queens—Radigund's beheading, Britomart's abandonment—as the principle behind Mutabilitie's downfall and hence behind eternal rest. But if apocalyptic allegorical conclusions require the grim armed forces that brought about Book 5's historic ends, then the final downstroke of that "Sabbaoth God" to whom the narrator prays might show us that we have shaken off the powerful embrace of *The Faerie Queene*'s last seductive queen only to lie down with Talus, Artegall's right–hand iron man.

3

Leading Ladies

Feminine Authority and Theatrical Effect
in Shakespeare's History Plays

TO MOVE FROM Spenser's epic-romance poem to Shakespeare's history plays, I wish to return to the moment in *The Faerie Queene* at which forward historical movement is first breached: Arthur's reading of history in Book 2. Before *The Faerie Queene* digresses from epic structure, the poem momentarily makes a proposal contrary to both the seductively digressive poetics of Books 3 and 4 and the unattractively direct poetics of Book 5. This is a proposal that Shakespeare's histories will reach for and elaborate: that a reader or audience member may be ravished just as much by a literary work when it details the orderly, masculine, teleological progress of history as when it suspends that orderly progress.

We remember that the volume of chronicle history that Arthur peruses in Alma's castle turns out to be his own history, the chronicle of his kingly ancestors the Britons. We also remember that Arthur remains ignorant of his connection to this chronicle because its account of his lineage halts just after it mentions Arthur's father, Uther Pendragon:

> After him *Vther*, which *Pendragon* hight,
>   Succeding There abruptly it did end,
>   Without full point, or other Cesure right,
>   As if the rest some wicked hand did rend,
>   Or th'Authour selfe could not at least attend
>   To finish it: that so vntimely breach
>   The Prince him selfe halfe seemeth to offend,
>   Yet secret pleasure did offence empeach,
> And wonder of antiquitie long stopt his speach.

(2.10.68)

Arthur is, understandably, frustrated at the "untimely breach" of his reading pleasure, a stoppage enforced unnaturally, "Without full point, or other Cesure right." A closer look at these lines, however, reveals an Acrasian cast to Arthur's reader response. Arthur's delight, it turns out, derives as much from the interruption in his reading as from its previous progress, anticipating the poetic ravishment I have discussed in regard to Book 3, where poetic success and reading pleasure are to be found when linear heroic narrative is interrupted or suspended, not determinedly completed. First of all, the double equivocation of the breach *half seeming* to offend—not only merely *seeming*, but *half* seeming—makes the harm appear small indeed; and second, the "secret pleasure" that accrues to Arthur and "empeaches" the interruption's offense in fact derives just as plausibly from the "untimely breach" that precedes the phrase, as from the "wonder of antiquitie" that follows it. The near homonymic substitution of "Authour" for "Arthur" in line 5, moreover, insinuates that the break in the text conforms to its princely reader's desires to dwell upon his secret pleasure, "as if . . . th'*Arthur* self could not at least attend to finish it." And because Arthur is reading a chronicle of England, the poetic reverberates within the political. In this first stanza, Arthur's "wonder of antiquitie" comes during an interrupted account of dynastic succession—a breach that conforms in poetic terms to the interruption that powerful, seductive women classically provide for epic action, and in political terms, as I will discuss in this chapter, to the dynastic interruption that Spenser's Virgin Queen clearly guaranteed for her country.

The very next stanza, however, enforces a diametrically opposed idea of what elicits reading pleasure, one that conforms to a masculine model both of textual power and of political authority:

> At last quite rauisht with delight, to heare
>   The royall Ofspring of his natiue land,
>   Cryde out, Deare countrey, O how dearely deare
>   Ought thy remembraunce, and perpetuall band
>   Be to thy foster Childe, that from thy hand
>   Did commun breath and nouriture receaue?
>   How brutish is it not to vnderstand,
>   How much to her we owe, that all vs gaue,
> That gaue vnto vs all, what euer good we haue.

(2.10.69)

Here Arthur as literary consumer is "quite rauisht with delight" very differently from the way other men in *The Faerie Queene* are ravished. Far from suspending his sense, the chronicle heightens it, so that he reacts with reasoned, rhetorically patterned patriotism to this mapping of monarchical lineage. Arthur's outburst manages to crown the way in which the chronicle he has just read has gradually effaced its own gynecocratic texture. At the beginning of the canto, which opened with a paean to Elizabeth, we were led to expect a genealogy ending with this Tudor queen: "Thy name O soueraigne Queene, thy realme and race, / From this renowmed Prince [i.e., Arthur] deriued arre" (2.10.4). Instead, the chronicle breaks off just after it recounts Uther Pendragon's conquest over his father's usurper and accession to his male forebears' throne. Admittedly, the chronicle before this point does tell of three female rulers of ancient Britain, but Arthur's response to his reading deflects what is female about England from its rulers onto the land itself.[1] His characterization of his "Deare countrey" as nourishing mother is highly conventional in both imagery and phrasing; both the didacticism and the repetitiveness of his speech ("Deare countrey, O how dearely deare"; "that all vs gaue, that gaue vnto vs all") indicate that this particular portrait of femininity is hardly the source of the reader's ravishment. Rather, Arthur's experience of poetic delight in this stanza derives from learning of this maternal land's "royall Ofspring," who are, in the end, men-children only.[2] Whereas in Books 3 and 4 that which is ravishing—both authoritative female characters, and the poetry infused with this female nature—is identified as anathematic to the epic cause, here the poem, if only for a stanza, offers an experience of literary ravishment that depends on male rule.

In this chapter, I shall be concerned with how Shakespeare's two major tetralogies of history plays (*1, 2,* and *3 Henry VI* and *Richard III*; and *Richard II, 1* and *2 Henry IV*, and *Henry V*) contend, as does *The Faerie Queene*, not only with the presence of female authority, but also with the potential alliances between female authority and ravishing literary effect. Produced in the same decade that *The Faerie Queene* was published, Shakespeare's histories, like the two Spenserian stanzas above, base their impact both on the anticipated progression of royal succession, and, conversely, also on the interruption, disruption, and contention of that succession.[3] In an association of interruption with ravishment that matches the dynamics of *The Faerie Queene*'s Book 3, the characters in the histories who are most theatrically compelling are, initially, those who most threaten this orderly succession of male rulers. (When I say "initially," I am referring to the histories as a sequence beginning with *1 Henry VI* and ending with *Henry V*, the order in which Shakespeare probably wrote the plays.)[4] As the histories progress, however, the plays echo the movement of the two anomalous Spenserian stanzas I have just analyzed in that they increasingly become an experiment in wresting theatrical authority from the unlawful female to the lawful male—in other words, a theatrical experiment in making what is *kingly* also *ravishing*. In the process of this experiment, the sequence of histories absorbs and shapes the political desires of its audience, which become theatrical desires as well: to witness and partake of a compelling masculine, rather than feminine, authority. At the same time, the histories progressively register the risk involved in that experiment, a risk that is elided in Spenser's two stanzas by the apparently easy supersession of the first stanza by the second, but that is recalled in the theater whenever literarily induced pleasure is identified with the feminine.

Evaluating the gendered character of these plays requires first addressing two topics, one having to do with the genre of the history play itself, the second having to do with the gendered nature of the exchange between actors and audience in the Elizabethan public theater. Much more than "epic" or "romance"—which, although they never exist in unadulterated literary incarnations, at least had impressive pedigrees prior to Shakespeare's era—"history" as an English literary form was invented in the sixteenth century. And arguably the history play, characterized by a plot that is drawn from English chronicles but that is not simply a transparent cover for a morality drama, was practically if not literally invented by Shakespeare.[5] Although (as critics since Tillyard have asserted) the genre of the history play was made possible only through the sixteenth-century revolution in historiography—with its new emphasis on human rather than divine causes for earthly events; its new recognition of historical temporality and anachronism; and its new questioning of textual authority[6]— the fact remains that no playwright besides Shakespeare was so interested in thematizing these issues in terms of the chronicle history of England. Further, as Jean Howard and Phyllis Rackin point out, of all the surviving history-play texts now known, only Shakespeare's ten forays into the genre are so obsessively concerned with the topic of monarchy (rather than with other topics such as the relation between the king and the city of London).[7]

My sense is that Shakespeare so fully embraces the history-play genre and so focuses his history plays on monarchy because this ploy allows him to adapt *The Faerie Queene* to the stage. Or more precisely, the history plays afford a venue for engaging Spenserian concerns with gender, with authority, and with the intersections between gender, authority, and a variety of heterogeneous literary modes. During the same decade, the 1590s, that his romantic comedies reproduce the more obviously feminine elements of Spenser's long poem—cross-dressed heroines, forests suited to wandering and enchantment, and even, in *A Midsummer Night's Dream*, the fairy queen herself—Shakespeare's histories enter into *The Faerie Queene*'s internal debate regarding how to construct a masculine literary form out of English history.

Upon the face of it, the history play, insofar as it indeed partakes of innovations in historiographical practice, seems to be the ideal vehicle for furthering the cause of masculine authority. Not only is the Renaissance writing of history devoted, of course, almost entirely to masculine pursuits,[8] but the very act of shaping the morass of human events into a condensed dramatic plot of a few hours' playing time implements what Julia Kristeva calls the cultural norm of "men's time": "time as project, teleology, linear and prospective unfolding: time as departure, progression and arrival—in other words, the time of history."[9] In this sense a dramatic play, with its short length and its capacity to produce a noticeable and singular climax in Act 5, might be an even more effective means of showcasing masculine heroic action than the potentially baggy structure of the Virgilian twelve-book epic poem. The trick for Shakespeare, as for Spenser, is that Virgilian epic defines masculine action not only as victory in a given battle on a given day, but also as the activity of nation-building, which in an imperial, patriarchal system—as Henry VIII knew all too well—necessarily involves the aid of women as bearers of male heirs. Hence Spenserian and Shakespearean histories' obsessive focus upon monarchical succession.

Hence, too, their focus upon the ruptures in that succession, given that sixteenth-century English history not only features a few authoritative women but also concludes in one authoritative woman, the stubbornly nonreproducing Elizabeth Tudor. In *The Faerie Queene*, the problem of discontinuous monarchical succession—a problem that only gained urgency in the 1590s, as Elizabeth passed her sixtieth birthday without having named an heir—tends to evince itself in two forms: in the concentrated recitations in Books 2 and 3 of England's and Faery land's genealogy of rule;[10] and more diffusely, as I suggested in Chapter 2, in femininity's propensity to disrupt the plans of male aristocratic heroes. In Shakespeare's history plays, in contrast, monarchical succession (meriting rule, achieving rule, holding onto rule, passing rule to one's son) is the entire topic of the

action, even by and large in the comedic, non-aristocratic tavern scenes of
1 and *2 Henry IV*. In fact, the freighted issues of monarchical succession
and of queenship's role in monarchical succession become, in these plays,
coterminous not only with the very course of history, but also, as I will
discuss below, with the very course of the plays themselves—the plot and
rhythm of each individual play, and also the succession of one play to the
next. Like Books 5 and 6 of *The Faerie Queene*, each of the plays in these
two history tetralogies suggests a variant upon the theme of the relation
between femininity and the furtherance of national epic.

As well, these plays cogitate upon potential connections among gender, epic, and theatrical success. At the same time that the history play
is trying, in epic fashion, to establish England's national character and
national history as masculine, its venue of production casts aspersions on
that masculinity. Not only was the public theater a disreputable institution,
one that flourished in the less-regulated "Liberties" of London alongside
taverns and brothels,[11] it was also one of very recent inception: the span
of time from James Burbage's construction in 1576 of the first permanent
playhouse in London, the Theatre, to the first of Shakespeare's history
plays is perhaps twelve or fourteen years. As adolescent in years as the boy
actors who took the parts of women, the public theater seemed an un-
likely place to approximate the character of that most advanced and adult
of Virgilian genres, epic. As well, contemporary analysts both pro- and
anti-theater worried at the question of what effect, exactly, the experience
of the theatrical event would have upon its audience. Stephen Orgel and
Laura Levine have recently discussed the Renaissance perception of the
theater as a sexualized exchange between actor and audience members.[12]
In this exchange any number of gender positions may be played out, given
that, as some Renaissance commentators saw it, not only the actors but
also the male audience members might transform, at least for the space of
the performance, from male to female. At issue with Shakespeare's history
plays, then—as I discuss in this chapter—is the drama's very suitability for
presenting England's history as national epic, and for honing its audience
into suitable participants in that epic project. For that reason, in my view,
the history plays often correlate their various presentations of masculine
and feminine authority with moments of metadiscourse upon theater's capacity to distract, seduce, and even transgender its audience.

Although I discuss both historical tetralogies in this chapter, I dwell
primarily on *1 Henry VI* and *Henry V*, the first and last plays in that se-

quence, which show the Shakespearean history play at its extremes of courting and refusing theater's alliances with the powerful woman.

Female Power and Its Alternatives in the
Henry VI Plays and Richard III

As Leah Marcus has analyzed in detail, Joan La Pucelle's appearance in *1 Henry VI* calls up a wealth of associations between the French woman warrior and the Queen of England.[13] Marcus focuses on the way Joan's martial skills, which violate gender distinctions, establish Joan as the counterpart of Elizabeth, who not only envisioned her public, ruling identity as male, but also was portrayed by England's own poets as "the Amazonian Queen."[14] This association of Joan with Elizabeth, reinforced by a host of topical references in the play, serves to air (and ultimately, Marcus asserts, to contain) an entire complex of anxieties about the purportedly oxymoronic phenomenon of female authority.[15] But whereas Marcus locates a queen's threat in her confusion of gender categories, her usurpation of male authority in a woman's body, my sense is that it is the prospect of a purely feminine authority, freely wielded, that is truly threatening. We may see this danger in Joan's first appearance in the play, when it is her perceived overwhelming sexuality as much as her prowess in arms that brings the Dauphin to his knees before her. "Impatiently I burn with thy desire," he tells her immediately after she has defeated him in combat, "My heart and hands thou hast at once subdu'd" (1.2.108–9)—as if she has ravished him, substituting her desire for his self-command. Here Joan seems the direct heir of all of Spenser's disturbingly authoritative females who suspend male self-consciousness. Foreign, marginal, and sexually loose, she is able, like Duessa or Acrasia, to entrance nearly every man she approaches, meanwhile enforcing her desires with the military skill of a Britomart or a Radigund.

But the character of Joan requires a reading in the light of not only Elizabethan fears about queenship, but also the theater's motives for dwelling upon those fears. Marcus offers no real reason for theater's desire to air such anxieties on stage, other than that they were anxieties culturally available to the English in the late 1580s. But such an explanation does not credit the theater with any agenda apart from, or more refined than, a cathartic one, as if the theater's aims were exactly coextensive with its audience's collective cultural psyche, or as if theater never sought to shape that psyche. More specifically, such an explanation of *1 Henry VI* does not account for the way in which Joan is compelling for the theater, as well as frightening for the audience—compelling not only as a leader for the misguided French, but as a theatrical presence. And not simply as a "strong character" within the play: rather, Joan is identified within the text as possessing a specifically theatrical power that depends upon her verbal, physical, and dramaturgical presentation of herself, one that unveils itself as unmistakably female.[16] Joan's histrionic skills, I will argue, set a puzzle for the play: is theatrical success necessarily bound up in the triumph of the female? Though *1 Henry VI* will work at this "puzzle" (a sobriquet punningly applied to Joan herself by the English) and will propose some provisional solutions, it will also bestow the terms of the problem upon its history-play successors, so that Richard III may be seen as an awful but in many ways convincing answer to the challenging precedent of Joan.[17]

To begin to investigate the association posed between theater and the powerful woman, let us return to Joan's first appearance in Act 1, scene 2, where she persuades the Dauphin and his companions that she can, indeed, aid their cause. Joan wins them over by means of a display that might be called magic, or trickery—but in either case, an adept, carefully managed performance. She convinces her on-stage French audience of what cannot be: that she can recognize the true Dauphin, even when he has put Reignier forward in his place; that she, an untutored girl, can defeat a trained swordsman. And these are only preludes to her verbal overthrow of the Dauphin, which conclusively proves her a master of rhetoric as well as of staged legerdemain.[18] Coupled with the thaumaturgy of her seeming omniscience and omnipotence, Joan's verbal power grants her the status of simultaneous dramaturge and theatrical spectacle. The progress of this scene in turn links the powerful woman's theatrical skill to her sexual charms, so that the experience of being her willing audience is one of being ravished. "Look gracious on thy prostrate thrall," exclaims the Dauphin, giving himself up as Verdant to Joan's Acrasia: "Bright star of Venus, fall'n down on the earth, / How may I reverent worship thee enough?" (1.2.117, 144–45). Joan's presentation of herself to the Dauphin, then, defines feminine theatricality as a mode of seduction. Faced with the combination of overwhelming feminine sexuality and entrancing speech, the audience can only surrender, producing a hierarchy of sexual authority entirely contrary to what the Renaissance perceived as normative and natural.

Overtly, this situation is entirely contrary to one of the primary moral

objections generally voiced by Elizabethan and Jacobean antitheatricalist writers: that *women* audience members would be the only ones easily
carried away by smooth talk from the stage, which would pave the way
for their literal seduction once they had left the theater. As Anthony Munday writes in his *Second and Third Blast of Retrait from Plaies and Theaters*,
"The Theater I found to be an appointed place of Bauderie; mine owne
eares have heard honest women allured with abhominable speeches." When
women venture into the theater's public arena, they open themselves up to
all manner of enticement.[19] Yet once drama's "abhominable speeches" have
been imagined as alluring, it is difficult to consider only the female members of an audience as ravished by theater. In *The Schoole of Abuse*, Stephen
Gosson objects to theater on the grounds of its sensual invasiveness, with
language that proceeds to convert the sensual into the sexual:

There set [poets] abroche straunge consortes of melody, to tickle the eare; costly
apparel, to flatter the sight; effeminate gesture, to ravish the sence: and wanton
speache, to whet desire too inordinate lust. Therefore of both barrelles, I judge
Cookes and Painters the better hearing, for the one extendeth his arte no farther
then to the tongue, palate, and nose, the other to the eye; and both are ended
in outwarde sense, which is common too us with bruite beasts. But these by the
privie entries of the eare, slip downe into the hart, & with gunshotte of affection
gaule the minde, where reason and vertue should rule the roste.[20]

With no gender specified, Gosson clearly means us to imagine all audience
members, men and women alike, sexually conquered—ravished through
"privie entries" with "gunshotte of affection."

　　When we consider that the scene Gosson describes is one of male
actors delivering honeyed speeches to a largely male audience, we might
label his ire as homophobic in origin. Such anxieties are more explicitly
expressed by the Oxford don John Rainolds, who is much concerned with
the homoerotic liaison established between a male audience and a playing company of boys dressed in women's clothes, playing women's parts.
And yet what is uppermost in Rainolds's argument is that the players,
though male, are effectively feminized by their actions and garb; and it is
as women that they work their invasive, debilitating seductions: "can wise
men be perswaded that there is no wantonnesse in the players partes, when
experience sheweth (as wise men have observed) that *men are made adul-
terers and enemies of all chastitie by comming to such playes? that the senses are
mooved, affections are delited, heartes though strong and constant are vanquished
by such players? that an effeminate stage-player, while hee faineth love, imprint-
eth wounds of love?*"[21] Later Rainolds makes the point that it hardly matters

who or what takes the woman's part, since the effect is the same: "For men may be ravished with love of stones, of dead stuffe, framed by cunning gravers to beautifull womens likenes."[22] Regardless of the absence of genuine women on the stage, the stage's own theatricality depends upon playing out the feminine, appropriating a "feminine" model of seduction to structure its own effect.[23]

For antitheatricalist writers—as Laura Levine has incisively analyzed the situation—what is ostensibly a fear for female spectators' chastity thus deconstructs itself into a fear for male spectators' sexual integrity. Levine describes the theater's dissolution of masculine gender as a kind of "dark side" of Renaissance self-fashioning: if the Renaissance self is not fixed or stable, as Stephen Greenblatt argues, then it may as easily be shaped by outside forces as it is capable of shaping itself.[24] The notion that the feminine actor can impress a feminine nature upon its male audience members exposes, as Levine points out, the fear that there is no such thing as essential masculinity.[25] In the sexualized relation between theater and its audience, the spectators too become increasingly feminized, so that the whorish nature of the theatrical spectacle transfers itself to its onlookers: "For while [the beholders] saie nought, but gladlie looke on, they al by sight and assent be actors. . . . So that in that representation of whoredome, al the people in mind plaie the whores."[26] In this process of sexual ravishment the male watcher is also ravished from his proper sense of self, from all that makes him solid and impermeable. As William Prynne thunders in his monumental volume, *Histrio-Mastix. The Players Scourge*, stage plays "so weaken and emasculate all the operations of the soule, with a prophane, if not an unnaturall dissolutenesse; that . . . they licentiously dissolve into wicked vanities and pleasures: and all hope of ever doing good either unto God, the Church, their Country, or owne soules, melteth as the Winter Ice, and floweth away as unprofitable waters.[27] As feminized, as whorish as it is, theater's operation is fundamentally rapine, creating in its audience an absence of male self-possession, then forcefully (if bewitchingly) transferring its own licentious nature into the gap it has created.

Opening just after the demise of the powerful king, Henry V, *1 Henry VI* begins with a vision of a world similar to that of the antitheatricalists' theater: one with no men left in it. Gloucester makes of the late Henry V a demigod, a dazzling, frightening icon whose mere gaze was enough to repel his foes:

England ne'er had a king until his time.
Virtue he had, deserving to command:
His brandish'd sword did blind men with his beams:
His arms spread wider than a dragon's wings:
His sparkling eyes, replete with wrathful fire,
More dazzled and drove back his enemies
Than mid-day sun fierce bent against their faces.

(1.1.8–14)

One wonders, upon reading these lines, what kind of play would ensue if the unrelievedly fearsome king they describe were its dominant character—perhaps another *Tamburlaine*, with its juggernaut of a conqueror, Talus-like, mowing down all that lies in his path.[28] In the end, a Henry V like the one Gloucester remembers blocks even the speech that could record his greatness: "What should I say? His deeds exceed all speech: / He ne'er lift up his hand but conquered" (1.1.15–16). We are reminded of the cautionary dictum of Aristotle regarding what might comfortably be contained in epic, but not in the theater: unlike in an epic poem, in a play "sameness of incident soon produces satiety, and makes tragedies fail on the stage."[29]

Although the play opens with longing for this mode of male authority, however, it also begins with no sense or hope that such an ideal king will ever return. Henry V's absence leaves *1 Henry VI* to match its aching nostalgia for the departed king with a foreboding sense of an approaching dismantling of order in the state—a dismantling that is almost immediately associated with what is feminine in the state: an "effeminate prince" (1.1.35); a proud Duchess of Gloucester who holds her husband in awe (1.1.39). Finally Bedford foretells a post-Henrician England inhabited by only women, in a nightmarish fantasy of nursing-turned-mourning:

> now that Henry's dead,
> Posterity, await for wretched years,
> When at their mothers' moist eyes babes shall suck,
> Our isle be made a nourish of salt tears,
> And none but women left to wail the dead.

(1.1.47–51)

The principle of female disorder in the play comes to be embodied, of course, in Joan. But her dramatic self-possession then implies an equivalence between female disorder and theatrical activity, both of which are enabled by the demise of the epic ruler. This equivalence comes to be borne out by the contrast and conflict in this play between Joan's schemes and conquests, which are nearly always acted out on stage, and Talbot's heroic deeds, which are nearly always reported. Talbot, the only honorable English warrior left in France, exercises the remaining fragment of Henry V-style heroism, as Gloucester's opening speech has portrayed it. But like Henry V, who in his ascent to iconic status has left only inadequate reportage to convey his memory, Talbot's actions achieve greatness primarily in the telling. Throughout the play, Talbot's authority continues to consist more in what is claimed for him, and by him, than in what he has actually done in our sight and hearing. Even when he does perform feats of arms on stage, like rescuing Young Talbot from his French assailants, the deed requires that Talbot retell what has presumably just transpired before us: "Then leaden age, / Quicken'd with youthful spleen and warlike rage, / . . . from the pride of Gallia rescu'd thee" (4.6.12–13, 15). In fact, the portrait of Talbot's heroism can best be painted after he is dead, when in Lucy's speech he comes to equal Henry V in awesome power. Lucy claims for Talbot's absence, not his presence, a truly ravishing power in which Talbot's representation alone would bereave his onlookers of sense: "Were but his picture left amongst you here, / It would amaze the proudest of you all" (4.7.83–84). The fact that Talbot's reputation as a man of valor is based on things recalled, not witnessed, associates him with the world of epic. Epic is, after all, always retrospective in nature, beginning in medias res and proceeding as a memorial reconstruction of events past; moreover, it also allows room for presenting heroic acts whose magnitude could never be reproduced on stage, or anywhere else but in memory.[30] Act 1's sequential *reporting* of Talbot's heroism (scene 1) and *staging* of Joan's seductiveness (scene 2) therefore establish what amounts to a contest of literary modes, epic versus dramatic, as well as a contest between masculine and feminine.

Nowhere is the initial contrast between Talbot's epic authority and Joan's dramatic authority more apparent than in their martial encounter in Act 1, scene 5. Here Talbot himself is ravished by Joan, driven out of his normal senses. And significantly, he attributes this influence not to her force of arms (though she has just equalled him in hand-to-hand combat) but to a kind of stage-trick, as if Joan fights using mirrors:

My thoughts are whirled like a potter's wheel;
I know not where I am, nor what I do:

A witch by fear, not force, like Hannibal,
Drives back our troops and conquers as she lists:
So bees with smoke, and doves with noisome stench,
Are from their hives and houses driven away.

(1.5.19–24)

Here, as in Joan's opening scene with the Dauphin, we find staged in small what the antitheatricalists claimed for the entire practice of theater: the conjuress steals the man's senses, leaving him not knowing where he is, or what he does. Joan's deeds are typically wrapped in charges of deceit—a common accusation against poetry as a whole, which feigns what is not true, but also against theater in particular, which embodies and clothes those feignings. Even Joan's compatriots accuse her of cunning and falsehood after the English take Orleans, a charge that seems hardly fair, considering she is the one hurriedly composing ways to recoup their loss (2.1.50–77). And yet it is true that even Joan's legitimate military stratagems have the air of Odyssean trickery. Her plan to recover Rouen, for example—by passing off herself and a few other French soldiers as grain-toting peasants—depends on her directing their disguise and accent. By referring to "Pucelle and her *practisants*" with what is evidently a Shakespearean neologism (3.2.20, my emphasis), the Bastard of Orleans directly labels Joan as either stage manager or play-actor, for the word "practise" in the Renaissance had as one of its meanings "to perform, act (a play)" (OED v. 1b).

Joan's finest dramatic hour is her persuasion of the Duke of Burgundy to the French cause, which is staged like an antitheatricalist writer's worst fantasy of being ravished by a seductive female theater. First Joan lays out her plan as depending on verbal cajolery: "By fair persuasions, mix'd with sugar'd words, / We will entice the Duke of Burgundy / To leave the Talbot and to follow us" (3.3.18–20). Then, as a skillful actor would, she uses her words to conjure up for Burgundy images of things invisible, impressing into him a concrete, tangible vision of a land not contained within the theater: "Look on thy country, look on fertile France, / And see the cities and the towns defac'd . . . / See, see . . . / Behold" (3.3.44–50). Her words prefigure those of the Chorus in *Henry V*, but with none of their implications of dramatic effect requiring strenuous imaginative effort from a disbelieving audience. Far from it: Burgundy's conversion under these blandishments is practically instantaneous, figured both as a bewitchment, and as a sexual capitulation in which he is the feminized partner:

Either she hath bewitch'd me with her words,
Or nature makes me suddenly relent.
. . . .
I am vanquished; these haughty words of hers
Have batter'd me like roaring cannon-shot
And made me almost yield upon my knees.

(3.3.58–59, 78–80)

Although at first the contest between Joan's and Talbot's literary modes is evenly matched, *1 Henry VI* comes to make provisional inroads on depriving the theatrical feminine of its power, by beginning to assimilate a different version of dramatic power to the male and the epic. Talbot's brand of heroism, even dependent as it is on what the stage cannot directly convey, accumulates a certain dramatic power of its own—a power paradoxically derived from the *absence* of visible, staged effects; and Joan's female, flamboyant, immediate brand of theater is increasingly disallowed.[31] To maintain his own masculine integrity, Talbot cannot, of course, practice Joan-like verbal seductions, which would immediately associate him with theatrical diversion and enchantment. Moreover, Talbot does not project a stage presence that immediately enthralls. The Countess of Auvergne makes much of his unprepossessing appearance, calling him nothing but "a silly dwarf . . . this weak and writhled shrimp" (2.3.21–22), and mocking him for bearing no resemblance to an epic hero: "I thought I should have seen some Hercules, / A second Hector, for his grim aspect / And large proportion of his strong-knit limbs" (2.3.18–20). Far from being ravishing, Talbot's person is shrunken, detumescent, inconsequential. But in this encounter with the Countess, Talbot begins to contrast that kind of ravishment with a new kind of theatrical creation, one that is manifestly *not* feminine in Joan's terms. Rather than seducing his audience into abandoning their right minds—as Burgundy follows Joan—Talbot projects a vision that requires his audience to exercise their minds, to follow him in imagining a world that the immediate surroundings cannot contain, but in this case a world where female allurement is supplanted by heroic imperviousness.

Talbot's response to the Countess illustrates this proposal of theater as an exercise in projection. When she declares she will clap him in irons, he tells her it is impossible to do so:

No, no, I am but shadow of myself:
You are deceiv'd, my substance is not here;
For what you see is but the smallest part

And least proportion of humanity:
I tell you, madam, were the whole frame here,
It is of such a spacious lofty pitch
Your roof were not sufficient to contain't.

(2.3.49–55)

Only then does he call in his men, actualizing on stage, we would expect,
the means to overpower her. But when we consider what Talbot is claiming—that he *can't* call in all his soldiers, there wouldn't be room for them—
we realize that his projection continues to depend on his audience, the
Countess, imagining more than his stage, her house, can hold. Like Joan,
Talbot anticipates *Henry V*'s Chorus, but whereas Joan's stratagem with
Burgundy depends on her spellbinding presence—that is, a presence that
binds his attention only to her, and to the sexualized bewitchment she acts
out before us—Talbot's design is to direct attention away from himself, to
what is beyond his ability himself to enact. At this moment, Talbot solves
the Aristotelian dilemma of how to represent epic heroism on stage without the presentation seeming ridiculous. When staged representation is
replaced by voiced projection, when a dwarfish Talbot refers to his massive
army, the audience stops sniggering and immediately responds as desired:
the Countess is cowed into firm belief, surrendering the stage to the English warrior. "I find thou art no less than fame hath bruited," she says in
capitulating, "And more than may be gather'd by thy shape" (2.3.67–68).

If Talbot can assume dramatic authority in this way, why, we might
wonder, can Joan not attempt a reciprocal appropriation? Why can feminine theatricality not seize hold of projective authority? The answer may
lie in the essential incompatibility between the immediate theatrical ravishment Joan controls, and the detached descriptions by which the epic
vision may be brought on stage. This incompatibility may be measured,
in fact, by what happens when such descriptions are brought to bear on
Joan herself. The French readily encomiate Joan as the English do Talbot.
But such tributes transform all too quickly into eulogy, and in the process demonstrate how any memorial project of this kind serves to control,
rather than to enhance, the feminine theatrical presence.[32] Immediately
after he deifies Joan as Astraea's daughter, the Dauphin imagines her dead,
shifting the object of his adoration from Joan herself, to the container he
will have made for her ashes:

A statelier pyramis to her I'll rear
Than Rhodope's of Memphis ever was;

> In memory of her, when she is dead,
> Her ashes, in an urn more precious
> Than the rich jewel-coffer of Darius,
> Transported shall be at high festivals
> Before the kings and queens of France.
>
> (1.6.21–27)

It is worth examining how this passage, although seeming to confer explicit forms of power upon Joan, progressively empties each form of any real influence. At first the Dauphin appears to cede Joan the place of highest honor, the place of epic: the coffer to which he compares Joan's funerary urn is the one in which Alexander the Great stored the treasured poems of Homer, progenitor (to the Renaissance mind) of all epic. Moreover, the image of how that urn will be displayed is evocative of a saint's remains, brought out in a precious reliquary "at high festivals" to elicit the crowd's devotion. But ashes are not poems, and although Joan's remains may be put in an urn befitting epic, they do not display in these lines an epic poem's ability to speak—the ability for which, we presume, Alexander valued the *Iliad* and the *Odyssey*. Nor do the Dauphin's words grant to Joan the power of saintly relics: we hear nothing of this urn having any effect on the kings and queens who will look on it. Thus, though the word "transported" promises religious ecstasy, it is a promise instantly reneged upon—here the word has only its mundane meaning. Hence the Dauphin's memorial construction of Joan, in its jewelled silence, shows none of the dramatic skill the not-dead Joan plies so well. In the Dauphin's vision, the Joan who has ravished him—skillfully improvisational, uncontrollably verbal, seductively coercive—is literally shut up in a vessel not of her own making. A panegyric to Joan, unlike one to Talbot, is therefore discontinuous with her kind of theatrical authority; it transforms her from an active maker of theater to a mere object of spectacle. The Dauphin's speech manipulates her, like *Tamburlaine*'s Zenocrate, into a dead image serving the male epic project, an inspiration for conquests not her own. Darius's jewel-coffer was Alexander's battle prize.[33]

The plot and the politics of *1 Henry VI* require Joan's eventual dismissal; but because her activities have been identified with one mode of theatricality, her removal also involves showing that mode to be both devalued and ineffectual. In short, the play as a whole enacts the desire voiced in the Dauphin's fantasy: a desire to cordon off the feminine as a ravishing force, projecting her instead as a mute and contained spectacle. Act 5, scene 3, in which Joan's loss of power is revealed, demonstrates this shift most visibly. Throughout the play, as we have seen, both the French praise and the English epithets attached to Joan have concentrated in large part upon the power of her voice. As prophesying daughter of Saint Philip, as "damned sorceress," or as "shameless courtezan" (1.2.143; 3.2.38, 45)—in other words, as Sibyl or as Siren—she is equally assigned a preternatural ability to enforce her desires through speech. Thus her demons' appearance in this scene, as well as their refusal to obey her commands, offers a commentary on the substitution of masculine for feminine voicings of power in the play. On the one hand, this episode occasions a significant dramatic moment for Joan, affording her a speech of some thirty lines; but on the other, it thematizes the evaporation of her dramatic effectiveness, since the demons as unwilling audience do not respond. And perhaps more importantly, the demons' mere appearance on stage, their first, signifies that Joan's power has been precipitated from an active, circulating linguistic and sexual energy into a gaggle of stagy fiends, whose dumb departure drives Joan to admit, "My ancient incantations are too weak" (5.3.27). Joan is still free to speak, of course, but her speech hereafter does not move her listeners. Her last exchange with York upon her capture by him both locates where her power has resided all along, in her tongue, and illustrates how this female verbal power will be increasingly circumscribed in the remaining plays of this first tetralogy.

York. Fell banning hag, enchantress, hold thy tongue!
Joan. I prithee, give me leave to curse awhile.
York. Curse, miscreant, when thou comest to the stake.

                                        (5.3.42–44)

Although women can curse, and their bitter prophesies often as not come true, cursing hardly equals the planning, instigation, and control of dramatic action, as the women of *Richard III* will bear out. Joan's last appearance, with her wildly dispatched and easily mocked attempts at saving herself from the flames, demonstrates even more strongly the extent to which female control in the play has dissipated. Her hastily composed excuses, far from ravishing her audience and substituting her will for theirs, are either ignored ("Ay, ay; away with her to execution!" [5.4.54]) or used to finish her off ("Strumpet, thy words condemn thy brat and thee" [5.4.84]).

The removal of both Joan and Talbot from the stage leaves the end of *1 Henry VI* in an interesting vacuum of authority, one with which the final three plays of this tetralogy must contend, even as the persons represented in them contend for the crown. Although Talbot the hero is mourned, we are left nonetheless with the sense that his mode of epic action has been discarded as ultimately unsuited to the theater, even as this "great exemplar of chivalric masculinity," as Coppélia Kahn describes him, is "no longer viable in this twilight of feudalism."[34] Both the chivalry for which Talbot is famous and the reportage that conveys that heroism become awkward and overblown in his last scene, whose strain is evident in its poetry, fifty lines of stilted, endstopped couplets. It is afterward too easy for Joan to point to Talbot's corpse as only that, "Stinking and fly-blown," fallen too far for the audience's epic desires to project him as other than what the stage can present (4.7.76).

But neither is theatrical authority readily vested in another Joan, someone else who inflicts feminine dramatic ravishment as she does. Several critics have seen Margaret of Anjou, who first appears between Joan's capture and condemnation, as a one-for-one replacement of Joan, one French witch for another; but Margaret's scope of action is immediately established in *1 Henry VI* as far more limited than Joan's, so that she cannot possibly call up the entire range of anxieties applicable to a female figure of authority.[35] In Margaret's first scene at the end of the play, her encounter with Suffolk has nothing of the air of Joan's with the Dauphin or with Burgundy, a dissimilarity that primarily has to do with whose words orchestrate the event. Although Suffolk is besotted with love for Margaret, it remains his language, not hers, that is the controlling agent: taking the role of the hapless lover, his voice is that of a Petrarchan sonneteer who claims inarticulateness even while he speaks volumes about his beloved (5.3.65–71).[36] And it is therefore Suffolk who, though speaking of Margaret, will rob his audience of their senses with his speech. He trains himself for this prospect even while Margaret is before him:

> Bethink thee on her virtues that surmount,
> And natural graces that extinguish art;
> Repeat their semblance often on the seas,
> That, when thou com'st to kneel at Henry's feet,
> Thou may'st bereave him of his wits with wonder.
>
> (5.3.191–95)

Henry in turn is "astonish'd" by Suffolk's report—the same word the Dauphin had used to describe his reaction to Joan (1.2.93)—and is "driven by breath of her renown" to marry her (5.5.2, 7).

The remaining plays of this first historical tetralogy, even while they stage several remarkably authoritative (even rampaging) women, will never again invest theatrical control in a single woman as *1 Henry VI* did in Joan La Pucelle. Joan's other, more easily identifiable talents are splintered into several different persons: her witchcraft becomes the Duchess of Gloucester's practice in *2 Henry VI*; her sexual, martial, and prophetic propensities become the portion of the early, middle, and late versions of Queen Margaret—the Margarets of, respectively, *2 Henry VI*, *3 Henry VI*, and *Richard III*. Missing from all of these women, however, is a sense of controlling the scene around them as a theatrical performance. Most inadequate in this regard is the Duchess of Gloucester, whose witchcraft as we see it is never entirely her own. In *2 Henry VI*'s conjuring scene (Act 1, scene 4) Bolingbroke and the other men are in charge of the proceedings; moreover, the entire episode seems to have been set up by Gloucester's enemies. Nor does it much seem to matter to the Duchess's prestige that the conjurations are successful. Even more immediately than with Joan's fiends, the staged appearance of the woman's demonic familiars indicates not the height of her influence, but rather her imminent fall from grace. And most importantly, the whole affair with the Duchess ultimately has little to do with eliminating a powerful woman, and everything to do with unseating a powerful man. Later, Suffolk and Margaret will assert that Gloucester put his wife up to performing witchcraft, or at least put her in the frame of mind to do so (3.1.45–52). Though mendacious, their contentions point toward the accelerating impoverishment of female authority in this play. The Duchess is finally reduced to the kind of dumb object of scrutiny paraded through the streets that also marked the waning of Joan La Pucelle's potency, both in fact and in the Dauphin's fantasy.

Margaret, unlike the Duchess, remains an audible as well as visible presence throughout the tetralogy, but her effect never becomes quite as incantatory as Joan La Pucelle's. *2 Henry VI* provides a striking example. Though Margaret defends herself and Suffolk in a protracted and conceivably persuasive speech to King Henry, her protestations—however long and eloquent—fail to move her husband (3.2.55–120). Only in *3 Henry VI* does Margaret come close to equalling Joan in this aspect, when she enters a kind of persuasion contest with Warwick for the support of the King of France (Act 3, scene 3). Immediately afterward, Margaret assumes a martial resemblance to Joan by resolving to don armor and project authentic ruling authority. Edward, learning of this decision, interprets it as a theatrical (and Joan-like) one: "Belike she minds to play the Amazon" (4.1.105). But Margaret never displays any awareness of her own drama-

turgical potential. Margaret does wield language freely, it is true: but persuasive rhetoric is attributed to her by male voices rather than deliberately
claimed by her, and in ways that serve more to reinforce than to overcome
a male consciousness. For example, after Margaret makes a speech worthy
of Queen Elizabeth before the troops at Tilbury, the Prince of Wales asserts that her words inspire tumescent manly valor:

> Methinks a woman of this valiant spirit
> Should, if a coward heard her speak these words,
> Infuse his breast with magnanimity
> And make him, naked, foil a man at arms.

> (5.4.39–42)

In *Richard III*, Margaret is stripped of even this influence upon men.
Although she becomes, if anything, a creature entirely of language—one
who is able only to curse—she does so as a hectoring Cassandra, doomed
always to be right but never to be heeded, or as the Chorus of a Greek
drama, who foreshadows and illuminates the main action but never directs
it. After Joan, females are stripped of conscious theatrical authority.[37]

But it does not likewise follow that theatrical authority is stripped of
the feminine. The conclusion of this tetralogy with *Richard III*, in fact,
makes a novel and terrifying proposition in terms of the alternative and
seemingly incompatible modes of theatrical authority first attempted in
1 Henry VI: that dramatic ravishment in the manner of Joan might equally
well be embodied in a man. Richard's histrionic prowess seems a direct inheritance from Joan La Pucelle; certainly he is the first figure of authority
since Joan who both commands the stage and is conscious of that command. My task here will be not so much to demonstrate Richard's awareness of his own theatricality, which has been well proved elsewhere,[38] but
to explore how this awareness, in not sufficiently differentiating Richard
from the theatrical feminine, doubly problematizes his accession to the
throne.

Richard's direct revelations of histrionic consciousness begin in
3 Henry VI, when he resolves in his "murderous Machiavel" speech to
"wet my cheeks with artificial tears, / And frame my face to all occasions" (3.2.184–85). From this assertion alone, we might suspect Richard
of edging towards the feminine, as he adopts tactics of deliberate falsehood that, up to this point in the tetralogy, have been employed chiefly
by Joan and Margaret. But on his way to his climactic line in this speech,

Richard affiliates himself even more closely with a feminine manner of dramatic seduction. His final resolution to "set the murderous Machiavel to school" builds from the initial claim, "I'll drown more sailors than the mermaid shall," so that to be swayed by Richard is to heed the Sirens' call (3.2.186). Here Richard goes Talbot one better at usurping female power: whereas Talbot's epic mode of projective speech simply supplanted Joan's seductive mode, Richard willfully integrates feminine theatrical method, in all its sexual bewitchment, into his own modus operandi. What Richard gains thereby is an ability to ravish his courtly audience, diverting them from their right minds so that they willingly dash themselves on the rocks of his nefarious machinations. And like Joan's successful plots, Richard's are played out in full sight and hearing, with no projection of an unstageable power that reinforces his presence. We first see his fledgling use of his craft in *3 Henry VI*, where he wins his brother George back to the Yorkist cause in a way that nearly duplicates Joan's seduction of Burgundy. These talents emerge fully by the time of his shocking wooing of Anne in *Richard III*. In recalling her surrender, Anne describes a process of ravishment fully equal to any instigated by Joan: "my woman's heart / Grossly grew captive to his honey words" (4.1.78–79). The word "grossly" conveys not only Anne's disgust at having succumbed, but also the degree to which Richard's methods, like Joan's, are sexually, corporeally charged—a fact Richard mockingly acknowledges when he has overcome her defenses: "Upon my life, she finds—although I cannot—/ Myself to be a marvellous proper man" (1.2.258–59).[39]

To say that Richard's successful consummation of his seductions is distasteful, both to his victims and to his witnesses, would be understatement in the extreme. Yet *Richard III*'s experimental proposal of a man appropriating the theatrical feminine is, no doubt, not meant to inspire comfort; rather, it contradicts the prior example of Talbot by intimating that it is fruitless to conceive of a satisfactorily masculine theater, that all playacting is unavoidably seductive, deceiving, ravishing. Richard's "murderous Machiavel" speech, in fact, enacts this very proposal. Just after he announces he will outdo the Sirens, Richard proposes male models for his action: "I'll play the orator as well as Nestor, / Deceive more slily than Ulysses could, / And, like a Sinon, take another Troy" (*3 Henry VI*, 3.2.188–90). The shift from deploying feminine methods of seduction to adopting male models of deceit, from Siren to trickster, suggests that jumping out of the feminine frying pan only lands theater in the Ricardian fire.

But at the same time *Richard III*, though it builds this suggestion up to a tremendous pitch, does not ultimately confirm it. Even more than Richard's victims (who always realize, sooner or later, what has been perpetrated upon them) Richard's primary audience, those to whom he addresses those solo speeches baldly laying out his plans, are inoculated against being bewitched by him. His seductions are in this way contained, as he himself posits an audience whose senses are sharpened, not robbed, by having been made privy to his intentions.[40] What *Richard III* does not provide, however, is an alternative to those despicable Ricardian seductions. In the fratricidal confusion of the Wars of the Roses, no Talbot is on hand to deliver a new mode of theater suitable to epic ideals. In fact, because of this tetralogy's mounting emphasis on patriarchal bloodlines, on the connection between father and son, the requirements for epic have become doubly unfulfillable: the feuding between families not only corrupts the recall of heroic deeds (the structure of Homeric epic), but also disrupts the untrammeled passage of male lineage (the structure of Virgilian epic). And because *Richard III* insists that Richard himself, the only practicer of dramatic art in the last three plays of this tetralogy, is implicated in this interference in both history and genealogy, theater remains inescapably (if uncomfortably) identified only with that which interrupts epic, rather than that which transmits it.

At first, all disruptions of epic's memorial constructions after *1 Henry VI* continue to be located in women, even if their role in those disruptions is structural, not theatrical. Henry VI's marriage to Margaret is initially figured as obliterating history, cancelling Henry V's recorded heroism. Gloucester angrily declares,

> shameful is this league,
> Fatal this marriage, cancelling your fame,
> Blotting your names from books of memory,
> Razing the characters of your renown,
> Defacing monuments of conquer'd France,
> Undoing all, as all had never been!
>
> (*2 Henry VI*, 1.1.97–102)

What the marriage threatens is a reversal of the rhetorical domination the Dauphin perpetrated upon Joan. Whereas the Dauphin pictured Joan reduced to her remains within a man-made monument, Gloucester pictures English man-made monuments reduced to mere remains. In his phrase "Undoing all, as all had never been" we hear the despair of an epic truncated: Troy in flames, with no Aeneas left to build Rome from its ashes. Continued references to both the *Iliad* and the *Aeneid* cause this anxiety to reverberate throughout the tetralogy, as if the marriage with Margaret prompts England to begin severing its ties with its own national myth, Britain as Troynovaunt. Similarly, in *3 Henry VI*, it is Margaret in her role as mother whose presence serves to dismantle the epic project. As in other moments in Shakespeare, where the mere mention of one's mother calls into question the legitimacy of one's descent from one's father, Margaret's fierce sponsorship of her son seems seriously to damage the delicate linkages that comprise patriarchal lineage—a disastrous prospect for epic.[41] The future Richard III, ironically, associates Margaret's authority with her son's illegitimacy when he jeers at the Prince of Wales, "Whoever got thee, there thy mother stands; / For well I wot thou hast thy mother's tongue" (*3 Henry VI*, 2.2.133–34).

But of course Richard too, in his moves toward usurping the throne, is involved in disrupting patriarchy. Richard's linguistic seductiveness, in its attempts to suspend his victims' reason, finds its genealogical analogue in Richard's efforts to suspend normal rules of succession.[42] In his identification not only with the Sirens, but also with Nestor, Ulysses, and Sinon, Richard affiliates himself not with the Trojans, England's putative epic forebears, but with the constellation of Greeks whose trickery nearly canceled that heroic line. Structurally as well as theatrically, then, Richard poses as an alternative to female authority who is finally no real alternative at all. Both as practicer of the theatrical feminine and as usurper of the English throne, Richard denies the promise made by Arthur's reading of the Briton chronicle: that a reversion of power to the male necessarily ensures right order, either literary or dynastic.

Because it does not fully revise this tetralogy's initial equation of the theatrical with the feminine, *Richard III* leaves the theater with nowhere to turn. *Richard III* and Richard III both end upon the founding of a dynasty, but that event has nothing to do with the ways in which the operations of the theater have been defined in this play. We could hardly ask for a less theatrically compelling leader than Henry of Richmond, who (like Malcolm or Fortinbras) seems designed to remind us that rightful kingship demands a clean break from that which has held dramatic interest. But as long as theatrical belief involves seduction and bewitchment, it remains incompatible with both epic heroism and epic lineage. This first tetralogy as a whole, then, brackets theater and its illegitimate seductions by two heroic kings— the dead Henry V at the tetralogy's beginning, Richmond at its end—to

whom plays cannot do justice. *Richard III* leaves theater unable to perform the transformation enacted in Arthur's reading of his own history:
though Richard stands as a male monarch who can be ravishing, he is not
the king we have been looking for, one who will bear the weight of epic.

Once we see Richard III as a ruler unable to pose a satisfactory alternative to feminine rule, we may begin to hypothesize a constellation of
topical associations wholly opposed to the ones traditionally posited for
the play. For when Richard bars dynastic continuity as do the women of
epic and of the preceding history plays, he also takes up a position in relation to the monarchy eerily similar to Elizabeth Tudor's in the 1590s.[43]
Elizabeth's refusal to marry and bear children had been a national obsession since the beginning of her reign; we may track this concern in the
increasingly pleading, and sometimes threatening, rhetoric of Parliament,
which brought up the topic of Elizabeth's marriage whenever she had to
petition for funds.[44] But by the 1590s, with the queen's childbearing years
long over, no one could see Elizabeth as anything but the ruler who would,
by her own choice, end the House of Tudor. The voicing of anxiety over
succession came to a head beginning in 1594, with the publication and dis-
semination of *A conference about the next succession to the Crowne of Ingland*, a
polemical tract published under the pseudonym "R. Doleman," and probably written by the Jesuit propagandist Robert Parsons.[45] In an attempt to
put forward the Infanta of Spain, who was descended from John of Gaunt's
second wife, as the next legitimate (and Roman Catholic) ruler of England,
"Doleman" argues that a country may choose a ruler as it pleases, putting
aside those whose lineage puts them in the way of a more desirable candi-
date. In other words, "Doleman" proposes that each country may act in
its own self-interest (though more benevolently, of course) as Richard III
does for himself. Responders to Parsons's tract were not slow to identify
his plan as a return to Ricardian modes of determining monarchic succession. John Hayward, evidently trying to compensate for the trouble caused
by his history of Henry IV's reign, wrote an answer to Parsons supporting
the divine right of kings and recalling the "domestical warres, for excluding the neerest in bloud from the crowne, into which unquiet quarrell, you
doe now endevour againe to imbarke us."[46] Even Catholics recoiled from
Parsons's dismantling of the rules of royal lineage. Henry Constable similarly denounces Parsons by reference to the Wars of the Roses, declaring
that Parsons aims "to breed a devorse of frendship in kinred by disturbinge
the lawfall liniall course of consanguinitye provided by lawes, for passaige
of thinheritance & succession, & that in such a sorte as hath not bene

allowed by Judgement of law to passe in englande [,] though by violence some suche enormities haue bene intruded and bolstered for a whyle to the horrible ruyne of manye noble families not recoverable."[47]

Detractors of Parsons were necessarily defenders of Elizabeth; but some of those defenders, in their near-hysteric pleas that Elizabeth might settle the succession and hence close off Parsons-like proposals of disorder, came close to saying that Elizabeth, too, threatened to plunge her realm into the fatal bowels of Ricardian chaos. In his *Pithie exhortation to her majestie for establishing her successor to the crowne*, the ex-parliamentary leader Peter Wentworth asserts that Elizabeth, by not following the example of her father, would call forth again the turmoil that the House of Tudor originally halted: "your most noble father fore-saw that no better then the fore-rehearsed calamities, would be the state of this land, if hee had died before hee had made his heire knowne: yea, that hee imputed all the miseries that this land had abode, through the contention betwixt the two houses of Yorke and Lancaster, to this: to wit, that the order & right of succession, had not bene (in former time) carefullie enough looked unto, & made publikely knowne."[48] If we project this anxiety over Elizabeth promoting internal strife onto the end of *Richard III*, we can construct a local reading of this tetralogy dependent not only on a connection between Elizabeth and Joan La Pucelle, but also on a connection between Elizabeth and Richard III. We can envision a bizarre face-off between Henry of Richmond, the progenitor of a monarchical line that reestablished dynastic continuity, and his own granddaughter, who inherited that line's promise only to end it. The celebration occasioned by Richmond's triumph therefore rings hollow, since his victory historically only doubles back on itself. What good is this male hero's defeat of the dynastically interruptive Richard if it only makes way for an entirely feminine, dynastically disastrous queen? Patriarchally as well as dramatically, Richmond cannot be seen as a convincing alternative to the disruption he staves off.

Of course I do not mean to assert that Shakespeare's Richard III "is" Elizabeth, in the same sort of direct allegory by which she suspected herself to be Richard II in portrayals of that deposed king.[49] But the last moments of *Richard III*, in their unsustainable imposition of proper kingship, pose a problem that reverberates politically as well as dramatically: although the play inculcates a desire for an alternative to Richard, the opposition it maintains between its own operations and those of epic heroism prevents it from fulfilling this desire. In the second section of this chapter, I turn to a Shakespearean king who makes a far more impressive attempt at that task: Henry V, whose play both reworks the concerns of the first tetralogy and raises their stakes, wagering its entire success on its hero's appropriation of dramatic power to the epic king.

Nostalgia, Epic Theater, and the Not Yet Late Queen: Refusing Female Rule in the Second Tetralogy

Within the last decade and a half, *Henry V* has assumed a surprisingly prominent place not only in Shakespeare criticism, but in wider critical debates over the relations between literature and hegemonic political power. Prompted by Stephen Greenblatt's consideration of the *Henriad* in his essay "Invisible Bullets," various critics have staked out Shakespeare's war play as their own battlefield for contesting, as Jean Howard puts it, "how and why a culture produces and deals with challenges to its dominant ideologies."[50] Whatever their stance, however, these critics have largely left untested Greenblatt's crucial assumption that, in the *Henriad*'s counterpoint between hegemony and subversion (or at least imagined subversion), hegemony resides with and emerges from the Elizabethan monarchy, and subversion (even if illusory) resides with and emerges from the Elizabethan stage. My contention, in contrast, is that *Henry V* crowns an experiment conducted by Shakespeare's second historical tetralogy in exercising precisely the reverse relation between throne and theater. If we fully consider this tetralogy's historical moment—its production late in the reign of not simply a monarch, but a queen—then *Henry V*'s association between theatrical enterprise and the enterprises of a dauntingly masculine monarch grants theater not the power of subversion, but rather the power of patriarchy, which is asserted over and against the waning and increasingly disparaged power of female rule.

In its opening lines, *Henry V* demonstrates its intent to undertake what Aristotle warned could not satisfactorily be done: to put epic on stage. The Prologue, beginning as it does with an epic invocation of the Muse, immediately and specifically translates the epic poet's desire for a Muse's inspiration into the playwright's desire for an unmatched stage, actors, and audience:

> O, for a Muse of fire, that would ascend
> The brightest heaven of invention;

A kingdom for a stage, princes to act
And monarchs to behold the swelling scene!

(1.Pro.1–4)

Were all these wishes fulfilled, the result would be the appearance, rather than the representation, of a king, the same king who could exist only in memory at the opening of *1 Henry VI*. That king, who "ne'er lift up his hand but conquered," would live again in all his godlike grandeur: "Then should the warlike Harry, like himself, / Assume the port of Mars" (1.Pro.5–6).

Of course this brave beginning immediately runs aground upon the material inadequacies of the theater, which does not possess and cannot hold entire armies of men, much less the "vasty fields of France" on which they fought (1.Pro.12). The Prologue, in admitting the stage's short-comings, places itself in the position of Talbot, evoking for the Countess of Auvergne soldiers whose physical presence can never be realized. With Talbot, this moment constituted an innovative proposal of a masculine the-atrical audience whose sensibility, rather than being seduced by the stage, was practiced at overcoming the stage's shortcomings. But the Prologue's level of anxiety about whether this proposal can be reintroduced leads us to examine more closely the gender affiliations of the theater, of the audience, and of the theatrical creation itself. As David Willbern notes, the Pro-logue's claims of theatrical inefficacy are coupled with its portrayal of the theater as an essentially feminine space: a pregnant, womblike, crammable O that is expected to bring forth heroes of the past, full-blown.[51] Although the Prologue's reference to "this swelling scene" might be interpreted as phallic as much as gestatory, further lines develop the theater as a scene of feminine reproduction, as the "cockpit" that both holds ("girdles") and brings forth the theatrical scene. This passage is worth quoting at length for its remarkable constellation of images of gendered generation:

> But pardon, gentles all,
> The flat unraised spirits that hath dar'd
> On this unworthy scaffold to bring forth
> So great an object: can this cockpit hold
> The vasty fields of France? or may we cram
> Within this wooden O the very casques
> That did affright the air at Agincourt?

O, pardon! since a crooked figure may
Attest in little place a million;
And let us, ciphers to this great accompt,
On your imaginary forces work.
Suppose within the girdle of these walls
Are now confin'd two mighty monarchies,

. . . .

Piece out our imperfections with your thoughts;
Into a thousand parts divide one man,
And make imaginary puissance.

                              (1.Pro.8–20, 23–25)

In this speech, the Prologue both recalls and goes some way toward recuperating the first tetralogy's dilemma of how to present masculine heroes
in a feminized theater. At first the "crooked figure" of the stage's "O," the
zero that when placed at the end of a numeral may "attest in little place
a million," fleetingly recollects Richard III's own crooked figure, as well
as his deceiving habit of making something out of nothing. Moreover,
the continuing metaphor of the actors as little O's themselves, "ciphers to
this great accompt," goes on to construe the actors as enacting a theatrical
seduction in which the audience acts as the passive partner: "let us . . . on
your imaginary forces work." But the introduction of the word "forces"
signals a shift in the erotic energies of this proposed imaginative encounter.
If the "forces" at hand belong to the audience, not the stage, then the scene
is changed from one of theatrical seduction to one of theatrical conception.
This is an important if subtle shift, since with it the audience, no longer
a ravished victim, takes the role of the man in the Aristotelian theory of
human conception, imposing form upon the staged matter: "Piece out
our imperfections with your thoughts; / Into a thousand parts divide one
man, / And make imaginary puissance" (1.Pro.23–25).[52] This refiguration
of a feminine theater as a site of dramatic inability hence ironically proves
to be an enabling maneuver for *Henry V*. If the theater is feminine only
insofar as it is a womblike container, then the heroes it reproduces, like
the audience response that gives them life, may be characterized as men
untainted by feminine seductive skill. *Henry V* declares the stage feminine
only to turn attention away from that stage, so that it can propose masculine authority as the only, unassailable, authority—both kingly and dramatic—in a history play that intends to bring English national epic to life.
    With this beginning *Henry V* distances itself from the preceding plays

in Shakespeare's second tetralogy of histories, and from their concerns about the evident incompatibility between stable kingship and good theater. In fact the second tetralogy up to this point has in many ways replayed the anxieties of the first, in associating the feminine both with theatricality and with elements disrupting state affairs. Admittedly, *Richard II* and *1* and *2 Henry IV* do not embody the theatrical feminine in a single villainess like Joan, or even a villain like Richard III; as Jean Howard and Phyllis Rackin point out, the second tetralogy is remarkable for its near-total relegation of women to marginalized roles—homebound wives, tavern keepers, prostitutes.[53] And these women can themselves hardly account for these plays' anxiety over the male integrity of the monarchy, or their tendency to shadowbox with feminine principles that are never fully embodied in a staged female character. Instead, the second tetralogy offers two men who, in their associations with both the feminine and the theatrical, continue to demonstrate the first tetralogy's opposition between who is fit to rule and who can most compellingly hold the stage. Richard II, incompetent king as he is, is repeatedly referred to as womanish in his vacillation and vanity. But if these qualities justify Richard's removal from the throne, his deposition and subsequent murder also afford him the play's most lyric and affecting scenes, as well as those most conscious of Richard's manipulative self-staging.[54] And although Bolingbroke reportedly understands the advantage to be gained by showing himself to the common folk (*Richard II*, 1.4.24–36), what we see of him on stage fails to match the dramatic standard set by Richard's extravagantly voiced martyrdom.

In *1* and *2 Henry IV*, Falstaff replaces Richard as the alternative to Bolingbroke's (now Henry IV's) unitary language of kingship. As Valerie Traub points out, Falstaff bears a maternal, pre-Oedipal relation to Hal, one signified in the swollen belly Falstaff calls his "womb" (*2 Henry IV*, 4.3.22), as well as in his penchant for remarks to Hal such as "I knew ye as well as he that made ye," as if to imply that Falstaff was present with Hal's father at Hal's making (*1 Henry IV*, 2.4.263).[55] More important for my purposes, however, is Falstaff's assumption of what both *The Faerie Queene* and Shakespeare's first tetralogy define as a feminine propensity for disrupting heroic enterprise and suspending masculine self-command. Eastcheap, for Hal, is the place of ravishing theater, and the Boar's Head Inn is where, with sack and wit, one may willingly forget one's sense of station and duty for awhile. And Falstaff, presiding over this scene, is the chief propagator of theatrical activity. In its shifting, improvisational expansiveness, Falstaff's speech displays and amplifies the bewitching qualities so often attributed to Joan La Pucelle. Whether or not his postures finally compel belief, they remain attractive and continue to encourage dalliance among their endless, profligate fantasies. The Hostess, hearing Falstaff play at being Hal's father, makes clear the associations between Falstaff, the theater, and feminine seduction: "O Jesu, he doth it as like one of these harlotry players as ever I see!" (*1 Henry IV*, 2.4.390–91).[56] When Falstaff parodies first Hal's father and then Hal, he ends with a plea for the necessity of Eastcheap's theatricality, in all its multifarious seduction: "banish plump Jack, and banish all the world" (*1 Henry IV*, 2.4.473–74). We can hardly help associating that world, which Hal indeed eventually banishes, both with Falstaff's roundness and with the "wooden O" of Shakespeare's theater, a theater that soon (beginning sometime in 1599) would be the "Globe" itself.

Hal, though, knows there is a world elsewhere; he is alone in being able to inoculate himself against the charms of Eastcheap, just as one does against the moustache-twirling confidences of Richard III. In *Henry V*, the only vestige of the Falstaffian theatrical voice is an account of its dying. With Falstaff's babbling of green fields, the green world of comedy—and its respite from affairs of kingship—finally gives way to the grassy fields of France.[57] Falstaff's demise, though, touches again upon the issues advanced by *Henry V*'s Prologue. If theater is to be an effeminizing agent no longer, what shall it be? The Chorus's speeches in *Henry V*, to which I shall return, continue to address this issue more or less directly. But the action of the play itself worries at the problem as well. Here the question of the theatrical feminine is woven into the fabric of the monarchy itself, and into King Henry's right and ability to declare himself sovereign. In the remainder of this chapter, I explore how Henry V himself will propose a new language for theater: one suited to the epic mode, but achieved only by rooting out and disavowing any woman's part in shaping kingship.

I begin this exploration with a consideration of the first long speech in *Henry V*, and one of the longest in the play—that is, the Archbishop of Canterbury's disquisition on Salic law, the French tradition that kingship may never be claimed via descent from a woman. The mercenary motives behind Canterbury's speech, and their influence on how we view Henry's decision to fight for dominion of France, have been much debated; nevertheless, most critics have found it difficult to construe this speech itself as anything but a throwaway, a purely legalistic discussion that merely gives Henry the excuse to act.[58] But in truth, *Henry V* is deeply concerned with Salic law, and—the Archbishop to the contrary—interested in how the

English might safely take the *French* side of the Salic-law issue: that is to say, how an English king might legitimately claim political power without having derived any of that power from a woman. If monarchical power in *Henry V* is indeed intimately bound up with theatrical power, as Greenblatt contends, then the play's concern with the ruler's gender also becomes one of characterizing dramatic power as wholly and properly male.

Salic law is never again mentioned in the play after this early scene; but we may begin to investigate its submerged importance by following Leah Marcus's lead, and asking ourselves why Salic law might be an issue topical to the writing of *Henry V*. The far more obviously topical reference in *Henry V* is the one that pinpoints the date of the play to an unusually precise degree: that is, the allusion to the Earl of Essex, "the general of our gracious empress," and his anticipated triumph over the Irish (5.Chor.29–34), which locates the play as having been written in the late spring or early summer of 1599.[59] But this same allusion—in its chronological specificity, in its naming of Essex, and in its hopeful (if cautious) projection of male conquest—also serves to locate the play firmly in that time of increasing speculation I brought up in regard to *Richard III*, that is, speculation over who should rule when England's now-aged gracious empress would be gone. Essex himself was deeply embroiled in the controversy, as he and Elizabeth's Secretary Robert Cecil in turn sought favor from James VI of Scotland, Elizabeth's likely but by no means guaranteed successor. Parsons's *Conference about the next succession*, even while advocating a Catholic successor to the throne, is dedicated to Essex, because "no man [is] like to have a greater part or sway in deciding of this great affaire."[60] *Henry V*'s uniquely topical reference thus circles back, via Essex's ambition to influence royal succession, to the play's Salic law speech; Parsons's tract, like others produced in the succession debates of the 1580s and 1590s, mentions Salic law as a precedent for measures that might promote only desirable candidates to the throne.[61]

Behind the generally respectful pleas to Elizabeth to name a successor —pleas provoked by Parsons's tract—lay an anxiety about what the succession controversy might mean: not simply the hope of having a ruler after Elizabeth, but rather the desire to have a ruler instead of Elizabeth. Bishop Godfrey Goodman, writing during the reign of Charles I, remembered of this time that "The people were very generally weary of an old woman's government."[62] Testimony in the 1598 trial of one Edward Fraunces, accused of attempting to seduce a woman named Elizabeth Baylie, revealed that Fraunces had remarked "that the land had been happy if Her Majesty had been cut off 20 years since, so that some noble prince might have reigned in her stead."[63] The 1599 crisis in government later precipitated by Essex's Irish failure, a failure caused in part by his lack of support from either Cecil or his always-cautious queen, seems to have marked a watershed in the increase of the people's discontent. Oxford's Regius Professor of Divinity Thomas Holland, when he "printed in 1601 his accession-day sermon of two years earlier, . . . found it necessary to preface it with 'An Apologetical Discourse' against those who opposed the celebration of 17 November [Elizabeth's accession day] as a Holy Day."[64] Perhaps most telling of all is the bill passed by Parliament in 1601 "to prohibit the writing and publishing of books about the title to the Crown of this realm, and the authority of the Government thereof, subjects being thus led into false errors and traitorous attempts against the Queen, into private factions, unlawful bonds, &c."[65] This injunction may have prevented the publication of manuscripts like that of the Lincolnshire rector Henry Hooke, who in 1601 or 1602 wrote of his desire "that what corruptions in justice, what blemishes in religion, the infirmitie, and inconveniency of woemanhead, would not permitt to discover and discerne, the vigor, and conveniency of man sytting as king in the throne of aucthoritie; maye diligently search out, and speedylie reforme."[66]

Such grumblings about the Queen indicate a partial turn from the antigynecocratic sentiments of the beginning of her reign and their obsession with the possibility of a "female nature" overtaking its bounds when it took over a country, her sexuality ruling both her actions and her nation.[67] Writings polemically directed in particular against either Elizabeth or Mary, Queen of Scots had continued in this same vein: their ire, which came to a head in the circumstances surrounding Mary's 1587 execution, had focused on the dissipation of these two women's bodies, their lust for power commingling itself with physical venery. These invectives had imagined the indirection into which a queen's realm is led as a wild, careening path governed only by the whims of a woman's pernicious sexual desire—making her country into a "cuntry," as the expatriate Cardinal of England William Allen pointedly spelled the word in 1588.[68] In the 1590s, in contrast, England for the first time also considered its queen's body as a decaying body, and her rule as one that would lead the country nowhere at all. J. E. Neale identifies the late–Elizabethan ennui that enveloped the court and country as having been caused by "a credulous desire of novelty and change, hoping for better times, despising the present, and forgetting favours past."[69] In 1602, as England waited ever more impatiently for Elizabeth to hand over both state and succession to a king, her godson Sir John Harington wrote, "I find some less mindful of what they are soon to lose, than of what they may perchance hereafter get."[70] Carole Levin has studied how late Elizabethan unrest over the state of its monarchy prompted the revival of rumors from Mary Tudor's time—rumors that Edward VI, Mary and Elizabeth Tudor's brother, had not died in 1553 but was about to return as savior of his people.[71] If such desires could be attached to the figure of a less than mythic boy-king who had reigned only six years, the fantasy of the return of legitimate male rule must indeed have been powerful.

The wish for the return of a King Edward who had been dead some forty years—in this case, not Edward VI but Edward III—is eerily echoed in *Henry V*. The entire second historical tetralogy, of course, broods upon as well as enacts the movement of royal succession, but *Henry V*'s presentation of the succession question is remarkable for the temporal as well as territorial convolutions surrounding the topic. Canterbury's Salic law speech first brings up succession in regard to France, not England; and his determination of who ought to rule there in the future is initially based on a recitation of who has ruled there in the past. Because previous French kings have claimed the throne through descent from a female, so might Henry. Moreover, as Canterbury goes on to assert, Henry's English forebears, Edward III and Edward the Black Prince, conquered France; it is from them that Henry should take his inspiration. Though no one in the play will ever again discuss Salic law, several speakers will return to this backward-looking temporal argument as a prescriptive. Forward-moving, decisive action is to be had by recalling, even replicating the past; Henry will be victorious when he imitates his great-grandfather, Edward III.

But in the slippage between the two prongs of Canterbury's argument—his debunking of Salic law, and his invocation of Edward III—resides the issue with which *Henry V* must grapple, both in terms of England's edginess about its elderly queen and in terms of the gender affiliations of the theater itself. In a late Elizabethan context, this slippage is equivalent to a shift between first upholding Elizabeth's reign (via defending a woman's place in royal lineage), and then abandoning this loyalty to look forward, by looking back, to a restored male rule. Even more interesting for theater, however, is the altered tone that accompanies the shift. The stirring phrasing of Canterbury's reference to mythic Edward and his son, especially after the dry, convoluted, even specious recital of the French monarchy's derivation, has the immediate effect of associating male rule with compelling theater—unlike female rule, which in this scenario remains embedded in dull chronicle. Canterbury's imagery serves to reinforce his rhetorical pitch, as he describes an heir to the English throne who exercises consummate dramatic control:

> Edward the Black Prince,
> Who on the French ground play'd a tragedy,
> Making defeat on the full power of France;
> Whiles his most mighty father on a hill
> Stood smiling to behold his lion's whelp
> Forage in blood of French nobility.
>
> (1.2.105–10)

If Henry is to recapitulate Edward III's blend of high drama and English triumph, he must himself enact the shift in Canterbury's declamation, and leave behind the contingencies of female rule upon which he ostensibly bases his royal claim. The image of theatrical success Canterbury employs, moreover, hints that *Henry V*'s sense of its own triumph will involve an analogous rejection of the female as any ingredient whatsoever of theatrical effectiveness. Perhaps the rejection will be easier, now that the Prologue has reconceived the theater's femininity in an Aristotelian mode, either as merely the theater building's containing, womblike walls or as merely the shapeless matter of chronicle to which the audience's masculine imagination gives dramatic life. Nevertheless, the high stakes of this realignment of theatrical gender become encoded throughout *Henry V*, as the play's action, language, and imagery are equally bent on purging England and the English of all that is feminine.

In fact, the play seems highly devoted to affirming a kind of Salic law of its own, contrary though that may be to Henry's legal justification for action: by the end of the play, as we shall see, Canterbury's initial repudiation of Salic law is so far forgotten that it is easy for us too to forget what side Henry initially took. First of all, the play's language continues insistently to derive Henry's ancestry as solely patrilineal. Even in Canterbury's opening scene with Ely, before he has showcased his explication of Salic law, he promises to recall Henry's descent from Edward III for him by revealing "The severals and unhidden passages / Of his true titles to some certain dukedoms, / And generally to the crown and seat of France, / Deriv'd from Edward, his great-grandfather" (1.1.86–89). In the ensuing rehearsal of the reasons by which Salic law may be discounted, as Jonathan Dollimore and Alan Sinfield have noted, Henry's genealogy is never traced further back than this single shining male forebear.[72] In historical fact—which Shakespeare knew from Holinshed, not to mention from the Shakespeare-apocrypha play *The Reign of Edward III*, published in quarto in 1596 and 1599—Edward III's own claim to France was derived through his mother, Isabella of France (daughter of the French king Philip IV and wife of the ill-fated English king Edward II). But the play never so much as mentions this Isabella, the Frenchwoman whose womb bore England's great king and from whom he received his birthright.[73] Her name appears in *Henry V* only as a distant echo in Canterbury's genealogy of the French monarchy, as a different, more distant Isabella, the French "fair Queen Isabel" from whom "King Lewis the Tenth" derived his claim to the French throne (1.2.77–83). Later, she is reincarnated as the queen of France, whose name "Isabel" appears in the Folio stage directions heading Act 5, scene 2. The language of the play therefore manages to deflect all matrilinear contingencies from the English onto the French. Apparently only the French, not the English, claim their rule through the female, reversing the two countries' actual historical positions on Salic law.

Moreover, this reconfiguration of Henry's ancestry joins with England's imperial designs upon France to solidify the English monarchy's final identification with the male: if *France* is posited as female, Henry can then attribute phallic qualities to both England and its king. Henry imagines that his mere appearance will strike fear into the hearts of his enemies, blinding/castrating the Dauphin, the only man who seems to stand in the way of his conquest: "I will rise there with so full a glory / That I will dazzle all the eyes of France, / Yea, strike the Dauphin blind to look on us" (1.2.278–80).[74] The Dauphin's challenge brings relief in the form not only of a final excuse for invading France, but also of a welcome reassignment of England's gender identity: a country not the invaded, but the invader; led not by an indecisive group of squabbling nobles, but by a king who promises to replicate *1 Henry VI*'s memorial reconstruction of Henry V as fabled hero.

Not that France, upon Henry's arrival, assumes a female role without protest. The Dauphin's language, especially, begins by resisting an English accumulation of all male and patrilineal identity. The Dauphin characterizes the two countries' contest as one between French fathers who have been careless about spreading their seed, and their English sons, now eager to "out-spirt" their progenitors.

> O Dieu vivant! shall a few sprays of us,
> The emptying of our fathers' luxury,
> Our scions, put in wild and savage stock

Spirt up so suddenly into the clouds
And overlook their grafters?

(3.5.5—9)

Two editors of the play, Gary Taylor and J. H. Walter, gloss "spirt" as
"sprout," one of the word's sixteenth-century meanings; but in so doing
they gloss over another sense available to Shakespeare, the one now spelled
"spurt."[75] If we compound the English sprouting with their spurting, the
Dauphin's objection to the English seems to be that they are attempting an ejaculation contest with their fathers. Hence, his description of the
French-English rivalry points interestingly at a fact the English seem carefully to repress—that their remoter forefathers were not English heroes,
but Norman conquerors who at their will ravished English women. But
this account of English ancestry, countering as it does the national gender distinctions Henry is trying to enforce, is not allowed any free play in
Henry V. Instead, France is eventually reconceived on all fronts as match-
ing the English image of it. The Dauphin himself is increasingly portrayed
as laughably effeminate, a soldier more absorbed with praising his horse—
which is a "palfrey," a lady's horse (3.7.28)—than with encountering the
English in pitched battle. Meanwhile, the rest of the French often antici-
pate and thus seem to accept the feminization of their homeland and its
openness to English ravishment. When the French king refers to Henry's
ancestry, he describes not Henry's Norman forefathers, but rather the
Edward III whose memory the English also enshrine, and who saw his
"heroical seed" make hay of the seed of French fathers. With Henry as the
"stem" of this "stock," whatever contest of virility there may be between
the French and the English seems already decided:

[Henry] is bred out of that bloody strain
That haunted us in our familiar paths;
Witness our too much memorable shame
When Cressy battle fatally was struck,
And all our princes captiv'd by the hand
Of that black name, Edward, Black Prince of Wales;
Whiles that his mountain sire, on mountain standing,
Up in the air, crown'd with the golden sun,
Saw his heroical seed, and smil'd to see him,
Mangle the work of nature, and deface
The patterns that by God and by French fathers

Had twenty years been made. This is a stem
Of that victorious stock; and let us fear
The native mightiness and fate of him.

(2.4.51–64)

That Edward III had a French mother is forgotten in the recollection of this "mountain sire's" triumph.

As Henry's army advances into France, England's military conquest becomes even more baldly intertwined with England's own patrilineal identity and France's hapless effeminizing. By the time Henry threatens the siege of Harfleur, he unmistakably poses military conquest as the English violation of a French woman, first metaphorically, as he menaces the "half-achiev'd Harfleur" with the prospect of "the flesh'd soldier, rough and hard of heart" (3.3.8, 11), then literally, as he tosses off a prediction of the townswomen being raped by English troops. It is immediately upon the closure of this scene—a closure in which Harfleur's governor earns mercy by inviting Henry to "Enter [the] gates" of his now thoroughly feminized city (3.3.49)—that Katharine of France makes her first appearance. She will, by the end of the play, embody what Henry has come to France to achieve: not just a feminine France, but France in the person of a female. And as sweetly amusing as her "language lesson" scene may be, it contains extraordinarily dark hints of how Henry's conquest of her will stand in for a purely military rape of France. Contrary to the usual way of playing this "naming game" with a child, Katharine does not begin her instruction with the obvious features of the face—eye, nose, mouth, and so on. Rather, the words she learns echo, either directly or indirectly, earlier language pertaining to the invasion of her country. The word *hand* recalls the "bloody hand" and "foul hand" of English soldiery with which Henry has just threatened Harfleur (3.3.12, 34); she also learns *fingers, nails, arm,* and *elbow,* words that serve to give an image of that hand its full shape and extension. She learns *neck,* a word reminiscent of the throats Pistol and Nym longed to cut (2.1.22, 92); *chin,* which reminds us of the barely bearded chins of those who followed Henry to France (3.Chor.22–24); and *foot,* another echo of Pistol's and Nym's contentious exchange ("thy fore-foot to me give" [2.1.67]). And, as C. L. Barber and Richard Wheeler remark, the *foot* and *count* that so embarrass her invoke for us both the besieged walls of France's violated cities, and the soon-to-be-won Princess herself.[76] Even the mistakes Katharine makes serve to substitute military terms for the words she is supposed to be learning. Instead of *nails* she says *mails;*

instead of *elbow*, *bilbow*—which can refer either to a type of sword, or to iron fetters (perhaps a metaphor for the fetters of arranged matrimony in which the Princess will quite soon find herself). All of her bobblings of the language, then, are directed toward her upcoming part in Henry's project of conquest: as she learns English, her own speech absorbs the English military and sexual might that is being brought to bear on her country.[77]

Henry's peacemaking and wooing activities in Act 5 are therefore not romantic or comedic incongruities, as Samuel Johnson grumpily contended, but rather part and parcel of successfully reassigning English and French national gender.[78] First of all, the Dauphin—last seen in Act 4, scene 5 cursing the conquering English—is unaccountably absent in the treaty scene; and second, the language of this scene follows up previous imagery of masculine invasion with resultant imagery of fruition. The Queen of France's hope is for a generative "happy . . . issue" of "this gracious meeting" (5.2.12–13); and Burgundy speaks at length of France as a female garden that needs to be properly husbanded, asking why "Peace"

> Should not in this best garden of the world,
> Our fertile France, put up her lovely visage?
> Alas! she hath from France too long been chas'd
> And all her husbandry doth lie on heaps,
> Corrupting in it own fertility.
>
> (5.2.34, 36–40)

Henry, for his part, does not separate these two discourses, the art of husbandry from the art of military conquest. He is eager to establish the language of love as a male, soldierly language, in which he need relinquish none of his armor and none of his aggression. Even in his attempts to "woo" the French princess, and under pretense of loverlike surrender, he continues to make her precisely equivalent to the cities he has conquered: "for I love France so well that I will not part with a village of it; I will have it all mine: and Kate, when France is mine and I am yours, then yours is France and you are mine" (5.2.178–82). As Katharine's language lesson anticipated, accepting Henry means barely transposing the martial into the marital: "If I could win a lady at leap-frog, or by vaulting into my saddle with my armour on my back, under the correction of bragging be it spoken, I should quickly leap into a wife. Or if I might buffet for my love, or bound my horse for her favours, I could lay on like a butcher and sit like a jack-an-apes, never off" (5.2.138–45).[79]

Henry has been engaged since his Prince Hal days with languages other than his own directed speech of warfare—with the languages of Eastcheap and of his own multi-accented army, as well as of his bride. But as both Stephen Greenblatt and Steven Mullaney have argued, Henry ultimately seeks not to partake of these alternative and potentially troublesome languages, but rather to negate their effectiveness, in a process that Greenblatt calls "the recording of alien voices" and that Mullaney describes as ritually purifying all that is base and gross in those voices.[80] If we associate this project with Henry's project of gender purification, of sifting all that is female out of England and recording it as French, we see that Henry will also be obliged to establish his very language as purely masculine, as worthy of a king, not a queen. And in his efforts to do so, we also find the development of a masculine language for the theater, one that draws upon the Prologue's desideratum: to project into others' minds what cannot be physically shown. However, Henry goes beyond even the Prologue's precedent in yoking this projective theatrical technique to a complex of epic paradigms—not only epic's depiction of masculine warfare, of arms and the man, but also epic's obsession with epochal continuance. With the Prologue, as it was with Talbot in *1 Henry VI*, the hope for epic was confined to invoking the presence of soldiers the stage could not hold; but Henry projects onto the stage a vision that overgoes not only the limits of physical space but also the limits of time. As he speaks, Henry creates upon the stage he occupies a legend of himself that spans a continuum from the ancestral past to the distant future. In himself, he recalls the puissance of his forebears, and in his language he projects that glory into the time to come.

In short, Henry is the creator of epic theater because he is concerned not only with the immediate future of winning battles and conquering France, as some ordinary hero would be, but also with an extended future in which Henry and his army will be remembered as the "happy band of brothers" that did these heroic deeds. And in a radical break with Aristotelian norms and with the anxieties of the first tetralogy, Henry's rhetorical endeavors to become part of cultural memory cumulatively propose that epic action can remain culturally alive *only* through recognizably theatrical means. We may begin investigating this proposition by examining a passage in which Henry once again figures victory over France as victory over a woman, and muses on the alternative if such a victory is not forthcoming. Not triumphing means not being remembered; but not being remembered means that no tongue will tell one's tale:

> [either] there we'll sit,
> Ruling in large and ample empery
> O'er France and her almost kingly dukedoms,
> Or lay these bones in an unworthy urn,
> Tombless, with no remembrance over them:
> Either our history shall with full mouth
> Speak freely of our acts, or else our grave,
> Like Turkish mute, shall have a tongueless mouth,
> Not worshipp'd with a waxen epitaph.
>
> (1.2.225–33)

As in the Prologue's speech, the problem here is one of sufficient "attest-ing" to the deeds that Henry and his men will perform. For the Prologue, if those deeds were not attested to—that is, if the actors and audience did not together do their imaginative duty—those "flat unraised spirits" would have no life. Here, the opposition drawn is analogous: the living voice, the "full mouth," of historical memory staves off the silent efface-ment, the "tongueless mouth," of the grave.

From this speech alone, we could perhaps assume that the "history" to which Henry refers his future is a written one, and that its "full mouth" is only metaphorically able to "speak freely." But as the play progresses, and as Henry's concern with inculcating his epic into his culture's memory in-creases, the "history" he has in mind turns out to require embodiment and reenactment. As he rouses his troops in his celebrated St. Crispin's Day speech, his intent proves itself not one of erecting a textual monument of or to himself, but rather one of assuring his everlasting reanimation in the form of popular remembrance—in the form of a story that will always be replayed, carved on living bodies and in living minds:

> He that shall see this day, and live old age,
> Will yearly on the vigil feast his neighbours,
> And say, "To-morrow is Saint Crispian":
> Then will he strip his sleeve and show his scars,
> And say, "These wounds I had on Crispin's day."
> Old men forget; yet all shall be forgot,
> But he'll remember with advantages,
> What feats he did that day.
> . . . .
> This story shall the good man teach his son;
> And Crispin Crispian shall ne'er go by,

From this day to the ending of the world,
But we in it shall be remembered.

$$(4.3.44-52, 56-59)$$

The confidence of Henry's projections for the future causes his vision to override the theatrical shortcomings raised by the timorous Prologue.[81] His pronouncements of what shall be remembered enact both the appearance of the epic scene and its subsequent legendary status, in a way the Prologue protests it cannot. Whereas the Prologue throws up its hands at the idea that a cockpit might hold the vasty fields of France, Henry declares those fields to be already present, the site of a battle immediately recognizable as historic.

Henry.   What is this castle call'd that stands hard by?
Montjoy. They call it Agincourt.
Henry.   Then call we this the field of Agincourt,
            Fought on the day of Crispin Crispianus.

$$(4.7.90-93)$$

Henry continues to install himself in history in this way, referring to his own story as something that will be known, recited, and compared "with advantages" to other well-known stories. With advantages, because his version is a dramatic one: not Holinshed but *Henry V*, not a history but a history play. "When," he asks after hearing the numbers of the battle-dead, "without stratagem, / But in plain shock and even play of battle, / Was ever known so great and little loss / On one part and on th' other?" (4.8.110–14). Never, the audience is obliged to answer; for it knows his feats even as he recalls them for it. Henry here makes of himself a "famous memory," one that will carry him for all time—as if built into his character is an awareness of his being staged, over and over again, as the king who is England's savior.[82]

But this desire for epic extension in the theater brings Henry back to the issue of Salic law and its attendant concerns of gender and genealogy. For Henry is engaged in making history not only by being himself eternally remembered, but also by extending his male lineage into the future. As with *The Faerie Queene*'s genealogical shorings-up of national myth, epic in *Henry V* is as much a matter of fictionalized patrilineal descent as it is a matter of heroic action. Act 5 thus hangs Henry's epic hopes, as well as England's masculinity, on his conquest of the French princess. In Henry's wooing speech, despite his concern with the male offspring that he and

Katharine will produce, Katharine's part in this process is minimized, so the fact that the woman will be a part of the family tree is suppressed as much as possible. It is almost as if Henry himself, with the help of the soldier-saints Denis and George, can produce an heir, one who will finally carry out the crusading dream of Henry's father: "Shall not thou and I, between Saint Denis and Saint George, compound a boy, half French, half English, that shall go to Constantinople and take the Turk by the beard?" (5.2.215–18).

The extent to which Henry's effort at epic posterity is plausible, however, also depends on the power of his theatrical vision, since to be persuasive, Henry's projection of the future must convincingly rewrite that future—a future already known to a theater audience that had witnessed in the early 1590s the turmoil of Shakespeare's first historical tetralogy. As Christopher Pye remarks, "The sequence of the history plays makes Henry V the one king who returns from the grave."[83] Only by writing the two tetralogies in reverse historical order, the earlier segment of history after the later, could Shakespeare make this revision possible: in the theater's version of history, *Henry V* succeeds *Henry VI*, not the reverse. This reversal then further enables the erasure of the feminine from the English monarchy. With Henry V, the first tetralogy's rule of ravishing women and a monstrous man is finally succeeded by that of a glorious king, who promises to live on both in cultural memory and in his male progeny.

We might call this retrospective revival of kingship nostalgic, since it looks to England's heroic past for an antidote to more recent troubles: unwon wars, unrevivified kings. But it is more than nostalgic, for nostalgia, in its reiteration that things aren't what they used to be, presupposes that the past can never come again. As Exeter in *1 Henry VI* puts it, "Henry [the Fifth] is dead and never shall revive" (1.1.18). *Henry V*, in contrast, gives voice to the fantastical, irrational desires to which nostalgia, when intensified to the point of supersaturation, gives way: that the past may return, that the dead are indeed alive, that historic heroism may replace the feminine chaos and decay that are the audience's more recent memory— both their memory of what happened in Shakespeare's first historical tetralogy and, increasingly, their memory of what has been happening in the English monarchy of the late 1590s. Surely *Henry V* itself has a great stake in what we might term this "supernostalgia," for, as the Prologue demonstrates at the play's very beginning, only when the stage gives way to Henry's self-staging does the theater convey its object. Although the Prologue bemoans the lack of a genuine monarch—a "warlike Harry" who, "like himself," will "assume the port of Mars"—in the progress of the play we witness a Henry who self-consciously does just that, taking on the bearing of a soon-to-be-mythic hero.

Yet there is also a certain tension, as well as symbiosis, between the play's creation of Henry and Henry's creation of himself, a tension that keeps alive the question of whether the epic mode is entirely possible, or even desirable, for theater. I wish now to return to the play's affiliations with the feminine, and how they force *Henry V* to stand at a certain uneasy distance from Henry V and his Salic-law visions of male perpetuity. Once the stage has limited itself to being a womblike space that only contains, and does not disrupt, male epic activity, it raises doubts about its own ability to match Henry in his supernostalgic task, bringing forth a King Henry who will take his place in history. The Prologue identifies Henry as one of the "mighty monarchies" who are "now confin'd" in the playhouse, "within the girdle of these walls." But what if, after this pregnant image, the theater's confinement does not bring a living Henry into the world? As the Chorus reappears at the beginning of Acts 2 and 3, these fears begin to insinuate themselves deeply into its rhetoric, resulting in something more than traditional, offhand protestations of theatrical inadequacy. In Act 2, the Chorus's unsettling transformation of womb imagery to intestinal imagery hints that its presentation of Henry will not be so easy: "Linger your patience on; and we'll digest / Th' abuse of distance; force a play" (2.Chor.31–32). And the excessively pleading, insistent tone of the Chorus in Act 3 reinforces how the audience might not be able to meet its obligations in the act of theatrical engendering. Urging the audience to "O do but think," "follow, follow," "grapple," and "work, work," the Chorus takes on the tone of an extremely demanding lover, who hopes past all hope that her partner will provide the heat necessary for conception, since she cannot.

Even the Chorus's Act 4 speech, which seems to offer a chance at faith in theatrical generativity, ultimately corrodes any such confidence. A momentary glimpse of dramatic attainment comes about primarily because the Chorus applies the imagery of a womb-like space not solely to the walls of the theater building, as a "girdle" that holds the actors, but rather to "the wide vessel of the universe" that holds the opposing armies of the English and the French (4.Chor.3). With this transfer of images, the space of the theater expands to become coequal with the space of all creation; Henry and his band are alive, in the world, and on the verge of triumph. But if the Chorus in Act 4 refers to "the wide vessel of the universe" as one container for its hero, it also mentions "the foul womb of night" as another (4.Chor.4). And this image of a malevolent womb, with the force of female Nature behind it, calls into question the Prologue's notion that a womb, theatrical or not, can and ought to be imagined as a neutral "vessel," an artificed container that cannot influence its own contents. In Act 5 the epic vision contained in the theater's womb is shown in several ways to be far from impervious to forces from without. We might first divine the error of epic complacency from Burgundy's speech about France as a garden requiring husbandry. As Burgundy describes her, France is far from infertile even when not "husbanded"; rather, she is grotesquely fertile, since it is not the masculine scythe or coulter that has made her so:

> her fallow leas
> The darnel, hemlock, and rank fumitory
> Doth root upon, while that the coulter rusts
> That should deracinate such savagery;
> The even mead, that erst brought sweetly forth
> The freckled cowslip, burnet, and green clover,
> Wanting the scythe, all uncorrected, rank,
> Conceives by idleness, and nothing teems
> But hateful docks, rough thistles, kecksies, burrs,
> Losing both beauty and utility.
>
> (5.2.44–53)

Here the female is hardly a passive vessel of reproduction: left to her own devices, the result is a kind of female parthenogenesis, where nature's prickly products grow in the absence of men's tools.

Katharine of France herself, the particular Frenchwoman on whose womb Henry's epic project will depend, does not display this extremity of willfulness, but she does evince a skepticism that in itself chips away at Henry's epic plans. While Henry is engaged in spinning out a vision of himself as soldier-wooer and his son as triumphant Crusader, Princess Katharine remains reserved and unbelieving. In a single line she forces historical awareness upon the audience, in case Henry's hermetically sealed projection has caused them to forget their history. When Henry asks her what to him no doubt seems a rhetorical question, whether they shall "compound a boy, half French, half English, that shall go to Constantinople and take the Turk by the beard," she answers, with all the knowledge of a woman who has already seen Shakespeare's *Henry VI* plays, "I do not know dat" (5.2.216–18, 220).

The remainder of the play reinforces the Princess's unbelief by continuing to strain at a Renaissance audience's awareness of a future, both historical and dramatic, quite different from the one Henry believes he is forging. First of all, as Dollimore and Sinfield remind us, the play itself has argued for the improbability of a French king (as Henry's son will be) being man enough to take the Turk by the beard.[84] Moreover, after the French and English monarchs close their treaty the French queen makes a speech that, in its forced insistence on the two countries' future amicable relations, violates even the sketchiest grasp of Anglo-French history since Henry V's time. And finally, the Epilogue closes the play with multiple reminders of the coming evaporation of this proposed ideal kingship. One of these reminders comes about with the Epilogue reverting to imagining the theater itself as a womblike space, "In little room confining mighty men, / Mangling by starts the full course of their glory" (Epi.3–4). The image is a grisly one: this is a womb that maims its progeny, even as it convulsively, "by starts," attempts to bring them into the world. Here the earlier, frenetic tone of the Chorus, begging us to work, work our thoughts, changes to one of failure, as pregnancy results in stillbirth. The image of truncated epic—of a theater that cuts off glory's "full course"—is borne out when the Epilogue reverses the salutary effects of the second tetralogy's erasure of the first tetralogy, placing Henry V for the first time inalterably in the past tense: "Small time, but in that small most greatly lived / This star of England" (Epi.5–6). And the audience is reminded, to its regret, that what Henry projected as his epic destiny—his foundation of an ever-victorious male dynasty—cannot, and did not, take place in history. In fact the audience may have itself witnessed the unravelling of Henry's achievement:

> Henry the Sixth, in infant bands crown'd King
> Of France and England, did this king succeed;
> Whose state so many had the managing,
> That they lost France and made his England bleed;
> *Which oft our stage hath shown.*
>
> (Epi.9–13, my emphasis) [85]

And yet the Chorus's references to what is to come—or to what has come already, if we think of the audience's familiarity with the *Henry VI* cycle—are not fully revelatory. The audience is asked to remember the dissolution of powerful male rule under Henry VI, but does it remember the increasing dominance in the *Henry VI* plays of female rule? I would argue instead that *Henry V* is, in the end, eager to maintain a certain momentary, if fragile, integrity of masculine rule, to rewrite history so that what we continue to desire is the triumphant resolution, however denied to us, of King Henry. Not only does the Epilogue omit any reference to the ravishing women who will plague Henry VI's reign, it also neglects to address the future of the woman who has come to symbolize Henry V's fruitful posterity, his queen, Katharine of France. Shakespeare knew what happened to Katharine, as would any Elizabethan who had read the account in Holinshed's *Chronicles* of Henry VI's reign:

This woman, after the death of king Henrie the fift hir husband, being yoong and lustie, following more hir owne wanton appetite than freendlie counsell, and regarding more private affection than princelike honour, tooke to husband privilie a galant gentleman and a right beautifull person, indued with manie goodlie gifts both of bodie & mind, called Owen Teuther [Tudor], a man descended of the noble linage and ancient line of Cadwallader last king of the Britains. By this Owen she brought forth three goodlie sonnes, Edmund, Jasper, and another that was a monke in Westminster. . . . which Edmund of Margaret daughter and sole heire to John duke of Summerset begat Henrie, who after was king of this realme, called Henrie the seventh.[86]

In other words, Katharine of France lived to become the great-great-grandmother of Elizabeth I.

At first it seems odd that a playwright would let slip this chance to refer to the illustrious lineage of his gracious queen; like Spenser and others among his contemporaries, Shakespeare might have made much of Holinshed's tracing of the Tudor line from Elizabeth back through Owen Tudor to King Arthur himself. In 1603, for example, Hugh Holland published a small book that he declares had been meant to be dedicated to the just-deceased Elizabeth, entitled *Pancharis . . . The Preparation of the Love betweene Owen Tudyr, and the Queen, Long since intended to her Maiden Majestie*.[87] Michael Drayton's contemporaneous *Heroical Epistles* (1597–99) had similarly showcased Katharine's marriage to Owen Tudor as the conduit for the spiritual, if not the genetic, inheritance of Henry V.[88] Shakespeare's omission seems even odder when we consider that the only allusion in *Henry V* to Katharine of France's subsequent attachment to the descendant of Briton kings is an oblique and not particularly flattering one, when Pistol tells Fluellen he would not eat the proffered leek "for Cadwallader and all his goats" (5.1.29). Yet the reasoning for the exclusion becomes clearer with reference again to Holinshed. In tracing Katharine's future, Shakespeare would have had to confront both her indelible presence in English monarchical lineage—indelible unlike Henry's, whose line died with his son—and her changed nature. She proved to become neither simply the regrettably necessary female component of Henry V's progenitive project, nor even the skeptical commentator on his soldierly rhetoric. Rather, the Katharine of the *Chronicles* became the forerunner of Joan La Pucelle and Margaret of Anjou, ravishing Frenchwomen all: young, lusty, and following more their own wanton appetites than friendly counsel, and regarding more private affection than princelike honor. Had the *Henry VI* plays extended her story, these associations would inevitably have been drawn.

But so, too, would the association have been drawn between Katharine of France and Elizabeth Tudor herself, an association not only of blood, but of temperament. Elizabeth's "wanton appetites" continued in the 1590s to provide fodder for Catholic propagandists, who painted her as even more unnaturally lascivious because of her age.[89] Even more importantly, Elizabeth's independent will increasingly frustrated the members of her council, who were all by this point at least one generation younger than she, and were highly impatient at her stubborn refusal to follow their advice and chart a purposeful course. In its extreme their frustration led to comments like that of the ambitious Earl of Essex—the same Essex whose Irish triumph the play anticipates—who once remarked that the Queen's mind had become as crooked as her carcass,[90] and who told the French ambassador that "they laboured under two things at this Court, delay and inconstancy, which proceeded chiefly from the sex of the Queen."[91] Obscuring Katharine of France's subsequent career thus serves to seal *Henry V*'s refusal of female rule. Exemplifying as it does those traits that England most feared in its queen, the inclusion of Katharine's completed story would incurably compromise the play's presentation of a successful male conquest. Hence *Henry V* in the end does, in the largest sense, impose Salic law. By excluding Katharine's Tudor marriage, the play effectively cancels the woman's part in English succession, and instead hails Henry V as the sole shaper of kingship. Even if the play does not erase all memory of the first tetralogy's female rule, it does succeed in erasing Elizabeth, first by shaping England as an entirely male dominant body with France as its female victim, then by eliminating Katharine of France as Elizabeth's female forebear.

Henry V therefore rehearses and resolves English involvement with female authority on several fronts: politically, since through its silence on Katharine's future it finally asserts that both authority and its familial succession ought to be an entirely male purview; and dramatically, since with its choice of hero it counters the antitheatricalist anxiety that theater, feminine in itself, effeminizes its audience. In 1592 Thomas Nashe had brought up an earlier dramatic treatment of Henry V to contend, against the antitheatricalist writers, that theater can in fact correct national effeminacy—first simply by providing men an alternative to visiting whorehouses, but second by bringing England's male ancestry back to life: "Nay, what if I proove Playes to be no extreme; but a rare exercise of vertue? First, for the subject of them (for the most part) it is borrowed out of our English Chronicles, wherein our forefathers valiant acts (that have l[a]ine long buried in rustie brasse and worme-eaten bookes) are revived, and they themselves raised from the Grave of Oblivion, and brought to pleade their aged Honours in open presence: than which, what can be a sharper reproofe to these degenerate effeminate dayes of ours?"[92] In Nashe's terms, *Henry V* would encourage the late-Elizabethan theater audience to follow Henry's Salic law model and purge the feminine from themselves, and from their country. Nostalgia for patrilineage revives patriarchy out of its "grave of oblivion": Shakespeare's history declares the degenerate authority of queenship to be not merely subverted, but overcome.[93]

I wish to follow this seemingly resounding assertion of patriarchal authority, however, with a qualification. At the beginning of this chapter I suggested that the progression of the two tetralogies of history plays amounts to a Shakespearean experiment—an experiment that, I believe, itself demonstrates its own unrepeatability. In the end, the extreme, insistent quality of *Henry V*'s corrective revival of male authority exposes that revival as an undesirable model for theater. *Henry V*'s commitment to epic requires theater to marginalize and neutralize its identification with the feminine; but in that case, the theater runs the risk of disenabling or at least limiting its own power. For what if the audience does not believe? What if the play's protestations of being an inadequate womb prevail? If the play convinces, then its cancellation of female authority survives. But if the illusion does *not* succeed, and Henry V is still-born, then the theater has disabled its own enterprise rather than discontinued the waning enterprise of England's queen. For Shakespeare's resolution of this problem, we can only speculate on the fact that *Henry V* remains sui generis in the canon. Shakespeare undertook no other history play until he redefined history as romance in *Henry VIII*; nor did he so thoroughly conflate dramatic authority and masculine rule until *The Tempest*, a play that stages long before its epilogue the unraveling of that rule.

Norman Rabkin's well-known formulation about Henry V is that he is patterned like the Gestalt drawing that may be seen either as a rabbit or as a duck, either an exemplary monarch or a notorious Machiavel, but never as both at the same time.[94] My version of this conundrum involves theatrical rather than moral considerations: not whether Henry is a good king or a bad king, but whether theater should or should not attach its being and its success to a burgeoning kingship. The play raises unallayed anxieties about the achievability of Henry's heroic project at the same time that it registers a deep and abiding desire for that project. In this way *Henry V* situates itself most poignantly not as the play that most celebrates the Tudor myth, but as the play that most commemorates the approaching end of a Tudor queen. The looked-for exclusion of female authority leaves both nation and theater anxiously peering into the past, looking there for a recording of their own destiny. *Henry V* translates its culture's memory of a triumphant historical king into expectation for the future, and for future drama — and yet at the same time adulterates that expectation with anticipated disappointment.

4

Exclaiming Against Their Own Succession

Queenship, Genre, and What Happens in Hamlet

NEARLY THIRTY YEARS AGO Mark Rose characterized the Prince Hamlet of Acts 1 through 4 of the play as a refined fellow, eager to escape the crude demands of the dramatic genre in which he finds himself—that is, revenge tragedy. "[H]is sensibility rebels," Rose declares, "refusing to permit him to debase himself into a ranting simpleton."[1] Until the end of Act 4, when he resolves "my thoughts be bloody or be nothing worth," Hamlet wholly evades assuming the revenger's role himself; and even in Act 5, in the graveyard and the fencing arena, Hamlet spends more time upon contemplating death as a philosophical matter or as its simulacrum, fencing, than upon bringing anyone's death to pass. Rose concludes from this circumstance that both the byzantine murder plotting and the vulgar bombast required of the revenger's persona offend Hamlet; each violates the elegant economy of suiting the action to the word, the word to the action. Further, it is precisely Hamlet's extended evasions of the revenger's constricted part, Rose asserts, that lift this tragedy above the level of the creaky revenge conventions of a play like *The Spanish Tragedy*, or, for that matter, like *The Murder of Gonzago*. In the process of not becoming the revenge tragedy it promises to be, Rose argues, *Hamlet* invents a new and superior Elizabethan dramatic genre: psychological tragedy.

While most of us would not much argue with Rose's evaluation of *Hamlet*'s relative quality, I am interested in why, in the closing scene of the play, this marvelous new mode is abandoned. My sense is that *Hamlet* must ultimately recoil for gendered reasons from this new genre so fulsomely invented in the play. Like Spenserian romance and like feminine theater as I have described them in the previous chapters, Shakespeare's psychological tragedy depends for its effect on digression and delay—qualities that develop under the auspices, in this play as in the history plays and *The Faerie Queene*, of the rule of a queen. Cancelling those feminine qualities requires a return to a cruder genre defined as masculine: blood-soaked revenge.

As in my discussion of the history plays, my topic in this chapter is succession, as both a monarchical and a dramatic phenomenon. The first part of my argument has to do with correlating Hamlet's aims as a reluctant but eventually successful revenger with the aims of the new dramatic genre he both inhabits and effects. Hamlet's own ambiguous term to describe the players' reason for going on the road, the recent "innovation" in the city—meaning either *invention* or *insurrection*—proves a key pun in this case, since the most innovative thing about Prince Hamlet and the play *Hamlet* is their desire to reinvent their own succession. That is to say, the Danish prince seeks to replace a regnant queen with a male ruler; and the Danish play evidently aims to redesign revenge tragedy. These two modes of reinvention, monarchical and dramatic, are at cross purposes, however: in the closing scene of the play, Prince Hamlet's monarchical innovations require erasing what is truly innovative both in the kingdom of Denmark and in the late Elizabethan theater, a feminized mode of authority. As it turns out, that feminized mode is precisely what Rose and most other twentieth-century critics (with the exception of T. S. Eliot) value about the play, going so far as to assert that *Hamlet* invents or at least embodies a nascently modern sense of self—a self, I would then extrapolate, that is enabled by queenship and that therefore must be summarily repudiated at *Hamlet*'s end.

As most readers of the play have noticed, however, *Hamlet* so thoroughly conflates its hero's psychology with the activities of playacting and play-framing that it is difficult to separate Hamlet, if not from our idea of Shakespeare the man, then from our idea of Shakespeare the dramatic artist. How else can we understand a character who refers to his own mind as equivalent to the Shakespearean playspace on a bad rehearsal day, "this distracted globe" (1.5.97)?[2] In the second part of this chapter I shall indulge in this delimited version of the intentional fallacy, insofar as it usefully imbricates Hamlet's personal succession crisis with the succession controversies surrounding *Hamlet* as both a dramatic piece and a book-text. Placing Shakespeare's play within the context of the War of the Theaters, an incident Hamlet mentions, broadens the problem of succession to include the status of Shakespeare's theatrical company in relation to its chief competitors in London at the time, the boys' companies of

Blackfriars and St. Paul's. Seen in this light—and particularly in the light of John Marston's contemporaneous plays composed for boys' companies, *Antonio and Mellida*, *Antonio's Revenge*, and *The Malcontent*—Hamlet becomes not as self-sufficient or as sui generis as, I argue, Hamlet believes himself and attempts to be. Similarly, the unprecedented proliferation of texts of *Hamlet*, two quartos and a folio, complicates nearly beyond comprehension any theory of a clearly defined succession of versions of the play. Intertwined as they are with the intertheatrical wranglings surrounding the production of Shakespeare's play, the successive printed versions of *Hamlet* also gesture toward the concerns of the theatrical profession over its status and over its ever-tightening relation to the monarchy, a monarchy that, in the post-Elizabethan world in which the printed versions of *Hamlet* appear, includes the rival claims of a king and his queen. To be a Child of the Queen's Revels or to be a King's Man: that is Hamlet's choice, just as it becomes the choice of the professional player in Jacobean London.

Hamlet's Succession

In her powerful reading of *Hamlet*, Janet Adelman describes the play's inattention to the genre to which it ostensibly adheres as a matter of Prince Hamlet's own familial turmoil. "Despite his ostensible agenda of revenge, the main psychological task that Hamlet seems to set himself is not to avenge his father's death but to remake his mother . . . in the image of the Virgin Mother who could guarantee his father's purity, and his own, repairing the boundaries of his selfhood."[3] In brief, the process Adelman outlines by which Hamlet comes to this task is this. For Hamlet, the sexual desire evident in Gertrude's second marriage exposes the history of sexual desire inherent in her first marriage, and in her procreation of her son; hence, Gertrude's willful choice of Claudius sullies Hamlet's own paternity. Hamlet's fantasies of feminine sexual voraciousness therefore propel him into a crisis of undifferentiated fathers: if Gertrude does not care to distinguish between her objects of desire, her first husband and her second, then how can Hamlet distinguish between them? Wedding themselves as they do to the same contaminating feminine flesh, that unweeded garden, Hyperion and the satyr become of a piece. As a result, the task of revenge requires Hamlet to recompose his family tree. Insofar as he is able to shift the degradation of human sexuality from his godlike father to his fallen mother, and then successfully to direct Gertrude to eschew sexuality, Hamlet can reinvent his own bloodline as both free from fault and untainted by feminine desire. Only with this task accomplished can Hamlet recover his father's identity and hence assume his father's place, "making His will his own" and avenging his death.[4]

Adelman's account seems to me brilliant not only as a reading of Hamlet's psychic maneuverings, but also as a suggestive analogue to Hamlet's place within the Danish succession. I will return shortly to the transformation Gertrude instigates in the revenge-tragedy plot. For now, though, I want to investigate how Gertrude's place as "imperial jointress" to the Danish state, as Claudius introduces her (1.2.9), heightens certain aspects of her familial authority and contributes to her being an even more dominant and troubling figure as Hamlet's queen than she would be as simply Hamlet's mother—so much so that she nearly becomes, in Hamlet's mocking phrase, "ten times our mother" (3.2.324).[5] *Hamlet*'s editors are quick to discount the Shakespearean neologism "jointress" used to denominate Gertrude, since it creates the impression that she is a queen regnant, not a queen consort. After noting that "jointress" could only literally mean "a woman who is in joint possession," Harold Jenkins, editor of the second Arden *Hamlet*, cautions that "nothing else in the play gives Gertrude that status [of co-ruler]" (p. 179 n. 9). I would not want to assert that Gertrude is in charge of Danish monarchical policy in any significant way (although she certainly bears a considerable degree of royal self-possession); as well, I do not mean to imply I have discovered the true, factual basis behind Danish succession, any more than I have discovered the number of Lady Macbeth's children. But to dub Gertrude a "jointress," especially given the ambiguities of the succession process in Denmark, is to complicate the male-to-male succession to the crown that critics have assumed must be the case, whether the crown descends patrilineally, fraternally, or electorally.[6] Being a "jointress" gives Gertrude a specific sixteenth-century legal status that, although it has nothing to do with her exercising or not exercising monarchical power, has everything to do with Hamlet's position in relation to the throne: the status of a widow whose husband, before his death, gave her control over some share of his lands and possessions, to continue for the term of her life. As Eric Mallin wisely points out, the epithet "imperial jointress" "suggests at least the possibility that the king's rights go hand in hand with the queen's graces, her political indulgence."[7] It seems that in Denmark, where royal succession is never unequivocally derived either from election or from birth, the only empirically surefire way to acquire the throne is by marrying Gertrude. In terms of the crown as well as of psychology, it is thus not the usurper Claudius, but rather the too-authoritative Gertrude who blocks Hamlet from his father's place.

Jointure, which could be substituted for the common-law grant of the wife's dower, was an increasingly common practice in the sixteenth century, beginning with the Statute of Uses (1535) enacted during the reign of Henry VIII. Instead of the dower's provision of an estate for life in one-third of her deceased husband's lands (including land acquired or disposed of during their marriage), a widow who had been granted jointure was entitled to the use and income of lands designated in the jointure agreement, which as a rule had been drawn up before the marriage took place. In practice, jointure (rather like the modern prenuptial agreement) seems to have decreased widows' income considerably, especially given that as the practice developed in the seventeenth century, the jointure income began to be tagged to the portion (or "dowry") the wife had brought into the marriage—by 1750, jointure income per annum was typically set at 10 percent of the bride's portion.[8] Viewed this way, jointure became a way of sequestering the husband's entire estate away from the widow's use, except for that share that had accompanied her into the marriage.[9] Moreover, even her rightful jointure was often difficult for a widow to claim. One of the reasons historians know so much about this arrangement is that so many sixteenth-century widows had to seek legal redress against disgruntled sons like Hamlet who, thinking it high time their fathers' property be in their own control and not their mothers', were withholding the income.[10]

But in theory, and in individual factual cases, jointure could prove far more advantageous than dower to the widow, since the jointure could conceivably consist of far more than one-third of the husband's property. The anonymous compiler of *The Law's Resolutions of Women's Rights* (1632) assures his readership that English men are typically so besotted with their prospective wives that they are willing to give all away to joint possession: "so sweet, fair and pleasing are [English women], or so very good and prudent . . . that though some men get lands by them, most men are fain to assure part or all of such lands as they have (in jointure or otherwise) to them ere they can win their love."[11] Further, jointure had specific advantages over dower that held true even when the jointure was small. Well into the seventeenth century, jointure income was more secure than dower in that it often continued even if the widow remarried; further, unlike dower, it could not be withdrawn on the grounds of the widow's being proved to have committed adultery, elopement, or fornication.[12] For Gertrude, whose first husband loved her so ardently that "he might not beteem the

winds of heaven / Visit her face too roughly" (1.2.141–42), and who certainly is accused of adultery and fornication (if not also elopement), jointure seems to be the boon it promised in theory to be. If Claudius has
married a jointress, he has probably done so in order to get access to the
control of her land, which in this case seems to be all of Denmark. And
not surprisingly, since it was the queen consort who, in England, enjoyed
extraordinarily sweeping rights of jointure. Beginning in Henry VIII's
reign, the queen consort held special jointure privileges, including the
right to administer her own jointure lands, maintain her own household,
preside over her own Council, and make use of her own royal seal. Since
1540 queens consort had enjoyed a legal status denied to all other married
women: the status of *feme sole* rather than *feme covert*.[13] The one limiting
factor to an English queen consort's legal freedom, in fact, is one which
circumstances allow Gertrude to evade: under a law enacted (interestingly
enough) in response to the willful Katharine of France's remarriage, after
her husband Henry V's death, to Owen Tudor, a king's widow had to
get permission from the new king to remarry. But in Gertrude's case, of
course, the prospective bridegroom *is* the new king.

　　Whether Claudius marries Gertrude before or after he gains the
throne, then, the fact remains that she is uniquely in a position to bestow
both herself and Denmark on whom she pleases.[14] As a result, if we take
Hamlet's pun on "nothing" as the female genitals seriously, it is indeed
the case that "The King is a thing—. . . / Of nothing" (4.2.27–29). One
of Hamlet's even more egregious sexual puns in fact literalizes Gertrude's
status in the play. After confusing Ophelia with his request to lie in her
lap, he twits her with a scurrilous double entendre: "Do you think I meant
country matters?" (3.2.115). With its play on country as "cunt-ry" and its
matter-*mater* twist, this quip becomes exactly what Hamlet does mean: the
country/cuntry *mater*, Queen Gertrude, whose jointure and whose sexuality are the entree to rule in Denmark.

　　What Gertrude's good fortune means is that Hamlet's fears of his
father's having succumbed to his mother sexually have been manifested
economically, in his father's disposition of the family estate. As Lisa Jardine observes, Gertrude's marriage to Claudius is incestuous in English
ecclesiastical law not according to the law's table of consanguinity, but
according to its table of affinity, which lists unions that might produce
conflicting claims of inheritance.[15] Anticipating *King Lear*'s treatment of
political authority as merely the legal transmission of property, *Hamlet*
also anticipates what *King Lear* avoids only by making Regan and Goneril

so headstrong: that a woman who inherits this property will, upon marriage, cede its control to her husband, someone out of the immediate
patrimony.[16] Henry VIII's will, which similarly conceived of the crown
itself as property to be transmitted, unwittingly set up just this scenario
by placing as second in line to the throne Henry's older daughter, Mary
Tudor, even though she had been declared a bastard after Henry's marriage
to Anne Boleyn.[17] As queen, Mary Tudor ceded de facto joint royal authority to her husband, Philip II of Spain, whose rights—though always in
dispute—eventually expired only because his wife died childless.[18] Hence,
I think that with Gertrude as "imperial jointress" we are also meant to
hear a kind of slant reference to another Shakespearean queen: that is, the
"imperial votress" of *A Midsummer Night's Dream*, the missed target of
Cupid's arrow and the catalyst for Oberon's love potion manipulations.
A shadow for Mary Tudor's sister, Elizabeth, whose lifelong spinsterhood
had the political benefit of defending her rule and her nation from bound-
ers like Claudius, the "imperial votress" figures precisely the virginal status
to which Hamlet would like his mother to revert.[19] But as *Hamlet*'s "imperial jointress," Gertrude frighteningly unites the two queenly bodies that
A Midsummer Night's Dream so widely separates: the chaste imperial votress, the only woman in the play untouched by masculine desire; and
Titania, the besotted Faery Queen. Gertrude becomes what England had
not seen since the days, half a century before, of Mary Tudor: the queen
whom Cupid has hit.

Or perhaps England *had* recently seen such a queen: Scotland's Mary
Stuart, who although she had been executed in 1587 was still very much
alive in England's memory at the turn of the seventeenth century.[20] Although the Queen of Scots, unlike Mary Tudor, had resolutely maintained
supreme ruling status in Scotland during the brief time that she was in
residence there (1561–67), she was much more celebrated for allegedly let-
ting sexual desire command her most important ruling decisions—that is,
her marriage alliances. Henry Stuart, Lord Darnley, who became the second husband of Mary, Queen of Scots (and the first she chose herself)
was famously handsome: Mary called him "the properest and best propor-
tioned long [i.e., tall] man she had ever seen"; and Lord Burghley's agent
in Scotland, Thomas Randolph, reported her to be so entranced that she
had "all care of common wealth set apart, to the utter contempt of her best
subjects."[21] Her third husband, James Hepburn, Earl of Bothwell, gained
Mary's hand after abducting her—a scheme in which Mary was widely believed to have colluded—and raping her.[22] Given that Bothwell was widely

known to have conspired in Darnley's murder, it is small wonder that *Hamlet* has been read as either a direct or a displaced allegory of Mary Stuart's marital career, by Lilian Winstanley and, more recently and more subtly, by Eric Mallin.[23] Mallin finds the Queen of Scots/Gertrude analogy suggestive not because it makes the play reflective only of a murder and marriage from the 1560s, but because it aligns the play with the succession waiting-game of the early 1600s. Like Hamlet, who waits at the pleasure of his "imperial jointress" mother, James Stuart found himself in the last years of Elizabeth Tudor's reign waiting upon the will—both the desire and the last testament—of a queen who blocked his way to kingship. The play, as Mallin describes it, "merges two stages of [James's] life story, each of which is occupied, in a radically different way, with immense succession anxiety: the past horror of Darnley's murder and Mary's disgrace; and the contemporary crisis of James's blocked ascent to the throne."[24] And whereas Hamlet imagines that expunging Gertrude's sexuality will secure his own identity, James's diplomatic gyrations during his years of waiting demonstrated the dangers to masculine identity of depending upon any mother, whore queen or virgin queen, for one's title. Eager to disclaim his inheritance from his mother Mary Stuart, known in England as an oversexed traitor, James nevertheless could claim the English throne only through her blood, her descent from Henry VII. Equally eager to establish himself as a superior replacement to Elizabeth Tudor, James nevertheless styled himself, as Jonathan Goldberg has demonstrated, as her mirror image and her son.[25] Publicly, James declared filial devotion for Elizabeth; privately, in a letter to his ambassador in England, he referred disparagingly to Elizabeth's "wonted obstinacy" in not assigning the throne to him in advance of her death.[26] Like the "little eyases," the boy-players discussed in Act 2 as "berattl[ing] the common stages"—and to whom I shall return in the second half of this chapter—James "exclaim[s] against [his] own succession" (2.2.340, 349): he and Hamlet both decry the history of feminine authority on which their own claims to authority are based.

Hamlet's frustration at his mother's barring his way to the throne nicely shadows Jacobean monarchical neurosis, whether one puts *Hamlet*'s composition at the traditional date of 1600 or 1601, or whether, as Mallin does, one argues that *Hamlet*'s Second Quarto, printed in 1604 and usually taken as the editorial control-text for the play, reflects the new monarchical regime.[27] (Elizabeth had died in 1603.) Whether anticipated or already taken place, James's accession to kingship inexorably hinged upon the choices undertaken by two queens in their female bodies natural: to be virgin or wife, to confine sexual desire to the realm of courtly fiction or to engage in it in fact. Upon these accidents—one queen giving birth, and another queen refusing to do so—James's kingly future depended; the queen's natural body lingers on into the next reign. Quite unlike the comforting, normative cry of continuity, "The king is dead, long live the king," the queen's death complicates the issue of who will be next to reign. What if accepting the crown from a predecessor queen feminizes the very nature of rule? *Hamlet*'s current avatar of kingship bears out this suspicion: Claudius's very monarchy is ultimately undone by his feminine submission to his wife. He confesses to Laertes that he cannot simply kill Hamlet himself because

> The Queen his mother
> Lives almost by his looks, and for myself—
> My virtue or my plague, be it either which—
> She is so conjunctive to my life and soul
> That, as the star moves not but in his sphere,
> I could not but by her.
>
> (4.7.11–16)

From this admission, we begin to suspect that Claudius's royal "we" is less a signal of his encompassing the state in himself than it is merely a substitution for "my wife and I." Gertrude is *conjunctive* to his life and soul: the word's root is the same as that of *jointure* (L. *iungere* = "to join"), demonstrating, as Adelman argues, that in this play marriage's mingling of man and wife in one flesh disables masculine self-sufficiency.[28] Appropriately, then, except for the brief complaint to Laertes just cited, Claudius seems surprisingly comfortable with this state of affairs. For him, the marital union as a source of monarchical power usually merits nothing but praise; like the "union" (pearl) he drops into the wine during the duelling scene, his marriage is "Richer than that which four successive kings / In Denmark's crown have worn" (5.2.270–71). No wonder he is so certain that young Fortinbras is incorrect to suppose "Our state to be disjoint and out of frame" after Old Hamlet's death (1.2.20). Claudius's state is joined, not disjoint, and hence secure.

Not so for Hamlet, for whom the time is "out of joint"—or, we might read, "out *because* of joint," the joining to the feminine that is the conjugal state.[29] Hamlet's nightmare of succession is precisely the one Claudius offers to him, when he tells Hamlet in Gertrude's presence, "You are the most immediate to *our* throne" and then "Be as *ourself* in Denmark" (1.2.109, 122, my emphases). The ideal state of succession for Hamlet would be not a union, a crown matrimonial like Claudius's, but rather a one-for-one replacement such as that signalled by the duplication of father-son names: a Fortinbras for a Fortinbras, a Hamlet for a Hamlet. Even a Hamlet for a Fortinbras will do, however, especially when, as with Old King Hamlet's defeat of Old Fortinbras, the exchange is accompanied by an unimpeded legal transfer of property from man to man, king to king. Old Hamlet

> Did slay this Fortinbras, who by a seal'd compact
> Well ratified by law and heraldry
> Did forfeit, with his life, all those his lands
> Which he stood seiz'd of to the conqueror;
> Against the which a moiety competent
> Was gaged by our King, which had return'd
> To the inheritance of Fortinbras,
> Had he been vanquisher.
>
> (1.1.89–96)

The "sealed compact" of male-male inheritance—closed, well knit, concise—stands opposed to the "union" of male-female jointure, a union that excludes Claudius from the kind of power acquired through man-to-man combat or man-to-man contract. This "seal" is repeatedly associated with Old Hamlet—Hamlet describes his father's "form" as one "Where every god did seem to set his seal / To give the world assurance of a man" (3.4.61–62)—and with his son's potential occupancy of the father's place.[30] When Hamlet sends Rosencrantz and Guildenstern to their deaths by means of substitute letters that have been "Folded . . . up in the form" of the original letters and embossed with his father's signet, "The model of that Danish seal" (5.2.50–51), he is attempting to reproduce that "sealed compact" that is the vehicle of kingly command. Though his deed is dastardly, it is a kind of answer to the question Hamlet earlier posed himself to one of his future victims: "what replication should be made by the son of a king?" (4.2.11–12). One of the now-defunct meanings of "replication," a fold or the act of folding, puts Hamlet's idea of "replicating" his father in the vicinity, once again, of the "sealed compact" by which one man wills his property to another. This masculine transference of property, moreover, is related to the father's successfully imprinting himself on his child. As Margreta de Grazia has recently discussed, the image of a seal imprinting itself on wax was essential to early modern notions of both kinds of conception, "the having of thoughts and the having of children."[31]

Hamlet's difficulty in reproducing his father and thus succeeding to a masculine inheritance, though, is revealed when we realize that "replication" in Shakespeare's day was about one hundred years away from its modern sense of "replica": though "replication" can mean "echo" in 1600, it cannot mean "exact copy."[32] Hamlet's much remarked-upon penchants for metaphor and simile, for punning, and for more literal ways of remarking upon *likeness* only point out how things that are *like* are not *equivalent*.[33] The most impossible equivalences, as it turns out, have to do with Hamlet's father, who cannot be replicated in any form, even a spiritual emanation. Although Horatio initially tells Marcellus that the Ghost is as like Old Hamlet "As thou art to thyself" (1.1.62), this initial statement of tautology disintegrates in Horatio's later account to Hamlet of seeing "a figure like your father": "I knew your father, / These hands are not more like" (1.2.199, 211–12). Naturally, a person's two hands are *not* alike, but mirror images, so it is not surprising that the Ghost might be merely a demonic image of Hamlet's father (a possibility that the play never lays to rest). If the Ghost cannot equal Old Hamlet, neither, of course, can young Hamlet. Thus we recognize that the letters Hamlet substitutes for the ones in Rosencrantz and Guildenstern's keeping are not the real thing, but merely counterfeit royal decrees, copies of a king's orders. Even Hamlet's most resounding statement of self-identification and self-possession, his cry "This is I, Hamlet the Dane!" as he jumps into Ophelia's grave (5.1.250–51), has the ring of a copy, an echo of his identification of the Ghost: "I'll call thee Hamlet, / King, father, royal Dane" (1.5.44–45)—a naming of the Ghost that has the air of the White Knight's multiple titles for his song in *Through the Looking Glass*. What a song is *called* is not what it *is*; what a king is called is not what he is.

Quite ironically, then, Hamlet's identity lies not with an inheritance from his father (problematic as that may be), but in his being the subject of a queen. Patricia Parker comments on the resonance between the play's puns on "matter" as mother/*mater* and "Aristotelian notions of female frailty as a matter or *materia*. . . . that undermines and adulterates the perfect copying or reproduction of [paternal] parthenogenesis."[34] "Stand and *unfold* yourself," cries Francisco in panic as the play begins (1.1.2, my emphasis). As opposed to residing within the sealed, folded compact of a king's will, what's rotten in the state of Denmark unfolds as an unsealed compact, corresponding to a state in which land is held by neither a Hamlet nor a Fortinbras: the state of queenship, and of its feminine body. To kill the queen, Hamlet avers, would be to reimpose the seal: "How in my words somever she be shent, / To give them seals never my soul consent" (3.2.389–90). Yet as long as Hamlet speaks daggers to his mother but uses none, Denmark remains unsealed, and remains that unfolded, non-intact, grotesque "unweeded garden / That grows to seed," so closely identified with the desiring body of the queen herself (1.2.135–36).

There are certain advantages in *Hamlet*, though, to one's lineage and hence one's identity swerving from masculine derivation. To be a king in the masculine line means, putting it bluntly, to be dead, as Old Hamlet and Old Fortinbras are; their sole functions as they are remembered in this play—as living persons, not as ghosts—are to will their property and to die. (Norway, the play's other king to inherit rule from a man, is at death's door, "impotent and bedrid" [1.2.29].) And upon death they are, of course, no longer kings, only corpses. As Gertrude points out to Hamlet in a piece of wisdom he resists, "Do not for ever with thy vailed lids / Seek for thy noble father in the dust. / Thou know'st 'tis common: all that lives must die" (1.2.70–72). Later Hamlet does seek for his noble father in the dust, though, flirting with death in much more material terms than he does in his "suicide" soliloquy. In the graveyard he muses upon the fact that the great emperors Alexander and Caesar return "to dust, the dust is earth" (5.1.203), but it is into this very earth—the grave of his surrogate father, Yorick—that Hamlet leaps to declare his own name, "Hamlet the Dane" (5.1.251). Fully to become the father is to lose one's own name, just as to become the monarch in a Shakespeare play is typically to lose one's identity in the name of one's country. (The name of the current king of Norway is only that, "Norway.")

And in this play, to obey the father's command and to step into his place is to become a stock character, the Revenger, whose function is to replicate the past by killing and being killed in turn. Mallin, drawing from René Girard, describes revenge as a process of emulation: "The Ghost . . . imitates Claudius by trying to engineer a murder; he calls for filial loyalty, an enforced similarity that will produce a like-minded revenger and replicate regicide."[35] As a revenger-in-training, Hamlet promises the Ghost to discard all that he is—all his learning, all his memory—in order to replace it with the Ghost's command "Remember me":

> Remember thee?
> Yea, from the table of my memory
> I'll wipe away all trivial fond records,
> All saws of books, all forms, all pressures past

That youth and observation copied there,
And thy commandment all alone shall live
Within the book and volume of my brain,
Unmix'd with baser matter.

(1.5.97–104)

Richard Halpern, noting how this passage initially calls up the image of God's commandments carved into stone, points out "the fact that this recording surface is erasable means that it cannot be relied upon to sustain the new message. . . . The Father's commandment may fade, and it does precisely that over the course of the play."[36] The wax of the writing surface, Hamlet's "tables," denotes not the authoritative wax of the father's sealed compact, but rather a malleable, inconstant surface—precisely the "baser matter" that is supposed to be removed from Hamlet's brain. Associated not only with the seal but with "form" itself (as in the passage I noted above, where Hamlet describes his father as "A combination and a form indeed / Where every god did seem to set his seal / To give the world assurance of a man" [3.4.60–62]), Old Hamlet and the authenticity of his command are destined in Hamlet's brain to lose their shape and urgency. But "form," to Hamlet, is also associated with that which is premanufactured, and hence inauthentic. When Gertrude urges him to cast his nighted color off, Hamlet impatiently dismisses such "forms, moods, shapes of grief" as inessential to his sense of self: "I have that within which passes show, / These but the trappings and the suits of woe" (1.2.82, 85–86). Even though Hamlet's remark is made in rebuke to Gertrude, we should not ignore the fact that *she* is the occasion for his having something "within" himself at all—that seething, melancholic, basically formless morass of grief, bitterness, and despair that is brought about by her marriage, and that catalyzes all of Hamlet's extended meditations upon himself and conversations with others as the play stretches on. If he were to adopt the "form" of the revenger, in contrast, his conversation would consist of railing against his wrongers and plotting his retaliation—and he himself would be a cipher. His twitting of Rosencrantz and Guildenstern, in other words, turns out to be true. Beggars, like Hamlet, *have* nothing, but are solid bodies. (Hamlet "lack[s] advancement" [3.2.331] and calls himself a "Beggar . . . even poor in thanks" [2.2.272], but he still inhabits "too too sullied flesh" [1.2.129].) In contrast, "our monarchs and outstretched heroes" *are* nothing, "beggars' shadows" (2.2.263–64).

It is absolutely the case that Hamlet himself associates his delay with the horrifying and disgusting dalliance of his mother, and that his delay is thus shot through with misogyny. But Hamlet's misogyny should not blind us to the fact that his delay also both reflects and produces his personality. What I am proposing is that the ostensible *telos* of *Hamlet*, his prescribed carrying out of the Ghost's command and hence succession to his father's place, would constitute not Hamlet's successful resolution of psychic dilemmas and consolidation of self, as in the classic psychoanalytic account of the play, but rather his loss of self.[37] This is in some ways Lacan's point about Hamlet: the phallus can be immanently present only when the subject himself disappears.[38] But the Lacanian notion that the phallus, though always an impossible object of/in desire, is *still* that object does not really hold true for Hamlet. Halpern points out that Lacan's description of the work of mourning—whose *telos* is, similarly, the invocation of the lost object, the phallus—is somewhat ambiguous in locating where Hamlet is in that process: "We must attend to Lacan's precise formulation: 'The Oedipus [complex] enters its decline to the degree that the subject is obliged to do his mourning for the phallus' [*avoir à faire son deuil du phallus*]. . . . 'Avoir à faire' means 'to have to do' in the sense of being obligated to do something, but it also implies that this thing is still to be done, that it has not yet *been* done. Hence the 'decline' of the Oedipus seems to turn (if we read Lacan's phrasing exactly) not on the actual act of 'mourning the phallus' but on being under an injunction to mourn which has not been fulfilled."[39] If mourning the phallus properly involves invoking and trying to reconstitute its "form," this is a task that Hamlet has to do, in the sense of having *yet* to do. For mourning properly would amount to revenging, and that is the form Hamlet is unwilling, for most of the play, to copy. Hamlet's self, celebrated as the first literary "modern" self, is the one inattentive to the phallus, the one "bored with Oedipus," as Halpern puts it.[40] Instead, Hamlet truly is made up of all that "is in *excess* of the facts as they appear," as Eliot complains.[41]

I refer again to "form" in order to reiterate the point that Hamlet's self, conceived under the aegis of queenship, is not that of the revenger. But I also want to argue that Hamlet is actively engaged in composing another form, one that is modeled after the state of his own mind and that thus corresponds to the new form of "psychologized tragedy" that Mark Rose praises. If we return to Hamlet's response to the Ghost's command, we see that Hamlet swerves from action into this kind of authorship. Initially, of course, he promises to compose himself as a wholly masculine literary piece: "thy commandment all alone shall live / Within the book and volume of my brain, / Unmix'd with baser matter" (1.5.102–4)—here again the pun is on matter as *mater*. But immediately Hamlet's thoughts *do* slide from masculine forms to feminine matter, as he follows this vow with "O most pernicious woman! / O villain, villain, smiling damned villain!" (1.5.105–6). The villain is Claudius, we assume; but unjustly so, since the syntax offers no certain referent for villainy but the pernicious woman herself. Gertrude's presence revises revenge tragedy: the woman, and her willful villainy—for which the Ghost urges Hamlet *not* to take revenge— are indeed the matter of the play. Remembering his father becomes not the impetus for Hamlet's becoming Hieronymo, but rather the occasion for Hamlet's endless revisions of the parts he and others are to act. And in his punning and his plotting, one of the parts Hamlet takes on is what he perceives as Gertrude's own: "one may smile, and smile, and be a villain" (1.5.108).

Taking on a part, of course, is exactly what at first Hamlet refused to do, as he mocked those "forms, moods, shapes of grief" that "are actions that a man might play" (1.2.82, 84). But further consideration of an apposite passage in the play, Hamlet's response to the Player's speech about the death of Priam, makes it clear that playing a part in itself is not the problem—rather, it is playing the part of the revenger that poses the difficulty.[42] At first, Hamlet expresses disgust for the Player's display of inauthentic passion:

> Is it not monstrous that this player here,
> But in a fiction, in a dream of passion,
> Could force his soul so to his own conceit
> That from her working all his visage wann'd,
> Tears in his eyes, distraction in his aspect,
> A broken voice, and his whole function suiting
> With forms to his conceit?
>
> (2.2.545–51)

But Hamlet cannot successfully contrast himself, as the real McCoy of revengers, to the player. Rather, he can only imagine, contradictorily, a player who truly has a "motive and a cue for passion" and who would hence

> drown the stage with tears,
> And cleave the general ear with horrid speech,
> Make mad the guilty and appal the free,

Confound the ignorant, and amaze indeed
The very faculties of eyes and ears.

(2.2.556–60)

It is hard to discern any qualitative difference between the Player's performance as Aeneas and Hamlet's imagination of the Player as revenger. Far
from being an "authentic" revenger, the Player with the motive and the
cue for passion that Hamlet has would only be a better actor, one who
could evoke an even more extreme response from his audience. This *Über-
spieler* would be no better at killing Claudius, only at emoting. Therefore,
although Hamlet engages in many roles during the course of his career,
the revenger's part as we usually understand it—the revenger as killer—is
not one of them. Hamlet even commissions the actors to put on a play
that conspicuously does not contain a revenger's role. Rather, *The Murder
of Gonzago*'s dumb show, which (unlike the interrupted dialogue version of
the play) seems to tell the play's story of murder to its very end, concludes
with the queen accepting the poisoner's love—in short, it goes no further
in revenging the king's death than Hamlet has himself. And by identifying the murderer as "Lucianus, nephew to the King" (3.2.239), Hamlet (as
nephew to the king) inserts himself into the role of the original murderer,
Cain to his father's Abel, rather than into the revenger's part.[43] When the
Ghost reappears to Hamlet in his mother's closet, Hamlet goes so far as to
define himself as the one who has *not* "acted" in this sense: "Do you not
come your tardy son to chide, / That, laps'd in time and passion, lets go
by / Th'important *acting* of your dread command?" (3.4.107–9, my emphasis). Notably, at this point Hamlet viscerally resembles the Player speaking
Aeneas's part, with "distraction in his aspect" (2.2.549) and his hair standing on end. And all for nothing, Gertrude points out: "how is't with you, /
That you do bend your eye on vacancy, / And with th'incorporal air do
hold discourse?" (3.4.116–18).

The Ghost's appearance, though derived from the *Ur-Hamlet* and
hence the creakiest revenge-tragedy prop of all, thus only highlights the
real innovation of the play *Hamlet*: in swerving from the Ghost's command, Hamlet designs *Hamlet* as a play free from its remembered past, a
play as yet undreamt of in any Renaissance philosophy of dramatic genre.
I must emphasize, though, that this literary experiment is carried out only
in the space opened by the suspension of masculine rule. In the play's last
scene, Hamlet prepares to end this experiment by disavowing to Laertes
the entire self he has displayed during the course of *Hamlet*'s action:

Was't Hamlet wrong'd Laertes? Never Hamlet.
If Hamlet from himself be ta'en away,
And when he's not himself does wrong Laertes,
Then Hamlet does it not, Hamlet denies it.

                                              (5.2.229–33)

The queen's death, however, marks that moment at which revenge tragedy
can truly resume its course. Only when Gertrude has made her quietus can
Hamlet make open declaration of the Ghost's command, when he finally
says, exactly upon the moment of her expiring, "O villainy! . . . Treachery!
Seek it out" (5.2.317–18). At the same time, Gertrude's death occasions the
reformation of Denmark from a state under jointure to a state entailed to
male inheritance, from a woman's "cuntry" into a man's "king-dom." Suddenly the succession to the throne becomes a matter of Hamlet's will, not
the queen's. Forcing Claudius to drink the poison, Hamlet commands him,
"Follow my mother," and hence displaces the fact of female-determined
royal succession from himself onto the usurper (5.2.332). And finally,
Hamlet alone anoints the next king: Fortinbras, whose "strong arms"
promise for the kingdom a sense not of psychologized delay, but of active,
bounded closure. Hamlet's naming his successor reiterates in mirror fashion the "sealed compact" of his father's single combat with Fortinbras's
father. This time, Fortinbras wins, but masculine succession is nevertheless
restored, willed (significantly) to a prince who seems unacquainted with
queenship, since he is never mentioned as having any mother at all.

Hamlet paves the way for Fortinbras's kingdom, of course, by pronouncing some "king dooms" of his own; "I cannot live to hear the news
from England," says Hamlet, "But I do prophesy th'election lights / On
Fortinbras" (5.2.359–61). In this prophecy Hamlet joins a whole host of
other Elizabethans, from rural cranks to highly placed courtiers, who at the
time of the play's first performance in 1600 or 1601 were prophesying the
imminent return of a king. In 1598, both Oxford and Cambridge mounted
commencement debates "on one question that bewraied a kynde of weeri-
nes of this tyme, *mundus senescit*, that the world waxed old"—a commonplace enough sentiment, except that Elizabeth's godson Sir John Harington, who reported the events, snidely noted, "which question I know not
how well it was ment, but I knowe how ill it was taken."[44] The world's
decay was manifested in the queen's decay, and both portended an imminent upheaval in the state. That upheaval, though terrifying, seemed also
rather appealing to those who looked forward to James's succeeding to the

throne. Reformer and Church of Scotland official Robert Pont undertook elaborate calculations to prove that "[o]f the estate of this present 1600. yeare of Christ in particular . . . there is an appearant dangerous alteration, to fall out therein, and within few yeares thereafter."[45] That "alteration" turned out to be Elizabeth's death, of which Pont reportedly had instant, miraculous knowledge, coming to James late at night in order to salute him "King of Great Britain, France, and Ireland." "The king said 'I still told you you would go distracted with your learning, and now I see you are so.' 'No, no,' said Pont, 'I am not distempered. The thing is certain; she is dead, I assure you.' "[46]

Such prophesying *before* Elizabeth's death was certain was technically seditious. Beginning much earlier in Elizabeth's reign, Roman Catholic agitation over Mary, Queen of Scots's place in line to the throne prompted a statute that criminalized the writing of books about the succession; in the 1580s, the Earl of Northampton's implication in a book of prophesies concerning the succession necessitated his writing a *Defensative against the Poyson of Supposed Prophecies*.[47] Nevertheless, prognostications only increased as the queen grew older, voicing both opposition to the current monarch and anticipation of the coming one. Harington himself, in a manuscript dated 1602 but unpublished before the nineteenth century, quotes two prophecies of James's succession in the context of expressing severe dissatisfaction with the rule of children and women that had persisted since Edward VI's accession to the throne: "Long may [Elizabeth] live to [God's] glory: but whensoever God shall call hir, I perceive wee ar not like to be governed by a ladye shutt up in a chamber from all her subjects and most of her servantes, and seen seeld but on holie-daies; nor by a childe that must say as his uncle bydes him (for thus it hath bene 53 yeares togither), but by a man of spirit and learning of able bodye, of understanding mynde, that in the preceptes he doth give to his sonne shewes what we must looke for, what wee must trust to. Thus freindes that dare talk one to another."[48] The queen's death, however, burst the dam of prohibition and produced what Howard Dobin describes as a flood of pro-Jacobean prophecy.[49] What was sedition in 1602 was celebration in 1603, like the prognostication that

> . . . a chiftain unchosen [will] choose forth him selfe,
> And ride over the Region, and for Roy holden,
> Then his scutifiers [i.e., shield-bearers] shal skail al the
>   faire South . . .

He shal be kind conquerour, for he is kind Lord,
Of al Bretaine that bounds to the broad sea,
The conquesting shal be keeped & never conquest after.[50]

Safe enough to predict a conqueror from the north after Elizabeth's death
in 1603; but what about in *Hamlet*'s first performances in 1600 or 1601?
Hamlet's answer is a conservative one of converting prophecy into memory, a projection of the future into a restoration of the past. The play's
prophesied new realm will be the realm of the familiar, the known masculine quantity. "I have some rights of memory in this kingdom," Fortinbras
declares (5.2.394), unproblematically returning the play to the site from
which both Prince Hamlet and the play *Hamlet* digressed: the simple
rites of memory, the Ghost's ceremonial command of "Remember me!"
upon which all revenge tragedies depend. Debora Shuger, remarking on
"the tendency in the Renaissance for traditional stories to acquire simultaneously tragic form and psychological complexity," describes that process
as the natural result of those stories' dependence on an "end myth," a myth
that "does not validate traditional symbols but discloses their inadequacy
to provide moral coherence, stable boundaries between right and wrong,
strategies for escaping dread."[51] For most of *Hamlet*, the end myth is one
of kingship; but the play's effort in its final scene is to reconstruct that
myth as living, stable, and coherent.

Of course, the summation of our memory of Hamlet, and of *Hamlet*,
is not so simple as the play's final construction of an alternative history of
rule and a simpler dramatic form. Unlike Horatio, who seems truly to remember *Hamlet* only as a revenge tragedy ("So shall you hear / Of carnal,
bloody, and unnatural acts, / Of accidental judgments, casual slaughters, /
Of deaths put on by cunning and forc'd cause" [5.2.385–88]), we are more
likely to recollect Hamlet as the unwilling revenger, in whose reluctance
an early modern psyche comes to life. Our culture's obsessive returns to
Hamlet emerge from this memory, the wax writing tablet of a mind that
is first Hamlet's but becomes our own—the memory of a man who recalls
everything but the task before him. As Mallarmé describes him, Hamlet is a creature of our own remembrance: "L'adolescent évanoui de nous
aux commencements de la vie et qui hantera les esprits hauts ou pensifs
par le deuil qu'il se plaît à porter [that adolescent who vanished from us
at the beginning of life and who will always haunt lofty, pensive minds
with his mourning]."[52] But if Hamlet emerges from our remembrance,
that remembrance is, as Hazlitt denotes it, ironically prophetic, like Ham-

let's own memory/prophecy of the once and future king: "It is *we* who are Hamlet. The play has a prophetic truth, which is above that of history."[53] We remember not *Hamlet the Revenge Tragedy*, but *Hamlet* alone, sui generis: and in this way, *Hamlet*'s true innovation is to be the first play to manufacture, in advance, nostalgia for itself.

Hamlet's Succession

As repositories of Hamlet's memory, it is easy for us to scoff at Horatio's misapprehension of Hamlet's story as the formulaic blood-and-gore of revenge tragedy. For if that were true, *Hamlet*'s final innovation would reconstruct the entire play as merely a revival, after all—a return of masculine rule through univocal paternal command and filial obedience. "Remember me," and only me. And yet Horatio's perspective might be a useful one. Regarded in this way, *Hamlet*'s closure seems to be a kind of corrective not only to Denmark's queenly presence, but also to *Hamlet*'s place within the burgeoning family tree of Shakespeare's corpus of plays, where genealogy is also, and uncomfortably, a matter of feminine willfulness. Whereas the prince must confront the fact that his impure mother had a part in his making, the play is haunted by reminiscences of the impure, female-dominated origins of the Shakespearean corpus: that is, the *Henry VI* plays, whose emphasis on women's willful and sexually replete rule, I have argued, is expunged only at great length and after many revisions by the apotheosis of masculine rule in *Henry V*. Gertrude's imperial jointure qualifies her for queenly status co-equal to the king's—a circumstance unseen in Shakespeare's work since Margaret of Anjou, who in *2 Henry VI* is called "most master" of her country (1.3.146). *Hamlet*'s antecedents in the history plays are borne out by the play's being titled in both its first and second quarto versions a "tragical history." As a tragedy's successor to the history plays' desiring queens, Gertrude appears poised to boost the status of the relatively subordinate queen of the prototypical Elizabethan revenge tragedy, Bel-Imperia of *The Spanish Tragedy*, whose own initial motivations and plans for revenge inexplicably give way in Act 2 to Hieronymo's. (A similar shift occurs in Shakespeare's own early experiment in the revenge line, *Titus Andronicus*, where Queen Tamora literally plays the figure of Revenge just before she is revenged *upon* by Titus.) It is perhaps not too outlandish, then, to envision *Hamlet*, composed perhaps a year after *Henry V*, as a kind of sequel (until its closing scene) focusing upon what that history play refused to bring into view, Katharine of France's lust-driven second marriage: *Henry V, Part Two: The Queen's Revenge*. In terms of the succession of genres, then, what is new for *Hamlet*—the psychology of a man under queenship—revives what is old for Shakespeare; and contrariwise, the revival of revenge at *Hamlet*'s end looks like something new.

This perspective on *Hamlet*'s experimental status already somewhat muddles the prevailing critical perspective, which I have echoed up to this point in this chapter, that the revenge-tragedy pattern is entirely prior to *Hamlet*, a dull precedent that Hamlet himself for the most part disdains to follow. When trying to imagine Shakespeare writing *Hamlet*, most critics envision him sighing heavily over having to remodel Kyd's fusty, decade-or-more-old *Ur-Hamlet* into something smart and fashionable, perhaps in consequence of history plays' suddenly having become a dangerous business in the wake of the Earl of Essex's rebellion.[54] The revenge tragedy, declares Girard, was "as hackneyed and yet inescapable in Shakespeare's days as the 'thriller' in ours to a television writer. . . . [T]he tedium of revenge is really what [Shakespeare] wants to talk about."[55] And no doubt such boredom would have been the proper response to revenge tragedy in the early and mid-1590s, when Nashe satirized the "English Seneca" who could "afford you whole Hamlets, I should say handfuls of tragical speeches" and Lodge alluded to the *Ur-Hamlet*'s tiresome "ghost which cried so miserably at the Theatre, like an oyster-wife, *Hamlet, revenge*."[56]

The idea that Shakespeare has only these old plays in mind when writing *Hamlet* is a comforting one, since it reassures us of the Bard's transcendent originality. Citing Harold Bloom's exemption of Shakespeare from the "anxiety of influence," David Scott Kastan agrees that with *Hamlet*, "Shakespeare borrows, parodies, quotes, echoes—imitates, in its various senses—but always to make something that meaningfully can be said to be 'pure his owne.'"[57] But such a view requires us to ignore what was happening with Shakespeare's theatrical competition at the time. Certainly old-fashioned, straightforward revenge tragedy still had its audience at the turn of the seventeenth century, when Shakespeare's *Hamlet* was in the works; the Admiral's Men seemed to specialize in it, in fact, reviving *The Spanish Tragedy* in 1597 and paying Jonson for revisions to that play in 1602, as well as commissioning new plays in the standard revenge line.[58] But at the same time, revenge tragedy was already being refashioned into something new by the boys' theater companies, which had just been revived in London after a ban of some ten years. *Hamlet*'s company of adult players, we remember, have come to Elsinore because of a ban on acting, a ban brought about by something Rosencrantz calls "the late innovation" (2.2.331). If taken as a topical allusion to the Essex rebellion of 1601, that "innovation," in its usual Shakespearean sense of "insurrection," further embeds *Hamlet* in the succession-inspired broils of the last years of Elizabeth's reign.[59] But the late innovation also seems to be the boy players themselves, the "little eyases" who "cry out on the top of question, and are most tyrannically clapped for't" (2.2.337–39). Those boy players might be in the news for Shakespeare around 1600 or 1601 for several reasons. Not only because they were popular, not only because the War of the Theaters was garnering them much attention, but also because much of their repertoire at the time consisted of two kinds of plays: new satires, and revivals of old revenge tragedies, including a revival around 1600 of *The Spanish Tragedy*, a play that at that moment was owned by Shakespeare's company. One can only imagine that in the boys' companies' hands revenge tragedy *was* satire, and that when the Children of the Chapel pirated *The Spanish Tragedy* from the Lord Chamberlain's Men they did so in the spirit of "exclaim[ing] against their own succession" by "bèrattl[ing] the common stages," as Hamlet and Rosencrantz describe the boys' satirical remarks (2.2.340, 349).[60]

As Joseph Loewenstein argues, then, we must look past *Hamlet*'s gestures at "autocanonization" in order to discern how the play participates in the newly heightened competition of the London theater scene.[61] When we think of Shakespeare laboring over *Hamlet*, we should imagine him not despairing over how to bring a tired genre up to date, but rather worrying over how to compete with rival upstart companies who were already doing so. The boys' companies were taking unusual liberties with the genres they co-opted. Besides being a novelty act—because of their youth, and because of the enclosed, banqueting-hall-like theater spaces they used, more comfortable and more exclusive than the public theaters—the boys' companies took advantage, as Thomas Heywood put it, of "their juniority be[ing] a privilege for any railing, be it never so violent."[62] Such privilege, though not unlimited, derived from the boys' companies' still operating under licenses granted to their earlier incarnations (and ostensibly their current employment) as boys' choirs, either of St. Paul's or of the Chapel Royal. The raison d'être of the Children of the Chapel (the Blackfriars company) when they first began to present plays in 1600 was "to perform plays and interludes for the Queen"; the performances opened to a paying audience were, in theory, merely "rehearsals" for their courtly appearances.[63]

But besides "railing," a practice that crested in the ad hominem War of the Theaters salvoes in Jonson's *Poetaster* and Marston's *Satiromastix* (both 1601), the boys' companies' productions also took license in flouting stage convention and puncturing stage illusion. Marston's plays are especially notable for their comments on the spectacle of boys playing at being adults. In the induction to *Antonio and Mellida* (1599), the boy who is to play "Piero, Duke of Venice" is advised in how to "frame your exterior shape / To haughty form of elate majesty." And midway through *Antonio's Revenge* (1600), the Osric-like character Balurdo comes on stage complaining, "the tiring man hath not glued on my beard half fast enough. God's bores, it will not stick to fall off."[64] Acknowledging that the romance plot of *Antonio and Mellida* and the revenge plot of *Antonio's Revenge* are equally silly—at the end of the latter play, Antonio remarks, "Never more woe in lesser plot was found" (5.6.59)—these plays instead derive novelty from breathtaking shifts in style and mood and from Marston's delight at coining new words. The shift from romance to revenge between the two *Antonio* plays, for example, is itself quite shocking. At the end of *Antonio and Mellida*, the two lovers' betrothal has been blessed by her erstwhile disapproving father, Piero. At the beginning of the sequel *Antonio's Revenge*, however, Piero confides to the audience that he has killed Antonio's father and plans to marry his mother, and that he has killed another man and laid the corpse next to the sleeping Mellida so as to impugn his own daughter's virtue. Yet at the same time, these plays lampoon their own innovations. Another actor in *Antonio and Mellida* complains that his role, like the play's tone, is ridiculously variable: "unless I were possessed with a legion of spirits, 'tis impossible to be made perspicuous by any utterance. For sometimes he must take austere state as for the person of Galeazzo, the son of the Duke of Florence, and possess his exterior presence with a formal majesty, keep popularity in distance and, on the sudden, fling his honour so prodigally into a common arm that he may seem to give up his indiscretion to the mercy of vulgar censure; now as solemn as a traveller and as grave as a puritan's ruff, with the same breath as slight and scattered in his fashion as—as—as—a—a—anything" (Ind.122–33). Similarly, when introduced by other characters to Marstonian neologisms like "retort," "obtuse," "endear," and "intimate," Balurdo writes them down and takes pains to use (or misuse) them at every opportunity, like a young gallant trying out the new lingo he's just heard at the theater.

Much critical ink has flowed over *Hamlet*'s textual relation to Marston's plays, especially *Antonio's Revenge*, whose plot nearly duplicates *Hamlet*'s and whose action and language either echo or are echoed by *Hamlet*'s at a number of points. New Arden editor Harold Jenkins strenuously argues (on the slim evidence of undated marginalia in Gabriel Harvey's copy of Speght's Chaucer) that an early version of *Hamlet* existed in 1599, soon enough to influence *Antonio's Revenge*, which was almost certainly first staged in the winter of 1599–1600; this early version of *Hamlet*, says Jenkins, was later revised to include the passage reflecting the Essex rebellion and the War of the Theaters.[65] Philip Edwards, in contrast, argues in his New Cambridge edition that Marston is echoing not Shakespeare's *Hamlet*, but an older version of the play; hence Shakespeare's play has to follow Marston's, and perhaps was being composed at the same time Marston's was being performed.[66] While I have nothing to add to and no interest in adjudicating this debate, I must observe that asserting *Hamlet*'s absolute priority over other plays conforms to Hamlet's own propensity for declaring his precedence and idiosyncracy. Whereas in relation to the old revenge tragedy form, *Hamlet* has to distinguish itself as something new, in relation to the boys' companies *Hamlet* has to distinguish itself as something old—that is, something adult, a play that has gone before the boys' plays and hence can stand aloof from their efforts to imitate and satirize revenge convention. Like the play of Aeneas that Hamlet has so taken to heart, *Hamlet* takes pride in its supposed singularity: "it was never acted, or if it was, not above once" (2.2.430–31). As opposed to the boys' companies' highly mannered and self-referential commentary on their own practice, Hamlet urges the players to "hold as 'twere the mirror up to nature" (3.2.22).

But we should not take Prince Hamlet's word, for a thousand pound or anything else, about his own actions' maturity in this regard. For Hamlet is himself in the position of the boy players, especially of one boy player whose case was notorious in 1600: Thomas Clifton, who in that year was impressed into the service of the Children of the Chapel/Blackfriars. Impressment was the usual method of recruiting boys into the St. Paul's and Chapel/Blackfriars companies; their managers held royal warrants for that purpose, a manifestation of the companies' ties to the royal court and of the many royal monopolies that Elizabeth granted (to her subjects' great discontent) near the end of her reign. Unfortunately the managers of the Chapel company had made the mistake of impressing the son of a gentleman, Henry Clifton, Esq., of Norfolk, who promptly brought a complaint against the Chapel company in no less eminent a court than Star Chamber, and secured a warrant freeing his son from the players' service.[67] The temptation is to associate Hamlet with the boy actors, impressed against their will—generally, like Hamlet, on their way home from school—into acting.[68] But once we distinguish "acting" as performance in general from "acting" the revenger's part, we see that Hamlet is really more like the disimpressed young Clifton, whose father wished him *not* to be a performer, to "exercyse the base trade of a mercynary enterlude player, to his utter losse of tyme, ruyne and disparagment."[69] Hamlet himself would prefer to be a performer, and specifically to be a performer along the lines of the boys' companies' players. Though Hamlet admires the visiting adult players, when he stages *The Murder of Gonzago* he is mounting a production very like those of the Children of Paul's or of the Chapel/Blackfriars. Those companies, who performed in theaters remodeled to resemble the royal banqueting halls in which they also habitually played, specialized in insulting the monarch. In 1608 James's clerk wrote to the Privy Council that after seeing two plays deriding him, "his G[race] had vowed [the Children of the Chapel/Blackfriars] should never play more, but should first begg their bred and he wold have his vow performed, And therefore my lo[rd] chamberlain by himselfe or your l[ordships] at the table should take order to dissolve them, and to punish the maker besides."[70] No wonder Claudius asks Hamlet, after seeing the dumb show, "Have you heard the argument? Is there no offense in't?" (3.2.227–28). Hamlet's reply, "No, no, they do but jest—poison in jest. No offence i'th' world" (3.2.229–30), though rather sardonic, is apropos to the "railing" that the boys' companies simultaneously engaged in and undercut. After all, James and his brother-in-law, the King of Denmark, in 1606 had happily watched a play by the Children of Paul's called *Abuses*, "at which the Kinges seemed to take delight and be much pleased."[71] Nor did James, in the end, act upon his determination to dissolve the Chapel/Blackfriars company.[72]

If Hamlet were never to enter masculine succession but forever "exclaimed" against it instead, he might resemble the boys' companies as they were at their height of popularity in the early 1600s, troupes in an eternal state of adolescence. In some ways, the boys' companies at that historic moment embodied in a doubled and redoubled form the position that Stephen Orgel has assigned to the smaller number of boys who acted in each adult company. As "a middle term between men and women," the boy actor represents an oddly comforting all-purpose erotic object, desirable to all members of the audience.[73] Like Pyrocles in Sidney's *Arcadia*, Antonio spends most of *Antonio and Mellida* disguised as an Amazon; and while the actor playing the part complains in the introduction that he has no "voice to play a lady," another actor approves of his voice occupying the middle register, neither male nor female: "O, an Amazon would have such a voice, viragolike" (Ind.74–76). The fear, though, as Antonio goes on to explain, is that after too long in women's dress he'll forget how to play a man: "Aye, but when use hath taught me action to hit the right point of a lady's part, I shall grow ignorant, when I must turn young prince again, how but to truss my hose" (Ind.81–83). While the boy actor on the one hand provides a kind of "out" to the much more frightening spectacle (in the early modern view) of adult female sexuality, on the other hand his mode of arrested development threatens permanently to effeminize him. Similarly, although delay is advantageous in terms of giving Hamlet a broader role of parts to play, including in some respects the "woman's part" of all talk and no action, Hamlet must in the end remember how to play "the young prince" again, just as the boys' companies eventually did for real. In the first two decades of the seventeenth century the boys' companies became less and less distinguishable from the adult companies, as some of the actors (like the boy wonder Nathan Field) stayed on into their twenties, and as other adult actors were recruited.[74] Unlike Hamlet's, though, the boys' companies' adulthood does not necessarily require establishing an all-men's monarchy: that the now-overgrown boy players felt somewhat different than Hamlet does about congress with aristocratic women may be inferred from gossip, about 1602, that "the Dowager Countess of Leicester had married 'one of the playing boyes of the chappell.'"[75]

It is to the boys' companies' less lascivious associations with a powerful woman that I now want to turn, for these associations further reveal how textual editors of *Hamlet* share Hamlet's project of making succession a matter of paternity unsullied by queenship. *Hamlet*, as I mentioned at the beginning of this chapter, is the only Shakespearean text for which not just one or two but three significant early texts survive. The succession of these texts' printing dates is not disputed: the First Quarto (Q1), a "bad" quarto of some 2150 lines that appeared in 1603, was followed in 1604 by the Second Quarto (Q2)—whose title page advertises its being "enlarged to almost as much again as it was, according to the true and perfect copy"—and in 1623 by the First Folio (F) version of the play. The succession of the three texts' composition, however, is impossible to determine with complete certainty. Even leaving aside the compressed and unfamiliar form of the play we find in Q1, Q2 and F pose the frustrating problem of each containing unique passages—Q2 has some that are not in F, and vice versa. Somewhere, at some time, someone made cuts and additions. These three texts' complex relation has spawned a number of detailed and highly refined theories about which text occupies the originary position, how or if the other two are derived from it, and how texts with independent derivation might nevertheless "contaminate" one another in the printing house. I cannot possibly delineate the permutations of all the positions of the various scholars who have worked on this problem; however, the leading theory might be generalized in this fashion:

1. Q2 is the closest text to Shakespeare's original text, being derived from his "foul papers." Q1 and F, in contrast, are ultimately derived from a secondary transcript of the "foul" papers, perhaps one used as a prompt book for theatrical production. Q1, the "bad" quarto, is a "memorial reconstruction" of a performance by one of the bit players, probably the actor who doubled the parts of Marcellus, Voltemand, and Lucianus. F, however, is a "good" copy of the transcript. Whether an editor uses Q2 or F as the control-text for his or her *Hamlet*, then, depends on his or her opinion of the transcript that spawned F. Either

> 1a. this transcript reflects Shakespeare's "second thoughts" on the play, and F should be used as the control-text; or
> 1b. this transcript is someone else's work, and F should be weighed less heavily than Q2.[76]

As David Ward notes, this construction of textual transmission requires both Q2 and the transcript spawning its successor, F, to have been produced before Q1 appeared in 1603, since Q1 contains passages otherwise unique to F.[77] Two interesting contrarian theories, however, have been recently proposed that disrupt the "Q2, then F, then Q1" succession of texts:

2. Steven Urkowitz, defending the old theory that Q1 is not a memorial reconstruction but rather a first draft of *Hamlet*, sees the three versions as successive playhouse revisions by Shakespeare: Q1 grows into Q2, which with some cuts, additions, and other revisions becomes F.[78]
3. Ward thinks that F is the first version of the text, followed by Q1's "memorial reconstruction" of it. Q2, which derives from F, postdates both of the other texts and reflects strategic revisions by Shakespeare.[79]

As with the "who's on first" Marston-versus-Shakespeare controversy, adjudicating among these claims is not my bailiwick. I would like, instead, to focus on how all three theories collude in purifying the text of effeminizing, corrupting influences, attempting to associate the text as closely as possible with the paternity of Shakespeare, and to *dis*associate it, both literarily and historically, from the influence of queenship. Theory 2, Urkowitz's narrative of the texts, which has no historical dimension, is simplest in this regard: Shakespeare, the consummate playwright and dramaturge, is in control of *all* of the texts attributed to him, rethinking and rewriting until he creates the master text. Theory 1a above, subscribed to in the Wells/Taylor/Hibbard Oxford editions that have been influenced by Urkowitz's work on *King Lear*, is a "soft" version of Urkowitz's, unwilling to take the "bad" Q1 as Shakespeare's but otherwise eager to see Shakespeare's controlling hand in the F revisions of Q2. Theory 1b, in contrast, disputes the notion that revision is masterful; instead, revision would signify a vacillating Shakespeare and cannot be countenanced. Hence for Theory 1b all differences between Q2 and F are someone else's work, reflecting cuts made either in the prompt book or the printing house. In any case, though, texts are to be more discounted the further they are from Shakespeare's hand begetting them. Like the Ghost's cry of "murder most foul," which Hamlet must endeavor to remember, Shakespeare's "foul" papers are the paternal point of origin to which editors must struggle to return.

When we examine the "little eyases" passage, however—a passage whose Shakespearean authorship no one disputes—we see that Shakespeare's hand is not as steady as it seems, and that historical circumstances tend to return the text in all its variants to a site of feminine origin. This passage is in F and also (in truncated form) in Q1, but not in Q2, a fact that has prompted several kinds of speculation upon the dates of the three texts of *Hamlet* and the involvement of Shakespeare's company with the boys' companies and the War of the Theaters.[80] For Theory 1a, which prioritizes F over Q2, Shakespeare's "second thoughts" on this scene include his making his text more topical, more contingent on its historical moment of around 1601—therefore, on a historical moment in which effeminate boys, the darlings of Queen Elizabeth and her court, were more attractive than men to theatergoers and thus able to usurp the Globe, "carry[ing] away Hercules and his load too" (2.2.358). But Theory 1b, which prioritizes the Q2 version that does not contain this passage, still does not deliver the text into a masterly world. Unwilling to let F's "little eyases" passage be non-Shakespearean, Jenkins can only speculate that these passages were dropped from Q2 in the printing-house, after the text had escaped Shakespeare's fatherly control.[81]

Only Ward, who with Theory 3 inverts the usually accepted priority of Q2 before F, manages to erase the "little eyases" in a way that reinforces *Hamlet*'s masculine genealogy. Ward argues that Q2's omission of the passage reflects this text's being a revised version of F, one that was taken in hand in anticipation of James I's ascent to the English throne in May 1603.[82] In an effort to cater to the new king's intellectual and political predilections, which were well known in England through James's copious publications, Shakespeare alters his play to make revenge and tyrannicide less attractive, to include the possibility that the Ghost is a demonic manifestation, and to comment on the folly of overmanned and undermotivated military operations like Fortinbras's. The issue of the boys' companies, in contrast, was less than pressing in 1603: not only was the War of the Theaters over, but James had no interest in sponsoring the boys, whose patronage he passed to his wife. The new royal patent issued in 1604 by James to the Children of the Chapel/Blackfriars appointed them to serve "the Queene our deerest wief . . . when she shall thinke it fit to have any playes or shewes"; their new name was "Children of the Revells to the Queene."[83] Having been shunted aside from the monarch's patronage, the "little eyases" exit Shakespeare's text, as well.

But Ward's argument, before turning to James's taste in dramatic topics, reveals how James's passing off the children to Queen Anne does not expunge traces of feminine will from *Hamlet*'s Q2. Anne, a more avid playgoer than James, was no insignificant source of royal favor for theatrical companies. According to the French ambassador, it was she who allowed the renamed Children of the Queen's Revels such license in insulting her husband: "Consider for pity's sake, what must be the state and condition of a prince, whom . . . the comedians of the metropolis bring upon the stage, whose wife attends these representations in order to enjoy the laugh against her husband."[84] Andrew Gurr notes that at the time of the ambassador's report, the Queen's Revels boys were the only ones putting on such plays in London.[85] Hence if Q2 represents a Jacobean revision of *Hamlet*, its failure to disparage the "little eyases" might reflect Shakespeare's reluctance to insult a queen and the objects of her theatrical affection. In that case, it is probably no accident that Q2 also omits to have Hamlet say of Queen Anne's home country, "Denmark's a prison." No matter where *Hamlet*'s text turns, its case is thus altered by the exigencies of a controlling femininity, whether that of boys or that of queens.

Ironically, it is the most corrupt—or, for Urkowitz, the most immature—version of the play, the "bad" Q1, that most grants to Hamlet the queen he seems most to want. Announcing proudly on its title page that it has been "lately acted" by the newly rechristened King's Men, Q1 then goes about purifying the queen of independent desires. In this version, Gertrude is clearly apprised by her son of Claudius's crime, and in response she not only declares herself innocent of involvement in the murder, but also enlists herself in Hamlet's aid.

Hamlet, I vow by that majesty,
That knowes our thoughts, and lookes into our hearts,
I will conceale, consent, and doe my best,
What stratagem soe're thou shalt devise.[86]

Assisted by God's consummately patriarchal "majesty," Gertrude proceeds to dissemble against Claudius—"I will soothe and please him for a time / For murderous minds are alwayes jealous"; meanwhile, she sends word to Hamlet that Claudius is planning to have him killed.[87] Reversing the circumstances in Q2 and F, in Q1 it is not Hamlet who follows Gertrude's allegedly dissimulating lead—"One may smile, and smile, and be a villain"—but rather Gertrude who follows Hamlet's. Further, as Leah Marcus remarks, in Q1 Hamlet's sexual disgust for Gertrude is nearly absent, so that his obsession with the dominance of her appetites also disappears.[88] As a result, Q1's Hamlet has, in a sense, already become his queen's king. No wonder that Q1 features a much more compressed, orderly, and action-packed version of events: little remains to bar the prince from the business of revenge.

Q1 might be able to construct this fantasy because of its memorial reconstruction status. If, indeed, the "bad" quartos were assembled in order to be taken on the road, *The Tragicall Historie of Hamlet* might have found a performance space less impinged upon by queenly demands. With Queen Anne as a competing patron on the London theatrical scene, however, it is hardly the case that to be a King's Man, a "tragedian of the city," is to be free of feminine control. The other texts of *Hamlet*, seen in their local context, disrupt that fantasy even more than *Henry V*'s ambiguous conclusions did. Whereas *Henry V* could at least temporarily imagine a theater as birthing a nation for men only, including its all-man king, *Hamlet* offers no undiscovered all-male kingdom—of country, of mind, or of Globe. We can thus see the close of *Hamlet* as neurotically short-sighted in its attempt to overgo even the performances of the boys' companies by advocating a kind of return of the regressed: a return of revenge tragedy, of masculine rule, of univocal command and obedience: "Remember me."

Though retrograde in this way, however, this closing regression does proleptically usher in something new: a Jacobean age, not only of monarchy but also of the way drama is shaped. When Hamlet picks up the scepter Gertrude has dropped, he paves the way for Shakespeare's Jacobean tragedies, our reading of which must derive, at least in part, from what we make of the final suppression—the plays' willful forgettings—of "imperial join-tresses" like Regan, Goneril, and Lady Macbeth.[89] In the next chapter I turn, however, not to these characters but to two plays that seem the abso-lute inversion of Hamlet's and *Hamlet*'s rejection of monarchical jointure: *Antony and Cleopatra* and *The Winter's Tale*, which in very different ways hinge the creation and the preservation of the world itself upon the free rein and free reign of a queen.

5

The Late Queen
of Famous Memory

Nostalgic Form in Antony and Cleopatra *and*
The Winter's Tale

AMONG THE MANY elegies, epitaphs, and funeral songs composed upon Elizabeth Tudor's death in 1603 was poet and playwright Henry Chettle's *England's Mourning Garment*, a portmanteau document that features a pastoral eclogue mourning the queen's passing, a list of the participants in her funeral procession (from "the Knight Marshal's Man" to the "Second and third Clerk of the Kitchen"), and a long prose account of Elizabeth's virtues and monarchical accomplishments.[1] Chettle's aim in this work is not only to eulogize his late queen, but also to chide England's most talented poets for remaining mute on the subject: "I want but the *Arcadian* Shepherd's enchanting Phrase of Speaking, that was many Times Witness to her just Mercies and merciful Justice; yet, rude as I am, I have presumed to handle this excellent Theme, in Regard the Funeral hastens on, of that sometime most Serene Lady; and yet I see none, or, at least, not past one or two, that have sung any Thing, since her Departure, worth the Hearing; and, of them, they that are best able scarce remember her Majesty" (509). Included in the list of authors Chettle rebukes (under pastoral aliases) for not following the example of Sidney, "the Arcadian Shepherd," are Jonson, Chapman, Drayton, and Shakespeare, "the Silver-tongued *Melicert*" who has neglected to "Drop from his honied Muse one sable Tear, / To mourn her Death that graced his Desert, / And to his Lays open'd her Royal Ear" (510). Were these poets not so remiss in their duties, Chettle argues, "*Elisa* might have liv'd in every Eye, / Always beheld till Time and Poems die" (510). In fact, as Chettle's poet-shepherd Collin goes on to declare in his epitaph for the queen, Elizabeth's demise should be no real tragedy, for with death she ought to gain everlasting fame:

> *Elisa*, Maiden Mirror of this Age,
> Earth's true *Astraea*, while she liv'd and reign'd,
> Is thrown by Death from her triumphant Stage;
> But by that Fall hath endless Glory gain'd;
> And foolish Death would fain, if he could weep,
> For Killing her, he had no Power to keep.
>
> (514)

Chettle's claim is a conventional one in terms of both religious doctrine and poetic conceit: through death Elizabeth gains eternal life, both in heaven and upon the page. But his remark about the queen's having plummeted "from her triumphant Stage" calls attention to the theatrical means by which Elizabeth so skillfully kept her throne "while she liv'd and reign'd," and therefore calls into question whether a playwright like Shakespeare could, in fact, accept Chettle's invitation to celebrate her fall as fortunate. Shakespeare indeed did not memorialize Elizabeth upon her death, just as he did not, except in passing or in epilogue, encomiate her while she lived. But given the associations between female authority and modes of theatricality that Shakespeare had developed in his plays up to this point, associations that I have delineated in the previous two chapters, any remembrance of the queen would have to take the form of a meditation upon theater itself. Further, the very act of remembrance changes matters. Far unlike the circumstances pertaining to *The Faerie Queene*, the history plays, and *Hamlet*, where the queen's very *presentness* occasioned literary works configured around feminine authority, in a post-Elizabethan era the queen must be conjured up from the past in order to be addressed. The work of poiesis is hence complicated by the work of recovery.

All literary work, of course, involves remaking at least a literary, if not also a historical, past; and drama featuring historical persons must be especially conscious of bringing the dead to life in the form of living actors on the stage. But in the immediate aftermath of queenship, Shakespeare's theater bears some complicity in reviving the very phenomenon whose end it so often forecast and for whose end it so often, in plays like *Henry V* or in persons like Hamlet, expressed desire. For here theater lays claim to the ultimate kind of authority, the authority to create what its culture remembers—remembers not just of national history, but of theatrical history as well.[2] In *Antony and Cleopatra* and *The Winter's Tale*, I argue in this chapter, Shakespeare evokes very explicitly the way that his own dramatic oeuvre has manifested theatrical authority as a feminine and effeminizing phenomenon. Cleopatra and (to a lesser extent) Hermione seem to represent Joan of Arc and Gertrude rolled into one, so that sexuality, authority, marital or quasi-marital union, fecundity, and theatrical entrancement are inseparable from each other. Even more so, though, in these two plays all of these aspects of feminine authority are expanded to be precisely coextensive with the space of theater. There seems to be no alternative masculine theatrical mode counterposing them, like that of Talbot or Henry V or the finally revenging Hamlet, from which this theatricality may be disparaged and in favor of which it may be discarded.

And yet feminine theatricality *is* discarded, nevertheless, as *Antony and Cleopatra* and *The Winter's Tale* come to their conclusions. It may seem unfair, especially with these plays—where what has come before has been so magical and so marvelous—to privilege the plays' endings as much as I ultimately do in this chapter. I feel myself nearly adopting the point of view of Horatio, who sees in *Hamlet* only the carnage at its conclusion. But the historical vantage point that gives rise to nostalgia for queenship, I argue, requires a very careful examination of what brought about the passing of feminine theatricality's magic and marvels. Nostalgia involves not only the inevitable historical consciousness of how things turned out, of knowing when and how Cleopatra died, but also the recognition that her death is required so that we may remember her and revive her upon the stage. *The Winter's Tale* performs that revivification with such insistence that it almost allows us to forget the queen's prerequisite death. But the events following Hermione's return to life, in my view, reinforce her removal from the scene in a way that, though more benign than Leontes's virtual murder of her, similarly restores his sense of patriarchal order. In this sense, *The Winter's Tale* follows *Antony and Cleopatra*'s lead as an experiment in a new Shakespearean genre, feminine tragedy. By that I mean not simply tragedy that happens to women, but tragedy that happens when the very femininity that produces theater comes to an end.

My argument about each of these plays thus pulls in two directions, in that I detail how each play registers the immense appeal of the theater as a feminine place and activity, but also how each play reveals the preconditions for such appeal: the queen's passing. At each play's conclusion there is no adequate substitute for the living, breathing queen, but her demise both apotheosizes and demarcates the limits of a feminine authority of playing.

Mixing Memory and Desire: Cleopatra

I begin with two related but distinct questions. What did early Jacobean England remember of queenship? And how did such a memory reverberate within early Jacobean theater?

Combining these two questions into one, as one is easily tempted to do, might lead to the conclusion that Cleopatra represents the welcome farewell England had bid to queenship. Composed sometime between 1604 and 1608, *Antony and Cleopatra* summons up reminiscences of England's recently deceased Queen Elizabeth along the lines of Elizabeth's and Cleopatra's shared fondness for theatrical spectacle, a trait commonly discussed in new-historicist treatments of Elizabeth's reign. Such theatricality—the display of the queen's glittering, glamorous self in the court, the city, and the countryside, in portraits, pageants, and processions—was employed as an instrument of monarchical power, as Stephen Greenblatt influentially contends in *Renaissance Self-Fashioning*.[3] But such an association between queenly rule and theatrical shows did not always buttress the queen's authority. In the opinions of some of her subjects, as Louis Montrose argues, Elizabeth's dramatic self-showings would also have served to delegitimate her by associating her with the "theatricality and spectacle" of abhorred Roman Catholicism, so that "at the same time that the iconic, verbal, and performative arts played a central role in entertaining the sovereign and aggrandizing the state, they were also a potential liability to the very reverence and assent they were designed to procure."[4] When Shakespeare's audience saw Cleopatra sitting on her throne and decked in her royal robes and crown, they could easily have conjured up a picture of their former queen in all her magnificence, but also in all the ambivalence of her sensually pleasing splendor.

Further, Cleopatra's queenly sexuality might also carry reminders of Elizabeth's arranging her court as a scene of courtship of the Virgin Queen —a queen who, though unavailable, created a fiction of being available for sexual possession. Referring to the familiar Ditchley portrait of the figure of Elizabeth standing on a map of England, Leonard Tennenhouse argues that *Antony and Cleopatra* is "Shakespeare's elegy for the signs and symbols which legitimized Elizabethan power"—power vested in "the desiring and desired woman, her body valued for its ornamental surface, her feet rooted deep in a kingdom."[5] Like Elizabeth in her court, Cleopatra rules by means of an eroticized collapsing of the distinctions between the monarch's body natural and body politic, equating monarchical charisma and sexual sway.[6]

However, as with Cleopatra's theatricality, we must also question how uniformly "legitimating" this Elizabethan strategy really was. In the light of what the conjunction of monarchical rule and female sexuality had meant to some Elizabethan thinkers, Cleopatra takes on the aura of a truly frightening flashback. Rather than the decrepit, indecisive, queen-hidden-away about whom England had vociferously complained in the last decade of Elizabeth's reign, Cleopatra looks more like the willful, vibrant, and sexually alive queen invoked with horror in the mid-sixteenth century English debate over women's right to rule, when anti–queenship polemicists worried, Hamlet-like, over the consequences of a female sexual appetite being given charge of the country. To take the most famous example, John Knox wrote with great disdain in 1558 that "women are lifted up to be heads over realms and to rule above men at their pleasure and appetites."[7]

The cost of that rule is a nation's masculine identity. Most drastic of all Knox's attributions to female rule is the spectacle of the nation itself, and all the male subjects in it, effeminized in service to the queen. Referring to the classical and biblical authorities he martials in support of his argument, Knox claims that the sight of a queen "should so astonish them that they should judge the whole world to be transformed into Amazons, and that such a metamorphosis and change was made of all the men of that country (as poets do feign was made of the companions of Ulysses), or at least that albeit the outward form of men remained; yet should they judge that their hearts were changed from the wisdom, understanding, and courage of men to the foolish fondness and cowardice of women."[8] Although the polemics over the sheer fact of queenship died down, for the most part, as Elizabeth's rule wore on, Knox's fear of an effeminized nation resurfaced as ad feminam attacks upon particular queens. In England, as I noted in Chapter 4, the primary target for nearly thirty years was Mary, Queen of Scots, pilloried until her execution in 1587 (and thereafter) as sexually uncontrollable as often as she was portrayed as politically ambitious. Indeed, these two charges became practically indistinguishable, so that political diatribes against Mary were almost certain to shade off into accusations of her lasciviousness. George Buchanan, who was Mary's tutor in her teens but became her most vehement opponent, speaks in one breath of Mary's political machinations and of her "outragious lust," her "mair than princely or rather unprincely licentiousness."[9] Even in the relatively decorous setting of Parliament, Mary was proclaimed to be "the most notorious whore in all the world."[10]

At this extreme, however, attacks against Mary resemble similar attacks against Elizabeth, who like Mary was routinely charged with effeminizing her nation by means of her sexual appetites. Adam Blackwood, the Scots Catholic living in France who became Mary's most prominent apologist, accuses Elizabeth in most graphic terms of unmitigated licentiousness in company with her court nobles, concluding that her rapacious appetites have unmanned her entire country:

> Lasches peuples, effeminez. . . .
> Les François trop courageux sont
> Pour servir des peuples qui ont,
> Un joug de femme sus leurs testes.
> [Feeble people, effeminate. . . . The French are too courageous to
>   serve people who have a woman's yoke on their heads.] [11]

Expatriate Roman Catholic Cardinal of England William Allen, who accuses Elizabeth of "unspeakable and incredible variety of lust," asserts that Elizabeth also exerts her appetites by promising marriage to nobles she hopes to enslave: "[she] promised mariage to sum of the nobillity at home, makinge many of them in single lyfe to the danger of their soules, and decay of their famelies, to attend her pleasure: & no lesse depelie dallied & abused by dissembly almost all the great personages of Europe, to whom as wel by letters, as by sollemne Embasses, she proffered herself, to the mockery & final delusion of them all." [12] Here, however, Allen comes close to the truth of Elizabeth's sexual rule: Elizabeth unmans men not by indulging her lust, but through a pose of sexual availability. Hence the queen's ruling power was indeed, as her detractors feared, eroticized—as Francis Bacon would slyly acknowledge by writing of his late mistress's "wonderful art in keeping servants in satisfaction, and yet in appetite." [13] Or, as Enobarbus says of Cleopatra, "she makes hungry, / Where most she satisfies" (2.2.237–38).

Bacon's remark about his dead queen indicates that some Jacobeans, at least, remembered their queen in terms of her sexualized rule. The question is whether this memory was a fond one, or whether it inspired revulsion and consequent relief. Not surprisingly, historical evidence suggests that Jacobean recollections of the late queen oscillated between fond attachment to her memory, and a profound sense of good riddance. Intense longing for Elizabeth can be found relatively soon after James's accession in Thomas Dekker's Armada play *The Whore of Babylon* (1606), which stars as the Whore's antagonist "Titania, the Fairie Queen, under whom is figured our late Queen Elizabeth." [14] Along the same lines (as I shall discuss further in Chapter 6), Bishop Godfrey Goodman remembered that after

Elizabeth's death, "her memory [was] much magnified—such ringing of bells, such public joy and sermons in commemoration of her, the picture of her tomb painted in many churches; and, in effect, more solemnity and joy in memory of her coronation than was for the coming in of King James."[15] In 1612 Henry Peacham closed his emblem book *Minerva Britanna* with a vision of "Eliza's" Phoenix, an apparition that causes him to plead for the queen's return in the person of "Vertue": "By all the means we her allure, / To take her dwelling where she did."[16]

Peacham's allusion is telling, however: of all Elizabeth's mythological referents, the phoenix is the most devoid of erotic appeal, reproducing itself without recourse to the engulfing feminine sexuality that Elizabeth, like Mary, Queen of Scots, so often represented. James I himself, successor to these two powerfully and fearfully sexualized queens, did his best to distance himself from precisely this aspect of their rule, resulting in his seemingly incongruous responses to recollections of either queen, depending on the sexualized valence of the incident. For example, although he issued only pro forma protests against his mother's execution for treason, he vehemently objected to Spenser's allegorization of her as the sexually vile Duessa in *The Faerie Queene*'s Book 5.[17] Similarly, James often invoked Elizabeth's decisions before Parliament as precedent for his own political aims,[18] but when it came to defending the last queen against the "base and scandalous" words uttered against her sexual honor "by one Sheapheard, a barrister of Lincolns Inn, [and] a base Jesuited papist," James only ordered "that wee should talke no news nor talke of kings nor compare one king with another."[19] James's most public act of homage to his two female progenitors served both to equate and to marbleize their memories: in 1605 he commanded that tombs for both be erected in Westminster Abbey, ordering that the "like honour might be done to the body of his dearest mother, and the like monument be extant of her, that had been done to his dear sister, the late Queen Elizabeth."[20] The resulting monuments, which face each other from the north and south aisles of the Henry VII chapel, are similar in size, in design, and in cold, imposing stoniness (even though Mary's, as it turned out, cost a good deal more).

I shall have more to say later in this chapter, and at the beginning of Chapter 6, about statues of queens. For now, though, I want to comment that given James's own desexualization of the late queens' memory, it is understandable that Tennenhouse should come to the conclusion that the highly sexualized Cleopatra denotes a Jacobean dislocation of female authority from the center of power to the margins of illegitimacy. This argument is a corollary of the assumption I discussed in Chapter 1, that authors take up the topic of queenship out of the compulsion of her presence. Once the English state was reconfigured around a king, not a queen, Tennenhouse argues, any power held by a woman similarly *must* have been delegitimated, reconstituted as a pollution threatening the state from without—Egypt threatening Rome—rather than as a feminine principle upon which the state depended.[21] Presuming first that Shakespeare's Jacobean audience would automatically attach its sympathies, along with its political allegiance, to the play's Roman imperial victor, Tennenhouse secondly presumes that the theater's sympathies would automatically follow suit. I have already questioned the extent to which all English people under James preferred his rule to Elizabeth's. But Tennenhouse's second premise seems to me more crucial, since if it is ill-founded, then we may begin to see how the close of *Antony and Cleopatra* might mark an impending crisis, if not for the Jacobean state, then for the Jacobean stage. And as with the history plays, testing this theory of theatrical allegiance requires investigating where theater's gendered loyalties reside. In my view, far from transferring the stage's affiliations from a queen to a king, *Antony and Cleopatra* invests theater's entire operation in what queenship's detractors had feared most: an authoritative woman who wields, by means of her own person, the seductive power of the stage itself. Moreover, Shakespeare emphasizes with Cleopatra—as he did not with Joan La Pucelle, whose imaginative seductions were challenged by Talbot's (and eventually by Henry V's) epic projections—the solely, incontestably feminine nature of that power.

In order to establish the preeminence of feminine theatrical creation in the play, I must first dispute the prevailing critical notion that *Antony and Cleopatra*'s twin kingdoms of Egypt and Rome are engaged in a contest between two rivalrous orders, each of which the play—and its audience—might conceivably choose. In traditional evaluations of the play the names of its two milieux, Rome and Egypt, generally serve as headings for an entire set of dualisms, each of which corresponds to the opposition of masculine vs. feminine. G. L. Kittredge, for example, categorically states that "in [*Antony and Cleopatra*] are mirrored two directly contrasting visions of life and conceptions of value: those of Egypt opposed to those of Rome—the sensual and wasteful opulence of the East opposed to the cold, bare efficiency of the West. Egypt in this play stands for passion and human weakness, Rome for duty and self-denial: the world of the senses pitted against the world of reason and a fixed morality."[22] A slightly different but increasingly popular version of this conception of Rome versus Egypt is also slightly more insidious, since it mirrors the play's own intermittent spasms of Orientalism: the idea that the play is not so much about Rome's opposition to Egypt as it is solely about the state of Roman masculinity, embodied in the homoerotic attachment and competition of Antony and Caesar. In this scenario, Cleopatra is relegated to the margins of the story as Egypt is to the margins of the European map, whence her role is to precipitate Caesar's and Antony's struggles.[23] Egypt and Cleopatra would thus represent an erotic, sensual entropy that always lurks just beyond the Roman border—not a state in the national sense, but a state into which the Romans, if they drop their guard or neglect their imperial ambitions, might dissolve. As Northrop Frye puts it, "while there is one world [in the play], there are two aspects of it: the aspect of 'law and order' represented by Rome, and the aspect of sensual extravagance and licence represented by Egypt."[24] From the Roman viewpoint, of course, this is certainly the right way in which to conceive the threat Cleopatra poses, since it allows Rome to consider Antony the only Roman who could plunge into the fleshpots of Egypt. As the Roman Philo, observing Antony's conduct with Cleopatra, objects at the play's outset, "Nay, but this dotage of our general's / O'erflows the measure" (1.1.1–2). The Egyptian queen's sexual command of Antony, the Romans repeatedly assert, causes him to give up his self-command and hence his imperial self. Thus Philo's speech goes on to decry Antony's surrender of Rome to Egypt:

> those his goodly eyes,
> That o'er the files and musters of the war
> Have glow'd like plated Mars, now bend, now turn
> The office and devotion of their view
> Upon a tawny front: his captain's heart,
> Which in the scuffles of great fights hath burst
> The buckles on his breast, reneges all temper,
> And is become the bellows and the fan
> To cool a gypsy's lust. Look, where they come:
> Take but good note, and you shall see in him
> The triple pillar of the world transform'd
> Into a strumpet's fool: behold and see.
>
> (1.1.2–13)

In familiar Renaissance terms, Philo describes what happens when a man gives himself to a woman: Cleopatra, the "gipsy" and "strumpet," leaches from Antony the very physical powers that tempered his great general-ship—his sight, his "heart," his breath. In her presence, to cool her lust, Antony exhales his Roman being and becomes "a strumpet's fool."[25]

Another look at this speech, however, draws us to a different under-standing of the play's two realms, one that complicates the moralized choice Antony makes between virtuous Rome and licentious Egypt, or be-tween impervious Caesar and loose Cleopatra. In short, Philo's judgment of Antony begins to hint at a theatrical relation implicit in the coupling of Rome and Egypt. By emphasizing Antony's gaze—once directed toward his armies, now fixed upon the Cleopatran spectacle—Philo's rhetoric matches that of Tudor-Stuart antitheatricalist writers who, as I discussed in Chapter 3, feared the feminized theatrical scene's ability to unman its male audience. William Prynne's diatribe might as well be Philo's, or sub-sequently Caesar's, describing how Antony has given himself over to the feminine: "When both *his* [i.e., the spectator's] *eyes*, his eares, affections, heart, and all his senses shal be wholy taken up, with such amorous, *beauti-full lust-provoking objects as* are able to revive the most mortified carnall affec-tions; *to fire, the most frozen benummed* lusts; to overcome the most chaste and continent heart; (all which concurre at once in Stage-playes:) how can it but ingender, not onely a sparke or two, *but an whole flame, an Hell of filthy lusts within his soule*; and carry him on to all uncleannesse even with a full carere?"[26] It is not only Antony who is implicated in this lustful interchange between stage and audience, however. Philo can acquire his Roman com-patriot's concurrence in his disapproval only if Demetrius likewise attaches his gaze to the spectacle before them, the spectacle of Antony reneging all temper to Cleopatra. "Look, where they come," says Philo. "Take but good note . . . behold and see." If Antony seems to be drawn into the Eastern vortex that is Cleopatra, so too are those who watch him being drawn.

Indeed, *Antony and Cleopatra* is configured not as a set of imperial decisions and their repercussions, but as a set of Cleopatran displays and Roman reactions, as if the entire Roman empire is compelled to fix its eyes upon Egypt and its queen. On grounds that are the very basis of theatri-cal presentation, the grounds of the ocular, the traditional division of the play into two realms is shown to be spurious, only a red herring.[27] The play has really only one sphere, composed both of the Cleopatran enigma and of those who are, to a more or less complete degree, attracted to her. The play's two apparently discrete points of view join in a single, theatrical arena. Without exception, no Roman in the play can (or evidently wishes to) avoid commenting upon the Cleopatran spectacle; as the play progresses, in fact, its action eventually leaves Roman territory entirely and inhabits only Egypt.[28] In the end, even Caesar goes to see Cleopatra— a seemingly unnecessary circumstance, given the plethora of lieutenants and messengers who have hitherto conducted his business. Egypt may be politically and sensually marginal to Rome, the mysterious East of forbidden fantasies and unwise choices, but the theatrical in balance subsumes all notions of margins; Cleopatra's queenliness becomes defined as the entrancing spectacle at which all of Rome eventually finds itself. This definition, moreover, accounts for one of Shakespeare's few omissions of detail from Plutarch's delineation of Antony's character. Along with drunkenness, gluttony, lust, and wastefulness, Plutarch castigates Antony for his deplorable habit of "pass[ing] away the time in hearing of foolish playes," a pastime which he pursues both before and after his entanglement in Egyptian affairs, and which Plutarch clearly associates with his abnegation of his Roman duty.[29] Shakespeare's Antony does not go to the theater—he goes to Cleopatra.

On this level, then, Cleopatra effects a theatrical ravishment similar to the one Shakespeare ascribed in *1 Henry VI* to Joan La Pucelle: her male beholder, erotically and sensually invaded by her seemings, finds his quotidian sense of judgment snatched away from him. Laura Levine has beautifully detailed this aspect of *Antony and Cleopatra* in her study of English Renaissance antitheatricalism,[30] so I will cite only the example of Enobarbus's objecting to Cleopatra going to war alongside Antony, because of her ability thus to befuddle him: "Your presence needs must puzzle Antony, / Take from his heart, take from his brain, from's time, / What should not then be spar'd" (3.7.10–12). In Levine's view, the play dramatizes as Antony's life history the Renaissance fear that masculinity is merely a performance, and that effeminate behavior (such as one observes and learns in the theater) will thus bring about the inevitable: a man's dissolution into womanhood. "[I]f the first acts of the play present Antony's effeminization through the testimony of rumor and the center of the play offers a dramatization of the story of the dissolving warrior . . . , the last scenes of the play that Antony appears in offer a psychological portrait of what it feels like to be an effeminized man."[31] This effeminized self that Antony adopts is, in Levine's view, a kind of nothing. Having exposed the extent to which masculinity is an unstable and easily dissolved kind of theatricality, *Antony and Cleopatra* also exposes the fear of having no stable self at all. Such, I argued in Chapter 3, is indeed the temporary effect Joan La Pucelle has upon Talbot: by dissimulative technique she whirls his thought so much that he does not know who he is, or what he does (*1 Henry VI* 1.5.19–20). But Cleopatra's "puzzling" of her lover—as Enobarbus puts it—and of the other Romans who draw near her is more multifarious, and hence more theatrically resonant, than the "Puzzel" Joan's instantaneous sensual confusion of the Dauphin or of Talbot. With Cleopatra, feminine ravishment emerges into a more idealized conception of theatrical activity: as a fertile, multivalent inventiveness that does not simply seize the spectator's sense, but imparts a unique sensibility in its place.[32] To a Roman, this sensibility may feel like having no self at all, but the play reveals that to an Egyptian, it entails a very full sense of self indeed. That is to say, theater as *Antony and Cleopatra* construes it demands not just that its spectator abandon his masculine will, becoming a kind of mindless putty in theater's hands, but that he actively claim for his own the feminine will that Cleopatra personifies.

The linguistic constructions by which Cleopatra is characterized carefully distinguish between these two modes of engagement, one physical, the other metaphysical, by refuting the notion that Cleopatra's effect depends, as the antitheatricalists thought of theater, on sheer sensual surfeit. In fact, the play takes up two potentially sense-depriving activities to which antitheatricalist writers compare theatergoing—*eating* and *sleeping*—and converts them into metaphors that summon up this simplistic description only to flout it. Continually coupled both in Roman descriptions of Cleopatra and in her own language, these metaphors immediately indicate the sensuous, corporeal nature of her power; but they also begin, in their reiteration and increasing complexity, to point to a queenly sway that is imaginative as well as sexual, and that creates as much as it takes away.

At first, the Romans' metaphorical use of *eating* and *sleeping* primarily elaborates their equation of gaze and sexual surrender: just as looking upon Cleopatra leads to self-abandonment, sensually ingesting things Egyptian leads to oblivion. Caesar defines Antony's former Roman self, the one he has sloughed off for Cleopatra, as impervious to the effects of food. On campaign, Caesar says, Antony survived terrible privations, including "eat[ing] strange flesh, / Which some did die to look on" (1.4.67–68). But Caesar's recollection also resonates proleptically, as Cleopatra comes to embody the food to which Antony was formerly immune. She is the next "strange flesh" Antony has encountered, a "strange serpent" like the crocodile Antony describes for Lepidus (2.7.47), but this time around Antony has joined the ranks of those who succumbed, who (sexually) "died" after looking upon her. Cleopatra herself also compounds gazing, eating, and sexual climax when she remembers her past lovers: Julius Caesar, for whom she was "a morsel for a monarch"; and Pompey the Great, who "Would stand and make his eyes grow in my brow, / There would he anchor his aspect, and die / With looking on his life" (1.5.31–34). This Pompey's son (who never meets Cleopatra himself) associates her seducing Antony with an overfed, overindulged stupor that approaches death's oblivion:

> Let witchcraft join with beauty, lust with both,
> Tie up the libertine in a field of feasts,
> Keep his brain fuming; Epicurean cooks
> Sharpen with cloyless sauce his appetite,
> That sleep and feeding may prorogue his honour,
> Even till a Lethe'd dulness—
>
> (2.1.22–27)

Egyptian food and Egyptian sensuality unite in a pun involving Cleopatra's person. She is, as Enobarbus puts it, Antony's "Egyptian dish." The equivalence of victuals and woman suggests that such feeding does not take place except where Cleopatra herself is; and certainly Antony's attempt to provide his Roman allies with a taste of Egypt is, at best, unsatisfactory. At the Roman conference Antony tries to stage his own "Alexandrian feast," one in which consumption of food and drink culminates in sleeping—"Come, let's all take hands, / Till that the conquering wine hath steep'd our sense / In soft and delicate Lethe" (2.7.104–6)—but the result is only a kitschy, tawdry reproduction. Lepidus, one of the "triple pillars of the world," is borne off stone drunk, while the others dance to the ungainly chorus of "Cup us till the world go round, / Cup us till the world go round!" (2.7.115–16).[33]

The problem with equating women with food and sleep is that, as the Roman banquet indicates, one eventually gets enough. Such a woman is Shakespeare's Cressida, who after being turned over to Diomedes becomes a created object rather than a creative actor, and henceforth as mere object of spectacle is doomed utterly to revolt those who look upon her. Like Helen, called a "flat tamed piece," Cressida becomes for the Greeks and the Trojans alike the repellent leavings of a now-tiresome banquet (4.1.63). Troilus in horror declares that "The fractions of her faith, orts of her love, / The fragments, scraps, the bits, and greasy relics / Of her o'er-eaten faith are given to Diomed" (5.2.157–59).[34] In his anger at Cleopatra after his first loss to Caesar, Antony attempts to reduce her to the same level, that of a whorish leftover: "I found you as a morsel, cold upon / Dead Caesar's trencher: nay you were a fragment / Of Gnaeus Pompey's" (3.13.116–18). The pun on woman as spoiled food and woman as prostitute is a familiar Shakespearean one; as *The Taming of the Shrew*'s Katherina asks her father when he offers her as a possible wife to her sister's suitors, "I pray you, sir, is it your will / To make a stale of me amongst these mates?" (1.1.57–58).

The writer of the epistle published with the quarto of *Troilus and Cressida* equates theater and woman by evidently taking to heart the notion that plays themselves are whores that can become cloying with overuse, and by promising us "heere a new play, never stal'd with the Stage, never clapper-clawd with the palmes of the vulger" (p. 95). What finally distinguishes Cleopatra from the Roman notion of overeating and oversleeping, however, is the quality that the younger Pompey calls "cloyless," and this is also the quality that distinguishes Cleopatran theater from plays "stal'd with the stage." Cleopatra is irresistible not because she satiates the men who look upon her, conquering men as the wine does Lepidus, but because they can never get their fill of her. In Enobarbus's famous formulation about Cleopatra,

> Age cannot wither her, nor custom stale
> Her infinite variety: other women cloy
> The appetites they feed, but she makes hungry,
> Where most she satisfies.
>
>   (2.2.235–38)

"Cloylessness" here marks itself, even more than in Pompey's speech, as an attribute that dissolves the interface between the seductress and the seduced, and that begs the question of whose appetite is the insatiable one in their encounter. Because Cleopatra is "cloyless," Antony is never "cloyed," never ceases to desire her: her feeding and sleeping arouse rather than stupefy. The Romans' suspicion of Cleopatra, then, derives not from a fear that she might overwhelm a man's sense entirely, as Acrasia does Verdant's or Joan temporarily does Talbot's, but from an awareness that she can transform a man's sense into one that wishes to be ravished, over and over again. Like the mysterious wafer at the center of the (now-forbidden) Roman Catholic Mass, Cleopatra not only is transubstantiative in herself, but also changes the very being of those who ingest her.[35] The impervious warrior not only becomes permeable to the spectacle that feeds him, he also begins to emulate its nature. Like it, he is constantly unfinished in his desire, unstaled by any custom.

And like the theater, he gives desire voice. Part of what shocks Philo

and Demetrius in the play's opening scene is not only Antony's sheer be-
sottedness, but also his eschewing Roman speech (he will not listen or
respond to Caesar's ambassadors) in favor of an expansive language of
inventive passions and infinite wishes. If anything, Antony in this scene
speaks a more "Egyptian" language even than Cleopatra: it is he who uses
words of overreaching, overflowing, and boundlessness.

Cleopatra.   If it be love indeed, tell me how much.
Antony.   There's beggary in the love that can be reckon'd.
Cleopatra.   I'll set a bourn how far to be belov'd.
Antony.   Then must thou needs find out new heaven, new earth.

(1.1.14–17)

To join fully with Cleopatra is to metamorphose, like her, into one "Whom
every thing becomes": Antony's word "becomes" indicates both the appeal and the changeability that constitute the "cloylessness" shared with
her. To join fully with Cleopatra is to be a playgoer who admits oneself to
be an integral part of feminine playing.

Not that Antony is always comfortable, of course, with sharing so
fully in Cleopatran theatrics. When he is enraged at her, or when he feels
the need to assert a Roman self, he is eager to label her beguiling powers as
mere witchcraft and his engagement with her as mere stupefaction. Thus
when he apologizes to Caesar for being absent from Rome, he explains
that "poisoned hours had bound me up / From mine own knowledge"
(2.2.90–91). Once a speaker identifies Cleopatra not with stimulating food
but with stultifying "poison," he distances his volition from her effect. Unawares, he was invaded by her; unawares, he succumbed. Even in a more
contemplative mood Antony often cannot move past the Roman fashion of defining his union with Cleopatra only as a loss of self. Before his
botched suicide he speaks to Eros of a cloudlike world in which all certain
meanings, all categorizations—including the category named "Antony"—
have disintegrated: "here I am Antony, / Yet cannot hold this visible shape"
(4.14.13–14). A shape-shifting world of liquid enchantment and leading
falsehoods; Egypt and the theater—both are summed up in Antony's despairing cry upon his final loss to Caesar:

Betrayed I am.
O this false soul of Egypt! this grave charm,
Whose eye beck'd forth my wars, and call'd them home;
Whose bosom was my crownet, my chief end,

Like a right gipsy, that at fast and loose,
Beguil'd me, to the very heart of loss.

(4.12.24–29)

And yet Antony's own language partakes in Egyptian constructions to the
extent that it hints at an alternative, Egyptian mode of being that even he
cannot admit or understand. When he tells Caesar that in Egypt "poisoned
hours had bound me up / From my own knowledge," his phrasing offers
two meanings apart from the overt one: first, that his *own* knowledge was
to some degree complicit in his constriction ("from" = "by means of");[36]
but second, that another version of knowledge—something other than *his*
own—is available in Egypt, if only to those who do not mourn a lost
Roman shape. Antony has been led to a place whose insuperable contradictions are beyond his ken, a place where one loses a self-enclosed mind
but may gain another, more circulatory, sense of being: a place that is "the
very heart of loss." At the center of theater's hollow "O" is indeed loss,
nothing. But as in Stanley Cavell's account of the play, Cleopatra's theater
can overcome the skepticism that would see that nothing as a cue for mistrust in theater, and for mistrust in the very existence of a world outside
one's fearful mind and rapidly dissolving Roman self. For those who attend the theater and are "beguil'd," that nothing has a center, a heart, that
may become anything, and everything.[37]

"The very heart of loss" is, then, Cleopatra's space, her realm not of
politics but of possibility. And we can understand this realm best not by
referring to Roman pronouncements about Cleopatra (like Enobarbus's
description of her on her barge), which are designed more often to cordon off than to explore her nature,[38] but by focusing on the playacting
queen herself, who demonstrates in her own person both theater's attrac-
tions, and the desire to attend. Periodically throughout the play, Cleopatra
arrests the stage action to indulge in an act of imaginative reverie that demonstrates, in small, what she defines theater to be: a place where the future
comes to happen. Like King Henry V, Queen Cleopatra enacts upon the
stage a voiced projection of what shall be. But unlike Henry's constricted
epic view that allows for only one possible outcome, and one that is all
too easily discounted as the play ends, Cleopatra's projections depend on
foreseeing unrestricted futures whose "truth" value arises from their sheer
audacious proliferation, from their unbridled generativity.

In the first such moment Cleopatra indulges, not in the unconscious-
ness-inducing mandragora for which she initially asks, but in thoughts of

what Antony might be doing at that instant: "Stands he, or sits he? / Or does he walk? or is he on his horse?" (1.5.19–20). Here she identifies even her thinking as erotically motivated, contrasting herself with the eunuch Mardian. " '[T]is well for thee," she tells him, "That, being unseminar'd, thy freer thoughts / May not fly forth of Egypt" (1.5.10–12). The contrast at first seems unfair, as Mardian immediately points out: Cleopatra contends that, as someone "unseminar'd" (castrated), Mardian can have no desiring thoughts at all. But looking more closely at her phrasing clarifies the distinction Cleopatra is making. If a "seminary" in Renaissance usage is also a seed-plot (OED 1a), and if in Cleopatra's dangling modifier the word "unseminar'd" seems to modify "thoughts" as much as it does "thee" (i.e., Mardian), then she is contrasting not her libidinous self with an unmovable eunuch, but her fertile, growing thoughts with his sterile, unimaginative ones. Mardian may "think / What Venus did with Mars" (1.5.17–18), but this rather conventional sexual fantasy cannot compete with Cleopatra's, not only because hers is more elaborate, but because hers ripens from wish into certainty. From wondering what *might be*—"Stands he, or sits he?"—Cleopatra shifts effortlessly to declaring her last guess to be what *is*, even though this "truth" has no more basis in evidentiary reality than did her suppositions:

> Or does he walk? or is he on his horse?
> O happy horse to bear the weight of Antony!
> Do bravely, horse, for wot'st thou whom thou mov'st,
> The demi-Atlas of this earth, the arm
> And burgonet of men. He's speaking now,
> Or murmuring, "Where's my serpent of old Nile?"
> For so he calls me. Now I feed myself
> With most delicious poison. Think on me,
> That am with Phoebus' amorous pinches black,
> And wrinkled deep in time.
>
> (1.5.20–29)

Even while they "fly forth of Egypt" to project a far-off Antony ("Egypt" implicitly being here, as often in the play, synecdochic for Egypt's queen), Cleopatra's thoughts remain internally satisfying, even autoerotic, as she becomes not only the spectacular creator of theatrical illusion, but also the willingly seduced audience of the demi-Atlas Antony she has created. As both actor and audience she reflexively declares, "Now I feed myself / With most delicious poison," a statement that both confirms and confounds the Roman notion of theater's arrestive qualities. Her captivatingly "poison-ous" manipulation of imaginary scenarios is not only delicious but also sustaining, leading her not simply to surrender herself, but to extend herself both into the mind of this made-up Antony, and into time itself, into a seemingly bottomless history: "Think on me, / That am with Phoebus' amorous pinches black, / And wrinkled deep in time."[39]

Thus Cleopatra fulfills, more than either man suspects, the promise of one of Antony's and Enobarbus's conversations about her. Enobarbus first links Cleopatra's erotic susceptibility with her acting ability in this sarcastic comment: "Cleopatra catching but the least noise of this [i.e., Antony's departure from Egypt], dies instantly. I have seen her die twenty times upon far poorer moment: I do think there is mettle in death, which commits some loving act upon her, she hath such a celerity in dying" (1.2.137–42). To which Antony replies, "She is cunning past man's thought" (1.2.143). If, as Enobarbus implies, Egyptian theatrics constitute a kind of feminine orgasm—an endless series of climactic deaths—they also take her "past man's thought," past any contained, singular projection of future events. Thus when Charmian asks the Roman soothsayer, "Good sir, give me good fortune," and he replies, "I make not, but foresee," she refuses to recognize his distinction between imagined fancy and probable truth, insisting, "Pray then, foresee me one" (1.2.13–15). The soothsayer's later remark recognizes that in Egypt, mental projections are in some way interchangeable with boundless female fertility.

> *Charmian.*   . . . prithee, how many boys and wenches shall I have?
> *Soothsayer.*   If every of your wishes had a womb,
>   And fertile every wish, a million.
>
>   (1.2.35–38)

Rome abounds with rumors of spontaneous generation in Egypt; Lepidus at Antony's "Egyptian" banquet contends that "Your serpent of Egypt is bred now of your mud by the operation of your sun" (2.7.26). But however much the Renaissance might still have found the theory of spontaneous generation scientifically plausible, Shakespeare consigns it to the realm of the ridiculous, to Lepidus's drunkenness—except as a powerful *meta-phorical* description of how events, ideas, desires propagate in Cleopatra's land.[40] Antony parts from Cleopatra swearing allegiance to this principle: "By the fire / That quickens Nilus' slime, I go from hence / Thy soldier,

servant, making peace or war, / As thou affects" (1.3.68–71). The pun on
"affects" (desires, but also influences) makes Cleopatra's wishes themselves
the wondrously generative slime of Nile that moves Antony hence.

If Cleopatra can enact by herself the whole scope of playing, all at
once playwright, actor, and auditor of her reveries, then *Antony and Cleopatra*'s equation of the Egyptian/Cleopatran mind with an endlessly fertile
womb extends that figure to the theater itself. We have seen how *Henry V*
approaches the same proposition, but can do so comfortably only by imagining the womb in the Aristotelian mode, as an inert container passively
producing only what male intent has placed there. Once the alternative
possibility enters *Henry V*'s scheme—the possibility on which Hamlet
dwells incessantly, that wombs may alter or even determine the nature of
their contents—horror results: theater might betray audience expectations,
giving birth to monstrous deformities ("flat unraised spirits" or "crooked
figure[s]") who are not at all the king and soldiers we expected to witness
and applaud. *Antony and Cleopatra*, in a characteristically contrary move,
takes this "horrific" alternative and reverses the valence of its pleasure. Betrayal, in Cleopatran terms, is precisely what affords theatrical delight.[41]
Betrayal, that is, in both senses of the word: leading astray, but also divulging what has not yet been known. Renaissance theater converts diversion
into revelation; even as it defeats rational expectation at every turn, it compounds wonders far beyond the simple summation of actors and materiel,
form and content. Perhaps nowhere more than in *Antony and Cleopatra*, a
play in which almost no "events" occur on stage and in which messengers
and couriers bear the course of political action,[42] does Shakespeare insist
that theater's enterprise is not to parade a familiar story but to give surprising birth, out of the thin air of visionary (and revisionary) language. This
challenge is taken up again and again by Cleopatra, in whose language betrayal, fecundity, and startling invention interwrap themselves inextricably
both as modes of speaking and as metaphors in which to speak.

In another moment of self-induced reverie, to take one of many examples, Cleopatra transmutes "feminine" moodiness from a simple spell
of changeability into a complex act of re-creation. She first asks for music,
then wants to play billiards, then says she'll go fishing:

> Give me mine angle, we'll to the river there,
> My music playing far off. I will betray
> Tawny-finn'd fishes, my bended hook shall pierce
> Their slimy jaws; and as I draw them up,

I'll think them every one an Antony,
And say "Ah, ha! y'are caught."

(2.5.10–15)

Cleopatra momentarily offers up a Roman picture of herself, "betraying" an unwitting Antony with a deceitful hook, but she does so only to modify this image of seduction into one of imaginative power. The line "I'll think them every one an Antony" grants "to think" a transitive, performative status, as if *betrayal* were the necessary prologue to *creation*: thinking each hooked fish an Antony, she makes each thought of each fish into the man she desires. Once Cleopatra imagines an initial deceit, she can move past this conjecture to a kind of imaginative experience, marked by its acceptance of unexpected consequences. Egyptian fish, tawny and slimy, become a Roman Antony; many fishes become a single lover, who nevertheless appears to multiply as each fish, one after another, is caught. This embrace of unforeseen outcomes tightens in Cleopatra's next speech, in which she responds in this fashion to Charmian's memory of another fishing trick played on Antony:

That time? O times!
I laugh'd him out of patience; and that night
I laugh'd him into patience, and next morn,
Ere the ninth hour, I drunk him to his bed;
Then put my tires and mantles on him, whilst
I wore his sword Philippan.

(2.5.18–23)

The extremely striking image of the woman initiating transvestism, which has drawn a great deal of critical commentary, may cause us to overlook the odd phrasing with which Cleopatra begins this recollection: "That time? O times!" Even though she remembers one particular instance, that instance is simultaneously singular and multiple—"That *time*? O *times*!"—as if every mental act is always both focused and plenitudinous, both directed and digressive. Theatrical imagination, for Cleopatra, involves calling up a moment as a tangible entity, but its tangibility does not preclude calling up another, alternative vision, equally seductive and equally satisfying. Every fish may be an Antony.

Egyptian wishes themselves engage in a peculiar mode of betrayal, since they have a way of coming true, even while defeating the wisher's expectations. Charmian tells the soothsayer that she loves long life even better than figs (1.2.32), so she gets exactly as much of one as the other, and Cleopatra does indeed draw Antony up, not as a fish upon her hook, but as a dying man to her monument. (And comments as she does so, "Wishers were ever fools" [4.15.37].) Because Egypt acknowledges betrayal as a guiding creative principle, however, a past statement's eruption into present action does not, in this play, carry with it a sense of doomed foreclosure— not as in *Macbeth*, where the witches' prophecies seem to hem Macbeth in upon a dreadful path to a single end. In Adelman's incisive phrase, other Shakespearean tragedies reinforce tragedy as an "end-stopped genre."[43] But *Antony and Cleopatra* evades this Sophoclean aspect of tragedy to the extent that Cleopatra employs imaginative betrayal to reforge the past. In Cleopatra's telling, a memory emerges into the present, staged moment only to be diverted and transformed, like everything else in her utterance, into something else. The phrase by which she summons up her children, "the memory of my womb" (3.13.163), resonates as Cleopatran methodology: if memories on stage are conceived and birthed into being, then they serve not to recall the past as it was, but to make the past new.

Cleopatra employs this technique, in which any remembrance may lead to a new and better vision, upon Antony himself. As she remembers Antony, she remakes him into a "demi-Atlas" (1.5.23); as she remembers *for* Antony the fullness of their passion, she remakes their present parting into the twilight of the gods ("Eternity was in our lips, and eyes, / Bliss in our brows' bent; none our parts so poor, / But was a race of heaven" [1.3.35–37]). But when Caesar's increasing political power encroaches upon Egypt, memory becomes even more the stuff of Cleopatra's stagings, since memory is, at that point, what remains to her. Her final scene becomes the consummation of performative thought, as if she has taken to heart Enobarbus's suggestion:

Cleopatra.   What shall we do, Enobarbus?
Enobarbus.   Think, and die.

                                                                          (3.13.1)

But if she thinks herself into death, she also thinks herself going to meet an Antony she both remembers and recreates. Like the legendary Isis in Shakespeare's other Plutarchan source, Cleopatra "re-members" her dead lover, piecing together the fragments of his departed being to fashion a creature more god-like than ever before.[44] Antony becomes a colossal

"Emperor Antony" who "bestrid the ocean," strewing "realms and islands" upon the world "As plates dropp'd from his pocket" (5.2.76, 82, 91–92). But Cleopatra is also careful to insist that this Antony is not pure projection on her part, not just a dream recalled:

> *Cleopatra.*   Think you there was, or might be such a man
>   As this I dreamt of?
> *Dolabella.*   Gentle madam, no.
> *Cleopatra.*   You lie up to the hearing of the gods.
>   But if there be, or ever were one such,
>   It's past the size of dreaming: nature wants stuff
>   To vie strange forms with fancy, yet to imagine
>   An Antony were nature's piece, 'gainst fancy,
>   Condemning shadows quite.
>
> > (5.2.93–100)

Like Charmian with the soothsayer, Cleopatra will not admit an opposition between imaginative desire and truth, between theatrical retelling and reality. From her memory she has "dreamt" an Antony who is yet "past the size of dreaming"; imagined an Antony who is "nature's piece," yet " 'gainst fancy"; conjured a fictitious "piece" that yet condemns the "shadows" to which Macbeth consigns the walking player. The very extravagance of theater's capacity for remembrance, Cleopatra contends, vaults it past the limitations delineated by *Henry V*'s timorous Chorus. A play can deck dead kings as nature did, precisely (and contrarily) *because* a play outdoes nature's work.

   In her suicide, then, Cleopatra fuses memory with all that she has staked out as feminine theatrical territory: with queenly self-display, with reciprocated erotic desire, with visionary projection, and with fertility of mind. Wearing for the spectacle her majestic robe and crown ("Show me, my women, like a queen" [5.2.226]), she imagines death as an erotic meeting with the Antony she remembers: "I see him rouse himself / To praise my noble act. . . . / The stroke of death is as a lover's pinch, / Which hurts, and is desir'd" (5.2.283–84, 294–95). Once again, however, she controverts the Roman notion of seduction leading to stupefaction. She takes Caesar's magnanimous suggestion to her—"Make not your thoughts your prisons . . . feed, and sleep" (5.2.184–86)—and transforms it into a dramatic act of feeding and sleeping, of self-reflexive sustenance and mesmerization that, though achieved through poison, is far from the "poisoned hours" by which Romans mark Egyptian time. Once she asks the Clown, "Will it [i.e., the asp] eat me?" (5.2.270), Cleopatra sets up the final invocation of feeding and sleeping in the play: "Dost thou not see my baby at my breast, / That sucks the nurse asleep?" (5.2.309–10). Cleopatra's explicit expansion of feeding and sleeping from the realm of seduction (and Acrasia-like sucking) to the realm of maternity reinforces the idea that Cleopatra has not only *fed* her audience, but *birthed* it, as well. In other words, the spectacle gives the audience its being; they will not exist—or at least, not in this transcendent state—outside the magic circle the drama traces. Asp, Antony, audience; all are given life by her, all rouse themselves to praise her noble act. All are drawn, in her final gesture and last words of sexual desire, to the very heart of loss: "O Antony! Nay, I will take *thee* too" (5.2.311, my emphasis).

Even Caesar is momentarily brought within the circle that betrayal draws. One of the guards who comes upon the dead and dying women calls out, "Caesar's beguil'd" (5.2.322), as if for this instant Caesar's intentions are subverted and remade into Cleopatra's. His language momentarily becomes infused with the very contradictions she habitually wedded, as he remarks of her that "She hath pursued conclusions infinite / Of easy ways to die" (5.2.353–54). "Conclusions infinite" seems exactly the Cleopatran project: creating countless imaginative possibilities, each of which may be entirely fulfilled—just like thinking each fish an Antony. And "conclusions infinite" also stubbornly reverses the emphasis of Antony's suicidal wish for a finished Roman end, one reminiscent of the "sealed compact" of male inheritance and male rule in *Hamlet*: "seal then, and all is done" (4.14.49). Cleopatra's stress would be not on *done*, but on *all*.[45] With its transmutation of memory into vision, of concluded past into conclusions infinite, Cleopatra's suicide staves off, at least for this staged moment, the inevitabilities built into her story's putative generic categories. In fact, Cleopatra's death is marked as much by its generic flexibility as by its self-conscious theatricality. Cleopatra has crafted for herself a "tragedy" marked not by a fall, but by a transcendent, self-willed reunion. With her "delicious poison" Cleopatra seizes that single hopeful word from Juliet's desperate gesture— "Haply some poison yet doth hang on [thy lips] / To make me die with a *restorative*" (5.3.165–66)—and converts tragic parting into confident restoration, anticipating as she does so the improbable restorations of the romances. And in so doing, Cleopatra redeems the paralysis conferred upon Hamlet by his father's ghostly command of "Remember me."

Even more boldly, however, theatrical resolution in Cleopatran terms also revises the generic conventions of the history play, by contravening the very notion of *ending* that historical sources confer to drama. A history play, in staging an Edward III or a Henry V, must yoke the audience's memory of history with its foreknowledge of oblivion: every historical hero is, like Hotspur, now food for worms. But Cleopatra takes "joy o' the worm" (5.2.278); and her alchemical compounding of her own recollections with both feminine pleasure and feminine fertility offers a model for the way both the theater and its audience might remember history. For Cleopatra, death can be staged not as an episode over which one finally has no control, but as a regeneration and progeneration of past memory into present enjoyment.

Antony and Cleopatra's investment of memory in the theatrical feminine returns us, however, to the issue that began this chapter: the question of this play's historical moment. As long as Cleopatra's stagings continue, theater is profoundly central to existence, not only in the sense that humanity circles around Cleopatra's playacting, but also in the sense that Cleopatra's playacting redefines the conditions by which humanity records its being. Memory, Cleopatra demonstrates, is gestated not in official history, but in theater's womb. The queen's theater commands what culture remembers. In itself this proposition is sufficiently audacious, but it becomes even more so when we again consider the play's post-Elizabethan genesis. The history given birth by Cleopatra's playing is adamantly contrary to the one England had learned by the time of *Antony and Cleopatra*'s first production. Not only does this play manifestly not conjoin theatrical operation with the interests of an *arriviste* king (a topic to which I will shortly return), its queen acquires an indelible character not in spite of, but by means of death. The case for Britain's nonfictional queens of recent demise had been markedly the opposite: both Mary, Queen of Scots and Elizabeth Tudor had attempted and failed in death to engineer the ways they would be remembered. In each case, moreover, both the attempt and its failure were bound up with the queen's manipulating feminine attributes and accouterments as a strategy for controlling her fate.

Like Cleopatra's, Mary Stuart's efforts to orchestrate her death scene took the form in part of queenly costume: she was "apparrelled in a kind of joye," as Lord Burghley's representative sent to witness her execution reported, in a black and silver satin overdress that, when removed, revealed a kirtle and petticoat all of red—the color of martyrdom.[46] In addition she wore some kind of wig or headdress, so that when the executioner lifted up her lopped-off head to cry "God save the queen," the head and its covering parted ways, leaving the executioner holding the latter while the former remained on the scaffold.[47] Thus Mary posthumously converted a traditional reinscription of state power into a mockery of state decorum: instead of associating the spectacle of decapitation with legitimate royal authority, the spectators could be diverted by the spectacle itself, which thereby acquired its own, rival authority.[48] In this case the head of state, Elizabeth, was punningly usurped by the head of her rival queen. Burghley's witness comments on the grisly but compelling object Mary's death placed in view: "her head . . . appeared as gray as if she had bin threescore & tenn yeares old, polled very short, her face being in a moment so much altered from the forme which she had when she was alive as fewe could remember by her dead face. Her lipps stirred up & down almost a quarter of an hower after her head was cutt of."[49]

Here, of course, is where Mary's dramaturgical power had to end. After this brief anarchic interval, both Mary's body and her reputation became the property of an English government that deliberately defused and discredited the feminine attributes upon which her fame might rest. The last spectacle that Mary could author in itself delivered her into the authorship of others, as the display she anticipated was only temporarily foiled: contemporary woodcuts and engravings of the execution scene show the axman confidently holding up for all to behold the head of an old and no longer seductive woman, a head in death become a grotesque and defeminized object, a prop for a theater not her own. Moreover, those who could thus display her could also choose to prevent her display. The English immediately turned to curtailing Mary's unsanctioned spectacularization as saintly martyr or *mater dolorosa*, as onlookers were carefully prevented from acquiring any relics of the execution scene. Even Mary's lapdog, which had come to lie next to her corpse, "was carried awaie & washed as all things els were that had anie blood on them, [and] the executioners were sent awaie with mony for their fees, not haveing anie thing that belonged unto her."[50] Finally her coffin, encased in an inordinate amount of lead, was not buried in Mary's first resting place in Peterborough Cathedral until nearly five months later, and even then the funeral was concealed from the public by being held in the middle of the night.[51] All too aware of the symbology available to those who hoped to revivify Mary as a queenly martyr to the Catholic cause in the tradition of the seductively sanctified Mary Magdalene, the English removed her from sight in order to stave off that alternative Marian mythology.[52] Fifteen years after Mary's execution, the public spectacle of a drama extolling her virtues was still enough to provoke official English displeasure, even when that drama was played

across the Channel: "On March 17, 1602, Sir Ralph Winwood, at that time
the English ambassador in Paris, wrote to Sir Robert Cecil in London that
'certaine base Comedians have publicklie plaied in this Towne the Tragedy
of the late Queen of Scottes,' referring, it has been shown, to [Antoine de]
Montchrestien's drama [*Escossoise ou le Desastre Tragedie*]. Winwood continues that he complained to the French chancellor about 'so lewde an
Indiscretion' and was promised that 'this Folly should be punished, and
that the like hereafter should not be committed.'"[53] Evidently Elizabeth's
government was concerned that the Queen of Scots never again, even
in theatrical representation, gain the control of the scaffold that she had
shown upon her death.

Elizabeth, for her part, did not stage her end, but her death therefore more strikingly demonstrates the posthumous revision of a feminine
strategy of remembrance. Elizabeth's refusal to assume feminine destiny,
to marry and bear an heir, had insured for years that her subjects' minds
and memories dwelled upon her, not upon the rising sun of some successor. In addition, she had carefully cultivated an image of herself as eternally youthful and desirable as well as eternally virgin, a more symbolic
way of denying the end and replacement of female rule.[54] But like Mary's
scaffold theatrics, Elizabeth's succession strategy contained the seeds of its
own undoing: by not declaring her successor, she gave over the making
of her inheritance to her ambitious young male advisors. In her last years
her most trusted courtiers (Essex, Cecil, Ralegh, and Harington, among
others) secretly sought the favor of James of Scotland, all the while attempting to discredit each other's loyalty to the future king.[55] Harington,
the queen's godson, in 1603 sent a New Year's gift to James with the not-so-
subtle biblical inscription, "Lord remember me when thou comest in thy
Kingdom."[56] Robert Cecil proved the ablest at both winning James's confidence and advising him on the best way to secure his uncontested succession. Hence it was probably Cecil who promulgated the report that Elizabeth on her deathbed had indicated James as her successor with the words,
"Who should succeed me but a king . . . who, quoth she, but our cousin
of Scotland?"[57] Elizabeth's nearly forty-five-year creation of a queenly self
who would give way to no man was instantly replaced, upon her death, by
Cecil's story of her: a queen who preferred to give way to a rightful king.[58]

Once on the throne, James habitually referred to his royal predecessor as "the late Queen of famous memory"—a nicely ambiguous phrase,
in which "memory" might be a remembrance of the famous late queen,

but might equally be the famous capacity for remembrance of the one who recalls her, the supplanting king.[59] Act 5 of *Antony and Cleopatra* begins with Caesar attempting to absorb the memory of the dead Antony into a self-memory that he alone has constructed, a memory of the purified, triumphant Caesar: "O Antony, / I have follow'd thee to this, but we do launch / Diseases in our bodies" (5.1.35–37). Like James's phrase "famous memory," Caesar's royal "we" serves at first to point toward the existence and quality of his problematic royal opposite, but then to absorb that contender into his own project of self-mythologizing. And Caesar clearly intends to do the same with Cleopatra. Imagining himself as the Virgilian Augustus-to-be ("The time of universal peace is near" [4.6.5]), Caesar assimilates Cleopatran limitlessness into an imagined future that is very un-Cleopatran and hence very untheatrical in its static singularity. He converts her dramatic statement of everlasting passion ("Eternity was in our lips and eyes") into his projected everlasting conquest: "her life in Rome / Would be eternal in our triumph" (5.1.65–66). Caesar intends that Cleopatra's complex construction of *memory* give way upon her death to his simple and very literally constructed *memorial*:

> She shall be buried by her Antony.
> No grave upon the earth shall clip in it
> A pair so famous: high events as these
> Strike those that make them: and their story is
> No less in pity than his glory which
> Brought them to be lamented.
>
> (5.2.356–61)

For Cleopatra's embrace of the asp, Caesar substitutes the embrace of the grave that he designs to "clip" her—to hold her, but also to cut her off. His truncation of her memory will, he hopes, deliver into *his* provenance the "high events" that Antony and Cleopatra fashioned. Even as Caesar utters this speech, he is fashioning a memorial to himself, inscribing in the third person a historical record of "his glory [i.e., Caesar's glory] which / Brought them to be lamented." Evidently Caesar has regained the composure he lost when he came upon the dead Cleopatra and was "beguil'd." The Dauphin of *1 Henry VI* imagined crafty Joan La Pucelle already dead and cremated, her ashes encased in an urn surpassing the coffer in which Alexander carried Homer's epics. Similarly, Caesar hopes to disengage

Cleopatra's theatrical power by subsuming her memory within his epic vehicle: she and Antony are to be remembered only as ashen prelude to Caesar's Augustan glory.

Within the context of this play, however, we are compelled not to take Caesar's literary ambitions too seriously. Not only does theater as *Antony and Cleopatra* constructs it unabashedly derive its being and its efficacy from feminine authority, but in the process this play also renders untenable any other experiment at theatrical gender affiliation. In fact, *Antony and Cleopatra* rehearses the very desire for kingship's return, and the concomitant theatrical desire for a male epic stage, that permeated *Henry V*, only to discount such projects from the beginning as theatrically useless. First of all, the play assigns to the future Caesar Augustus, whom Renaissance England recognized and emulated as the quintessential inheritor of epic authority, attitudes suspiciously reminiscent of antitheatricalist polemics. Let us return to Caesar's nostalgic reminiscence of Antony's pre-Cleopatran warriorhood:

> Thou didst drink
> The stale of horses, and the gilded puddle
> Which beasts would cough at: thy palate then did deign
> The roughest berry, on the rudest hedge;
> Yea, like the stag, when snow the pasture sheets,
> The barks of trees thou browsed. On the Alps
> It is reported thou didst eat strange flesh
> Which some did die to look on: and all this—
> It wounds thine honour that I speak it now—
> Was borne so like a soldier, that thy cheek
> So much as lank'd not.

$$(1.4.61-71)$$

In his antitheatricalist tract *The Schoole of Abuse*, Stephen Gosson remembers the English before they were introduced to theater as warriors on a par with the not-yet-effeminized Antony. As Levine remarks, the phrasing of Shakespeare's Caesar is astonishingly similar to that of Gosson: "english men could suffer watching and labor, hunger & thirst, & beare of al stormes with hed and shoulders, they used slender weapons, went naked, and were good soldiours, they fed uppon rootes and barkes of trees, they woulde stand up to the chin many dayes in marishes without victualles: and they had a kind of sustinaunce in time of neede, of which if they had taken but the quantitie of a beane, or the weight of a pease, they did neyther gape after meate, nor long for the cuppe, a great while after."[60] Before the rise of theater, as before the sway of Cleopatra, men were truly men, not given to sensual indulgence.

But we have seen that construing Cleopatra's theater as mere sensual indulgence requires ignoring the scope and weight given to her dramatic being. To remember Cleopatra at play's end is to be nostalgic not for life *before* theater, but for life *as* theater, which, as Cleopatra has fashioned it, is the only life to remember. Theater such as Rome is able to imagine it, in contrast, would have little life in it at all. Caesar, as Levine points out, does occasionally envision monarchs on display, but I read his idea of royal theater, including the Roman "triumph," as tableau or procession, not as a creative, verbalized enactment. The purpose of such a show is solely to consolidate Caesar's power as it already exists. Thus he complains, when Octavia returns to Rome without benefit of a public parade, "the ostentation of our love . . . , left unshown, / Is often left unlov'd" (3.6.52–53). No more like Cleopatran theater is the popular drama that, Cleopatra imagines, will be staged in Rome as part of Caesar's victory celebration.

> The quick comedians
> Extemporally will stage us, and present
> Our Alexandrian revels: Antony
> Shall be brought drunken forth, and I shall see
> Some squeaking Cleopatra boy my greatness
> I' the posture of a whore.
>
> (5.2.215–20)

Critics have long pointed to this passage as the most self-conscious in Shakespeare's drama, since the actor playing Cleopatra is, like the Roman actor she disparages, a boy.[61] But Cleopatra's protest draws attention to the reality of stage practice only to contrast it to her own: her fear is not strictly that she will be played by a boy actor, but that the Roman representation of her will be debased, reducing Egyptian "feeding" to Antony's being made drunk, and reducing her seductiveness to a caricature of whoredom. Roman theater would shame her because, like Caesar's idea of "eternity," it is coarsely inadequate to her story.

Antony and Cleopatra therefore closes not with the sympathy that Tennenhouse assumes between stage and state, but with an insuperable separation between the two. Centralizing the theatrical feminine puts theater in a place hopelessly defiant of masculine-identified state power, both in the closing milieu of the play and in the prevailing milieu of James's England. As several critics have recently discussed, James himself was both suspicious of theatrical representation and anxious to assimilate its power to his: although he disliked the self-staging in which Elizabeth had evidently revelled, he encouraged drawing public theater companies under court control by making them the personal servants of various members of the royal family. Royal control over actual dramatic content may or may not have tightened as a result, but the fact remains that Jacobean theater operated under a heightened awareness of kingly interest and potential interference.[62] As Steven Mullaney discusses, the crown even began to press for incorporation of the Liberties—the physical suburban space in which theater, along with other semi-licit, marginal institutions, had grown up and flourished—into London's city limits.[63] With the partial exception of *Antony and Cleopatra*, Shakespeare's Jacobean plays reflect the increasing desire of royal authority to keep a tight rein upon dramatic representation. The dominant figures of monarchy in these plays do not celebrate infinite theatrical variety, as Cleopatra does; nor are they like Theseus and Hippolyta, content to give free play to (if to comment upon) others' bumblingly inventive theatrics. Instead, Duke Vincentio disguises himself in order to make all Vienna's liberties subject to his justice; instead, Prospero employs magical stagings to bend an entire island to his single will.[64] *Macbeth*'s procession of future kings may even have ended, in the play's court performance, by presenting King James with the singularity of present monarchy, with his own focused mirror image. Antony and Cleopatra's story, in comparison, is indeed a tragedy: not because they are dead (for as we have seen, Cleopatra confounds all notions of ending), but because in their Jacobean incarnation they are so anachronistic. They are, as Antony describes himself, "lated in this world" (3.11.3).

Here, however, I must turn toward the seamier side of this nostalgia. Even once we recognize that *Antony and Cleopatra* dramatizes—indeed, poses as existence itself—a mode of feminine authority that the Jacobean age has delegitimated, we would be mistaken simply to cast James or his administration as the villain and Shakespeare's drama, via Cleopatra, as the tragic hero/ine in this passing. Like the rest of his culture, Shakespeare could celebrate queenship with the full weight of nostalgia only when queenship was no longer a destabilizing, threatening reality. *Antony and Cleopatra*, temporally close enough to a living queen to remember her problematics, is also far enough to celebrate her with unmitigated delight.

Nostalgia is, in point of fact, a disease of seventeenth-century inception. David Lowenthal describes the affliction for which the word was coined: "Seventeenth-century nostalgia was a physical rather than a mental complaint, an illness with explicit symptoms and often lethal consequences. First medically diagnosed and coined (from the Greek *nosos* [sic] = return to native land, and *algos* = suffering or grief) in 1688 by Johannes Hofer, nostalgia was already common; once away from their native land, some people languished, wasted away, and even perished."[65] Lowenthal goes on to make clear that it was not just their physical displacement, but rather specific recollections of their past that caused Hofer's patients to suffer. Swiss mercenaries, for example, were apt to fall into fits of illness whenever they heard alpine tunes. Dying of and through memory, then, makes Cleopatra a peculiarly seventeenth-century heroine. And my sense is that a Protestant country such as England would feel nostalgia in an especially personal way, since in cancelling Purgatory and the possibility of improving the lot of the souls of departed family and friends, the Reformed religion had placed an insuperable barrier between the living and the dead.[66] But ethnographer Renato Rosaldo puts a darker cast on a seventeenth-century audience who, watching Cleopatra, might feel nostalgic for the theatrical queen they remember through her performance. Rosaldo describes a phenomenon peculiar to conquering cultures he calls "imperialist nostalgia," that is, the longing of colonialism's agents for the very culture they have destroyed: "Imperialist nostalgia revolves around a paradox: A person kills somebody, and then mourns the victim. In more attenuated form, someone deliberately alters a form of life, and then regrets that things have not remained as they were prior to the intervention. . . . In any of its versions, imperialist nostalgia uses a pose of 'innocent yearning' both to capture people's imaginations and to conceal its complicity with often brutal domination. . . . 'We' (who believe in progress) valorize innovation and then yearn for more stable worlds, whether these reside in our own past, in other cultures, or in the conflation of the two."[67]

No doubt Johannes Hofer's patients did not experience their nostalgia as Rosaldo describes, but Shakespeare's theater, unlike those early sufferers, was already alive to this more modern aspect of nostalgia as memory combined with regret. Shakespeare's Jacobean audience had not killed their late queen of famous memory, but they had eagerly anticipated the new age of kingship brought on by her passing: over the years of her reign they had agitated for her marriage, for her bearing children, and for her appointing an heir, all tactics designed to bring the institution of queenship to an end. As Nietzsche was later to remark (with characteristic apocalyptic cynicism) of modern nostalgia for God, "We have left the land and have embarked. We have burned our bridges behind us—indeed, we have gone farther and destroyed the land behind us. . . . Woe, when you feel homesick for the land as if it had offered more *freedom*—and there is no longer any 'land.'"[68] No matter that *Antony and Cleopatra* lodges theatrical (and audience) remembrance with the queen; it remains a play whose staging depends on queenship's demise. This is Shakespeare's elegy for female rule, quite the opposite of the conventional poetic trope that Henry Chettle conceived: not that a play might give the queen eternal life, but that she, in giving up her life, gives life to playing.

"The Statue Is But Newly Fix'd": Hermione

Antony and Cleopatra's retroactive imposition of safe distance between the present moment and the remembered queen designs the entire plot of *The Winter's Tale*. As Valerie Traub has argued, it is Hermione's nature as a sexual woman, manifested in her pregnancy, that sparks Leontes's fit of jealousy.[69] To the horrifying prospect of that sexuality we must also add, however, her ability as a queen to command others' desires. "A lady's Verily's / As potent as a lord's," says Hermione in convincing Polixenes to remain in Sicily—an assertion that brings up the shadow of Gertrude's jointure, in that a queen's word seems as powerful as a king's in this realm (1.2.50–51).[70] Or even more powerful, since only upon her urging, as Leontes points out, does Polixenes delay his departure: "At my request he would not" (1.2.87). In uniting insubordinate queenship with erotic desire, Hermione at the play's beginning reminds us of precisely those characteristics of female monarchy that the Elizabethans had found most potentially troublesome: she speaks a language of desire and bodily presence, a language of eagerness and excess that Leontes can interpret only as *sexually* eager and excessive. "[C]ram's with praise, and make's / As fat as tame things," Hermione suggests to her husband, "You may ride's / With one soft kiss a thousand furlongs ere / With spur we heat an acre" (1.2.91–92, 94–96). We can hardly help remembering Cleopatra's likening herself to Antony's happy horse. Moreover, Leontes's immediate leap from Hermione's seemingly uncontrolled sexuality to the physical fact of her pregnancy means that royal patrilineage is bound up in a feminine erotic nature. As king and as man, Leontes finds this prospect unbearable. As

Adelman argues, Leontes accuses his wife of infidelity, even though such charges convert him into a cuckold, because her unfaithfulness would dissociate him from her sexuality: "he can imagine her pregnant body as the sign of her infidelity, rather than the sign of his sexual concourse with her; and the baby she carries thus becomes no part of him."[71] As for Mamillius's likeness to his mother, Leontes seeks to expunge this conection by repeatedly, and anxiously, declaring his own resemblance to the boy (1.2.130, 135, 159). Adelman considers these lines as evidence of Leontes's fantasy of having produced Mamillius himself, paternal parthenogenesis and maternal infidelity being inverted strategies for purging the true royal line of the stain of feminine sexuality.[72]

As befits a Jacobean play, *The Winter's Tale* places the queen's death early, an event that at the play's beginning is almost already a foregone conclusion. Leontes's remorse is immediate and profound, serving as explicit occasion for a full-fledged meditation upon nostalgia for an irreplaceable queen. Clearly though, as with Queen Elizabeth, it is not her sexuality that is missed. Rather, Leontes confronts with the loss of his wife the end of his royal line, and it is the damage he has done in this regard that comprises most of his memories of her:

> Whilst I remember
> Her, and her virtues, I cannot forget
> My blemishes in them, and so still think of
> The wrong I did myself: which was so much,
> That heirless it hath made my kingdom, and
> Destroy'd the sweet'st companion that e'er man
> Bred his hopes out of.
>
> (5.1.6–12)

A dead queen seems to leave the kingdom heirless, since in Sicily no young Fortinbras or Octavius Caesar is in the wings, eager to seize the occasion of the queen's passing as a deliverance of monarchy into male inheritance.

Rather, *The Winter's Tale* requires that queenship be reworked into a principle of genealogical continuity. If life and rule are to go on, the feminine must be reincorporated in at least some sense, both within the society of the play and within the horizons of theatrical possibility. On one level, as Lindsay Kaplan and I have argued elsewhere, such a reincorporation is a truly radical statement of early modern women's right to defend themselves against sexual slanders like the one Leontes promulgates. At the same time, however, such a defense is successful only when it is accompanied by the queen's desexualization.[73] Produced by and starring aristocratic women, Paulina's and Hermione's theater of statuary is an undeniably feminine one, and it proves to be stunning both as a theatrical moment and as a metatheatrical commentary on drama's capacity for bringing the dead to life. Nevertheless, this is a theater that demands the exclusion of feminine erotic desire from an otherwise Cleopatran conjunction of memory, physicality, and imagination.[74] Leontes's earlier remark about Hermione as sexually forthcoming—"Too hot, too hot!" (1.2.108)—transforms, therefore, into his remark about her flesh not being marble any longer: "O, she's warm!" (5.3.109). Whereas previously Hermione eagerly addressed Polixenes in a courtier's expert language of combined *politesse* and wooing, now Paulina urges Leontes to take Hermione's hand, rather than vice versa, so as to avoid the unseemly spectacle of a mature aristocratic woman displaying desire: "Nay, present your hand: / When she was young you woo'd her; now, in age, / Is she become the suitor?" (5.3.107–9).

Such circumstances compromise the truly extraordinary longing Leontes expresses for his queen to inhabit a body again. Undeniably, Leontes's remarks are pleasantly shocking in that one can hardly imagine them in the mouth of any other Shakespearean man, except perhaps for Romeo: "What you can make her do, / I am content to look on: what to speak, / I am content to hear" (5.3.91–93). And there is the strongest possible echo of Cleopatra in Leontes's approving acceptance of feminine enchantment as food: "If this be magic, let it be an art / Lawful as eating" (5.3.110–11). But how Leontes is fed by Hermione is not, at this point in the play, made clear—quite different from his earlier graphic metaphor for Hermione's sexual waywardness, a spider steeped in a man's drinking cup: "if one present / Th' abhorr'd ingredient to his eye, make known / How he hath drunk, he cracks his gorge, his sides, / With violent hefts. I have drunk, and seen the spider" (2.1.42–45). A similar but redeemed extended metaphor of ingesting his wife's sexual desire is not available in the play's final scene. Evidently, the food now presented to him has no effect upon him, as nothing alters in his personality as his wife rejoins him; instead, there is something passingly chilling in Leontes's final speech, which returns the play to its initial situation of Leontes's ordering his wife to make contact with Polixenes. But whereas Leontes earlier made the mistake of commanding his wife's speech—"Tongue-tied our queen? speak you" (1.2.27)—now he confines his wife to a probably less erotic mode of exchange: "What! look upon my brother: both your pardons, / That e'er

I put between your holy looks / My ill suspicion" (5.3.147–49). Even the desexualized performance of feminine theater that Paulina and Hermione have just mounted is now disallowed, in that even feminine speech (such as Paulina and Hermione have both so ably wielded) is discontinued. For Leontes, Hermione is now still essentially a statue, just one that happily is warm and moves.

The de-eroticizing of Hermione's body enforces an ideal seldom realized in Elizabethan portrayals of queenship: the monarch's female body natural really is transumed by the body politic and its needs. In this case, what the body politic requires is the queen's genealogical presence, but with her body purified to the point of its near absence. By the time of her resurrection Hermione thus no longer represents a threat, either sexual or successional, to masculine rule. In contrast to her public presence and courtly efficacy at the play's beginning, she has now become a purely private creature; her only words upon her revival are to her daughter, Perdita. And that daughter's own potential sexual unruliness has already been reined in, engaged in the marriage that will join Leontes's and Polixenes's kingdoms, as brother to brother, under Florizel's single kingship.[75] We might recall that Shakespeare's source for *The Winter's Tale*, Robert Greene's *Pandosto*, ambiguously ends its story by hinting at the death of Perdita's prototype.[76] Shakespeare is not so eager as that to excise femininity from *The Winter's Tale*'s conclusion; after all, it is Shakespeare's innovation upon *Pandosto* to have the queen return to life, and there is no hint in Shakespeare's retelling of Perdita's imminent demise. But *The Winter's Tale*, having marked a distinction between queenship's past and its future, the erotic and the modest queen, also clearly marks a distinction between mother's and daughter's experience of the time to come. For Hermione herself, there is no future now but remembrance—not, as with Cleopatra, her own memories, but memories *of* her and of her end. Leontes closes the play promising to recall what each person in the company has "Perform'd in this wide gap of time, since first / We were dissever'd" (5.3.153–54). What has Hermione done in that time, except die and be memorialized? Does nothing else remain to her?[77]

David Bergeron, following W. W. Greg, has proposed that *The Winter's Tale* as we know it represents a revised version of the original 1611 play, presented for the wedding of King James's daughter Elizabeth in early 1613. In its showcasing of a lifelike statue, Bergeron argues, the final scene of the play refers its Jacobean audience to recent developments in funerary art: the novel realism of monumental statues such as those on the Abbey tombs of Elizabeth Tudor and Mary, Queen of Scots; and the striking effigies borne at the 1603 funeral of Elizabeth Tudor and the 1612 funeral of young Elizabeth's brother, Henry Stuart.[78] Given this multiplicity of references, the revival of Hermione's sculpted figure could be encouraging a cultural desire quite other than wishing its dead queen alive again: the Jacobean audience wishes for and is granted the prince it has lost. Not Henry Stuart himself, not the irrecoverable Mamillius; but Florizel as Princess Elizabeth Stuart's new husband Frederick the Elector Palatine, whose marriage to the king's daughter promises the nation that the male monarchical image will continue to be displayed in more than "lifelike" monumental form. We might read in the passing of genealogical influence from Hermione to Perdita, then, the strongly felt Stuart reformation of the old Elizabeth Tudor into Elizabeth Stuart as a young, docile, and soon-to-be-fruitful wife. Princess Elizabeth's wedding, according to Frances Yates, consciously conjured up the queen for whom James had named her, only to differentiate the new Elizabeth from the old: "She was a phoenix bride, in whom the old Virgin Queen became young again, reborn as a bride."[79] Further, James's choice of a Protestant husband for his single surviving daughter represented a real triumph for English radical Protestants who had feared her union with a powerful Catholic prince such as the King of Spain. In terms of James's own family, the princess's marriage posthumously fulfilled the desires of her brother Henry, who had been, as Bergeron describes him, "the great white hope of England and Protestantism."[80] This reformation of the queen was thus also a reformation of Elizabethan religious compromise into post-Elizabethan Protestant expansionism. Roy Strong describes Henry Stuart's assimilation of the dead queen's mythology into his own Protestant militarism, and the further refocus of that mythology, once Henry was gone, around Elizabeth's namesake.[81] Such militarism, the pursuit of which required Spenser's Artegall to flee his own bride, in *The Winter's Tale* is potentially enabled by the bride's willing subordination to the masculinist project.

Whether Shakespeare's theater shares that masculinist project is a question *The Winter's Tale* deliberately leaves open to debate. Unlike Henry V's epic theater or Hamlet's revenge tragedy, *The Winter's Tale* does not promote a kind of masculine theatricality to supplant the feminine. Nonetheless, on the level of plot such supplantation certainly takes place, not only in this play but in all of Shakespeare's last plays, which feature a remarkable parade of fathers redeemed, reprieved, restored to crowns and families. And as Adelman points out, that redemption and restoration is achieved at the cost of women's authority being either remade as chaste, as Marina, Thaisa, Hermione, and Imogen are, or altogether demonized, as are Antiochus's daughter, Cymbeline's wife, and the witch Sycorax.[82] Even Cranmer's prophecy at the end of the romance-history *Henry VIII* makes clear that the Virgin Queen, just a baby at this moment in the play, has her future written for her, a future that, whatever its intrinsic glories, is aimed primarily at the queen's rule giving way to a king. In this case, Elizabeth Tudor's wonted self-mythologizing is even more radically revised than it was in Elizabeth's Stuart's wedding pageantry, so that the dying phoenix gives birth not to a new Elizabeth, but to a king—a notably phallic James himself:

> but, as when
> The bird of wonder dies, the maiden phoenix,
> Her ashes new create another heir
> As great in admiration as herself,
> So shall [Elizabeth] leave her blessedness to one
> (When heaven shall call her from this cloud of darkness)
> Who from the sacred ashes of her honour
> Shall star-like rise, as great in fame as she was,
> And so stand fix'd.[83]
>
> (5.4.39–47)

It seems grimly appropriate, in the wake of Cleopatra's equation of theater with queenship, that the ashes *Henry VIII* ultimately produced were not those of Elizabeth the maiden phoenix, but those of the Globe itself, burned to the ground during a performance of the play in June 1613. However, *The Winter's Tale*'s new dramatic form of romance resists this premonition of the theatrical world gone bad. If *Antony and Cleopatra* engages in nostalgia for queenship only to reveal (after strenuous critical detective work) how the theater is invested in the queen's passing, *The Winter's Tale* as romance lays claim to that proposition from the very start, creating tragicomic form out of the two responses England was exhibiting for the death of its sexual and theatrical queen, mourning and joy.[84] In other words, although it lays bare the bad faith behind *Antony and Cleopatra*'s reliance on the death of feminine authority, *The Winter's Tale* derives not just its conclusion but its entire shape from that bad faith. By compressing the work of an entire tragedy—Leontes's jealousy, Mamillius's and Hermione's premature deaths, Perdita's abandonment—into its first three acts, *The Winter's Tale* leaves room for the new pastoral-tragical-comedy form of Acts 4 and 5. But it also leaves room for pastoral tragi-comedy's *display* of itself as a new form, a conspicuous exhibition of what we would now call the avant-garde.[85] "[T]hou met'st with things dying, I with things new born," says the Shepherd at the moment in the play that establishes that generic shift, as the sea drowns the mariners, the bear masticates Antigonus, and the Shepherd discovers Perdita and her trea-sure (3.3.112–13). What has died, of course, is also Hermione as a sexual queen. What is new born, then, is a mode of theater that reminds us of that which has died, as often as Paulina reminds Leontes of his guilt. This new tragicomic mode of theater, for all its pleasures and satisfactions, iden-tifies itself as new precisely in that it freely acknowledges that something has to perish to make it work. Like the avant-garde as Philip Fisher has discussed it, the romance form is engaged in "imagining [the present] as the future's past."[86] This role of being the "future's past" is one Hermione claims for herself when she tells Leontes, "My life stands in the level of your dreams, / Which I'll lay down" (3.2.81–82). Laying down her life for the sake of Leontes's dreams, Hermione also gives up her self so that the dream of romance's happy endings may endure.

6

Milton's Queenly Paradise

MONUMENTS OF ELIZABETH TUDOR by no means lost their importance in England after the queen's reign faded from recent memory. On November 17, 1678, the one-hundred-twentieth anniversary of Elizabeth's accession to the throne, the queen was remembered in an unusual event that took place precisely at the site of her statue. Catalyzing this spectacle was the rumored (and entirely trumped-up) "Popish Plot" to burn London, raise the Irish Roman Catholics, conquer England with French and Irish forces, massacre every unrepentant Protestant, and murder King Charles II. On October 17 of that year Sir Edmund Berry Godfrey, the magistrate with whom the informant of the alleged plot had deposed his evidence, was found strangled to death and stabbed through the heart. The date of Godfrey's murder was fortuitous: exactly one month before Elizabeth's Accession Day, it prompted London's anti-Catholic Whigs to choose that Elizabethan anniversary to mount a torchlight parade and burning of the Pope in effigy. In a curious (though no doubt unintentional) parody of a Catholic saint's-day processional, the crowd made its way to Temple Bar, where they chanted beneath the statue of their long-dead queen:

> Your Popish plot, and Smithfield threat,
> We do not fear at all;
> For lo, beneath Queen Bess's feet
> You fall, you fall, you fall.

G. M. Trevelyan, in recounting this scene, tells us that "By midnight the vast mob was so highly wrought that many supposed the proceedings had been designed to end in a revolution before the dawn."[1] As Andrew Marvell would more cheerfully put it, "A Tudor a Tudor! wee've had Stuarts enough; / None ever Reign'd like old Besse in the Ruffe."[2]

The posthumous affiliation between Elizabeth and Parliamentary revolution is a telling instance of the seventeenth-century metamorphosis of Elizabeth's monarchical reputation. During her life, Elizabeth had favored religious compromise over religious zeal, and was a reluctant foot-dragger in the cause of Protestant expansionism. As well, she would naturally have found the potentially seditious violence enacted in her name by the 1678 crowd unbearable; no doubt she would have urged her cousin Charles II, "You are the Pope; know ye not that?" I have already demonstrated, in my discussion of *The Winter's Tale*, how the late Queen Elizabeth could be coopted for the cause of hard-line Protestantism in the new Jacobean era; significantly, with the passing of years Elizabeth no longer required the mediating royal reincarnation of a marriageable Princess Elizabeth Stuart or of a patriarchal King James I in order for this metamorphosis to be effected. Once detached from its association with current members of the monarchical line, nostalgia for the late queen, even while endorsing the Protestant cause, need not also necessarily endorse the absolutist, patriarchal monarchy that James I sought to bring about. Rather, Elizabeth's memory sponsors decidedly antimonarchist principles—in the case of the anti-papist protesters of 1678, the principle of militant Protestantism against the Catholic sympathizer Charles II. This Accession Day scene led almost immediately to action that, though more orderly than the mob's gathering, equally sought to bring populist desires to bear upon the monarch's will: the people's furor fed Whig resolve in the House of Commons to reintroduce legislation excluding Charles II's Catholic brother, James, from the line of royal succession. Three bills of Exclusion, each more successful than its predecessor, were introduced between 1679 and 1681: the first bogged down in the Commons; the second was approved by the Commons but rejected by the House of Lords; and the third was stalled only by the King's dissolving Parliament in 1681. As Edward Norman describes it, the Whigs in planning the 1678 Elizabethan Accession Day spectacle and in engineering the subsequent Exclusion crisis demonstrated their "insistence on linking popery and absolutist government."[3] The irony of conducting pope-burning in Elizabeth's statuesque presence thus was magnified, for although Elizabeth had been too canny to indulge in her successors' expressions of absolutism, she had consistently opposed demands for a Presbyterian church government by insisting upon her reign's replication of divine will. For example, against the Commons committee proposing Presbyterianism in 1585 the queen had declared, via the Speaker Serjeant Puckering, "'She knows—and thinks you know—she is Supreme Governor of this Church, next under God. . . . [A]s she hath power so hath she good will to . . . examine and to redress whatsoever may be found amiss.'"[4]

Citing the precedent of Elizabeth as a guarantor of Presbyterian religion and antimonarchist government was not a phenomenon new to the Restoration, however. In fact, this strategy had been steadily and increasingly employed since the 1620s, when Charles I ascended the throne accompanied by his Catholic queen, Henrietta Maria. It was at the start of Charles I's reign that Elizabeth's Accession Day, now marked in almanacs as a "red-letter day," began to be popularly celebrated as what David Cressy calls "a safe and discreet way to criticize the current regime."[5] Because the new king had ordered church-bell ringing on November 16 and November 19, the birthdays of his wife and himself, respectively, the newly widespread, unmandated ringing of bells on Elizabeth's day of November 17 was especially politically charged.[6] As Charles I's increasingly pro-Catholic and pro-absolutist reign continued, Elizabeth's Accession Day became a much less covert occasion for expressing defiance of the king. On that date in 1640, for example, two preachers urged Parliament, which was then debating the impeachment of the Earl of Strafford and Archbishop Laud, to replicate Elizabeth in their Protestant zeal and "make this another blessed seventeenth of November."[7] By 1641 nostalgia for Elizabeth had reached the improbable point of Charles I's being pressured by Parliament to promise "to reduce all matters of religion and government to what they were in the purest times of Queen Elizabeth's days."[8] Referring their actions to the model of good Queen Bess was practically de rigueur for Oliver Cromwell's generation of religious and governmental reformers, who conveniently forgot her repression of Puritans.[9] At the beginning of the Long Parliament, for example, November 17 was chosen as a fast day, "upon which the clergy would seasonably remind members of their duty to resume the great queen's interrupted work."[10]

Conveniently forgotten, as well, was Elizabeth's reputation as not only a religiously conservative monarch, but a female monarch. In the 1620s, Henry King quite decidedly declared Elizabeth a more than honorary king, the masculine equal of epic heroes like Edward III and Henry V: "Our Elizabeth, that unpatterned mirror of her sex, that only example of masculine heroic virtue, which the latter or indeed any times produced, hath as many pennons, as many streamers hung about her hearse, as many trophies of conquest to adorn her precious memory, as any of those whose names who whilst they lived were wedded to victory, the Edwards or the Henrys."[11] Posthumously, then, Elizabeth acquired what I argued in

Chapter 1 was never really a successful royal fiction while she lived: a transhistorically masculine body politic that subsumed her incidentally female
body natural.[12] Like Henry King, would-be reformers of the Civil War
era and the Restoration could reify the queen only by disregarding the
specifically feminine elements that, during her lifetime, had contributed
to radical Protestant fear and rage: her troublingly eroticized feminine
self-presentation; her tendency to vacillate and compromise on matters of
militant Protestant expansionism; and her structural blocking of a securely
masculine (and Protestant) genealogical line of rule. Instead, long after her
death Elizabeth's feminine identity calcified into an asexual image that pre-
sided over and even enacted the demolition of elements opposed to Protestant government: "beneath Queen Bess's feet / You fall, you fall, you fall."

Not surprisingly, Milton's historical memory was better. Upon the
eve of Charles II's restoration, Milton accurately remarked in *The Readie
and Easie Way to Establish a Free Commonwealth* that "Queen *Elizabeth*
though her self accounted so good a Protestant, so moderate, so confident of her Subjects love would never give way so much as to Presbyterian
reformation in this land, though once and again besought, as *Camden* relates, but imprisond and persecuted the very proposers therof; alleaging it
as her minde & maxim unalterable, that such reformation would diminish
regal autoritie" (*CPW* 7:457).[13] Nor did Milton forget the fundamental
anxiety that the very femininity of women's rule had provoked. In fact, as
I argue in this chapter, the memory of female rule haunts two major topics of Milton's prose: his arguments in favor of divorce, and his arguments
against monarchy. Milton's polemical connections between divorce and
regicide are complex in many respects, but particularly so in that both the
divorce tracts and the antimonarchical tracts recollect queenly rule as a condition that must be corrected. Thus when we turn to *Paradise Lost*, we must
view the question of Eve's subjection not merely as a matter of Milton's
view of women in general, but more specifically as a meditation upon the
relation between femininity and sovereignty. And once again, queenship
becomes the pivot upon which issues of poetry's form and efficacy turn.
Milton intends to design an epic form quite superior to the feminized romance of his predecessor Spenser or the more trivial tragic subjects of his
predecessor Shakespeare. At the same time, however, Eve's point of view,
with all its reminiscences of the expansive, inventive feminine imagination
developed in *The Faerie Queene* and in *Antony and Cleopatra*, becomes in
important ways the epitome of human invention in the poem. Hence, despite Eve's undeniable subordination to Adam as woman to man and wife

to husband, the "paradise within" toward which Adam and Eve aim at the poem's conclusion has largely been designed by her sovereign female will.

Divorcing the Queen: The Prose Tracts and *A Mask*

Milton's divorce tracts, as nearly everyone concedes, adhere to the Pauline doctrine of wives' subjection to their husbands, even going so far as to disavow other biblical evidence (including evidence from Paul himself) of equality between the sexes.[14] What is less recognized is that Milton depicts such male sovereignty as won only with great effort. Although Milton in these tracts ostensibly assumes woman to be naturally subject to man — perhaps so much so that, as Janet E. Halley argues, whatever subjectivity a wife possesses is produced by her husband — he also describes her as preternaturally, and perhaps ab initio, liable to seize rule within marriage.[15] Although Milton's prime brief against non-companionate marriage is the lack of spiritual and social solace accruing to both unhappy parties, chief among the injuries suffered *uniquely* by the husband in such a union is "to be contended with in point of house-rule who shall be the head, not for any parity of wisdom, for that were somthing reasonable, but out of a female pride" (*CPW* 2:324). Trapped in uncongenial wedlock, the husband becomes his wife's subject and even bondsman, suffering a state of "enthrallment to one who either cannot, or will not bee mutual . . . the ignoblest and lowest slavery that a human shape can bee put to" (*CPW* 2:625–26). Divorce, then, is a process of restoring male rule over the female usurper, "that he may acquitt himself to freedom by his naturall birthright, and that indeleble character of priority which God crown'd ·him with" (*CPW* 2:589–90).[16] "Restoration," however, may not be the accurate term to attach to the husband's assumption of authority. Woman's propensity to act as a tyrant in the household, combined with the legal restrictions on divorce that Milton is seeking to overturn, complicates the notion of the wife's "natural" submission to her husband. In Milton's description of the ideal marriage, precedent for this paradisal state can be found literally only in paradise; only Adam and Eve's union can be held up as a standard for the way "that serene and blisfull condition [marriage] was in at the beginning" (*CPW* 2:240). But there's trouble in paradise, as well. In the shadows of the marriage of Adam and Eve, as James Grantham Turner points out, lurks Adam's first wife: Lilith, who (in rabbinical legend familiar to Renaissance biblical scholars) "refused to accept a subordinate position in the household and in bed, and was therefore replaced by the more compliant Eve."[17] Adam thus may join all postlapsarian husbands in struggling against bonds of female rule, bonds that, though unnatural, are also (quite paradoxically) ontologically anterior. Only divorce at will—that is, male will—could right this ubiquitous human wrong.

Even as early as the divorce tracts, it is clear that Milton aligns freedom from unwanted wives with freedom from unwanted rulers: "He who marries, intends as little to conspire his own ruine, as he that swears Allegiance: and as a whole people is in proportion to an ill Government, so is one man to an ill mariage" (*CPW* 2:229).[18] What begins as an analogy, however, turns out to be a reformative process. The first manumission, husband from tyrannous wife, must take place before the second, country from tyrannous ruler, can be contemplated. "[T]he constitution and reformation of a commonwealth . . . is, like a building, to begin orderly from the foundation therof, which is mariage and the family, to set right first what ever is amisse therein" (*CPW* 2:431).[19] When Milton turns in the late 1640s, then, from promoting legalized divorce to justifying the execution of a king, the tyrant who is to be toppled from rule exhibits the qualities of both a wife and a queen.

In some ways, Milton marks out the despised Charles I merely as a husband overcome by uxoriousness. In *Eikonoklastes* he argues that Charles's letters (captured and published by Parliament in 1645), for example, "shewd him govern'd by a Woman," and he recounts the story from the Apocryphal 1 Esdras of "*Zorobabel* Prince of the Captive Jewes . . . [who] proov'd Women to be stronger then the King [Darius], for that he himself had seen a Concubin take [Darius's] Crown from off his head to set it upon her own" (*CPW* 3:538, 583). It almost seems as if Charles himself is in need of a divorce: "Examples are not farr to seek, how great mischeif and dishonour hath befall'n to Nations under the Goverment of effeminate and Uxorious Magistrates. Who being themselves govern'd and overswaid at home under a Feminine usurpation, cannot but be farr short of spirit and autority without dores, to govern a whole Nation" (*CPW* 3:421). Milton's contempt in *Eikonoklastes* for a nation led by women also finds vent in his (perhaps contemporaneous) account in *The History of Britain* of the Roman historians' fascination with Boadicea: "this they do out of a vanity, hoping to embellish and set out thir Historie with the strangness of our manners, not careing in the mean while to brand us with the rankest note of Barbarism, as if in *Britain* Woemen were Men, and Men Woemen" (*CPW* 5:79).[20] Milton's characteristic choice of the variant spelling "woeman," as Stevie Davies notes, crystallizes his general opinion about the unfortunate consequences of women's rule.[21]

But this last remark, that under women's rule women are men, and men women, leads us to the point that for Milton, Charles—in his unreasonable exertions of erratic will, in his disregard for his country's best interests, and especially in the associations made by his supporters between the king and the feminized Christ of the Roman Catholic Passion—is not a king at all, but a queen.[22] Back of this point of view surely lies the ubiquitous Renaissance fear that a man who caters too much to women finally becomes one himself.[23] But Milton's conversion of Charles I into a female ruler has a political history, as well as a psychosexual one. Indeed, among Milton's sources for a people's right to depose unsatisfactory leaders are the premier antigynecocratic Calvinist writers of the mid-sixteenth century: Christopher Goodman, George Buchanan, and John Knox.[24] And correspondingly, the executed Charles is described in details that associate him with authoritative women in general, and with specific queens who figured in that sixteenth-century debate over women's right to rule. When Milton jeers in *Eikonoklastes* at *Eikon Basilike*—the 1649 tract condemning the regicides that was written in Charles's voice—he calls Charles's avowed "pregnant motives" for arresting five members of Parliament "a Queen *Maries* cushion," that is, a false pregnancy like the one Mary Tudor claimed in the mid-1550s (*CPW* 3:379). Similarly Charles's meditations on death, praised by his supporters as "the most vertuous, most manly, most Christian, and most Martyr-like both of his words and speeches heer, and of his answers and behaviour at his Tryall," are revealed by Milton to have been cribbed from "not our Saviour, but his Grand-mother *Mary* Queen of Scots . . . from whom he seems to have learnt, as it were by heart, or els by kind" (*CPW* 3:597). Abandoning Parliamentary rule for a restoration of kingship thus amounts to abandoning the Edenic state, in which Adam had proper sovereignty over Eve, in favor of a return to queenship. Or as Milton puts it in *The Readie and Easie Way to Establish a Free Commonwealth*, restoring monarchy is like volunteering to retrogress from a type of Eden, the Mosaic Promised Land, to an Egypt of female rule: "the same reason shall pass for current to put our necks again under kingship, as was made use of by the *Jews* to returne back to *Egypt* and to the worship of thir idol queen, because they falsly imagind that they then livd in more plentie and prosperitie" (*CPW* 7:462).

Why would men ever subject themselves to the illegitimate but pervasive rule of queenly wives and queenly kings? In the case of marriage,

Milton surprisingly does not charge women with using their feminine wiles
to trap unwary men; the furthest he goes in this direction is to note that
men sometimes choose wives inadvisably because "the bashfull mutenes
of a virgin may oft-times hide all the unlivelines & naturall sloth which is
really unfit for conversation" (*CPW* 2:249). Nevertheless, the blame falls
upon a different type of feminine authority. Milton indicts "Custom," a
feminine figure who has no body but only a face, and who thus must
seek out the company of another allegorical figure: "shee accorporat[es]
her selfe with error, who being a blind and Serpentine body without a
head, willingly accepts what he wants, and supplies what her incompleat-
nesse went seeking" (*CPW* 2:223). The image pointedly reincarnates (as I
will discuss below) Spenser's Error, a monster half maternal serpent, half
woman—with the important difference that for Milton the serpent is decidedly male. This transsexualization of Error has a political use, since it
allows Milton to describe all of English society, in its opposition to divorce, as prone to a kind of rampant uxoriousness: masculine Error cedes
authority to feminine Custom. In the same way, an unenlightened rabble
prefers the customary rule of a feminine king to an enlightened, masculine Parliamentary government. In a very conscious echo of his earlier
reference, Milton opens his *Tenure of Kings and Magistrates* with the observation that men "generally give up thir understanding to a double
tyrannie, of Custom from without, and blind affections within" (*CPW*
3:190). Strikingly, in both these indictments of "Custom" Milton is alluding to a similarly worded argument in William Whittingham's preface to
Goodman's 1558 *How Superior Powers Oght to Be Obeyd*, an antimonarchical
and antigynecocratic tract advocating the disallowance of women's rule in
general, as well as the deposition of two especially despised queens, Mary
Tudor of England and Marie de Guise, regent in Scotland for her daughter
Mary, Queen of Scots. Whittingham's Custom is herself a seductive, blind-
ing woman—she "so bewitcheth us, that althogh we wallowe and walter
in darcke blyndenes, yet as it were by dreaming we seme to walke in the
bright sunne shyning"—from whom we must seek an instant divorce: "if
Custome be wicked and withholde us from God, we must spedely reject
her and cleave unto God."[25] Otherwise, as Milton puts it in *The Tenure of
Kings and Magistrates*, those very men living under the tyranny of "Custom from without, and blind affections within" are subject to a domestic,
quasimarital servitude, "being slaves within doors" (*CPW* 3:190).

For Whittingham as for Goodman, choosing a king according to right
principles is enough to effect such a dissolution of unlawful marriage. But

for Milton, who takes Goodman's advocacy of a popular monarchy to its logical extreme, any king at all is actually that seeming-bashful wife who turns out to be a monster with a woman's face. Gloomily awaiting the restoration of Charles II, Milton describes him as a nightmare return of the spectacularly theatrical Queen Elizabeth, a monarch who "will have little els to do, but to . . . set a pompous face upon the superficial actings of State, to pageant himself up and down in progress among the perpetual bowings and cringings of an abject people, on either side deifying and adoring him for nothing don that can deserve it." Like Custom supplying a face to Error, the monarch supplies a face to his misguided State. For Milton, the king is to the Parliament, the proper ruler, as the theater was to the king in *Henry V*'s Prologue—a feminine nothing to a masculine sufficiency: "a great cypher set to no purpose before a long row of other significant figures" (*CPW* 7:426).[26] The difference between the king as cipher and the fertile theater as cipher, of course, is the king's barrenness, his incapacity to make something from his nothing. Placed uselessly at the head of the state, the monarchical nullity is hardly a "crooked figure [that] may / Attest in little place a million" (*Henry V* 1.Pro.15–16).

Ironically, however, the specter of the feminine monarch can be countervailed by one particular attribute of the queen whom Milton's co-revolutionaries claimed as patron saint. While he did not join his compatriots in eulogizing Elizabeth's devotion to the Protestant cause, Milton in his early writing does evidence interest in reviving, in a way, precisely the type of rule that Queen Elizabeth in the latter portion of her reign fashioned for herself, even though her detractors doubted her veracity: the reign of the Virgin. A specifically Elizabethan cult of virginity, in fact, informs Milton's first public authorial production in 1634, the *Mask Presented at Ludlow Castle*. While scholars have generally found literary precedent for the *Mask* in Stuart-era productions like the court masques and Inner Temple entertainments of Ben Jonson and William Browne, its more relevant predecessor influence is, in my view, the Elizabethan entertainment addressed to and occasioned by the presence of the queen. (Milton's own father, incidentally, may have helped embellish a late incarnation of such an entertainment with his contribution to Thomas Morley's madrigal collection *The Triumphs of Oriana* [1601].)[27] While masques from the latter decades of Elizabeth's reign celebrate her virginity in astoundingly diversiform fashion, several of the most memorable (and most publicized) masques showcase Elizabeth or her stand-in utterly defeating a rapine assault upon another female virgin, also a duplicate of Elizabeth. For example, in Philip Sidney's 1581 pageant *The Four Foster Children of Desire*, later written up in Holinshed's *Chronicles*, the four knights (Sidney, Fulke Greville, and two others) staged a two-day assault on the fortress of Perfect Beauty, which proved "[s]o invincible . . . that it did not yield even to Virtuous Desire, although cannons bombarded it with sweet powder and perfume."[28] (The point was to persuade the queen not to marry the French duc d'Alençon, whose representatives were in attendance.) In 1592 a similar pageant reached print, describing an entertainment at Sudeley in which Elizabeth replaces the father of the virgin nymph Daphne in rescuing her from Apollo's lustful embrace.[29] More appositely, at his estate of Kenilworth in 1575 Sir Robert Dudley engineered a series of entertainments — recorded for print distribution by George Gascoigne, who authored some of them — at the core of which was a device whose plot even more fully anticipates the *Mask*'s: Queen Elizabeth herself rescues the Lady of the Lake from being raped by "Sir Bruse, sans pittie."[30] As in the *Mask*, it takes a virgin to save a virgin. This requisite dual virginity of savior and saved accounts, it seems to me, for Milton's altering his source narrative, Geoffrey of Monmouth's *History of Britain*, in which "Sabrina's death had nothing to do with refusing to give up her virginity."[31] Furthermore, the *Mask* recollects the Elizabethan cult of virginity on the level of phrase, as well as of plot. *A Midsummer Night's Dream*, whose influence on *A Mask* has long been recognized, is quoted in such a way as to replicate the queen in the Lady: Shakespeare's "imperial votress," the vestal who avoided Cupid's shaft and "passed on, / In maiden meditation, fancy-free" (*MND* 2.1.163–64), is reincarnated as the Lady who "may pass on with unblench't majesty" whatever rapine threat looms near (430).[32] Spenser's literary evocations of Elizabeth are in place as well. Steeped in linguistic and situational reminiscences of *The Faerie Queene*, the *Mask*, like Spenser's poem, similarly centers on a ravishing virgin, whom Comus even declares "my Queen" (265). It is hardly accidental, then, that the *Mask* particularly draws on *The Faerie Queene*'s Book 3, which details the adventures of the female Knight of Chastity.

These surprising recollections of Elizabethan iconography in Miltonic masque counterpose Milton's equivalence elsewhere between female monarchy and uncompanionate marriage, where unlucky or unthinking men submit to a womanish rule. Here, queenliness instead becomes a state of being that a man might profitably occupy. This is, needless to say, a very unusual position in the 1630s. For Elizabeth, queenly virginity had signified regal power; for nostalgic post-Elizabethan subjects of the Stuart and Commonwealth regimes, it merely indicated the morality, patriotism, and pure Protestant faith that were posthumously attributed to her. For high-church-inclined Stuart subjects, Elizabeth's virginity was referred to primarily as an excuse for reviving the cult of the Virgin Mary.[33] Indeed, as the seventeenth century wore on Elizabeth's virginity became a much less emphasized aspect of her hagiography. Milton himself, for example, in his early poem on the Gunpowder Plot "In Quintum Novembris" alludes to Elizabeth's virgin status only in the context of the defeat of the Spanish Armada, alluding to events "Thermodoontea nuper regnante puella [during the recent reign of the Amazonian virgin]" (105).

But Milton was not uneager to claim the "feminine" virtue of chastity: he was himself called "Lady" at Cambridge, he surmises in his Sixth Prolusion (on "Sportive Exercises"), "because I never showed my virility in the way that these brothellers do" (*CPW* 1:284). Milton's Latin for "Lady" in this Prolusion is *Domina*, with all its connotations of female rule—a status preferable, he asserts, to being one of those unruly rout who have unjustly impugned his manhood.[34] In the *Mask*, then, Milton resurrects queenly virginity because for him, it signifies a sufficient defense against a similarly unjust and degraded monarchy. As the Elder Brother rightly asserts about the *Mask*'s Lady, "Virtue may be assail'd but never hurt, / Surpris'd by unjust force but not enthrall'd" (589–90). John Rogers has recently argued that the Lady's chastity, which Milton even intensified in his 1637 printed edition of the *Mask* by adding the Lady's impassioned commentary on "the sage / And serious doctrine of Virginity" (786–87), in fact signals Milton's momentary engagement with a subset of radical sectarian thought that held virginity to be "a symbolic model for the specifically seventeenth-century image of the autonomous liberal self."[35] At its most extreme, says Rogers, retaining one's virginity "could also be imagined, far more radically, as an actual historical precipitant for a spiritual, even political, revolution."[36] Milton did not go so far as to enlist perpetual celibacy as an active revolutionary force; nor does the *Mask* itself finally endorse perpetual celibacy, since the Lady's return to her parents is followed by the Spirit's celebration of the fruitful marriage of Cupid and Psyche. But the embodiment of individual liberty in a belated avatar of Elizabeth, the virgin Lady, has a perhaps more interesting political resonance. For if Elizabeth's sacrosanct virginity was an attempt to rewrite the theory of the King's Two Bodies as the Queen's Single Body—where the inviolable entity of the queen's corporal person is magnified into the impermeable body of the state—then the Lady's erstwhile virginity converts the Queen's

Single Body into a model and a means for the liberated nation: the individual subject as virginal and hence free occupies the queen's place in being apotheosized into the body of England itself.

Milton flirts briefly in the divorce tracts, Stephen Fallon argues, with the idea that virginity within marriage might expunge the unavoidable indignities of the conjugal state.[37] In that case, the divorce tracts at least fleetingly take up the *Mask*'s concerns, hinting that the Miltonic recollection of historical queenship bifurcates into two figures: the wife as queen, as we have seen; but also the perhaps better-off virgin husband, who might, through either abstinence or divorce, escape the servitude of his body even as he escapes servitude to his wife.[38] Indeed, among his commonplace book entries under "Marriage, See of Divorce," Milton praises the virgin Elizabeth as a model not for the incompatible wife, but for the husband who rids himself of her, citing "the reply of Elizabeth in her refusal of marriage with the Duke of Anjou [i.e., Alençon] on account of the difference in religion" (*CPW* 1:398). The free will of the husband, which precedes and enables the free will of the subject who overthrows his monarch, is thus based, quite ironically, on the precedent of feminine authority. As an alternative to the fallen world of female rule we are given a different kind of queenship, virginity as prelapsarian condition.

My point is a rather eccentric one, I am aware, and I would not want to press it far in the context of the divorce tracts themselves. But looking ahead to *Paradise Lost*, even though in that poem physical virginity is no longer a precondition for innocence from sin, we might begin to see the inherent tensions in Eve's character as a product of the heritage I have been tracing. On the one hand, the extent to which she refuses companionate marriage with Adam associates her with not only the domineering wife of the divorce tracts (and later of *Samson Agonistes*), but also the womanish king of the antimonarchist tracts.[39] But on the other hand, the freedom from subjugation she seeks—and to which, I shall argue, *Paradise Lost* is deeply committed, for poetic as well as republican reasons—ascends, in a Miltonic genealogy of texts, from Eve back to the enlightened republican antimonarchist, back to the enfranchised ex-husband, back through the *Mask*'s Lady to England's remembered Virgin Queen. Further, the complicated crossing and re-crossing of gender lines in this genealogy (where a usurping queen becomes a tyrannous wife becomes a feminine king becomes an unruly Eve, but also where a virgin queen becomes a virgin Lady becomes an enfranchised husband becomes a free-thinking Eve) calls into question any analysis of Milton's idea of femininity that strictly segregates

Milton's characters by sex.[40] Bound up in this Miltonic textual genealogy I have been describing is not only a story of accepting or rejecting previous models of state government and self-government, but also a story of accepting or rejecting previous models of poetic authority. In this latter story, Milton remembers feminine sovereignty not only in terms of the late Queen Elizabeth, but also in terms of his literary forebears Shakespeare and especially Spenser, themselves associated with female rule.

The Paradise of Woman

In the note on verse that prefaces *Paradise Lost*, Milton once again echoes the Whittingham preface to the antigynecocratic Christopher Goodman tract, this time rejecting the "Custom" of rhyme, which Milton calls "the Invention of a barbarous Age, to set off wretched matter and lame Meter; grac't indeed since by the use of some famous modern Poets, carried away by Custom, but much to their own vexation, hindrance, and constraint to express many things otherwise, and for the most part worse than else they would have exprest them." The "troublesome and modern bondage of Riming," like the domineering wife of the uncompanionate marriage, not only constrained "some famous modern poets" but "carried [them] away" in its thrall (p. 210). The issue is more than one of poetic style, however. As in Milton's prose tracts, where the illegality of divorce is intertwined with the fate of the nation under monarchy, rhyme turns out to have consequence for England's conception of itself. Milton's reference here is to Samuel Daniel's *Defence of Ryme* (1603), which in reply to Thomas Campion's advocacy of English quantitative verse defended the "Generall Custome, and use of Ryme in this kingdome" in terms that look to have been borrowed by seventeenth-century monarchists: "*Ill customes are to be left*, I graunt it: but I see not howe that can be taken for an ill custome, which nature hath thus ratified, all nations received, time so long confirmed, the effects such as it performes those offices of motion for which it is imployed; delighting the eare, stirring the heart, and satisfying the judgement in such sort as I doubt whether ever single numbers will do in our Climate."[41] As Richard Helgerson points out, choosing blank over rhymed verse is more than a merely literary decision for Milton; rather, it has the force of wresting imperial authority away from "Custom" and placing it in the hands of the individual agent.[42] In Milton's poetic cosmology, God alone is allowed to claim the priority of what Satan in *Paradise Lost* mockingly calls the "old repute, / Consent or custom" (1.639–40) arrogated by other writers to rhyming or to kingship.

Milton seems to have in mind particularly the master rhymer Spenser, Milton's "original," whose romance is slighted even while it is echoed throughout *Paradise Lost*.[43] My sense is that Milton's revisions of romance, and especially Spenserian romance, are intertwined with the Miltonic politics of queenship that I have been outlining. Certainly late in his career Milton seems to have agreed with Marx that Spenser, "Elizabeth's arse-kissing poet," was not to be imitated in glorifying monarchical government. But the issue of contention between Milton and his predecessor poet also has to do with something other than the royal object of Spenser's authorial address. If romance, like uxoriousness within marriage and within monarchies, is wedded to "custom," then Milton's ideal and innovative poem ought to present as best it can an unfallen state of poetry—poetry that is not romance—as well as of marriage and of human society. Romance, in other words, is the genre of bad marriages and bad monarchies. Romance, however, unlike the end-directed epic that generally proves in *Paradise Lost* to be a Satanic mode, also comes to represent the freedom of the individual human will, which, like the Lady of *A Mask*, may be "surpris'd by unjust force but not enthrall'd." All of these issues are bound up in the contradictory character of Eve, who unlawfully usurps sovereignty within her marriage but who also inaugurates a future of human choice.

Milton's great poem is not consistently charitable to any previous, non-biblical mode of tale-telling. It is generally recognized, for example, that Milton was out to "exorcize the reader's false notion of epic heroism"; and indeed, Homeric and Virgilian models are rejected in Milton's plea to his muse for an "answerable style" at the beginning of Book 9.[44] But Milton reserves special and extended scorn for the genre of chivalric romance, declaring himself "Not sedulous"

> to describe Races and Games,
> Or tilting Furniture, emblazon'd Shields,
> Impreses quaint, Caparisons and Steeds;
> Bases and tinsel Trappings, gorgeous Knights
> At Joust and Tournament; then marshall'd Feast
> Serv'd up in Hall with Sewers, and Seneschals;
> The skill of Artifice or Office mean,

Not that which justly gives Heroic name
To Person or to Poem.

(9.27, 33–41)

A dig at Spenser is more than generically implied here, as Milton puns on Spenser's initial knightly hero, "gorgeous" George, the Redcrosse Knight (9.36). Partly at issue is merely the anxiety—hardly unique to Milton, as I discussed in Chapters 1 and 2—that romance is by nature dangerous to one's upright, moral self-possession. In his retrospective account in the *Apology for Smectymnuus* of his own youthful reading of *The Faerie Queene*, inferentially included in "those lofty Fables and Romances, which recount in solemne canto's the deeds of Knighthood founded by our victorious Kings," Milton dodges depravity only by divine intervention: "even those books which to many others have bin the fuell of wantonnesse and loose living, I cannot think how unless by divine indulgence prov'd to me so many incitements . . . to the love and stedfast observation of that vertue [i.e., chastity] which abhorres the society of Bordello's" (*CPW* 1:891). Somehow ignoring Spenser's ostentatious celebrations of Elizabeth's chastity, Milton barely escapes with his own.[45] No wonder, then, that romance is often infernal in *Paradise Lost*, where allusions to Tasso, Ariosto, and *The Song of Roland*, among other examples of the genre, cluster around the descriptions of Satan's demonic forces. Likewise Satan, who mistakenly believes himself to occupy an epic role, is doomed to what David Quint calls "bad romance," that is, "the losers' condition of endless, circular repetition."[46]

But Spenser is to be indicted not merely for writing romance, but for writing romance in celebration of a female monarch. If the "gorgeous Knights" in the passage cited above are Spenser's, then the "impreses quaint" that Milton disdains to employ slight Spenser's entire poem as a heraldic device blazoning the "queynt" of a queen (9.35). Part of Milton's contempt, no doubt, derives from Elizabeth's having conducted at least the surface goings-on of her rule as if she were the fair lady to whom all her male courtiers must direct knightly adoration. For some in the Stuart era, this memory fueled nostalgia for that supposedly chivalric age. For others, however, like Francis Bacon in his 1608 essay eulogizing Elizabeth, the queen's conduct in this regard provoked some embarrassment and had to be excused: "As for those lighter points of character,—as that she allowed herself to be wooed and courted, and even to have love made to her; and

liked it; and continued it beyond the natural age for such vanities. . . . if
viewed indulgently, they are much like the accounts we find in romances, of
the Queen in the blessed islands, and her court and institutions, who allows
of amorous admiration but prohibits desire. But . . . certain it is that these
dalliances detracted but little from her fame and nothing at all from her
majesty, and neither weakened her power nor sensibly hindered her business."[47] Remembering Elizabeth's fashioning of her court on the model of
Arthurian romance might alone, I suspect, have prompted Milton to abandon his plan of writing a great English epic in the Arthurian mode, and, in
his *History of Britain*, to deride the Brutus myth with which Spenser associates Arthur's history as "the whole *Trojan* pretence" (*CPW* 5:8).

And yet the association between monarchy and chivalric romance had
hardly died with Elizabeth. Indeed, as Annabel Patterson discusses, Charles
I shaped his reign around the fiction of himself as not just any romance
hero, but a Spenserian St. George.[48] In *Eikonoklastes* Milton ridicules just
this association between Charles and the romance genre, revealing that a
prayer attributed to him in *Eikon Basilike* was in fact lifted from "no serious
Book, but the vain amatorious Poem of Sr *Philip Sidneys Arcadia*" (*CPW*
3:362). Charles's prayer is, in fact, one spoken by the *Arcadia*'s Pamela; as
if reading romance were not feminizing enough, Charles actually speaks in
the voice of a lovelorn woman, once again styling himself as a feminized
king. In the second edition of *Eikonoklastes*, in fact, Milton adds that by
culling one prayer from the *Arcadia* Charles casts doubt upon any other
prayers credited to him, citing other romance titles, the first two of which
connote goddesses that had been amalgamated to the cult of Elizabeth:
"For he . . . might gather up the rest God knows from whence; one perhaps out of the French *Astraea*, another out of the Spanish *Diana*; *Amadis*
and *Palmerin* could hardly scape him" (*CPW* 3:366–67).[49]

We must look for *Paradise Lost*'s attitude toward latter-day monarchy, then, not only in those details in the poem that associate Charles with
Satan, but also in those moments that associate romance with feminine
authority.[50] Correlating genre, femininity, and monarchy is another thing
that Milton has learned from Spenser, his great teacher; but the first moral
Milton takes away from this lesson is that this multiple conjunction signifies the worst kinds of sin, or at least of moral danger. Recall that the
most overt reference to *The Faerie Queene* in *Paradise Lost* is to replicate
Error, the half-woman-half-serpent, in a figure actually anterior in time
to Error, who exists in Spenser's post-fallen world: Satan's daughter and
lover, Sin.[51] Similarly, the one episode from *The Faerie Queene* that Milton

singles out for praise in *Areopagitica* (though he erroneously recalls its specifics) is Guyon's passing "with his palmer through the cave of Mammon, and the bowr of earthly blisse that he might see and know, and yet abstain" (*CPW* 2:516). Guyon's journey, Maureen Quilligan points out, derives from the *Odyssey*; but "it is an odyssey that ends not with a homecoming to a loyal wife, but with the destruction of a queen's power. (No wonder Milton singled it out.)"[52] I might add that Guyon's destruction of the bower represents not only the reassertion of patriarchy over female rule; it also represents that last moment in *The Faerie Queene*, as I argued in Chapter 2, before the poem "degenerates" into Britomartian-inspired romance—romance that is itself dismantled in Book 5 only by *The Faerie Queene*'s abandoning both the female quest for marriage, and the feminizing language of lush poetry. Thus it is that one of the most convincingly Spenserian passages in *Paradise Lost*, Satan's greeting to Eve in Book 9, ascribes to Eve the power of ravishment in language that duplicates Spenser's description of his ravishing queen in the Proem to Book 3. Satan's speech, too, is a proem:

> Thee all things living gaze on, all things thine
> By gift, and thy Celestial Beauty adore
> With ravishment beheld, there best beheld
> Where universally admired . . .
>
> .   .   .   .
>   [thou] shouldst be seen
> A Goddess among Gods, ador'd and serv'd
> By Angels numberless, thy daily Train.
>   So gloz'd the Tempter, and his *Proem* tun'd;
> Into the heart of Eve his words made way.
>
> (9.539–42, 546–48, my emphasis)

And as in Spenser's proem, the ravishing queen is addressed herself in words that ravish, "making way" into Eve's heart so that, as Spenser might put it, all her "senses lulled are in slomber of delight" (*Faerie Queene* 3.Pr.4) The divine queen of Paradise summons forth the very romance poetry that, in seducing her, threatens to undo her.

Romance's associations with a feminine monarchy help account for the odd timbre of another subset of Miltonic allusions: the references in *Paradise Lost* to some of those plays of Shakespeare that are most concerned with feminine rule. I have in mind first of all *A Midsummer Night's Dream*, which (as I noted above) Milton remembers specifically in *A Mask* for its description of Elizabeth as "imperial votress"—a remembrance helped along, most probably, by Thomas Dekker's incongruously giving the name "Titania" to his triumphant Virgin Queen figure in *The Whore of Babylon* (1606). But in *Paradise Lost* the characters associated with queenship in Shakespeare's play—the fairies; the "peasant" Bottom who "dreams" he attends on Titania; the "imperial votress" whom Oberon sees juxtaposed with the "cold moon" that quenches Cupid's dart—are demonically recalled in this description of Satan's minions in Pandaemonium, swarming in miniature like

> Faery Elves,
> Whose midnight Revels, by a Forest side
> Or Fountain some belated Peasant sees,
> Or dreams he sees, while over-head the Moon
> Sits Arbitress, and nearer to the Earth
> Wheels her pale course.
>
>   (1.781–86)

The other Shakespearean play on which Milton seems to cast most aspersion is *Antony and Cleopatra*, whose evocations of the late queen I discussed in Chapter 5. Milton generally admires Shakespearean tragedy, implicitly praising it along with other of "our best *English* Tragedies" for precisely its freedom from the "troublesome and modern bondage of Riming" of Spenserian-style poetry (p. 210), and declaring "tragic notes" the fit medium for his narration of the Fall (9.6). But the tragedy of a man overcome by female seduction bodes nothing but ill for Milton. Hence Satan reviewing his demonic army takes on the aspect of Shakespeare's Antony, remembered by Philo at the play's opening as the general whose "goodly eyes, / . . . o'er the files and musters of the war / Have glow'd like plated Mars," and whose "captain's heart, / . . . in the scuffles of great fights hath burst / The buckles on his breast" (*Antony and Cleopatra* 1.1.2–4, 6–8). Similarly, Satan

> through the armed Files
> Darts his experienc't eye, and soon traverse
> The whole Battalion views, thir order due,
>
> . . . .

And now his heart
Distends with pride, and hard'ning in his strength
Glories.

                                            (1.567–69, 571–73)

Hell is, of course, populated by Egyptian deities as it is by other pagan gods, but the Egyptian gods Milton picks out by name are those specifically associated with the goddess claimed by Shakespeare's Cleopatra: "*Osiris, Isis, Orus* and their Train" (1.478). That Horus is the son of Isis and Osiris renders especially demonic the fecundity of body and of thought that Shakespeare's Cleopatra possessed. And whereas Spenser reserved some approving (or at least fascinated) commentary for the supergenerative bounty of Egypt's Nile, later associated by Shakespeare with Cleopatra herself, Milton takes care to inform us that, just as Eden is not whence Proserpina was snatched, nor is it near the Nile (4.268–72, 280–84). In Hell, quite the contrary, Isis and Osiris march in company with a recognizably Spenserian crew of demons, all of them symbolizing female desire and/or female dominance as sin. *The Faerie Queene*'s Adonis, whose coupling with the desiring goddess Venus generates the procreative and poetic effusions of Book 3's Garden, in *Paradise Lost* appears as Thammuz, who inspires the "amorous ditties" and "wanton passions" of the women of Syria and Sion (1.449, 454). And perhaps most startlingly, a Belphoebean image of Elizabeth herself, crowned with Diana's crescent moon, crops up in the figure of "*Astarte*, queen of Heav'n, with crescent Horns; / To whose bright Image nightly by the Moon / *Sidonian* Virgins paid thir Vows and Songs" (1.439–41). In Milton's infernal theogony the Queen of Virgins is assimilated, as in the divorce tracts and antimonarchist tracts, to the portrayal of the "uxorious king" (in this case, Solomon) ruined by his feminine attachments: his "heart though large, / Beguil'd by fair Idolatresses, fell / To idols foul" (1.444–46).[53]

When Milton turns, then, to hailing the wedded love of Adam and Eve, he is extraordinarily circumspect about distinguishing the epithalamic setting of their bridal bower from any suggestion of queens Spenserian or Shakespearean. Their "blissful Bower" (4.690) is pointedly not the "bowr of earthly blisse" from which, Milton approvingly noted, Guyon abstained. And their Cupid is pointedly not "*Venus* dearling doue" who softens Elizabeth's heart in *The Faerie Queene* (4.Pr.5); nor do his "revels," unlike Antony's and Cleopatra's, promote "casual fruition":

Here Love his golden shafts imploys, here lights
His constant Lamp, and waves his purple wings,
Reigns here and revels; not in the bought smile
Of Harlots, loveless, joyless, unindear'd,
Casual fruition, nor in Court Amours,
Mixt Dance, or wanton Mask, or Midnight Ball,
Or Serenate, which the starv'd Lover sings
To his proud fair, best quitted with disdain.

(4.763–70)

Most of all, of course, this passage dismisses the entire apparatus—the songs, the masques, the entertainments, even the very "court amours"— by which a monarch, either Elizabeth or Charles I, conveys regal power as chivalric fiction. What the narrative voice enacts in Adam and Eve's bower seems like a successful Miltonic divorce-prevention program: the marital space of the poem is inoculated against Milton's poetic predecessors' engagements with female authority. It is understandable, then, that several critics have explained Milton's treatment of female subordination, and indeed of readerly subjectivity itself, as contingent upon the absence of Queen Elizabeth from his literary and monarchical purview. Linda Gregerson remarks that as *Paradise Lost* supplants *The Faerie Queene*, God replaces Elizabeth as supreme authority. Quilligan similarly argues that since Milton does not have to cater to a queen, the poem's "fit audience though few" can be narrowed to male readers alone.[54]

As we have seen, however, queenship remains even when the Queen is dead. I suggest we pay close attention when Eve is addressed, as she often is, in discourse that seems a holdover from *The Faerie Queene*, language that appears particularly when Eve is disposed to exert her own will. The most blatant instance occurs when Eve proposes she and Adam set about their labor separately: her very being becomes that of queenship, as her sobriquet becomes "the Virgin Majesty of *Eve*" (9.270). And then, as she heads off to her temptation, she metamorphoses into a series of chaste nymphs and goddesses worthy of a tribute to Elizabeth herself: Delia/Diana, Pomona escaping rape, and even a young Ceres, "Yet Virgin of *Proserpina* from *Jove*" (9.396). But even before this loaded conversation, Eve's acting upon her own desires is haunted by Elizabeth-like address. For example, she leaves Adam and Raphael alone to talk celestial shop as a matter of her own preference—"her Husband the Relater she *preferr'd* / Before the Angel, and of him to ask / *Chose* rather" (8.53–54, my emphases)—and transforms at that very moment into an iconic figure of Elizabeth as queen and goddess, complete with attendant Graces:

> With Goddess-like demeanor forth she went;
> Not unattended, for on her as Queen
> A pomp of winning Graces waited still,
> And from about her shot Darts of desire
> Into all Eyes to wish her still in sight.
>
> (8.59–63)

From such instances we might read backward, then, to find the queenly subtext in the famous first description of Eve's appearance. Even as her status as subject to Adam is asserted, the poetry reverts to a Spenserian mood—that is, it rhymes. Her hair

> in wanton ringlets wav'd   (a)
> As the Vine curls her tendrils, which impli'd (b)
> Subjection, but requir'd with gentle sway,   (c)
> And by her yielded, by him best receiv'd,   (a)
> Yielded with coy submission, modest pride,   (b)
> And sweet reluctant amorous delay.   (c)
>
> (4.306–11)

The tyrannous rhyme employed here hints at Eve's elevation to queenly status. As in the divorce tracts, in this marriage the wife, though inferior, is all too likely to take charge.

Albert C. Labriola discerns in these reminiscences of Elizabeth a Miltonic yearning for replacing the patriarchy of God-Son-Adam with "a consensual model of governance . . . in which power is less an affirmation or an enforcement of authority than a coefficient of reciprocal attraction and an index of mutual dependence"—a kind of Cixousian *autorité féminine*.[55] But for Milton, as we have seen, feminine authority within marriage is a precondition not for "mutual dependence" but for tyranny in the state, and hence is coded as illegitimate. And as we have also seen, the divorce tracts are haunted by the fear that a wife's sovereignty, even though illegitimate, is the initial marital state. As it turns out, Adam's first wife indeed exerts control over him from the very beginning of their matrimony—and that wife is not Lilith, but Eve. As Quint puts it, "Adam has already made Eve his queen and his goddess before Satan tells her that she is one."[56] And one

of the ways we know she is his queen is that she prompts from him effusions of extraordinary courtierlike poetry, such as this beautiful response
to Raphael's warning him against uxoriousness:

> yet when I approach
> Her loveliness, so absolute she seems
> And in herself complete, so well to know
> Her own, that what she wills to do or say,
> Seems wisest, virtuousest, discreetest, best;
> All higher knowledge in her presence falls
> Degraded, Wisdom in discourse with her
> Loses discount'nanc't, and like folly shows;
> Authority and Reason on her wait,
> As one intended first, not after made
> Occasionally.
>
> (8.546–56)

As we can see from this reverie, it takes some time for Adam to understand his wife's authority over him as tyranny. We are reading wrongly if we
descry a misogyny latent in Adam's lyric utterance; it is not that she *lacks*
wisdom, authority, reason, but rather that she, queenlike, is *served by* these
qualities and hence owns them. Like the impermeable Elizabeth herself,
Eve to Adam is "absolute" and "in herself complete." And he, confessing
his rapture in her presence, finds himself "in all enjoyments else / Superior
and unmov'd, here only weak / Against the charm of Beauty's powerful
glance" (8.531–32). As Patricia Parker points out in her fine analysis of
Adam's sense of self-deficiency (perhaps, he says, "Nature fail'd in mee,
and left some part / Not proof enough such Object to sustain" [8.534–
35]), Adam inverts even the priority of their creation, declaring Eve "As
one intended first, not after made / Occasionally."[57] When Eve suggests
their laboring separately—the same point at which she becomes "Virgin
Majesty"—Adam's own assertion of strength in numbers betrays his sup-
position that she is already his superior. He proposes that, if Satan were to
tempt them while they were together, "shame, thou looking on, / Shame
to be overcome or over-reacht / Would utmost vigor raise, and rais'd unite"
(9.312–14); but the syntax leaves it quite unspoken *who* would "over-reach"
him in this case: perhaps not Satan, but Eve herself. Thus Eve's rather
modest postlapsarian hopes of acquiring occasional rule over Adam, of
being "more equal, and perhaps, / A thing not undesirable, sometime /

Superior," prove superfluous (9.823–25). Even part of the Son's judgment on Eve, that "to thy Husband's will / Thine shall submit, hee over thee shall rule" (10.195–96), suggests that heretofore, in the prelapsarian state of marriage, this has not been the case. Milton's neat, subordinative inversion of Tasso's description of Armida's sway over Rinaldo—"L'uno di servitù, l'altra d'impero / si gloria, ella in se stessa ed egli in lei [One glories in slavery, the other in command, / She in herself and he in her]"—into "Hee for God only, shee for God in him" (4.299) proves highly susceptible to re-inversion.[58] It is not simply that, as Chrystostom argued, Eve was not subject to Adam before the fall.[59] Rather, she has, in fact, been his queen all along.

Eve's prelapsarian monarchy helps account for the heavy-handedness with which Adam, the Son, and even the narrative voice itself seek her subordination after the fall. It is as if all of them, Eve included, have dipped into Milton's divorce tracts to understand that female rule, however primal, not only is undesirable but can be overthrown. Immediately after sinning, Eve, in considering whether she will elevate Adam into sapience alongside her, realizes for the first time that she can be replaced. She imagines being Lilith, the first wife whom the patriarch (not Adam in this case, but God Almighty) puts aside:

> but what if God have seen,
> And Death ensue? then I shall be no more,
> And *Adam* wedded to another *Eve*,
> Shall live with her enjoying, I extinct.
>
> (9.826–29)

Before he clues in to the potentiality of male sovereignty, Adam chooses sin as someone who, like the polemicists Milton derides in the divorce tracts, assumes "Our State cannot be sever'd, we are one, / One Flesh; to lose thee were to lose myself" (9.958–59). But a marriage in which the wife holds sway, the divorce tracts argue, is already one in which "one flesh" is never joined, since it is not one that sorts with companionacy as Milton sees it. The Son, for his part, echoes Milton's prose in deracinating the rhetoric of wife-as-queen that has been deployed so far in the poem. Owning that "Adorn'd / [Eve] was indeed," the Son declares that she was "lovely to attract / Thy Love, not thy Subjection" (10.151–53). In this way he dismantles the *Faerie Queene*-inspired descriptions of Eve as "Majesty" by separating, in a way never employed in Elizabeth's milieu, the poetry of courtiership from the fact of queenly superiority, and woman's beauty from her monarchy. His lesson is one that Adam has himself anticipated, when in his post-fall enlightenment he distinguishes his wife's *worth* from her *precedence* over him: "Thus it shall befall / Him who to worth in Woman overtrusting / Lets her Will rule" (9.1182–84).

I wish now, however, to consider the other strand of Elizabethan inheritance that comes into play in *Paradise Lost*, and that causes us to think about Eve's sovereignty in quite another fashion. Remember that Eve takes on aspects of monarchy at precisely those moments when she is exerting self-will. In these cases, as I suggested above in my discussion of Milton's *Mask*, her "Virgin Majesty" figures forth not only the divorce tracts' domineering shrew, but also their newly emancipated husband, who scorns external determination of his fate in the manner of the *Mask*'s virgin Lady and who hence becomes an essential constituent of the republican state. It is only through considering all of these texts in sequence, Milton's prose as well as his poetry, that Eve and the Lady seem anything but diametric opposites, since the Lady, quite unlike Eve, refuses all of Comus's Satan-like persuasions meant to override her "well-govern'd and wise appetite" (705). But (Henny Youngman to the contrary) the intervening textual connections I have traced above make it clear that a Lady may also be a wife, in the sense that Eve's power to decide and to consent derives from the Lady's self-governance, which itself (quite ironically) recollects Queen Elizabeth's virginal self-sufficiency. Like the Lady, and like the "true wayfaring Christian" of *Areopagitica* who sallies forth with uncloistered virtue into the bookstalls, Eve stands "Virtue-proof" (5.384). This phrase does not, as it turns out, mean that she is forever safe from sinning. Rather, being "Virtue-proof" appears in the context of her having just conducted her first foray into choosing which fruit to pick, action prefaced with her unprompted resolution, "I *will* haste and from each bough and brake, / Each Plant and juiciest Gourd will pluck such *choice* / To entertain our Angel guest" (5.326–28, my emphasis). "Proof" thus has to do both with the *trials* of adversity and with *experiment*; to be "Virtue-proof" is to have one's virtue tested, but also to undertake such testing of one's own accord.

My purpose here is to intervene, although in a somewhat limited fashion, in the now long–running debates among Miltonists about the mutuality or hierarchization of the Adam-Eve marriage, and about the state and function of Eve's subjectivity within that marriage. On one side stand critics like Diane McColley, who seeks "to show that Milton has fashioned an Eve who in all the prelapsarian scenes is not only sufficient to stand

and able to grow, but . . . is a pattern and composition of active good-
ness."[60] Critics like Mary Nyquist, on the other side of the issue, describe
McColley's reading as symptomatic of the exact liberal-humanist version
of female equality-within-hierarchy that Milton's poem helped to create.
In a brilliant essay connecting the biblical hermeneutics of the divorce
tracts to the psychotextual structure of *Paradise Lost*, Nyquist has argued
that although Eve possesses subjectivity and in fact also comes to represent
Adam's subjectivity, her subjection is a necessary condition of that subjectivity.[61] One of the primary issues in this disagreement is one of how to
evaluate *firstness* within the poem. McColley and others believe that Eve's
account of her creation and coming to self-knowledge—appearing as it
does before Adam's similar account in the poem, even though God made
him first—bespeaks the shaping of her independent psychology. Against
this perception, however, Nyquist points out that Eve is created out of
God's fulfilling Adam's desire for a companion. Hence Eve's coming-into-
being scene and its flavor of psychological development is merely a component of Adam's personhood, says Nyquist: "if Eve is created to satisfy
the psychological needs of a lonely Adam, then it is necessary that *Paradise
Lost*'s readers experience her from the first as expressing an intimately sub-
jective sense of self."[62] Nyquist grounds her reading on Milton's byzantine
argument in the divorce tracts privileging God's decision to make "an help
meet" for Adam (Genesis 2:18) over all other biblical discussions of the reason for marriage, including Christ's own injunction against divorce. Linda
Gregerson both counters and extends Nyquist's perception of the poem's
invention of bourgeois subjectivity, contending that the patriarchalism en-
dorsed in the divorce tracts and enacted in *Paradise Lost* is precisely what
makes Eve the "normative" postlapsarian subject, that is, the subject who
occupies every Christian's postlapsarian relationship to God, a relationship
of "reciprocity within hierarchy." Central to Gregerson's own historicizing of Eve-as-subject is her cogent observation that our post-Romantic
valorization of the individual psyche ought not to color our reading of a
seventeenth-century society that "could posit the self as a *contested* political construct and could envision a positive, reciprocal reformation of self
and community."[63]

This debate is a fascinating one and clearly awaits further analysis of
seventeenth-century conceptions of the self, and particularly of the gendered self. I propose to sidestep the question somewhat, however, to suggest that Nyquist's and other critics' one-to-one alignment, according to
sex, between the husbands and the wives of the divorce tracts and *Para-*

dise Lost is not the only way to explore the question of subjectivity in the poem, and that the relation between gender and subjectivity is thus even more complicated than it looks. If Eve's attributes of queenship, as I have been arguing, correlate her not only with the wife of the divorce tracts and the feminized king of the antimonarchist tracts, but also with the newly autarchic husband who divorces the wife and topples the king, then her exertions of self-will—*because* they are associated as they are with a feminine sovereignty reminiscent of Elizabeth's—form a foundation in Paradise for a republican government. I am not arguing, to be sure, for a new conception in this manner of the entirety of Eve's characterization. But perhaps my reading will help shed light on why it is that Miltonists, both feminist critics and others, have found liberatory qualities in exactly those actions of Eve's that doom humankind and justify her subordination. Her sovereign will is parallel to her mediated relation to God, which demonstrates on the one hand that she is in need of proper husbandly restraint, but on the other hand that she is in the position of having to make out for herself who she is and what she desires to do.

Adam, in contrast, in his prelapsarian condition never exactly chooses to do anything at all. The most he does is express a desire, a lack, or a curiosity, at which point God or one of his angelic emissaries provides Adam with knowledge or fulfillment. Paradigmatic of Adam's singular lack of volition is his account of awakening in the Garden from his first post-creation nap:

> Each Tree
> Load'n with Fairest Fruit, that hung to the Eye
> Tempting, stirr'd in me sudden appetite
> To pluck and eat; whereat I wak'd, and found
> Before mine Eyes all real, as the dream
> Had lively shadow'd.
>
> (8.306–11)

Even without the word "tempting" we would recognize the parallels between Adam's appetite for hanging fruit and Eve's later sin. But here, as always, Adam is provided for without ever having to think "I will." Eve, in contrast, even while being shunted away from her "vain desire" for her own watery reflection, is promised a future of self-directed forward movement with no specified goal ("I will bring thee where no shadow stays / Thy coming"), but equally a future of active pleasure ("hee / Whose image thou art, him thou shalt enjoy / Inseparably thine" [4.470–73]). The impression we are sometimes given, in fact, is one that flies in the face of the very terms of the debate over whether Eve is ontologically subordinate to Adam, or whether she possesses an independent psychology. Increasingly as the poem moves toward its end, it seems that neither of these is the case, and that Eve's mind has actually brought Adam into existence, in much the same way that Shakespeare's Cleopatra thinks a mythical Antony into being. Even while Adam receives the "foresight" of all of human history from Michael, for example, Eve's concurrent sleep is compared to the sleep of Adam out of which *she* was made: "let *Eve* . . . / Here sleep below while thou to foresight wak'st, / As once thou slep'st, while Shee to life was form'd" (11.368–69). The last words spoken in the poem are hers, as she commands him to take his place as head of the human race:

> but now lead on;
> In mee is no delay; with thee to go,
> Is to stay here; without thee here to stay,
> Is to go hence unwilling; thou to mee
> Art all things under Heav'n, all places thou,
> Who for my wilful crime art banisht hence.
>
> (12.614–19)

Her crime was "wilful," yes, but she shall continue in that willfulness, leaving Eden with Adam *not* "unwilling" in their existence thereafter. Life after Paradise, like life in Paradise, seems to bear an aspect of *Hamlet*'s jointure, where governance in the "unweeded garden" of Denmark is at least in part a matter of the will of a queen. In that case, Adam's subjectivity, like Hamlet's, comes into being and emerges from the Garden only because female will has *ab origine* been given sway. Even his postlapsarian resolution to shoulder his burden manfully—"My *labor* will sustain me"—seems to take both heart and shape from Eve's own destiny, to labor in childbirth: "to thee / Pains only in Child-bearing were foretold, / And, bringing forth, soon recompens't with joy, / Fruit of thy Womb" (10.1056, 1050–53, my emphasis). What there is of outward- and onward-directed human motion in the poem is entirely at Eve's instigation—not only the human fall into sin, but also their apprehension of choice, possibility, and even joy.[64]

Just as Eve's female sovereignty demands a kind of double vision, so we must also take a different look at the associations between Milton's poem and the romance mode associated with memories of queenship.

Here is where Milton's innovative epic starts not only to acknowledge, but also to depend on its fundamental debts to his Elizabethan and Jacobean predecessors. As with the works of Spenser and Shakespeare I have addressed in the preceding chapters, then, the question with *Paradise Lost* becomes whether literary enterprise is less hobbled than it is enabled by its associations with feminine authority.

First of all, we must recognize that the poem's male authority figures offer untenable models for human poetic imitation—untenable, as it turns out, precisely because they conform, to the greatest degree possible, to the teleological pattern of epic and of epic history as I have described them in the foregoing chapters. Satan's relentless counter-epic, initially attractive, is deflated by his inability to see beyond the limitations God has set for him. Satan's will is only a version of God's will, since all he can imagine, really, is a hidebound reversal of God's plan:

> If then his Providence
> Out of our evil seek to bring forth good,
> Our labor must be to pervert that end,
> And out of good still to find means of evil.
>
> (1.162–65)

God's omniscient pronouncements, for their part, are in fact incapable of expressing will. Will requires recognizing a present desire and hoping for its future fulfillment, but neither desire nor hope has any meaning for an eternal, omnipotent being. Hence God's dialogue is famously static, to the point of either tautology or incomprehensibility. Occasionally God will even speak essentially the same line twice in a row, as if being God consists (and why would it not?) of expressing the same truth over and over again. However, we see that both God's tautologous repetition and Satan's perverse syntax are versions of the same epic linearity—since linear quests, even Satanic ones, are a subset of the *grand récit* of God's eternity. Betraying this similarity between divine and damned poetry is God's penchant for chiasmus, a figure of both Godly repetition and Satanic reversal—as when God sends Raphael to advise Adam "of his happy state, / Happiness in his power left free to will, / Left to his own free Will, his Will though free, / Yet mutable" (5.234–37). By the end of this declaration, Adam's will seems hardly free at all, trapped as it is within the closed-term strictures of divine poetic form.[65] Christ's language is similar to the expression of Adam's fate in this respect. With the exception of his one astounding resolution to his father—"I for [man's] sake will leave / Thy bosom, and this glory next to thee / Freely put off, and for him lastly die" (3.238–40)—Christ uses the word *will* solely in its sense of futurity, not in its sense of desire and fulfillment. This futurity is, of course, that which God has already foreseen and foreordained. God's poetic discipline reappears, in extended manner, in Michael's minimally figurative recitation of the course of human history, a recitation analogous in poetic terms to the unornamented and distinctly unpleasurable poetics of historical allegory in *The Faerie Queene*'s Book 5.[66] Like Book 5's historical allegory, Michael's speech is designed to counteract the female agency that has dominated both the content and the form of the previous stretch of the poem. Perhaps because of its poetic structure as well as its postlapsarian occasion, it may be no accident that Michael's narration of human woe is also the site of the most unalloyedly misogynistic passages in the poem.

Consequently it is neither heaven nor hell, but rather Eve's presence that prompts—from Adam, from the narrator, and from herself—the most riveting, impassioned, and expansive stretches of poetry in *Paradise Lost*. This is the kind of poetry the Lady in *A Mask* utters in her song, prompting Comus to remark upon its "Divine enchanting ravishment" (245). As well, however, it is the kind of poetry Milton attributed to Shakespeare in "L'Allegro":

Lap me in soft *Lydian* Airs,

. . . .

with many a winding bout
Of linked sweetness long drawn out,
With wanton heed, and giddy cunning,
The melting voice through mazes running.

(136, 139–42)

Here the Shakespearean "melting voice" matches the "melting sweetnesse" that Spenser ascribes to poetry that may ravish even the queen (*Faerie Queene* 3.Pr.4). Both invent a poetics of "giddy cunning," the pun on *cunny* identifying poetry as emerging from the very locus of feminine sexuality. Correspondingly, poetic fecundity in Eden arises from the uncontrolled creativity of the Garden, which is itself associated with the body (and the culinary artistry) of Eve:

Nature here
Wanton'd as in her prime, and play'd at will
Her Virgin Fancies, pouring forth more sweet,
Wild above Rule or Art, enormous bliss. . . .
And *Eve* within [her bower], due at her hour prepar'd
For dinner savoury fruits, of taste to please
True appetite.

(5.294–97, 303–5)

Although Eve, unlike Shakespeare's Cleopatra, cannot be classified as the *supreme* creative intelligence in her universe, she is so identified with the verdant poetics of Eden that it almost seems as if Eve, the Garden, and the poetry are equal participants and products of a feminine mode of invention. As McColley points out, Eve's naming the flowers of the Garden reminds us that "[t]he art of poesy was habitually troped during the Renaissance by the art of gardening. Posies pun the connection."[67] In tandem, Eve and Eden espouse a "wanton" poetics: undisciplined, unbound by "custom," full of desire—a poetry that is "wantin'" and hence creates that which is "of taste to please / True appetite." Milton's customary pun on want/wanton initially suggests that both Eve and Eden "lack" a discipline that must be supplied by an external agency; the word "wanton," in fact, is used in the poem almost exclusively in connection with either Eve, Eden, or some other agent of feminine seduction.[68] John Guillory even suggests that Eve herself might be the agent of discipline, as she stands for both Edenic superfluity and the new domestic economy of frugal gardening.[69] For me, however, fruit-producing and fruit-picking are two versions of the same impulse: the impulse to make, and then to choose among, a multitude of possibilities. Lack, for Eve, promotes desire, so that we almost hear a prescient pun on "wanton/want" as "wish for" (even though this meaning of "want" seems not to have been in use until the turn of the eighteenth century).

Further, feminine desire connotes and propels a particular form of poetic effort. It is always the case in *Paradise Lost* that poetry might originate from a feminine source; and indeed, the Muse Urania takes on the aspect of a wife-as-bedmate to the poetic voice that at the beginning of Book 7 finds himself "yet not alone, while thou / Visit'st my slumbers Nightly, or when Morn / Purples the East" (7.28–30). He even implores her to be his poetic queen: "still govern thou my Song" (7.30).[70] With Eve and the Garden, however, we find further that feminine "governance" is a matter not of straight, or strait, direction, but of expansively exerted will. And this mode of invention, associated with feminine desire but *not* teleologically directed, is, we remember, precisely how Spenser, in the person of Britomart, designed romance as a creation of feminine authority. It is not the case—as Heather James argues—that Eve is associated with romance simply because she is figured as a text open to inexhaustible interpretation.[71] Rather, Eve's romance genre consists of her operating within a world of choice. As Patricia Parker puts it, Eve's tendencies (in diction repeatedly attached to her) either to "stay" or to "stray" associate her with the realm of "evening," a middle state between darkness and light that is analogous to the stage of reading in which signs have not yet been assigned their singular, "true" meaning. Neither "staying" nor "straying" will lead one, quest-like, to the foreordained end of revelation.[72] Rather, each leads to the kind of unlimited, laterally spread perspective that—more than Satan's promise of goddesshood, in my view—appeals to Eve in her dream: "The Earth outstretcht immense, a prospect wide / And various" (5.88–89). This is the wide prospect into which Adam and Eve venture at the end of the poem, with the enjambment of the closing lines emphasizing it as an open vista of infinite choice: "The World was all before them, where to choose / Thir place of rest, and Providence thir guide" (12.646–47). Divine guidance now appears not in the form of Michael divulging the ends of human history, but rather in the form of the much less determinative (and perhaps even self-chosen) "Providence," a word that carries the limitless bounty of Eden even into the "subjected plain" of their future habitation (12.640).

Against Stanley Fish's influential reading of *Paradise Lost*, in which even poetry itself is a mode of fallen knowledge that must be superseded and discarded as the reader moves closer to revelation, Parker calls the romance mode of the poem, its non-revelatory poetry, a necessary and even desirable state of being, both for poetry and for the human beings whom the poetry describes: "The decisive level [in *Paradise Lost*] remains the moral one, the interval of temptation and trial: the dramatic locus of paradise regained is not Paradise but the wilderness, the counterpart of the 'woody maze' of romance."[73] Quint, in turn, emphasizes "the *political* ramifications of this in-between ground of romance: it allows the poem to enact—at the level of its narrative structure—an Arminian middle way that avoids the all or nothing extremes of Calvinist orthodoxy and preserves the liberty of its human protagonists."[74] Republican liberty, like the genre of romance, is radically contingent; governed as it is by the will of individuals, the republican state, like the romance mode, generally doesn't know where it's heading. This feminine poetic wandering may, in fact, be the way to grace, a way to reapprehend Paradise.[75] It is Eve, after all, who first takes on the labor of reconciling herself with Adam and then assumes the poetic persona of Orpheus as she, reversing Adam's gesture as he first called her to him in Book 4, recalls the spouse who has turned away (4.480–82, 10.909–36).[76] But she goes Orpheus one better, as she does indeed usher herself and her spouse out of the depths of despair and into the wide world. Romance and feminine authority are reunited and revitalized in their newly healed wedlock.

As has often been noted about *Paradise Lost*, the poem's conclusion is one of romance, as Adam and Eve "with wand'ring steps and slow" proceed digressively into the uncertainties of the future.[77] And yet oddly, though in much-mediated fashion, this romance that Eve has caused to come into being is the product of monarchy, not of feminine submission: the monarchy of a Virgin Queen, the queen who took her solitary way. Dryden observed that *Paradise Lost* ends where *The Faerie Queene* begins, with Adam as a "knight . . . wander[ing] through the world with his lady errant"; but the connection to Spenser is even stronger than this.[78] Milton's last Spenserian allusion in *Paradise Lost* calls to mind, very faintly, the remembrance of queens past: just as Spenser closed *The Faerie Queene* by invoking Elizabeth's name—Eli-sabbath, "God's rest"—in hopes of "rest[ing] eternally / With Him that is the God of Sabbaoth hight" (*Faerie Queene* 7.8.2), Milton sends Adam and Eve out in quest of their own sabbath, "Thir place of rest" (12.647). There is, however, an important difference in these two conclusions. Spenser decapitates his queen's name in order to clear away the possibility of feminine, romantic mutability and prepare for an unchanging "Sabaoths sight," an epic view of the angelic host. Milton, in contrast, identifies that place of rest with an infinitude—through an infinitive—of earthly choice: "where *to choose* / Thir place of rest" (12.646–47, my emphasis). Elizabeth's sovereign virginity, which sponsors the freedom of the Lady's mind in the *Mask* then metamorphoses into the "Virgin Fancies" of *Paradise Lost*'s "wanton" Nature and equally "wanton" Eve, now becomes the will and the imagination, the "Fancy," required to make a choice. In our search for subjectivity in *Paradise Lost*, we can find Elizabeth herself as predecessor monarch of the paradise within.

Afterword

Queenship and New Feminine Genres

MY CONSIDERATION OF QUEENSHIP as a model (or countermodel) for literary experiment has traversed nearly a hundred years of literary history, and I would like nothing better than to be able to say that the experiment continues, that female authority continues to be a touchstone for the way new kinds of writing are conceived. Women writers, in particular, might stand to benefit from a revaluation of the associations between femininity, authority, and literary imagination.

We have to ask ourselves, however, when such a revaluation might have occurred. During Elizabeth's lifetime, there does not seem to have been much to be gained by a woman's attaching her literary production to the phenomenon of a female ruler. Elizabeth's own stance of exceptionality—in which her wisdom, her learning, her self-possession were not the lot of ordinary women, only of one extraordinary one—left little room for other women who wished to be exceptional in composing themselves as authors. Mary Sidney Herbert's "Dialogue between Two Shepherds, Thenot and Piers, In Praise of Astrea" (published in Francis Davison's *Poetical Rhapsody* [1602]), a wonderfully tongue-in-cheek mockery of the Spenserian-style pastoral paean to Elizabeth, underscores the point. Thenot, who undertakes a stereotypically lavish praise of the Queen, is repeatedly identified by his singing partner, Piers, as a habitual prevaricator:

Thenot. I sing divine Astrea's praise;
   O Muses! help my wits to raise,
   And heave my verses higher.
Piers. Thou need'st the truth but plainly tell,
   Which much I doubt thou canst not well,
   Thou art so oft a liar.

Praising Elizabeth so extremely plays right into the presumption that a
poet everything affirms, and therefore always lies—a surefire way for a
woman's writing to be dismissed as idle fantasy. Having reprimanded
Thenot for his continuing hyperbole, Piers proceeds to discount poetic
imagination entirely: "Words from conceit do only rise; / Above conceit
her honour flies: / But silence, nought can praise her."[1] As in Merlin's recitation of Elizabeth's genealogy in Book 3 of *The Faerie Queene*, here the
presence of Elizabeth leads to an end that is "nought." The rest is silence.

The window of opportunity for women writers to profit by association with female rule seems to have coincided, in large part, with the era
of most intense nostalgia for queenship that I delineated in Chapter 6:
the Commonwealth period, in which Elizabeth was frequently held up
as a model of personal and national rectitude. Anne Bradstreet's poetic
elegy of the Queen (dated "1643" in her 1650 volume of poems, *The Tenth
Muse*) delights in Elizabeth's exceptionalism precisely because the queen's
worth excuses Bradstreet's own writing. After declaring herself, like Mary
Sidney's Piers, unable to relate the queen's "personal perfections" ("Which
I may not, my pride doth but aspire / To read what others write and so
admire"), Bradstreet makes an abrupt volte-face to claim, through Elizabeth's example, the very mental faculties that are patently in play as she
writes this elegy:

> Now say, have women worth? or have they none?
> Or had they some, but with our Queen is't gone?
> Nay masculines, you have thus taxed us long,
> But she, though dead, will vindicate our wrong.
> Let such as say our sex is void of reason,
> Know 'tis a slander now but once was treason.[2]

Bradstreet's poem is an important early example of what Catherine Gallagher describes as a significant wrinkle in the history of early feminism:
women writers' looking to monarchy as a source not of subjection but of
liberty, in that monarchy provides an exemplum for a woman's subjectivity,
her sovereignty over her own mind.[3] Elizabeth "hath wiped off th' aspersion of her sex," declares Bradstreet, "That women wisdom lack to play the
rex" (196). The remark that Elizabeth *played* the rex is an interesting one,
however, since it signals Bradstreet's recognition that both monarchy and
reason itself are a matter not just of fiction, but of a feminine, theatrical fiction, with all its connotations of falsehood and changeability. Bradstreet's

attaching herself to Elizabeth, in other words, is a precursor to the customary practice of Tory women writers like Margaret Cavendish and Aphra Behn, who, Gallagher argues, paradoxically derive from their disempowered *male* monarch Charles II—disempowered in exile but also in his restored kingdom, where he was saddled with debt—a sense of feminine autonomy and writerly identity, even though it is an identity based on lack.[4]

Behn's affiliations between herself and a feminized monarch are also assimilated, Gallagher asserts, to the role of the female writer—specifically, the female playwright—as a prostitute, who creates and engages in erotic literary play for financial gain. This is a compelling argument; but in that case,Behn would be the final writer in England, in my view, to amalgamate a feminized monarchy with literary creation as the spinning out of endless sensual pleasures. For Bradstreet, as for most seventeenth-century admirers of the late Elizabeth, a rogue feminine sexuality drops out of the picture, and hence out of the association between queenship and authorship. And once the queen has been de-eroticized, as I argued at the end of Chapter 5, she can be dethroned from her position at the locus of literary creativity. In the place of Queen Hermione, whose language and imagination are equally sexually eager and whose resurrection embodies the life-giving capacities of theater, we are given Princess Perdita, whose productive capacities will be strictly limited to the reproduction of children.

As the seventeenth century turns into the eighteenth, developments in both philosophy and medicine encourage what the end of *The Winter's Tale* anticipates: the abandonment of the notion of the feminine mind as a source of powerful, fascinating, perhaps even dangerous fictions. Descartes' definition of the mind as that which has no substance degenders it; and meanwhile, advances in the understanding of human anatomy begin to debunk the theory that all human bodies, as well as the minds that inhabit them, are liable to degrade into a feminine state of being.[5] In the Restoration and beyond, then, queen's bodies became babymaking apparatuses— one thinks of the poor, overweight Queen Anne's nineteen pregnancies— not sites of spectacular erotic attraction. Or if they inspire erotic attraction, the erotic fictions that are created thereby are managed by the masculine minds who make them. One outstanding example illustrates what I mean here: Dryden's *All for Love* (1678), which in its rewriting of Shakespeare's Cleopatra emphasizes her beauty at the expense of her imagination, to the point of reassigning her best dialogue of speculative fiction-making to male characters. (Hence beginning a tradition that continues to this day, I have argued elsewhere, in film adaptations of *Antony and Cleopatra*.)[6] It is

Antony's Roman friend Ventidius, for example, who describes him in the terms of Cleopatra's "Emperor Antony" speech ("Could'st thou but make new Worlds, so wouldst thou give 'em / As bounty were thy being"); and it is Antony's friend Dolabella who prompts from Antony a formerly Cleopatran remembrance of legendary love ("we were so mixt, / As meeting streams, both to our selves were lost"). Meanwhile Cleopatra, whose actions throughout the play are entirely manipulated by her eunuch Alexas, disclaims fiction-making skill of any kind: "Nature meant me / A Wife, a silly harmless houshold Dove, / Fond without art."[7]

Cleopatra's labelling herself "a silly harmless houshold Dove" points to the other way in which queenship no longer proves important to literary innovation after the Restoration. The eighteenth and nineteenth centuries' major new innovation is, of course, the novel: a pointedly nonaristocratic form, but also a domestic form. Nancy Armstrong and Leonard Tennenhouse, in fact, trace the evolution of the novel from *Paradise Lost*, describing Milton's poem in ways that correspond to some of my assertions in Chapter 6. Eve's mode of domestic, commonplace knowledge, they argue, becomes the salvation of humankind.[8] But the domesticity that the novel form derives from *Paradise Lost* is a domesticity without Eve's sexualized imaginative force behind it. Eventually, in Armstrong's and Tennenhouse's view, *Paradise Lost*'s privileging of the female subject emerges in the trials of Pamela, who (like the Lady in *A Mask*) possesses an independent will precisely because her body resists all kinds of erotic desire.[9]

If Milton helps invent the novel, then, his invention forgets its creator's deployment of a peculiarly sixteenth-century mode of female rule as the model for independent human will. But since *Paradise Lost* is a poem that designs itself as belated, we should not be surprised that it does not whole-cloth take on the mantle of the avant-garde.[10] Indeed, the closing of *Paradise Lost* fashions the whole of human history as a product of Miltonic nostalgia. Hence Milton is, truly, the last Elizabethan: nostalgia for the queen finds its final resting place, so to speak, in the "place of rest" for which our first parents seek. In terms of literary form as well as of English history, reviving feminine authority as Spenser, Shakespeare, and Milton have inhabited it would mean living in the past. Or, as Bradstreet puts it,

> But happiness lies in a higher sphere,
> Then wonder not Eliza moves not here.
> Full fraught with honor, riches and with days

She set, she set, like Titan in his rays.
No more shall rise or set so glorious sun
Until the heaven's great revolution;
If then new things their old forms shall retain,
Eliza shall rule Albion again.

(198)

Notes

Chapter 1: Forms of Queenship

1. Stephen Greenblatt, *Renaissance Self-Fashioning*, 167.

2. Spenser's portrayal of Elizabeth, Montrose argues, "suggests the dialectic by which poetic power helps to create and sustain the political power to which it is subservient" (Louis Montrose, " 'Eliza, Queene of shepheardes,' and the Pastoral of Power," 168).

3. Louis Montrose, *The Purpose of Playing*, 160. I quote from the most recent and revised version of Montrose's work on *A Midsummer Night's Dream*, which was published in 1983 as " 'Shaping Fantasies': Figurations of Gender and Power in Elizabethan Culture," and in revised form in 1986 as "*A Midsummer Night's Dream* and the Shaping Fantasies of Elizabethan Culture: Gender, Power, Form." For Montrose's explication of a similar reciprocity between poet and queen in *The Shepheardes Calender* and *The Faerie Queene*, see "The Elizabethan Subject and the Spenserian Text."

4. For Lavinia as Queen Elizabeth, see Leonard Tennenhouse, *Power on Display*, 106–12; for Joan of Arc as Elizabeth, see Leah Marcus, *Puzzling Shakespeare*, 51–105; for Amoret as Elizabeth, see Susan Frye, *Elizabeth I*, 122–24; for Radigund as Elizabeth, see Mary Villeponteaux, " 'Not as women wonted be': Spenser's Amazon Queen."

5. Tennenhouse, *Power on Display*, 6.

6. I should emphasize that this critical viewpoint has produced several fine studies of Elizabethan literature, including especially Susan Frye's *Elizabeth I*. For an excellent analysis of how English Renaissance theater portrayed anxious masculinity's fear of reverting to femininity, see Laura Levine, *Men in Women's Clothing*.

7. See, for example, Richard Helgerson, *Forms of Nationhood*, for commentary on jurisprudence's and cartography's relation to the crown.

8. Edmund Plowden, *The Commentaries, or Reports*, 213a; quoted in Ernst Kantorowicz, *The King's Two Bodies*, 9–10.

9. For a literary analysis that turns on this aspect of the king's two bodies see, for example, Leah Marcus, "Shakespeare's Comic Heroines, Elizabeth I, and the Political Uses of Androgyny." Marcus delineates how "[Elizabeth's] participation in the undying principle of kingship outranks [her subjects'] masculinity" (139). See also Allison Heisch, "Queen Elizabeth I: Parliamentary Rhetoric and the Exercise of Power," for Elizabeth's evocation of a kingly self in her speeches to Parliament. In *The Poem's Two Bodies*, David Lee Miller reads the allegory of *The Faerie Queene* according to the doctrine of the king's two bodies; in this case, the

body natural is the imperfect present moment of allegorical reading, and the body politic is the anticipated closure of perfect reading, as well as of perfect individual and corporate being, to which the poem directs its readers.

10. Frye, *Elizabeth I*, 13. Frye goes on to detail how the queen's profession of virginity similarly contributed to a unique conception of what must have seemed an oxymoron, female monarchy (15–16 and passim).

11. Plowden, *The Commentaries, or Reports*, 212a; quoted in Kantorowicz, *The King's Two Bodies*, 7; see Marie Axton, *The Queen's Two Bodies*, 11–37. Plowden articulated the king's two bodies theory most clearly in a manuscript defending Mary, Queen of Scots's claim to the English throne entitled *A treatise of the two Bodies of the king, vis. natural and politic . . . The whole intending to prove the title of Mary Quene of Scotts to the succession of the crown of England and that the Scots are not out of the allegiance of England* (Axton, *The Queen's Two Bodies*, 19).

12. Henry VIII's will excluded the descendants of his older sister, Margaret Tudor, and hence the entire Scots succession that led to James VI of Scotland's ascending the English throne as James I. Edward VI ignored his father's will to exclude his own sisters, Mary and Elizabeth Tudor, from the throne, in favor of his cousin, Jane Grey. Both Henry's and Edward's decisions had the force of removing Roman Catholics, among others, from the line of succession.

13. Christopher Goodman, *How Superior Powers Oght to Be Obeyd*, D2v. The force of Goodman's argument is made clear in his own retraction of his book, made after his return to England, in which he more or less predicts the fate of monarchy under Charles I: "I do protest and confess, that good and godly women may lawfully govern whole realms and nations. . . . Neither did I ever mean to affirm, that any person or persons of their own private authority ought or might lawfully have punished queen Mary [Tudor] with death: nor that the people of their own authority may lawfully punish their magistrates, transgressing the Lord's precepts" (John Strype, *Annals of the Reformation and Establishment of Religion*, 1:185).

14. Lily B. Campbell, ed., *A Mirror for Magistrates*, 420. First published in 1559, *A Mirror for Magistrates* appeared in augmented editions in 1563, 1578, and 1587. The quoted text, which first appeared in the 1563 edition, is from an address "To the Reader" that follows the verse tragedy "The Blacksmith," whose moral ("To the Reader") is "to teach all people as well offycers as subjectes to . . . lyve in love and obedience to the hygheste powers, whatsoever they be, whom god eyther by byrth, lawe, succession, or universal eleccion, doth or shall aucthorise" (419). For queenship's role in furthering the cause of Parliamentary rule, see Constance Jordan, *Renaissance Feminism*, 131–33.

15. John Aylmer, *An Harborowe for Faithfull and Trewe Subjectes*, H3r-v.

16. Nina S. Levine, *Women's Matters*, 15.

17. C. H. McIlwain, *The High Court of Parliament*, 389, quoted in Kantorowicz, *The King's Two Bodies*, 21. David Norbrook disputes the plausibility of Kantorowicz's conclusions here, based on the fact that the document Kantorowicz cites does not refer to the king's "body" per se ("The Emperor's New Body?"). I think Norbrook is splitting hairs here, although his argument that the Parliamentary forces in the Civil War did not frequently or consistently invoke the king's two bodies theory as a way of opposing the king is an important one. Norbrook's larger

point is that new historicism, in its fondness for employing Kantorowicz's argument, unwittingly buys into Kantorowicz's idea of the mystical union of the king's body natural and body politic—and hence buys into an absolutist paradigm that, for example, discounts the republican ideologies behind the English Revolution. But Norbrook, like Kantorowicz, fails to consider the Elizabethan circumstances of female monarchy surrounding the king's two bodies theory, origins that promote the severance of the body politic and body natural over their mystical union.

18. Jane Tylus proposes a more general version of this assertion by exploring the conditions—economic, social, and gendered—of "vulnerability" experienced by Renaissance writers from Cellini to Corneille: "late Renaissance writers are aware not only of their own historical vulnerability, but of ways in which they might use their vulnerability and that of others to their advantage" (*Writing and Vulnerability in the Late Renaissance*, 6).

19. Philip Sidney, *A Defence of Poetry*, in *Miscellaneous Prose of Sir Philip Sidney*, 110.

20. Richard Helgerson, *Self-Crowned Laureates*, 3.

21. Harold Bloom, *The Anxiety of Influence*. The phenomenon of the continual shifting and regrouping of literary form is what encourages me *not* to apply a precise taxonomy to the broad outlines of form—epic, romance, history, tragedy—that I discuss in this study. For the flexibility of form in Renaissance literature, see Rosalie Colie, *The Resources of Kind*.

22. Raphael Falco, *Conceived Presences*.

23. See, e.g., Fredric Jameson, who argues that the romance mode comes about as a means of repressing the uncomfortable pressures of the historical present (*The Political Unconscious*, 103–50); my discussion of *The Faerie Queene* in Chapter 2 incorporates Jameson's theory. Annabel Patterson understands the Renaissance's creation of new genres and adaptation of old ones as a response to the perceived restrictions of a particular historical pressure, censorship (*Censorship and Interpretation*, 128–240). For a fine recent study of Renaissance literature that turns on Jameson's theory of the cultural work of literary form, see Rosemary Kegl, *The Rhetoric of Concealment*.

24. See Wendy Wall, *The Imprint of Gender*, 14–16.

25. See Gail Kern Paster, *The Body Embarrassed*, 45–46, 52.

26. See Thomas Laqueur, *Making Sex*, 25–113.

27. Indeed, Richard Rambuss points out the folly of classifying bodies represented in literature as either "masculine" or "feminine" based on those bodies' possessing or not possessing penetrable orifices ("Pleasure and Devotion: The Body of Jesus and Seventeenth-Century Religious Lyric").

28. In *Inescapable Romance*, Patricia Parker details the qualities of deferral and dilation inherent in the romance mode, qualities that Parker in a later study connects with Renaissance theories of lyric as effeminizing (Parker, *Literary Fat Ladies*, 54–66). For the feminine qualities of lyric and the ways in which twentieth-century critics have often reproduced Renaissance critics' misogynistic disdain for the lyric form, see Diana Henderson, *Passion Made Public*, 14–21.

29. Parker, *Literary Fat Ladies*, 244 n. 7; quoting Ludovico Ariosto, *Orlando Furioso*, trans. Sir John Harington, 14–15.

30. Stephen Gosson, *The School of Abuse*, quoted in Laura Levine, *Men in Women's Clothing*, 10. Levine's book is an excellent discussion of the prospect of theater as effeminizing agent; I discuss this topic further in Chapters 3 and 5 below.

31. Thomas Nashe, *Pierce Penilesse, His Supplication to the Divell*, in *The Works of Thomas Nashe*, 2:212.

32. Catherine Gallagher, *Nobody's Story*.

33. Poems by Elizabeth I first appeared in *The Norton Anthology of English Literature* beginning with the fifth edition in 1986. Mary, Queen of Scots's poems were written in French and thus are excluded from consideration for such anthologies (although one might argue that early Scots writers in general are slighted in standard anthologies of British literature).

34. For a cogent and concise summation of such critiques see Steven Mullaney, "After the New Historicism," especially 31–33.

35. Timothy Hampton, *Writing from History*.

36. Richard Halpern, in one of the most subtle critiques of the monarchocentrism of early new-historicist studies, argues that their focus is necessarily only partial, given that their juridico-political model draws attention only to relations "between unequal hierarchical subjects" (*The Poetics of Primitive Accumulation*, 3). Halpern is attentive to exchanges of economic and cultural capital that involve perhaps only latent, and certainly not always coercive, modes of domination. My concern is similarly to focus on those literary moments in which the relation between author and female monarch transforms into something other than subjection.

37. Henderson, *Passion Made Public*, 113. Philippa Berry's study of the various crises of masculinity proposed by Elizabethan love poetry includes one chapter on John Lyly, whose pastoral courtly comedies (e.g., *Endymion: or the Man in the Moon* and *Gallathea*) redefine courtship as contemplation and hence construct certain alliances between male courtly authorship and feminized pastimes, if not feminine power (Philippa Berry, *Of Chastity and Power*, 111–33). Most of Berry's study, however, describes male authors as developing a masculine style in resentment toward and defiance of their queen.

38. Leah Marcus, *Puzzling Shakespeare*, 1–50.

39. See especially Montrose, " 'Eliza, Queene of shepheardes' and the Pastoral of Power."

40. See Jenny Wormold, *Mary Queen of Scots*, 167–89.

41. For Elizabeth's being accused of sexual licentiousness see James E. Phillips, *Images of a Queen*, 143–97; and Carole Levin, *The Heart and Stomach of a King*, 65–90.

42. The Scots lords who deposed Mary maintained the fiction that she had voluntarily resigned the throne to her son (Wormold, *Mary Queen of Scots*, 174–75). For a fascinating account of how one of Elizabeth's own chaplains, Richard Fletcher (who had preached before Mary at her execution), admonished Elizabeth about her duty to commit a fellow monarch to death, see Peter E. McCullough, "Out of Egypt: Richard Fletcher's Sermon Before Elizabeth I after the Execution of Mary Queen of Scots."

43. Nancy Armstrong and Leonard Tennenhouse, *The Imaginary Puritan*, 7.

44. Harry Berger, Jr., "Sneak's Noise, or, Rumor and Detextualization in *2 Henry IV*," in *Making Trifles of Terrors*, 130.

45. For a comprehensive account and analysis of English Renaissance notions of women's myriad faults, see Linda Woodbridge, *Women and the English Renaissance*.

46. *The deceyte of women, to the instruction and ensample of all men, yonge and old*, K2r.

Chapter 2: Genre and the Repeal of Queenship in Spenser's Faerie Queene

1. A. C. Hamilton, *The Structure of Allegory in "The Faerie Queene,"* 170, 173. Hamilton's sentiments are echoed by Michael O'Connell, who takes care to distinguish between the remainder of the poem's historical *allusion* and Book 5's historical *allegory*, which features "an almost obsessive desire to celebrate and defend the policies of Elizabeth" (*Mirror and Veil*, 13).

2. Hamilton himself attempts to rescue Book 5 from history by asserting that "[t]he last three cantos are distanced from fact by the increasing element of fairy tale . . . and the obvious emphasis on the ideal" (*The Structure of Allegory*, 190). I will discuss below the question of these cantos' adherence to and departure from the historical record. Critics since Hamilton have similarly tried to massage the last cantos of Book 5 into an idealized form. T. K. Dunseath extends a traditional moral interpretation of the poem into an analysis of Book 5's character development, arguing that its final cantos crown the moral development of Artegall, who gives up pride, wrath, and concupiscence to be worthy to redeem Irena (*Spenser's Allegory of Justice*, 17–140). Jane Aptekar unifies her analysis of Book 5 by tracing the recurrence of certain iconographic patterns; for example, Hercules is the heroic prototype for both Artegall and Arthur (*Icons of Justice*, 153–71). Angus Fletcher defends the historical episodes as culminating an idealized progression of legal codification and imperial absolutism (*The Prophetic Moment*, 135–214). Kenneth Borris asserts that Spenser's apocalyptic imagery critiques English ecclesiastic and social institutions (*Spenser's Poetics of Prophecy in "The Faerie Queene"s*). But Borris's reliance on reading Spenser in conjunction with non-Spenserian projections, in sixteenth-century historiography and topical allegory, of apocalyptic success leads him to depict an optimistic Spenser whose fiction overgoes the worrisome failure of those endeavors in the present moment.

3. Studies of Spenser and Ireland have proliferated in recent years; see Willy Maley, "Spenser and Ireland: An Annotated Bibliography, 1986–96," as well as two major post-1996 studies: Maley, *Salvaging Spenser*; and Christopher Highley, *Shakespeare, Spenser, and the Crisis in Ireland*. The other historical episodes of the last five cantos have received less attention; important studies include David Norbrook, *Poetry and Politics in the English Renaissance*, 109–56; Richard McCabe, "The Masks of Duessa: Spenser, Mary Queen of Scots, and James VI"; and Jonathan Goldberg, *James I and the Politics of Literature*, 1–17.

4. See, for example, Maureen Quilligan, "The Comedy of Female Authority in *The Faerie Queene*"; Mihoko Suzuki, *Metamorphoses of Helen*, 178–209; Mary R.

Bowman, " 'she there as Princess rained': Spenser's Figure of Elizabeth"; Sheila T. Cavanagh, *Wanton Eyes and Chaste Desires*, 167–71; Mary Villeponteaux, " 'Not as women wonted be': Spenser's Amazon Queen"; Susanne Woods, "Amazonian Tyranny: Spenser's Radigund and Diachronic Mimesis"; and Susanne Woods, "Spenser and the Problem of Women's Rule." In the latter essay, Woods disputes James E. Phillips's view that Spenser conformed to Calvin's position that women might rule only if ordained to that position by God (Phillips, "The Background of Spenser's Attitude Toward Women Rulers" and "The Woman Ruler in Spenser's *Faerie Queene*"). In an important treatment of this episode, Clare Carroll bridges historicist and feminist perspectives by arguing that Artegall's imprisonment reveals Spenser's critique of Elizabeth's "womanish" policies toward Ireland, as well as of the "Old English" (Anglo-Normans) who have been enthralled by the barbarous Irish; see "The Construction of Gender and the Cultural and Political Other in *The Faerie Queene* 5 and *A View of the Present State of Ireland*," as well as Carroll's consideration of other sixteenth-century authors' views on the subject, "Representations of Women in Some Early Modern English Tracts on the Colonization of Ireland." Also see Highley's discussion of how Spenser and other English officials in Ireland resented their female sovereign (*Spenser, Shakespeare, and the Crisis in Ireland*, 110–33).

5. An important exception is Richard Rambuss, who briefly addresses the second mode of Book 5 as a critical response to the first (*Spenser's Secret Career*, 107–14); I discuss Rambuss's readings below.

6. "Degendered" and "degenerated," along with "degenered," were interchangeably available usages in the late sixteenth century.

7. Sigmund Freud, "Medusa's Head," in *The Standard Edition of the Complete Psychological Works of Sigmund Freud*, 18:273–74. Rambuss also focuses upon 5.Pr.2 as anticipating Spenser's critique of feminine authority (*Spenser's Secret Career*, 109–10).

8. Fredric Jameson, *The Political Unconscious*, 103–59.

9. Jameson, *The Political Unconscious*, 148.

10. Harry Berger, Jr., " 'Kidnapped Romance': Discourse in *The Faerie Queene*." Building on Northrop Frye's account in *The Secular Scripture* of romance as a genre "kidnapped" by the ascendant Protestant revolution, Berger describes *The Faerie Queene* as a poem that reveals its own kidnapping of the discourses it uses, and through that revelation analyzes and critiques both those discourses and the historical moment that demands them. Berger warns us that "the poem does not always maintain its critical distance but frequently weakens, melts, embraces the kidnapped forms. The fluid variations between distance and embrace are, however, consistently sustained within the perspective of analysis and critique, and this means that whenever embrace dominates, the critique becomes reflexive" (237).

11. David Underdown suggests that the English obsession with assertive women in the early modern period resulted at least in part from women's increasing participation in capitalist endeavors; see "The Taming of the Scold: The Enforcement of Patriarchal Authority in Early Modern England."

12. Patricia Parker, *Inescapable Romance*.

13. Patricia Parker, *Literary Fat Ladies*, 65.

14. For Guyon's destruction of the Bower as a simultaneous imposition of civilization over disorder, and iconoclasm over beauteous poetic art, see Stephen Greenblatt, *Renaissance Self-Fashioning*, 170–92.

15. Sir Richard Blackmore, preface to *Prince Arthur, an Heroicke Poem* (1695), quoted in John Watkins, *The Specter of Dido*, 1, emphasis in original.

16. Richard Helgerson, *Forms of Nationhood*, 40–59.

17. David Quint, *Epic and Empire*, 9. Susanne Lindgren Wofford's thesis in *The Choice of Achilles* complements Quint's in that Wofford finds in epic tropes potential challenges to the epic value of heroic action. Combining Wofford's and Quint's insights would imply that in the epic, tropes belong (at least potentially) to the losers—and by extension, for my purposes, that the micro-units that make up the poem, from single words to individual stanzas, are ripe for investigating how the poem builds identification with the usually disesteemed feminine.

18. For a study of how the representation of female characters disrupts the norms of epic, in the process redefining the author's relation to political authority and poetic predecessors, see Suzuki, *Metamorphoses of Helen*. Elizabeth J. Bellamy describes the "epic versus romance" paradigm in terms of a Lacanian psychoanalytic model in which "epic expresses the urge to situate the hero in the cultural order of the Symbolic" and "romance seemingly remains suspended on the threshold of ego formation, at the point of the denial of castration" (*Translations of Power*, 29). Bellamy goes on to analyze the traces of romance within epic as a kind of "narrative unconscious within epic history" (*Translations of Power*, 32).

19. Watkins, *The Specter of Dido*, 8.

20. Bellamy, *Translations of Power*, 221–33. David Lee Miller, who reads the 1590 *Faerie Queene* after the model of the queen's two bodies—one "natural," imperfect, and prone to error and deferral, and one "politic," perfect, and typologically conclusive—reads this breach as potentially, if not actually fulfilled by Arthur, who "is invested with the function of converting [this] negative moment" (*The Poem's Two Bodies*, 203). Miller recognizes the "radical imperfection" of the break in *Briton moniments*, but declares that "[i]f Arthur 'perfects' this imperfect history by responding to it properly (st. 69) and by mightily upholding the royal mace in his turn (st. 4), then his conversion of the past into the future will be in effect a conversion of successiveness into success" (206). That *if* is a momentous one; unlike Miller, I do not find that the stanzas in question justify even a hope of *conditional* success for Arthur.

21. Jon A. Quitslund, message to the "Spenser-L" electronic discussion list, December 11, 1996; available at the Spenser-L Archive, http://darkwing.uoregon. edu/~rbear/archive1.btxt.

22. The OED does not cite "plot" as meaning "literary plan" before 1649; nevertheless, the sense remains that Glauce and Britomart are proceeding according to baroque design.

23. John Guillory identifies Britomart's vision of Artegall as a moment of danger for Spenser, in that it proposes poetry as something other than mere mimesis and hence displaces the poet's privileged vatic role (*Poetic Authority*, 37). I would add that the moment of imaginative invention is marked out as even more dangerous in its originating from a female mind. For a provocative reading of Alma's castle

(Book 2, Cantos 9–11) in terms of its investment not in masculine rationality but in feminine wandering thought, see Dorothy Stephens, "'Newes of devils': Feminine Sprights in Masculine Minds in *The Faerie Queene*." For the alliances between Britomart's improvisational actions and story-telling skills and Spenser's own narrative technique in Book 3, see Lauren Silberman, *Transforming Desire*, 19–21.

24. Quilligan, *Milton's Spenser*, 191–94; and Silberman, "Singing Unsung Heroines: Androgynous Discourse in Book 3 of *The Faerie Queene*." Silberman's later work is less sanguine about the Garden's inclusive incorporation of male and female dualism; see *Transforming Desire*, 35–48.

25. Jonathan Goldberg, *Endlesse Worke*, 11. Silberman, like Goldberg, reads Book 4 as culminating in a delightful play of textual signification (*Transforming Desire*, 130–36).

26. Harry Berger, Jr., "Actaeon at the Hinder Gate: The Stag Party in Spenser's Gardens of Adonis." In this essay Berger cautions that what looks to Quilligan like a female perspective in Book 3's Garden is actually a "peculiarly male perspective of the narrative occasionally addressed to female readers to whose interests it is clearly sympathetic" (109). Silberman's recent work also emphasizes the Garden's riskiness; see *Transforming Desire*, 40–48.

27. For an interesting reading of Argante as a parody both of the Faery Queen and of Elizabeth herself, see Judith H. Anderson, "Arthur, Argante, and the Ideal Vision: An Exercise in Speculation and Parody."

28. Berger, "Actaeon at the Hinder Gate," 115.

29. Quilligan, *Milton's Spenser*, 198.

30. Only in the Cambell-Cambina, Triamond-Canacee union is the wedding vow itself included: the couples are "Allide with bands of mutuall couplement" (4.3.52). The rivers' wedding, for its part, seems to stop after the bridal procession; no vows are taken. Richard Mallette has suggested to me that the Cambelline marriage tetrad is stabilized, as is the Poeana-Squire marriage, by its absorption of desire for the Same rather than the Other—for one's sibling or one's same-sex friend.

31. The wishful thinking that is most evident at the end of Book 3, of course, belongs not to Britomart but to Busirane, who constructs representation as a matter of masculine sexual violence. For an analysis of the House of Busirane as a scenario of rapine poetics, see Susan Frye, "Of Chastity and Violence: Elizabeth I and Edmund Spenser in the House of Busirane."

32. Dorothy Stephens has argued that Book 4 does indeed offer a space for women expressing and exerting their will—the space of their (sometimes erotic) friendships with one another; see "Into Other Arms: Amoret's Evasion." Stephens's readings of Amoret's confidences with Britomart and, in Lust's Cave, with Aemylia are sensitive and persuasive, but I must disagree with her assertion that this short-term clearing of a wholly feminine space of will troubles patriarchy on more than a local level.

33. Since Venus's Temple is portrayed in Canto 10, the canto that in each book of *The Faerie Queene* typically offers an educative or sacred vision, it is particularly ironic that Venus's appearance is one not of revealing, but re-veiling.

34. For Artegall's implementation of *doome* see, for example, 5.1.12, 5.1.25, 5.1.29, 5.2.47, 5.3.35, 5.4.1, 5.4.16, and 5.4.20.

35. For Britomart's battle with Radigund as psychomachia, see Suzuki, *Metamorphoses of Helen*, 187–89; for the specific resemblances between the two women, see Bowman, "she there as Princess rained." Philippa Berry points out that the defeat of Radigund signifies a defeat of the female independence offered to women by the pre-Reformation religious life: "The historical Radegund was a sixth-century saint . . . . [who] became a nun on leaving the brutal Merovingian king she had been married to against her will, and later founded a famous monastery for women near Poitiers" (*Of Chastity and Power*, 162). Radigund's name thus puts her somewhat at odds with her desire for Artegall—a contradiction that argues even further for her equivalence to Britomart, another chaste Amazon who nevertheless has Artegall in mind.

36. Clare Regan Kinney, *Strategies of Poetic Narrative*, 84.

37. Dunseath, *Spenser's Allegory of Justice*, 142.

38. "Of the parts of Osiris's body the only one which Isis did not find was the male member, for the reason that this had been at once tossed into the river. . . . But Isis made a replica of the member to take its place, and consecrated the phallus, in honour of which the Egyptians even at the present day celebrate a festival" (Plutarch, "Of Isis and Osiris" 358, in *Plutarch's Moralia*, 5: 47).

39. Quilligan also notes that Britomart lays Radigund low first by a blow to the head, then by complete decapitation—acts that amount to "capital punishment for the usurping female ruler" who against all order becomes head of state ("The Comedy of Female Authority," 169). The catalogue of abused heads in Book 5 includes the decapitated lady of 5.1.18; the aptly named Pollente's "groome of euill guize," who both is bald himself and "pols and pils the poore in piteous wize" (5.2.6); and the ignominiously bareheaded Terpine (5.4.22), whom Radigund smites "on his head-peece" (5.4.40) and whom the Amazons eventually hang not by the neck, but "by the hed" (5.5.18). In such a crew, headbashing appropriately becomes the most common punishment for usurping authority. Radigund is not the only upstart either beheaded or otherwise beaten in the head: Artegall decapitates Pollente and raises his head on a pole (5.2.19), tilts the Paynim out of his saddle so that "on his head vnhappily he pight" (5.8.8), and finally beheads Grantorto (5.12.23). I discuss this last beheading below. For an ingenious but eccentric attempt to see Radigund's beheading as the last element in a detailed Spenserian allegory of Mary Queen of Scots's career from 1558 to 1571, see Donald V. Stump, "The Two Deaths of Mary Stuart: Historical Allegory in Spenser's Book of Justice."

40. The marriage canto ends with the promise that "when as time to *Artegall* shall tend, / We on his *first* aduenture may him forward send" (5.3.40, my emphasis). The next canto begins by reiterating the point: Artegall goes on "To follow his aduentures *first* intent, / Which *long agoe* he taken had in hond" (5.4.3, my emphases). After Artegall settles the dispute of Amidas and Bracidas, he once more "Departed on his way, as did befall, / To follow *his old quest*, the which him forth did call" (5.4.20, my emphasis). In the very next stanza, he encounters the Amazons.

41. Before Artegall defeats Adicia and her husband the Souldan, her crimes are described with no sexual valence: she merely counsels her husband "through confidence of might, / To break all bonds of law, and rules of right" (5.8.20).

42. Fletcher, *The Prophetic Moment*, 137.

43. Dunseath, *Spenser's Allegory of Justice*, 4.

44. Fletcher, *The Prophetic Moment*, 31, quoting Hazlitt's "Lectures on the English Poets" (1818).

45. Hamilton, *The Structure of Allegory*, 175. Hamilton acerbically notes of these monotonous reminders of Artegall's shield and how battered it is, "No wonder it is battered."

46. Norbrook, *Poetry and Politics*, 124.

47. Borris, *Spenser's Poetics of Prophecy*, 9.

48. Norbrook, *Poetry and Politics*, 33–36. For Leicester's radical Protestant sympathies and for Spenser's praise of Leicester in *The Shepheardes Calender*, see Norbrook, *Poetry and Politics*, 82–90. For a magisterial history of England's post-Armada war against Spain see Wallace T. MacCaffrey, *Elizabeth I: War and Politics, 1588–1603*, 73–302. MacCaffrey's account is indispensable for its detailing of how England's military exploits against Spain were from moment to moment fraught with a sense of failure or of impending disaster, even though by the late 1590s its aims on the Continent had been largely accomplished.

49. Whereas the massacre in Book 5 is commonly taken as merely fulfilling the genocidal policies in Spenser's *View of the Present State of Ireland*, Jonathan Goldberg astutely comments on the distinctions between the two: whereas both set out in open view the premises upon which sovereign power operates, the *View* describes those premises too unambiguously and thus could not be published; Book 5, on the other hand, hedges those premises with portrayals of their simultaneous justice/injustice, thus duplicating the internal contradictions upon which sovereign power depends and thus (ironically) allowing those contradictions to be promulgated (*James I*, 9–11). Like his reading of Duessa's trial (which I discuss below), however, Goldberg's description of Book 5's concluding battles tends too fully to totalize "power" and the poem's acquiescence in it; significantly, Goldberg does not discuss how Book 5's victories run along the lines of policies that Spenser's government did not advocate. Rambuss offers a convincing rebuttal to Goldberg in *Spenser's Secret Career*, 110–12. Norbrook reminds us, too, that in the 1590s even the defeat of the Armada did not seem the resounding victory for imperialist power that it does now (*Poetry and Politics*, 128–29).

50. Hamilton's note to 5.10.4 tells us that "thereto" refers to Duessa's being beheaded, but the text does not support this assumption. Emphasizing a beheading that the poem elides can lead to a skewed reading of the operations of authority in this episode: Goldberg, for example, asserts that the fact that "Duessa is beheaded all the same" despite Mercilla's show of pity demonstrates "the sustaining contradictions by which power is represented and by which it represents itself" (*James I*, 5), a reading that does not sufficiently address how this episode shows that power may work its will only when the feminine is overridden. History, however, may bear out Goldberg's reading more than *The Faerie Queene* does: Elizabeth, who was not above claiming feminine weakness when it suited her, delayed as long as she could in signing Mary Queen of Scots's death warrant; and after the deed had been done, she "declared that she had never meant to send it, that [second Secretary William] Davison had acted improperly in showing it to other councillors, and they in dispatching it" (J. E. Neale, *Queen Elizabeth I*, 291). Whether

Elizabeth's wrath was real or feigned, Mary's death was certainly something Elizabeth urgently desired, though she probably hoped that some loyal subject would covertly do the deed, in the time-honored tradition of Thomas à Becket or Shakespeare's Richard II (Neale, *Queen Elizabeth I*, 288–89).

51. R. B. Wernham, *The Making of Elizabethan Foreign Policy, 1558–1603*, 84.

52. Neale, *Queen Elizabeth I*, 351.

53. On Burghley's and Elizabeth's cautious approach to military action, see MacCaffrey, *Elizabeth I: War and Politics*, 555–72. For the discontents within the militant Protestant cause and the increasingly serious disputes within the court in the 1590s see, for example, MacCaffrey, *Elizabeth I: War and Politics*, 453–536; Patrick McGrath, *Papists and Puritans under Elizabeth I*, 299–338; and Simon Adams, "Faction, Clientage and Party: English Politics, 1550–1603." M. Lindsay Kaplan has argued convincingly that Spenser's depiction of Artegall as the "slandered" Lord Grey runs contrary to historical fact: Grey in fact made known to the court his urgent desire to be recalled, and went on to enjoy a prosperous career in England. Hence Spenser's portrayal of Artegall's recall has more to do with the poet's 1590s sense of frustrated politics and poetics than it does with a factual depiction of Grey's career in the 1580s (*The Culture of Slander in Early Modern England*, 34–63).

54. Henry Hooke, *Of the succession to the Crowne of England*. For further commentary on Hooke and on the English desire for kingship in the 1590s, see Chapter 3.

55. Highley, *Spenser, Shakespeare, and the Crisis in Ireland*, 110–33. For the problem of absentee monarchy in Ireland, see Maley, *Salvaging Spenser*, 99–117.

56. Paul Alpers has argued that Book 6 is conceived specifically as an alternative to heroic poetic form ("Spenser's Late Pastorals"). For a similar view see also Richard Helgerson, *Self-Crowned Laureates*, 82–100. Rambuss contends, in contrast, that Mount Acidale must be considered in conjunction with Calidore's mediation between public and private (courtly and pastoral) worlds, so that "[w]hat we find in Book 6 is a divided or doubled poetic persona, incorporating both the questing knight of the open, serendipitous romance world of the poem, and the retired shepherd of its closed, occluded pastoral domain" (*Spenser's Secret Career*, 123). Whether private or public, however, Book 6 is conspicuous in defining a poetic mode free from feminine determinations. Even if Mount Acidale is not a private matter at all, but rather continues to promote the colonization of a pastoral Ireland, as Robert E. Stillman has contended ("Spenserian Autonomy and the Trial of New Historicism: Book Six of *The Faerie Queene*"), then Spenser is continuing to advocate policies contrary to those of his queen.

57. For *The Shepheardes Calender*'s appropriation of Elizabeth, see Louis Montrose, "The Elizabethan Subject and the Spenserian Text." Thomas H. Cain analyzes in detail how the dance of the Graces in Book 6 appropriates Elizabeth's queenly symbology; see *Praise in "The Faerie Queene,"* 156–61. Elizabeth Bellamy regards Colin's non-naming of Elizabeth as merely another instance of *The Faerie Queene*'s replacement of Spenser's queen with a series of supplementary metonymies; for Bellamy, *The Faerie Queene*'s failure to address Elizabeth by her proper name both indicates and originates Spenser's vocational frustration, signified by the erosion

of the quest structure and the unfinishedness of the poem (Bellamy, "The Vocative and the Vocational: The Unreadability of Elizabeth in *The Faerie Queene*"). Bellamy seems to me correct concerning anxiety in earlier episodes at not revealing Elizabeth, but in this case Colin's confident replacement of Elizabeth with the country lass provides the poet with another *telos* superior to that of naming the queen.

58. Harry Berger, Jr., "Narrative as Rhetoric in *The Faerie Queene*," 11, 12, 41. Berger quotes Paul Alpers, *The Poetry of "The Faerie Queene*," 5.

59. For allegorical meaning as premature end, see Parker, *Inescapable Romance*, 98–100. Not that *The Faerie Queene* therefore proposes no allegory at all as a poetically satisfying alternative: as Quilligan has argued, part of the confusion about Book 6 is that its romance events have little allegorical referent and thus destroy *The Faerie Queene*'s "world of heightened significations" (*The Language of Allegory*, 170). Quilligan describes the complex allegory that Spenser generally commands as based on punning, on multiple but deftly controlled referentiality (*The Language of Allegory*, 25–96). But Wofford makes the point that Spenser's allegorical figuration aspires to an extratextual closure of meaning, even while "his poetics require that 'ends' . . . not be made accessible within the text" (*The Choice of Achilles*, 277).

60. Hamilton quotes William Blissett, "Spenser's Mutabilitie," 253.

61. Gordon Teskey, *Allegory and Violence*, 179. Blissett hypothesizes that *Mutabilitie*'s final stanzas are a kind of retraction; and though he does not say in so many words that what is retracted is Elizabeth's rule, he comes close: "what does the poet retract? The presumptuous and demonic in Ann [*sic*] Boleyn's daughter, in Gloriana, in *The Faerie Queene*" ("Spenser's Mutabilitie," 265).

62. Teskey, *Allegory and Violence*, 171–84.

63. Harry Berger, Jr., "The *Mutabilitie Cantos*: Archaism and Evolution in Retrospect," in *Revisionary Play*, 269.

64. Wofford, *The Choice of Achilles*, 303–10. Wofford, however, associates Elizabeth's rule with such compulsion, and hence associates the poem's usurpations of female rule with resisting the compulsion required by allegory (353–71). In contrast, my argument depends on noticing allegory's alliance with the unthroning of queens.

65. Bellamy, "The Vocative and the Vocational," 23.

Chapter 3: Leading Ladies

1. The three female rulers of Britain in the *Briton moniments* are Guendolene, who killed her unfaithful husband and acted as regent for her son (2.10.17–20); Cordelia, who in this version reigned after King Lear's death (2.10.32); and Bunduca (or Boadicea), who fought valiantly against the Romans (2.10.54–56).

2. Arguably, portraying England as maternal might point toward Elizabeth, who was occasionally emblematized as the self-sacrificing pelican who feeds her children from the blood of her breast. In *Euphues and His England* Lyly writes in praise of her, "This is that good Pelican that to feede hir people spareth not to rend hir owne personne" (quoted in E. C. Wilson, *England's Eliza*, 238; see also 217–19). However, as Stephen Orgel points out, this emblem is highly unstable, evoking

as easily images of filial murder and vengeance—hardly the bland maternal nurturance that Arthur summons up ("Gendering the Crown").

3. Although the first installment of *The Faerie Queene* was not published until 1590, some portions of the poem evidently circulated in London in manuscript before that date. *The Faerie Queene*'s influence upon even the earliest of Shakespeare's histories, either Part 1 or Part 2 of *Henry VI*, can be demonstrated through verbal allusion. The Arden editor of *1 Henry VI*, Andrew S. Cairncross, suspects Shakespeare indeed had access to the first installment of Spenser's poem in manuscript (xliv).

4. It is practically certain that Shakespeare wrote all of the historically later tetralogy of histories—*1, 2,* and *3 Henry VI* and *Richard III*—before composing the historically earlier tetralogy—*Richard II, 1* and *2 Henry IV*, and *Henry V*. Parts 2 and 3 of *Henry VI* were most likely both composed before 1590–91, with *Richard III* following close at their heels. (Antony Hammond, in his Arden edition of *Richard III*, makes a case for this whole tetralogy having been completed by late in 1591 [54–61].) The next set of histories was composed between 1595, the earliest date for *Richard II*, and 1599, the virtually certain date for *Henry V*. When I refer in this chapter to the "first tetralogy" and the "second tetralogy," I am labeling them according to their order of composition. The most problematic history play in terms of its date is *1 Henry VI*, which some critics argue to have been composed after Parts 2 and 3, out of historical sequence. As will become evident from my progressive account of the plays, I would prefer to date *1 Henry VI* as Shakespeare's earliest history play. For arguments supporting such a chronology, see *King Henry VI Part 1*, ed. Andrew Cairncross, xxviii–lvii; and Hanspeter Born, "The Date of *2, 3 Henry VI*," who argues that all three parts of *Henry VI* were first performed, in sequence, between March and September 1592. However, even if *1 Henry VI* was composed out of sequence, it would still signify a logical if post hoc initiation of the themes that Parts 2 and 3 had begun to develop.

5. As Robert Ornstein notes, "So preeminent was his contribution that, if we omit his History Plays, the tradition very nearly ceases to be artistically significant" (*A Kingdom for a Stage*, 6).

6. See Phyllis Rackin, *Stages of History*, 5–12. Rackin draws this summation of the new historiography's governing principles from Peter Burke, *The Renaissance Sense of the Past*. For the literary challenges posed by new notions of the relationship between past and present, see Thomas M. Greene, *The Light in Troy*.

7. Jean E. Howard and Phyllis Rackin, *Engendering a Nation*, 160. Richard Helgerson also contrasts Shakespeare's histories with those of Munday, Chettle, Heywood, Dekker, et al., whose focus is on "common people and their upperclass champions" (*Forms of Nationhood*, 234).

8. As Rackin points out, "Renaissance historiography . . . [was] written by men, devoted to the deeds of men, glorifying the masculine virtues of courage, honor, and patriotism, and dedicated to preserving the names of past heroes and recording their patriarchal genealogies" (*Stages of History*, 147).

9. Julia Kristeva, "Women's Time," in *The Kristeva Reader*, 192.

10. See *The Faerie Queene*, 2.10.5–76, 3.3.27–49, and 3.9.33–51.

11. See Steven Mullaney, *The Place of the Stage*.

12. Laura Levine, *Men in Women's Clothing*; and Stephen Orgel, *Imperson-ations*.

13. Leah Marcus, *Puzzling Shakespeare*, 52–105.

14. Marcus, *Puzzling Shakespeare*, 53–61. For Elizabeth as "Amazonian Queen" see James Aske, *Elizabetha Triumphans* (London, 1588), in John Nichols, *The Progresses and Public Processions of Queen Elizabeth*, 2:545–82, cited in Marcus, *Puzzling Shakespeare*, 231 n. 30; and Winfried Schleiner, "*Divina Virago*: Queen Elizabeth as an Amazon."

15. Joan is hailed as Astraea's daughter, where Elizabeth was identified with Astraea (in, for example, the 1591 London pageant, *Descensus Astraeae*); Joan is re-puted to have an insatiable sexual appetite, like the one Catholic detractors attrib-uted to Elizabeth; and Joan claims as lovers the Dukes of Alençon and Anjou, titles belonging to Elizabeth's French suitor of the 1570s and 1580s (Marcus, *Puzzling Shakespeare*, 67–83). The reference to Joan's "sword of Deborah" would also tie her to Elizabeth, since Deborah was one of the biblical and mythological heroines to whom Elizabeth was most often compared. See E. C. Wilson, *England's Eliza*, 61–95. Gabrielle Bernhard Jackson also examines Elizabeth I's connections with Joan in "Topical Ideology: Witches, Amazons, and Shakespeare's Joan of Arc." Nina S. Levine's study of Joan argues incisively, against Marcus, that fears of female power in this play are not ultimately contained, since the male aristocratic world that coun-ters her is patently riven with factionalism and bad faith (*Women's Matters*, 26–46).

16. When I refer in the following pages to Joan's theatrical power, I am de-scribing the effect that she has within the context of the play—that is, her effect upon her auditors in the French and English armies. I am not attempting to mea-sure her effect upon *1 Henry VI*'s theater audience, either Elizabethan or modern; in point of fact, I find few of Joan's lines especially "powerful" in the sense that they move me, as armchair auditor. I find myself in this chapter quoting more of the responses to Joan's speeches than her speeches themselves; what Joan's auditors *per-ceive* as her dramatic power is exactly the issue here. What I have in mind is a study of what Harry Berger, Jr. calls "imaginary audition," which derives from Shake-spearean characters' "sense that even in their most formal and public utterances they seem often to be listening to and acting on themselves" (*Imaginary Audition*, 75). But because *1 Henry VI*'s language does not create the well-developed con-sciousnesses that can be attributed to characters in later history plays, particularly in the second tetralogy, our "imaginary audition" of someone like Joan is formed primarily by other characters' voiced reactions to her, rather than by her reactions to herself.

17. Talbot puns on Joan's appellation of "Pucelle" as meaning in English both "maid" and "slut" (OED n. 1a, 2): "Puzzel or Pucelle, dolphin or dogfish, / Your hearts I'll stamp out with my horse's heels" (1.4.106–107). But at this point Talbot does not yet know what or who Joan is, so that she is as much a puzzle as a puzzel.

18. Reignier and Alençon assume it is the Dauphin whose speech controls his tête-à-tête with Joan. When Alençon remarks "Doubtless he shrives this woman to her smock; / Else ne'er could he so long protract his speech" (1.2.119–20), lengthy speech becomes part of a quibble on the Dauphin's sexual prowess. But Joan's next

lines establish that the verbal control is in fact hers: when Reignier asks the Dauphin a question, *she* answers (1.2.124–27).

19. Anthony Munday, *A Second and Third Blast of Retrait from Plaies and Theaters*, 56. Jean Howard wisely argues that the fear of women playgoers' endangering their sexual purity is a kind of "cover" for the fear that women might claim more public presence and critical power by joining the theatrical audience (*The Stage and Social Struggle in Early Modern England*, 73–85).

20. Stephen Gosson, *The Schoole of Abuse*, B6v-B7r.

21. John Rainolds, *Th'Overthrow of Stage-Playes*, D1v, emphasis in original.

22. Rainolds, *Th'Overthrow of Stage-Playes*, E3v.

23. Orgel in fact proposes that the employment of transvestite boys on the English Renaissance stage was not so much a problem as the solution to a problem: a homoerotic affinity between the actors and the audience was far less socially threatening than the equivalent heterosexual alliance would have been. However, insofar as an audience was willing to believe that the boys-playing-women *were* women, a heteroerotic relation between the two would be reinscribed; hence perhaps Shakespeare's reluctance, as Orgel points out, to allow female transvestite characters like Rosalind or Viola to reassume female garb and female identity at play's end (*Impersonations*, 50–51).

24. Stephen Greenblatt, *Renaissance Self-Fashioning*, 2.

25. Laura Levine, *Men in Women's Clothing*, 10–25. Levine expands upon Katharine Eisaman Maus's suggestion that the antitheatricalists pose audience response as "sexual capitulation": "[a]t the foundation of the antitheatrical fear of histrionic display is a fear of losing male identity" ("Horns of Dilemma: Jealousy, Gender, and Spectatorship in English Renaissance Drama," 569).

26. Munday, *A Second and Third Blast*, 3–4.

27. William Prynne, *Histrio-Mastix. The Players Scourge*, Aaa2r-v. Prynne is quoting here, not entirely accurately, from Robert Bolton's sermon *Discourse about the State of True Happinesse* (London, 1611). Most of Prynne's relentless text is composed of quotations and references strung together from other texts, both classic and contemporary.

28. In his introduction to *Tamburlaine*, for example, J. W. Harper discusses the monotony of the play, referring to the hero as "an historical personage whose character seemed as single as his unbroken series of victories" (Christopher Marlowe, *Tamburlaine*, xii). However one might disagree with Harper's assessment, it is one that *1 Henry VI* seems to endorse.

29. Aristotle, *Poetics*, 63.

30. "The irrational . . . has wider scope in epic poetry, because there the person acting is not seen. Thus, the pursuit of Hector would be ludicrous if placed upon the stage—the Greeks standing still and not joining in the pursuit, and Achilles waving them back. But in the epic poem the absurdity passes unnoticed" (Aristotle, *Poetics*, 63).

31. Rackin makes a point similar to mine above, in that she identifies the male voices in the history plays with the historiographic record they attempt to establish, and the female voices with their attempts to disrupt that record. Rackin, however, aligns these female voices not with dramatic power, but with a "physi-

cal reality" to which the women often refer (*Stages of History*, 146–200). Because she does not associate women with imaginative verbal construction, which would more forcefully oppose them to static verbal recollection, Rackin cannot credit them with having any real effect at all within the plays, since drama, of course, in many ways departs from "physical reality." For a pioneering reading of *1 Henry VI* as a contest between male order embodied in Talbot and female disorder embodied in Joan, see Leslie Fiedler, *The Stranger in Shakespeare*, 43–81. Fiedler's account differs from mine most obviously in that he argues that plays like *1 Henry VI* more or less successfully exorcise the threatening female, and that such exorcism is *always* desirable for Shakespeare's psyche; he does not discuss what is desirable for Shakespeare as a maker of theater.

32. This kind of memorial control happens nowhere more strikingly than at the end of *Antony and Cleopatra*, which I discuss in Chapter 5.

33. Cf. *Tamburlaine Part 2*, 3.2.36–42, where Tamburlaine's speech to Zenocrate's effigy makes it clear that he has realized the Dauphin's fantasy, by having the memorial of a dead woman as his heroic inspiration (Marlowe, *Tamburlaine*, 126). Norman Rabkin, by referring to Joan as a "mock-Tamburlaine, a shepherd's daughter risen to military command," points toward the urgency of controlling Joan by imagining her in the traditional female role that Zenocrate occupies in death (*Shakespeare and the Problem of Meaning*, 88). The simple fact that the Dauphin's words metaphorically deprive Joan of speech has a more immediate metatheatrical valence, as well. As Andrew Gurr discusses, the sixteenth century debated whether theater was primarily an auditory or a visual experience, whether those who attended theater were primarily listeners or spectators. Poets (chief among them Ben Jonson) highly preferred to think of their dramatic creations as chiefly verbal ones that could therefore approach the literary status of poetry, not as vulgar "shows" for the common playgoer (*Playgoing in Shakespeare's London*, 85–97). Hence the Dauphin's lines silencing Joan, enclosing her in a spectacular object to be put on view, imply a desire for her to be no longer the producer of theatrical effect, but a mere production, and an inferior dumb show, at that.

34. Coppélia Kahn, *Man's Estate*, 52.

35. For Margaret's equivalence to Joan, see Patricia Silber, "The Unnatural Woman and the Disordered State in Shakespeare's Histories." Fiedler more cleverly reads Margaret as an "archetypal daughter-alter ego" to Joan: Margaret is related to Joan "in the nighttime illogic of dream and myth," since Joan claims to be bearing the bastard child of the King of Naples, and Margaret is the daughter of that very king (*The Stranger in Shakespeare*, 48–49). But for Margaret's and Joan's nonequivalence, see Marcus, who persuasively argues that Margaret, unlike Joan, "takes on none of Elizabeth's explicit symbology of power" (*Puzzling Shakespeare*, 93).

36. In his later scene with King Henry, Suffolk will take on what Nancy Vickers describes as the blazon's rhetorical strategy of men talking to men about women ("'The blazon of sweet beauty's best': Shakespeare's *Lucrece*").

37. Margaret's curse upon the Yorkists who are to meet their doom in *Richard III* (1.3.196–246) predicts the action of the play and in that sense organizes it; but at the time, no one pays her heed. Ironically, the only complete identification of Margaret with theater comes in Robert Greene's blast at the young Shakespeare, "with

his tiger's heart wrapped in a player's hide." In parodying York's cry in *3 Henry VI*, "O tiger's heart wrapp'd in a woman's hide" (1.4.137), Greene proposes an identity between Margaret and a stage-player, and by extension between Margaret and Shakespeare the audacious dramatist.

38. See, for example, Thomas F. Van Laan, *Role-Playing in Shakespeare*, 132–51. For Richard's theatricality as an inheritance from Joan and Margaret, see also Howard and Rackin, *Engendering a Nation*, 107–12.

39. Nor is Richard's effect limited to women. Hastings's admission of how Richard has seduced him echoes deeply with fears we may piece out as sexual, though somewhat discordant: fears simultaneously of falling from a great height, hence losing his own erect masculinity, and of homoerotically plunging into the "fatal bowels" of the Ricardian danger he faces:

O momentary grace of mortal men, . . .
Who builds his hope in air of your good looks
Lives like a drunken sailor on a mast,
Ready with every nod to tumble down
Into the fatal bowels of the deep.

                                                        (3.4.96, 98–101)

One of the earliest (though perhaps apocryphal) surviving anecdotes about *Richard III*'s performance, though it digresses from the play itself, attests similarly to the sexual nature of Richard's ability to ravish, even as it comically attaches that ability to a dramatist's prowess. John Manningham noted in his diary entry of 13 March 1601/1602 that "Upon a tyme when Burbidge played Rich. 3. there was a citizen greue soe farr in liking with him, that before shee went from the play shee appointed him to come that night unto hir by the name of Ri: the 3. Shakespeare overhearing their conclusion went before, was intertained, and at his game ere Burbidge came. Then message being brought that Rich. the 3.d was at the dore, Shakespeare caused returne to be made that William the Conqueror was before Rich. the 3" (*Richard III*, ed. Hammond, 67).

40. This heightening of awareness is not necessarily what Richard intends. As Marguerite Waller points out, Richard claims to be self-determining in a way that ignores his own demystifications of others' power; he seems blind to how his own power might similarly be demystified ("Usurpation, Seduction, and the Problematics of the Proper: A 'Deconstructive,' 'Feminist' Rereading of the Seductions of Richard and Anne in Shakespeare's *Richard III*").

41. For an astute reading of this tetralogy as delineating the dissolution of the father-son bonds of patriarchy, see the first half of Chapter 3 of Kahn's *Man's Estate*, especially 50–66. Richard III, she concludes, exemplifies "the dissolution of masculine identity paternally defined" (66). Rabkin also discusses the tetralogy as manifesting the collapse of benign patriarchy once signified in the idealized father-son bonds of the Talbots (*Shakespeare and the Problem of Meaning*, 85–97).

42. Waller provocatively argues that Richard's seductions and his usurpation are linguistically equivalent, since both involve creating identity by doing violence to the established order ("Usurpation, Seduction, and the Problematics of the

Proper"). I would expand the scope of discussion, however, to include sexual and political as well as linguistic disruption.

43. Nina S. Levine also connects Richard and Elizabeth, on the grounds not of her canceling dynastic continuity, but of her portrayal by some of her subjects as a monstrous mother (*Women's Matters*, 109–22).

44. See J. E. Neale, *Queen Elizabeth I*, 69–84, 137–55, and 243–63; also Mortimer Levine, *The Early Elizabethan Succession Question*.

45. Robert Parsons ["R. Doleman," pseud.], *A Conference about the Next Succession to the Crowne of Ingland*. Richard Dutton discusses this tract and its relation to how the duchy of Lancaster is bestowed in *Richard II* ("Shakespeare and Lancaster").

46. John Hayward, *An answer to the first part of a certaine conference*, F4r-v. Hayward's efforts to justify an orderly succession paid off under the king to whom this volume was dedicated, the future James I. Hayward earned the patronage of Prince Henry Stuart and was knighted in 1619.

47. Henry Constable, *A Discoverye of a Conterfecte Conference*, 19.

48. Peter Wentworth, *A Pithie exhortation to her majestie for establishing her successor to the crowne*, 27–28; probably first drafted in 1587, when Wentworth began the activities to force determination of the succession that finally led to his 1593 confinement in the Tower, where he died in 1597. Once Parsons had published his tract in 1594, Wentworth wrote an answer entitled *A Discourse containing the Author's opinion of the true and lawful successor to her Majesty*; this answer and the *Pithie exhortation* were published together in 1598. See J. E. Neale's chapter on "Peter Wentworth and the Succession Question" in *Elizabeth I and Her Parliaments, 1584-1601*, 251–56.

49. The queen once responded to a reference in her presence to Richard II, "I am Richard II; know ye not that? . . . this tragedy was played forty times in open streets and houses." For an examination and critique of this passage's use in critical analyses of Shakespeare's *Richard II*, see Leeds Barroll, "A New History for Shakespeare and His Time."

50. Jean E. Howard, "The New Historicism in Renaissance Studies," 39. The first version of Greenblatt's essay appeared in *Glyph* 8 (1981): 40–61; the most recent is included in his *Shakespearean Negotiations*, 21–65. Another influential treatment of *Henry V*'s strategies of ideological containment is Jonathan Dollimore and Alan Sinfield's 1985 essay, "History and Ideology: The Instance of *Henry V*," an extended version of which appeared in 1992 as "History and Ideology, Masculinity and Miscegenation." Further references to this essay are to the 1992 version. Carolyn Porter's essay "Are We Being Historical Yet?" is typical in its treatment of "Invisible Bullets" as paradigmatic of new historicist theories of hegemonic political and literary forces; see also her extension of that essay's argument, "History and Literature: 'After the New Historicism.'"

51. David Willbern, "Shakespeare's Nothing," 255–56.

52. For the Aristotelian model of conception and its employment in Renaissance medical theory, see Thomas Laqueur, *Making Sex*, 25–113. In other contexts, unlike this one, the maternal connection to Aristotelian "matter" conjures up fantasies of death and decay; see Janet Adelman, *Suffocating Mothers*, 6. Joel Altman also analyzes *Henry V*'s Prologue as a sexualized exchange, describing the Pro-

logue's "solicitings as invitations to violent appropriation," i.e., rape, on the part of a presumably masculinized audience ("Vile Participation," 20). Indeed, it seems difficult even to describe the Prologue's operations without entering into its sexualized phrase-world; Robert Weimann, for example, uses the Prologue to illustrate how an audience provides the stage spectacle with what he unselfconsciously calls "performative thrust" ("Bifold Authority in Shakespeare's Theatre," 413).

53. Howard and Rackin, *Engendering a Nation*, 137–41.

54. See Harry Berger Jr.'s analysis of *Richard II* in *Imaginary Audition*, 45–137.

55. Valerie Traub, *Desire and Anxiety*, 54–61.

56. The word "harlot" was just slippery enough in Renaissance usage to convey all of Falstaff's roles. The OED defines "harlot" in late sixteenth-century usage as, among other things, vagabond, knave, menial servant, jester, juggler, buffoon, and good fellow, as well as fornicator or female prostitute.

57. I am indebted to Oliver Arnold for the suggestion that Falstaff's last words indicate the death of comedy's "green world."

58. In his Oxford edition of *Henry V*, Gary Taylor, in contrast, defends the Salic law speech as not all that obscure to an Elizabethan audience, which would have been far more familiar with its historical references: "the speech's reputation for tedium has become such a critical commonplace that reports of its obscurity have been greatly exaggerated" (35). Rackin is among the few critics who do not simply pass over this speech, arguing that this recitation of genealogy, like Henry's winning of the French princess in Act 5, signifies "the appropriation of the indispensable female ground of patriarchal authority" (*Stages of History*, 168). It will become clear below that I both agree and disagree with Rackin's point: I contend that Henry wishes to *appropriate* feminine authority without *associating* himself with what is feminine about it. My argument in this regard parallels that of Dollimore and Sinfield, who describe the Salic law speech as part of *Henry V*'s fractured ideological attempts to banish the female and the feminine ("History and Ideology, Masculinity and Miscegenation," 127–42).

59. Gary Taylor describes these lines as "the only explicit, extra-dramatic, incontestable reference to a contemporary event anywhere in the [Shakespearean] canon" (*Henry V*, ed. Taylor, 7). For the dating of the play, see *King Henry V*, ed. Walter, xi–xiv; and *Henry V*, ed. Taylor, 3–7.

60. Parsons, *A Conference about the Next Succession*, A3r. J. E. Neale describes Parsons's work as "an important and disturbing book, repudiating the doctrine of divine hereditary right, placing election alongside birth as a way to the succession, and by implication arguing that Parliament could take away the King of Scots' right to the English throne" (*Elizabeth and Her Parliaments, 1584–1601*, 262). Essex did not solicit or welcome Parsons's dedication; nevertheless, its comment on Essex's involvement in the succession question is telling. For James's late-Elizabethan correspondence and intrigues with Essex and Cecil, see David Harris Willson, *King James VI and I*, 149–57. Essex in fact intended one of the results of his rebellion to be Parliament's recognition of James as Elizabeth's successor. Cecil, whose influence prevailed upon James after Essex's arrest, rightly urged caution: if James would flatter Elizabeth rather than press her for a decision, he would be assured of the throne. See also Joel Hurstfield, "The Succession Struggle in Late Elizabethan

England." For a reading of *Henry V* as skeptical toward the Essex expedition and toward English militarism in Ireland, see Christopher Highley, *Shakespeare, Spenser, and the Crisis in Ireland*, 133–63.

61. Even Thomas Wilson's fairly casual *The State of England, Anno Dom. 1600* begins by discussing the succession, mentioning Parsons, and then undertaking a refutation of Salic law: "the Lawe is that if a man decease without heyre male haveing many daughters, his lands shall be parted equally among them all, but in the succession of the Crowne the eldest shall inheritt all" (7). For the role of Salic law in the sixteenth-century debate over women's rule, see Constance Jordan, *Renaissance Feminism*, 244–45.

62. Godfrey Goodman, *The Court of King James I*, 1:97, quoted in Hurstfield, "The Succession Struggle," 370.

63. *Calendar of State Papers, Domestic Series, of the Reign of Elizabeth, 1598–1601*, 137, cited in Carole Levin, *The Heart and Stomach of a King*, 84. Fraunces's felonious remark was prefaced in his seductive technique by the argument "that the best in England, *i.e.* the Queen, had done so, and had three bastards by noblemen of the Court" (Levin, 83–84).

64. Joel Hurstfield, "The Succession Struggle in Late Elizabethan England," 370.

65. *Calendar of State Papers, Domestic Series, of the Reign of Elizabeth, 1601–1603*, 115–16.

66. Henry Hooke, *Of the succession to the Crowne of England*. This manuscript includes a dedication to James I, apparently added after his accession to the English throne. Hooke evidently found favor with the new king, as attested to by the publication of his sermon "Jerusalem's peace" under the title *Sermon preached before the King at White-hall, the eight of May. 1604*, which reiterates publicly what Hooke had, during Elizabeth's reign, been able to declare only privately: "[God] hath made broad signes, that all the world might see, especially his elect might hope, that what was not possible for a woman to effect, man should be both able and industrious to performe" (C4r).

67. In his virulent *First Blast of the Trumpet Against the Monstrous Regiment of Women*, for example, John Knox writes with horror that "women are lifted up to be heads over realms and to rule above men at their pleasure and appetites" (*The Political Writings of John Knox*, 46). Christopher Goodman, Knox's equally fervent compatriot in Geneva, accuses Queen Mary Tudor's councilors of having no other goal but to seek "how to accomplishe and satisfie the ungodly lustes of their ungodly and unlawful Governesse" (*How Superior Powers Oght to Be Obeyd*, Civ). For accounts and analyses of the 1550s debate over women's rule see especially Paula Scalingi, "The Scepter or the Distaff: The Question of Female Sovereignty, 1516–1607"; and Constance Jordan, "Woman's Rule in Sixteenth-Century British Political Thought."

68. William Allen, *An admonition to the Nobility and People of England and Ireland Concerninge the Present Warres*, B2r. For an invaluable compendium of 1570s and 1580s propaganda for and against Elizabeth and Mary, Queen of Scots, see James E. Phillips, *Images of a Queen*.

69. Neale, *Queen Elizabeth I*, 403. Neale is quoting an Elizabethan source that

he does not identify. For England's "fin-de-siècle" sense of discontent with Eliza-beth and her government, see Peter C. Herman, "'O, 'tis a gallant king': Shake-speare's *Henry V* and the Crisis of the 1590s"; John Guy, "The 1590s: The Second Reign of Elizabeth I?"; and Margreta de Grazia, "Fin-de-Siècle Renaissance En-gland."

70. Sir John Harington, *Nugae Antiquae*, 1:321.

71. Levin, *The Heart and Stomach of a King*, 92–104.

72. Dollimore and Sinfield, "History and Ideology, Masculinity and Misce-genation," 129.

73. *Edward III* opens with a Salic-law discussion that is very similar to *Henry V's*, with the notable difference that Edward III's mother Isabel is prominently named. In response to Edward's question about whether his "pedigree" grants him the succession to the French throne, Robert of Artois makes the matter crystal clear:

Edward.   Who next succeeded Phillip of Bew?
Artois.   Three sonnes of his, which all successfully,
            Did sit upon their fathers regall Throne:
            Yet dyed and left no issue of their loynes.
Edward.   But was my mother sister unto those?
Artois.   Shee was my Lord, and onely Issabel,
            Was all the daughters that this Phillip had,
            Whome afterward your father tooke to wife:
            And from the fragrant garden of her wombe,
            Your gratious selfe the flower of Europes hope:
            Derived is inheritor to Fraunce.

(*The Raigne of King Edward the Third*, 86) Karl P. Wentersdorf points out that Henry's descent from Isabella had also been made clear in another Elizabethan play, *The Famous Victories of Henry V* ("The Conspiracy of Silence in *Henry V*," 266 n. 5). Wentersdorf also explains how Shakespeare suppresses the part female descent played in Scroop's rebellion: Cambridge, one of the plotters, historically claimed the throne through his wife Anne Mortimer's descent from Edward III's third son. The son of Anne Mortimer and Cambridge was the Richard, Duke of York, who challenged Henry VI's rule. Rackin reminds us, "the Yorkist claim . . . hovers at the edge of consciousness, lending a suppressed irony to Henry's reliance on female inheritance to justify his claims to France" (*Stages of History*, 168).

74. For comments on the sexual rivalry between Henry and the Dauphin, see Peter Erickson, *Patriarchal Structures in Shakespeare's Drama*, 60–61; and Dollimore and Sinfield, "History and Ideology, Masculinity and Miscegenation," 132–33.

75. Taylor rejects a modernization of "spirt" to "spurt," calling it misleading because it obscures the sense "sprout" (*Henry V*, ed. Taylor, 180, note to 3.5.8); but dismissing "spurt" similarly obscures the sense "to issue in a jet," a meaning avail-able in the 1590s (see OED *spirt* v[i], 1 and 2a).

76. See C. L. Barber and Richard Wheeler, *The Whole Journey*, 219. Taylor's

Oxford edition preserves the Quarto spelling *cown*, which better conveys the bilingual pun achieved through Alice's mispronunciation, gown-*con*. But *count* retains the suggestion of the obscene pun on feminized nationhood, cunt/cuntry, that was commonly used in diatribes against Elizabeth, Mary, Queen of Scots, and the institution of queenship in general. In an essay on Peter Erondell's 1605 French phrasebook, Juliet Fleming demonstrates how the entirety of the Princess's language lesson is a lesson in dirty talk: "The first two words that she asks her teacher to translate, *le pied* and *la robe*, were used in England to mean respectively one who commits buggery (from pied, meaning variegated), and a female prostitute. . . . *D'elbow* sounds like *dildo*, *neck* and *nick* were synonyms for *vulva*, and *sin* was a euphemism for *fornication*. Finally, *excellent* had lewd connotations, and was especially associated with buggery, as was *assez*, understood to mean ass-y enough" (*"The French Garden*: An Introduction to Women's French," 45).

77. Altman connects the Princess's "litany of dismemberment" with the play's efforts to make King Henry's battle *present* to the audience, and hence to offer the audience the satisfaction of illusory participation in the battle, of not being "gentlemen in England now a-bed" ("Vile Participation," 18–19).

78. "The truth is, that the poet's matter failed him in the fifth act, and he was glad to fill it up with whatever he could get; and not even Shakespeare can write well without a proper subject" (Samuel Johnson, *Selections from Johnson on Shakespeare*, 205). For a history of the critical debate instigated by Johnson's remark, see *Henry V*, ed. Taylor, 70–72; *King Henry V*, ed. Walter, xxviii–xxix; and Marilyn Williamson, "The Courtship of Katherine and the Second Tetralogy."

79. For an account of the Princess's scenes similar in many respects to mine, see Lance Wilcox, "Katherine of France as Victim and Bride." Wilcox, however, makes an effort to prove that Henry's wooing of the Princess is satisfyingly mutual: "anything short of vigorously rejecting [Henry's] suggestions must inevitably be seen as avouching similar fantasies of her own" (71)—an assertion tantamount to blaming a rape victim for not screaming loud enough. And yet Wilcox's views seem to be shared by modern directors of *Henry V*, all of whom (to my knowledge) have staged Henry's exchange with Katharine as mutually romantic. (Kenneth Branagh's 1989 film of *Henry V* is symptomatic; by casting his then-wife, Emma Thompson, as the Princess, Branagh effectively forestalled any but a romantic conclusion to Henry's courtship.) For Henry's courtship of Katharine as an exercise in the "traffic in women," see also Karen Newman, *Fashioning Femininity and Renaissance Drama*, 97–108. Christopher Pye suggests that Salic law itself generates the erotic energies by which Henry woos and claims the Princess. As a "female bar" (1.2.42) to male occupation of the throne—a bar that both does and does not impede Henry's progress—Salic law is embodied in the contradictions of Henry's erotic desire: the Princess must be wooed, but in Henry's and Burgundy's subsequent bawdy repartee (5.2.298–337), she seems always already to have surrendered (*The Regal Phantasm*, 29–33).

80. Greenblatt, "Invisible Bullets," in *Shakespearean Negotiations*, 21–65; and Steven Mullaney, "Strange Things, Gross Terms, Curious Customs: The Rehearsal of Cultures in the Late Renaissance." For *Henry V*'s treatment of the problems and the advantages accruing to a "common language" in Renaissance England,

see Claire McEachern, *The Poetics of English Nationhood, 1590–1612*, 83–137. For another analysis of the relation between Henry's language, kingship, and theater, see James L. Calderwood, *Metadrama in Shakespeare's Henriad: "Richard II" to "Henry V,"* 162–81.

81. Several critics have noticed that Henry's tone and the Chorus's are similar. Michael Goldman remarks, for example, that the King rousing his troops sounds very like the Chorus "rousing the audience to cooperation and excitement" (*Shakespeare and the Energies of Drama*, 61). See also Lawrence Danson, "*Henry V*: King, Chorus, and Critics." The difference between Henry and the Chorus is, of course, that Henry never displays any doubt that his troops will arise.

82. For Henry's attempts to manipulate national memory—based on forgetting what is contrary to what he would like remembered—see Jonathan Baldo, "Wars of Memory in *Henry V.*"

83. Pye, *The Regal Phantasm*, 19.

84. Dollimore and Sinfield, "History and Ideology, Masculinity and Miscegenation," 140.

85. Edward I. Berry sees this historical disruption of epic as the play's primary mode ("'True Things and Mock'ries': Epic and History in *Henry V*"). For further commentary on how *Henry V* both sustains and deflates a Tudor fantasy of absolute state power, see also David Scott Kastan, "Proud Majesty Made a Subject: Shakespeare and the Spectacle of Rule." Marjorie Garber, noting the two tetralogies' reversal, remarks that "in [*Henry V*'s] epilogue the audience is invited, not to imagine, but to remember—and specifically to remember Shakespeare's *Henry VI* plays . . . as well as the historical events contained in them" ("'What's Past Is Prologue': Temporality and Prophecy in Shakespeare's History Plays," 324).

86. Raphael Holinshed, *The Chronicles of England, Scotland, and Ireland*, 3:615.

87. E. C. Wilson, *England's Eliza*, 435.

88. Herman, "'O, 'tis a gallant king',"223.

89. See the tirades published in the wake of Mary, Queen of Scots's 1587 execution, cited in Phillips, *Images of a Queen*, 171–97.

90. Walter B. Devereux, *Lives and Letters of the Devereux, Earls of Essex*, 2:131, quoted in R. B. Wernham, *The Making of Elizabethan Foreign Policy*, 93.

91. André Hurault, Sieur de Maisse, *De Maisse: A Journal*, 155, quoted in Helen Hackett, *Virgin Mother, Maiden Queen*, 181.

92. Thomas Nashe, *Pierce Penilesse, His Supplication to the Divell*, in *The Works of Thomas Nashe*, 2:212. For history plays as capable of fashioning valiant men, see Howard and Rackin, *Engendering a Nation*, 18–19.

93. To assert that *Henry V* only shores up Elizabethan monarchical authority, then, is to disregard the monarch's gender. Leonard Tennenhouse, for example, argues that Shakespeare's history plays maintain the unity of the king's two bodies in the face of late-Elizabethan anxiety over the queen's decaying corporeal body (*Power on Display*, 76–88). But only because Tennenhouse does not identify that queenly body as female can he continue to associate Elizabeth with Henry V rather than with the feminine selves that Henry consistently either repudiates or identifies as entirely other, absolutely not English. Near the beginning of his interesting analysis of how the accommodation of female authority in *All's Well That Ends Well*

remains uncomfortable and disturbing, Peter Erickson briefly suggests the formulation of authority in *Henry V* that I am proposing: "Henry V . . . is both chivalric warrior and monarch, and his dual role displaces Elizabeth as a specifically female ruler. This effect is confirmed by the way subsequent dramatic events assert male domination in Henry V's high-handed appropriation of Katherine: Henry V in the most decisive manner reverses Essex's subordinate position" (*Rewriting Shakespeare, Rewriting Ourselves*, 60).

94. Rabkin, *Shakespeare and the Problem of Meaning*, 33–62.

Chapter 4: Exclaiming Against Their Own Succession

1. Mark Rose, "*Hamlet* and the Shape of Revenge," 13. Rose's essay was first published in 1971.

2. I use a modern, conflated edition of the *Hamlet* text (the New Arden edition, ed. Harold Jenkins) for convenience's and familiarity's sake, but I will highlight Jenkins's editorial choices and the differences among the two quarto and the folio texts as they become significant for my argument.

3. Janet Adelman, *Suffocating Mothers*, 31.

4. Adelman, *Suffocating Mothers*, 35.

5. In emphasizing Gertrude's status as queen, I am following the lead of Peter Erickson, who aligns *Hamlet*'s final reformation into an all-male pastoral elegy with the Earl of Essex's attempts to upstage and displace his queen (*Rewriting Shakespeare, Rewriting Ourselves*, 74–91); and Steven Mullaney, who reads Hamlet's misogyny toward his sexualized mother as reflecting antipathy toward the aging Elizabeth's continuing to compel expressions of erotic desire from her male subjects ("Mourning and Misogyny: *Hamlet, The Revenger's Tragedy*, and the Final Progress of Elizabeth, 1600–1607").

6. For the controversy over whether the Danish kingship is an elective office and hence whether Claudius ought be considered a usurper of Hamlet's throne, see E. A. J. Honigmann, "The Politics in *Hamlet* and 'The World of the Play' "; and A. P. Stabler, "Elective Monarchy in the Sources of *Hamlet*." J. Dover Wilson noticed the connection between "jointress" and Gertrude's jointure long ago; see *What Happens in "Hamlet*," 38.

7. Eric Mallin, *Inscribing the Time*, 113.

8. Eileen Spring, *Law, Land, and Family*, 50.

9. Amy Louise Erickson, *Women and Property in Early Modern England*, 119–22.

10. Susan Staves, *Married Women's Separate Property in England*, 27–55.

11. *The Law's Resolutions of Women's Rights* (excerpts), in *Daughters, Wives, and Widows*, ed. Joan Larson Klein, 41.

12. Staves, *Married Women's Separate Property in England*, 33.

13. See N. R. R. Fisher, "The Queenes Courte in her Councell Chamber at Westminster," 316–17. These laws seem to have been put in place so that the king might avoid being sued for his wife's debts.

14. Edward Coke explains that this law has been in effect since the reign of Henry VI: "at the Parliament holden in anno 6 H. 6. it is enacted by the King, the

Lords Temporall, and the Commons, that no man should contract with or marry himself to any Queen of *England*, without the speciall licence or assent of the King" (*The Second Part of the Institutes of the Laws of England*, 18). Coke is clarifying that the King's widow is the exception to this rule: in England, "Widowes are presently after the decease of their Husbands without any difficulty to have their marriages (that is, to marry where they will without any license or assent of their Lords) and their inheritance" (16).

15. Lisa Jardine, *Reading Shakespeare Historically*, 40. Bruce Thomas Boehrer aligns Gertrude both with Henry VIII's many legally incestuous marriages (to Catherine of Aragon, Anne Boleyn, and Catherine Howard) and with the supposed punishment for incest, a female rather than a male heir to the throne—i.e., Elizabeth I (*Monarchy and Incest in Renaissance England*, 62–77). Boehrer uses the play's references to monarchical incest to explain the decentering of Gertrude/Elizabeth from sovereign influence.

16. For *King Lear*'s materialist conception of kingship and its relation to James I's grounding of absolutist rule in feudal property rights, see Richard Halpern, *The Poetics of Primitive Accumulation*, 218–34.

17. The Succession Act of 1543 formally restored Mary and Elizabeth after Edward VI in Henry's line of succession; however, each had been declared a bastard in a previous Succession Act (of 1534 and 1536, respectively), and in each case the relevant Act was not repealed before the queen's succession. A will of any kind was rather a novelty in England at the time, being permitted only after the 1545 Statute of Wills. For the dubious authenticity and legality of Henry VIII's will, see Mortimer Levine, *The Early Elizabethan Succession Question*, 147–62.

18. For the ambiguous status of Philip II's royal authority in England see David Loades, *The Reign of Mary Tudor*, 164, 185–86, and 334–35.

19. On Elizabeth as the "imperial votress" see Louis Montrose, *The Purpose of Playing*, 151–78; for Elizabeth's chastity as symbolic of national integrity, see Peter Stallybrass, "Patriarchal Territories: The Body Enclosed."

20. For Mary's posthumous portrayal in England see James E. Phillips, *Images of a Queen*, 198–223. An interesting historical sidebar to my argument is that Mary enjoyed a generous jointure as the widow of France's François II. See M. Greengrass, "Mary, Dowager Queen of France."

21. Sir James Melville, *Memoirs of Sir James Melville of Halhill*, 107, quoted in Antonia Fraser, *Mary Queen of Scots*, 223; and *Calendar of State Papers Relating to Scotland and Mary, Queen of Scots, 1547–1603*, 2:166, quoted in Fraser, 227.

22. Fraser, *Mary Queen of Scots*, 315–19.

23. Lilian Winstanley, *Hamlet and the Scottish Succession*; and Mallin, *Inscribing the Time*, 111–66. See also Roland Mushat Frye, *The Renaissance "Hamlet,"* 31–37 and 102–10; and Alvin Kernan, *Shakespeare, the King's Playwright*, 32–42.

24. Mallin, *Inscribing the Time*, 129.

25. Jonathan Goldberg, *James I and the Politics of Literature*, 12–17. For James's view of his monarchy as a set of familial relations, see Boehrer, *Monarchy and Incest*, 86–93.

26. Alan G. R. Smith, *The Last Years of Mary Queen of Scots*, 83.

27. Mallin's reading of Q2 as a 1604 play is reflected in his treatment of the

play's omnipresent images of disease and fleshly corruption; he connects Hamlet's delay not only to James's waiting for Elizabeth to die, but also to James's delayed entrance into London and coronation, necessitated by a severe outbreak of plague in the city (*Inscribing the Time*, 61–65, 106–11, and 162–63).

28. Adelman, *Suffocating Mothers*, 11–37. See also Boehrer, who argues "there is something distinctly feminine in Claudius's strategy for social advancement . . . [since he assails] the patrilinear basis of personal identity" (*Monarchy and Incest*, 73).

29. In this phrase, "out" might even carry the specific legal sense of "not in the hands or occupation of the owner; let or leased; in other hands or occupation" (OED adv. I.15.f). The OED's first citation of this usage is Shakespeare's, from *The Two Gentlemen of Verona*: "Considers she my possessions? . . . they are out by lease" (5.2.25, 29). Such an inflection would intensify the sense of Hamlet's considering the state of things in Denmark as a kind of jointure gone terribly awry.

30. For the seal as an instrument of exact duplication, as opposed to the changeable and copyable handwritten signature, see Jonathan Goldberg, *Writing Matter*, 244. Louise Cary constructs a clever reading of repetition in *Hamlet* on the level of the letter, both alphabetical and epistolary ("*Hamlet* Recycled, or the Tragical History of the Prince's Prints").

31. Margreta de Grazia, "Imprints: Shakespeare, Gutenberg and Descartes," 70.

32. For "replication" as "fold/folding," as "reply," and as "echo" in sixteenth-century usage see, respectively, OED 1, 2a, and 5.

33. On Hamlet's use of puns to draw distinctions, see Margaret W. Ferguson, "*Hamlet*: Letters and Spirits."

34. Patricia Parker, *Shakespeare from the Margins*, 263.

35. Mallin, *Inscribing the Time*, 69. For Hamlet's resistance to the revenger's emulative mode, of which I shall speak more below, see David Scott Kastan, " 'His semblable is his mirror': *Hamlet* and the Imitation of Revenge."

36. Richard Halpern, *Shakespeare Among the Moderns*, 281. Halpern connects this passage to Freud's "Note upon the 'Mystic Writing Pad' " and compares Gertrude to the mystic writing pad's celluloid, which does not retain its writing (282–83).

37. David Leverenz, who views femininity as integral to Hamlet's personality, offers an important counter to the traditional psychoanalytic perspective, however ("The Woman in Hamlet: An Interpersonal View"). I am also inverting Stephen Greenblatt's suggestion that the Renaissance self was constituted by property—land, movables, and the physical properties of one's body included; see Greenblatt, "Psychoanalysis and Renaissance Culture," in *Learning to Curse*, 131–45. It is in his *lack* of physical property, not his possession of it, that Hamlet's identity resides.

38. Jacques Lacan, "Desire and the Interpretation of Desire in *Hamlet*," 34.

39. Halpern, *Shakespeare Among the Moderns*, 264–65. Halpern cites and translates Jacques Lacan, "Hamlet, par Lacan," *Orincar?* 26–27 (1983): 37. The Hulbert translation of this passage tersely and rather misleadingly translates *avoir à faire* as "must," not "has [yet] to" (Lacan, "Desire and the Interpretation of Desire," 46).

40. References to Hamlet as the originary modern self are too numerous to cite. A trend in criticism for about the last fifteen years has been to describe *Hamlet*

as a signal, but anticipatory, text in the transition between the medieval "corporate" self and the modern "individual" self. See Catherine Belsey, *The Subject of Tragedy*, 26–29, 41–42, and 112–16. For Hamlet's inwardness as anachronistic within early modern culture and within *Hamlet* itself, see Francis Barker, *The Tremulous Private Body*, 22–37. Katharine Eisaman Maus refutes Barker's contention that Hamlet's inwardness is novel or unmatched in the early modern period (*Inwardness and Theater in the English Renaissance*). Halpern brilliantly investigates, not Hamlet as a modern self, but Hamlet's importance to modernism and postmodernism (*Shakespeare Among the Moderns*, 227–88).

41. T. S. Eliot, "*Hamlet*," in *Selected Prose of T. S. Eliot*, 48. Though Jacqueline Rose is quite right to discern that by "excess" Eliot means Gertrude and femininity, she wrongly assumes that such a critical identification is *necessarily* a misogynist move. A misogynist move on Prince Hamlet's part, yes, and on Eliot's too—but not one, I think, that *Hamlet* requires us to make (Jacqueline Rose, "Sexuality in the Reading of Shakespeare: *Hamlet* and *Measure for Measure*"). A revised version of Rose's essay implicates the play in the misogyny it showcases and elicits ("Hamlet—the *Mona Lisa* of Literature").

42. For commentary on Hamlet's disbelief in revenge, see René Girard, "Hamlet's Dull Revenge." Robert Weimann discusses Hamlet's role-playing as a manifestation of a crisis in "representativity" itself ("Mimesis in *Hamlet*"). If "representativity" is equivalent to Hamlet's representation of the revenger, I quite agree with Weimann that Hamlet's " 'antic disposition' . . . is another mode of release from representativity" ("Mimesis in *Hamlet*," 284).

43. Leonard Tennenhouse interestingly observes that when Hamlet interrupts the play with "A poisons him i'th' garden for his estate. . . . You shall see *anon* how the murderer gets the love of Gonzago's wife" (3.2.255–58, my emphasis), he separates, by sequentializing, "the seizure of royal property and the possession of the queen's body" that seem united in Claudius's accession to the throne (*Power on Display*, 113).

44. Sir John Harington, *A Tract on the Succession to the Crown*, 104.

45. Robert Pont, *A Newe Treatise of the Right Reckoning of Yeares*, K3v. Although Margreta de Grazia is right to point out that the year 1600 could have meant nothing in terms of its being the end of a century—the concept of a century of years not being invented until the eighteenth century—the year could still be numerically significant; for example, Pont's treatise was designed to refute Catholic calculations of 1600 as a year of jubilee. See de Grazia, "Fin-de-Siècle Renaissance England." For the sixteenth-century contention that the world was decaying and perhaps ending, see Victor Harris, *All Coherence Gone*, 86–172. Katharine R. Firth details the prevailing belief that "1600 would be a very important date. Luther and Melanchthon thought the world would not last much beyond then; Fox, Napier, and Pont, that it must mark at least the beginning of a quick series of events completing the prophecies of the Apocalypse and preparing the world for the kingdom of the Last Judgment" (*The Apocalyptic Tradition in Reformation Britain*, 195).

46. Robert Wodrow, *Analecta*, 2:341–42.

47. Henry Howard, Earl of Northampton, *A Defensative against the Poyson of Supposed Prophecies*.

48. Harington, *A Tract on the Succession to the Crown*, 69.

49. Howard Dobin, *Merlin's Disciples*, 105. For the function of prophecy in Tudor-Stuart England see Dobin's book as a whole; and Keith Thomas, *Religion and the Decline of Magic*, 389–432.

50. *Collection of Ancient Scottish Prophecies, in Alliterative Verse*, 13.

51. Debora Keller Shuger, *The Renaissance Bible*, 90.

52. Stéphane Mallarmé, *Oeuvres Complètes*, 299, quoted and translated in Marjorie Garber, *Shakespeare's Ghost Writers*, 151.

53. William Hazlitt, *Characters of Shakespeare's Plays*, 80.

54. For the theory that the Essex rebellion in effect shut down the history play, see James Forse, *Art Imitates Business*, 205–29.

55. Girard, "Hamlet's Dull Revenge," 282–83. For *Hamlet* as a response to the outdatedness of the revenge tragedy see also, e.g., Garber, *Shakespeare's Ghost Writers*, 172–75; and Halpern, *Shakespeare among the Moderns*, 283–84. For a more traditional view of why the revenge command stymies Hamlet, see Eleanor Prosser's study of revenge as an ethical dilemma, *Hamlet and Revenge*. Prosser refutes Fredson Thayer Bowers's classic account of the imperative to revenge in *Elizabethan Revenge Tragedy*, a volume still indispensable for its survey of the genre.

56. Thomas Nashe, *The Works of Thomas Nashe*, 3:315–16; and Thomas Lodge, *Wit's Misery*, 56, both cited in *Hamlet*, ed. Jenkins, 83.

57. Kastan, "'His semblable is his mirror,'" 122.

58. Two new but old-style revenge plays put on by the Admiral's Men at about this time were *Lust's Dominion*, by Marston, Dekker, et al. (1600), and *The Tragedy of Hoffman*, by Henry Chettle (1602). See David Farley-Hills, *Shakespeare and the Rival Playwrights*, 11–15.

59. See Erickson, *Rewriting Shakespeare, Rewriting Ourselves*, 74–91, for a fine analysis of the play's reflections upon the Essex rebellion; and also Montrose, *The Purpose of Playing*, 99–105.

60. The induction to *The Malcontent* makes clear that Marston's play had originally been written for a boys' company, as *The Spanish Tragedy* had for an adults' company, but that each play had switched venues, perhaps through reciprocal piracy. Referring to the height advantage the men had over the boys, Henry Condell remarks, "Why not Malevole in folio with us, as Jeronimo in decimo-sexto with them?" (John Marston, *The Malcontent*, Ind.75–76). For the argument that the Blackfriars' Boys' recorded performance of the play *The First Part of Hieronimo* was a burlesque of *The Spanish Tragedy*, see J. Reibetanz, "Hieronimo in Decimo-sexto: A Private-theater Burlesque." In this section's discussion of *Hamlet* and the War of the Theaters I am much indebted to work in progress by my colleague, John Murphy.

61. Joseph Loewenstein, "Plays Agonistic and Competitive: The Textual Approach to Elsinore."

62. Thomas Heywood, *An Apology for Actors*, 61, quoted in E. K. Chambers, *The Elizabethan Stage*, 4:253.

63. Forse, *Art Imitates Business*, 192.

64. John Marston, *Antonio and Mellida*, Ind.7–8; and Marston, *Antonio's Re-*

venge, 2.1.30–32; both editions hereafter cited parenthetically in the text. Balurdo's remark about his beard being half stuck on is even more remarkable if, as editor W. Reavley Gair contends, the Paul's boys who performed this play did not use false beards. Gair's evidence comes from a manuscript play by William Percy, *Arabia Sitience* (Alnwick Castle MS 509), which gives the stage direction, "Here he held him by the Bearde, or clawd him on the face. If for Poules this, Bearde for th'other" (Marston, *Antonio's Revenge*, 45 n. 100).

65. *Hamlet*, ed. Jenkins, 7–13. *The Malcontent's* first incarnation, too, may have been composed before *Hamlet's*, but it is difficult to pin down its date within the parameters of 1600–1604. See Marston, *The Malcontent*, xiv.

66. *Hamlet*, ed. Philip Edwards, 6–7.

67. For the Clifton episode see Forse, *Art Imitates Business*, 191–204; for the companies' writs of impressment, see Harold Newcomb Hillebrand, *The Child Actors*, 138, 158–59, and 190–91.

68. The Clifton Star Chamber complaint lists three boy actors who, like young Clifton himself, were waylaid on their route to or from school (Frederick Fleay, *A Chronicle History of the London Stage*, 128–29). Fleay reproduces the entire text of the Clifton complaint, which makes for wonderfully lurid reading (127–32).

69. Fleay, *A Chronicle History of the London Stage*, 129.

70. Letter of 11 March 1608 from Sir Thomas Lake to Lord Salisbury, quoted in Chambers, *The Elizabethan Stage*, 2:53–54.

71. *The King of Denmark's Welcome* (1606), quoted in Chambers, *The Elizabethan Stage*, 2:22 n. 2.

72. There is some evidence that James, through Yeoman of the Revels Edward Kirkham, put pressure on Henry Evans, manager of the Chapel/Blackfriars company, to quit his position, which he did later in 1608. However, even under new management the company maintained the same repertoire of plays. See Andrew Gurr, *The Shakespearian Playing Companies*, 354–56.

73. Stephen Orgel, *Impersonations*, 63.

74. Gurr, *The Shakespearian Playing Companies*, 358–61. It is not the case, though, that most boy actors stayed on in the profession as adults; instead, most were apprenticed into and entered other trades. See Orgel, *Impersonations*, 64–68; and Gerald Eades Bentley, *The Professions of Dramatist and Player in Shakespeare's Time*, 113–46.

75. Philip Gawdy, *Letters*, 117, quoted in Chambers, *The Elizabethan Stage*, 2:48.

76. This summation, though I have effaced some smaller disagreements, applies to the major principles behind three prominent recent editions of *Hamlet*, those by Jenkins (New Arden), Gary Taylor, Stanley Wells, and G. R. Hibbard (Oxford), and Philip Edwards (New Cambridge). See *Hamlet*, ed. Jenkins, 13–82; Stanley Wells and Gary Taylor, *William Shakespeare: A Textual Companion*, 396–402; *Hamlet*, ed. G. R. Hibbard, 67–130; and *Hamlet*, ed. Philip Edwards, 8–31. Hibbard's work greatly influenced the Oxford old-spelling edition of Wells and Taylor, so for my purposes these two editions may be considered as one. Hibbard, however, has since changed his mind about the relation between Q1 and F: it is

not that Q1 is a (later) memorial reconstruction stemming from the same text that F does, but that Q1 derives from a text that *precedes* the text from which F stems ("The Chronology of the Three Substantive Texts of Shakespeare's *Hamlet*").

77. David Ward, "The King and *Hamlet*."

78. Steven Urkowitz, "'Well-sayd olde Mole': Burying Three *Hamlets* in Modern Editions"; "Good News about 'Bad' Quartos"; and "Back to Basics: Thinking about the *Hamlet* First Quarto." Eric Sams argues that Q1, written in or before 1589, represents the *Ur-Hamlet*, which Shakespeare wrote ("Taboo or Not Taboo? The Text, Dating, and Authorship of *Hamlet*, 1589–1623").

79. Ward, "The King and *Hamlet*."

80. For side-by-side comparison of this passage in Q1 and F (and its omission in Q2), see Paul Bertram and Bernice W. Kliman, eds., *The Three-Text "Hamlet,"* 102–5.

81. For a fascinating account of the Renaissance printing house as modeled after the Aristotelian process of conception, masculine form imprinting itself on feminine matter, see de Grazia, "Imprints." Because printing mechanisms were far from perfect, misconceptions inevitably worked their way into the printed text, frustrating Shakespearean editors ever after. In the case of *Hamlet*, for example, some "contamination" of the three texts may have occurred in the printing process. Q2 seems to have been "contaminated" by the printers' consulting Q1 for certain details, while F seems to have been "contaminated" either by Q2 or by a later Q3, published in 1611, that derives from but differs slightly from Q2. Such feminized "contamination" is still in play. Lisa Jardine cleverly argues that the common twentieth-century editorial practice of conflating *Hamlet*'s Q2 and F in itself creates an "excessive" text that, like Gertrude, is just far too much (*Reading Shakespeare Historically*, 155). For the history and consequences of the editorial conflation of Q2 and F, see Paul Werstine, "The Textual Mystery of *Hamlet*"; and Barbara Mowat, "The Form of *Hamlet*'s Fortunes."

82. Mallin's treatment of Q2 as a text composed in 1603–4 thus at base duplicates Ward's method, referring *Hamlet* to the circumstances of Jacobean kingship.

83. *Collections, Part III*, ed. W. W. Greg, 267.

84. Friedrich von Raumer, *History of the Sixteenth and Seventeenth Centuries*, 2:206; quoted in Chambers, 1:325.

85. Gurr, *The Shakespearian Playing Companies*, 351.

86. *The Tragicall Historie of Hamlet*, G3r-v.

87. *The Tragicall Historie of Hamlet*, H2v.

88. Leah Marcus, *Unediting the Renaissance*, 141–43.

89. See Jodi Mikalachki's analysis, for example, of the repression of female sovereignty in *King Lear* (*The Legacy of Boadicea*, 68–95).

Chapter 5: The Late Queen of Famous Memory

1. Henry Chettle, *England's Mourning Garment*, 3:509. Hereafter cited parenthetically in the text.

2. I am indebted in my thinking here to Gordon Teskey's account of the

Tudor monarchy's efforts to manipulate both national memory and national amnesia (*Allegory and Violence*, 168–88).

3. Stephen Greenblatt, *Renaissance Self-Fashioning*, 167–69.

4. Louis Montrose, *The Purpose of Playing*, 61. Montrose's book synthesizes and extends his previous important work on the complex relation between the stage and the state; see especially 76–105. For the relation between theater and the delegitimation of "popish" Roman Catholic displays see also Greenblatt, "Shakespeare and the Exorcists," in *Shakespearean Negotiations*, 94–128.

5. Leonard Tennenhouse, *Power on Display*, 146.

6. Theodora A. Jankowski also connects Cleopatra's sexual mode of rule to Elizabeth's employment of sexual strategies to control men who sought to influence her (*Women in Power in the Early Modern Drama*, 147–63). Clare Kinney points toward a similar argument in "The Queen's Two Bodies and the Divided Emperor: Some Problems of Identity in *Antony and Cleopatra*." Several critics have suggested that certain aspects of the play deliberately recall incidents involving Elizabeth. In particular, Cleopatra's inquiring after the height and looks of Octavia parallels Elizabeth's doing the same in 1564 about Mary Stuart; the ambassador from Scotland, Sir James Melville, took the place of Cleopatra's unfortunate messenger. (Melville's memoirs recording this incident, however, were not published until 1683.) Like Elizabeth, Cleopatra is fond of histrionics and self-display; easily (if strategically) flies into rages; and attaches her ruling symbology to that of the moon goddess—Isis, instead of Diana. See Helen Morris, "Queen Elizabeth I 'Shadowed' in Cleopatra"; and Keith Rinehart, "Shakespeare's Cleopatra and England's Elizabeth."

7. John Knox, *The Political Writings of John Knox*, 46. For accounts and analyses of the mid-sixteenth century debate over women's right to rule see James E. Phillips, "The Background of Spenser's Attitude toward Women Rulers"; Paula Scalingi, "The Scepter or the Distaff: The Question of Female Sovereignty, 1516–1607"; Mortimer Levine, "The Place of Women in Tudor Government"; Constance Jordan, "Woman's Rule in Sixteenth-Century British Political Thought"; and Jordan, *Renaissance Feminism*, 116–33.

8. Knox, *Political Writings*, 43–44.

9. George Buchanan, *Ane Detectioun of the Duinges of Marie Quene of Scottes*, Biv.

10. J. E. Neale, *Elizabeth I and Her Parliaments, 1559–1581*, 328.

11. Adam Blackwood, *Martyre de la Royne d'Escosse*, Aa4r. For a fascinating account of rumors and seditions of Elizabeth's non-virginity, see Carole Levin, *The Heart and Stomach of a King*, 66–90.

12. William Allen, *An Admonition to the Nobility and People of England and Ireland Concerninge the Present Warres*, B3r.

13. Francis Bacon, "Mr. Bacon's Discourse in the Praise of His Sovereign," in *The Works of Francis Bacon*, ed. Basil Montagu, 2:450.

14. Thomas Dekker, *The Whore of Babylon*, 96. For early Jacobean nostalgia for Elizabeth see Anne Barton, *Ben Jonson, Dramatist*, 300–320. There is some argument over whether and when such longing developed into a desire or an active

consensus for monarchical change. Barton claims that nostalgia for Elizabeth became politically barbed only in the later years of James's reign, whereas D. R. Woolf contends that even these later Jacobean evocations of Elizabeth, though politically charged, were designed only as didactic admonitions to the king, not as the calls to revolution they became during the reign of Charles I ("Two Elizabeths? James I and the Late Queen's Famous Memory"). Curtis Perry distinguishes in this regard between the nostalgia expressed by aristocrats, and that expressed by London citizens, the latter being more critical of the king ("The Citizen Politics of Nostalgia").

15. Godfrey Goodman, *The Court of King James I*, 1:97–98; quoted in Christopher Haigh, *Elizabeth I*, 167. For the politics of celebrating Queen Elizabeth's accession day both during and after her reign, see my Chapter 6.

16. Henry Peacham, *Minerva Britanna*, 212.

17. James's official anger at Mary's execution lasted only a few weeks. Immediately after her death on February 8, 1587 he refused to see Sir Robert Carey, who had been sent to deliver Elizabeth's story that she had not personally authorized the execution. "But by the end of February [Patrick] Grey [James's close advisor] was writing to [Archibald] Douglas in London, indicating that James would now be susceptible to further arguments from Elizabeth and that the old Latin tag—*necessa est unum mori pro populo*—it is necessary for one person to die for the sake of the people—might perhaps be brought into play" (Antonia Fraser, *Mary Queen of Scots*, 546–47). At the same time James wrote a letter to Elizabeth accepting her implausible claims of innocence; see G. P. V. Akrigg, ed., *Letters of King James VI and I*, 84–85. In the case of Spenser, in contrast, he demanded to one of Elizabeth's agents in Edinburgh "[t]hat Edward Spencer [sic] for his faulte, may be duly tried and punished" (James E. Phillips, *Images of a Queen*, 202).

18. See Woolf, "Two Elizabeths?" 176–77.

19. *The Diary of Sir Simonds D'Ewes*, 142, quoted in Woolf, "Two Elizabeths?" 179. For further analysis of posthumous slanders of Queen Elizabeth see M. Lindsay Kaplan and Katherine Eggert, "'Good queen, my lord, good queen': Sexual Slander and the Trials of Female Authority in *The Winter's Tale*"; and Julia M. Walker, "Bones of Contention: Posthumous Images of Elizabeth and Stuart Politics."

20. Arthur Penrhyn Stanley, *Historical Memorials of Westminster Abbey*, 154–55.

21. For an interesting study of how seventeenth-century historiography and political theory similarly erased the authority of queens from England's past, see Jodi Mikalachki, *The Legacy of Boadicea*.

22. *Antony and Cleopatra*, ed. G. L. Kittredge, rev. ed. Irving Ribner, xiii. Rosalie Colie reads the contrast between the two realms as requiring a linguistic as well as a moral choice ("*Antony and Cleopatra*: The Significance of Style," in *Shakespeare's Living Art*, 168–207). However, Janet Adelman incisively points out that the play itself both encodes and shows as unreliable the process of judging, including the process of choosing between one realm and another: "it is no wonder that the critics have spent so long trying to judge between Rome and Egypt when the characters themselves are so concerned with right judgment" (*The Common Liar*, 24–25).

23. Coppélia Kahn, for example, describes Cleopatra as "an alibi for gaining the distance from Caesar that [Antony] seeks in order to excel him" (Kahn, *Roman Shakespeare*, 114). Jonathan Gil Harris determines that the Romans have entirely manufactured Cleopatra to fill the space of their own (at base homoerotic) desire, an argument that carries marginalization of the feminine to the point of erasure ("'Narcissus in thy face': Roman Desire and the Difference it Fakes in *Antony and Cleopatra*.") For analyses of Orientalism in the play, see Ania Loomba, *Gender, Race, Renaissance Drama*, 78–79 and 124–30; and Kim F. Hall, *Things of Darkness*, 153–60. Hall also discusses, however, how Cleopatra tends to defeat or escape the Oriental categories into which the Romans like to place her (159–60).

24. Northrop Frye, *Northrop Frye on Shakespeare*, 123.

25. Ridley notes that in contemporary parlance the word "gipsy" could be applied to any woman, not just an Egyptian one (*Antony and Cleopatra*, ed. Ridley, 4). See "gipsy," OED 2b: "A contemptuous term for a woman, as being cunning, deceitful, fickle, or the like: a 'baggage', 'hussy', etc."

26. William Prynne, *Histrio-Mastix*, Bbb2v, emphasis in original.

27. See John Michael Archer's fascinating essay, "Antiquity and Degeneration in *Antony and Cleopatra*," for the ways in which writers of Shakespeare's era—through Plutarch and Herodotus—were well aware of how much classical Greek and Roman culture had in common with ancient Egypt.

28. The more or less regular distribution of scenes between "Rome" and "Egypt" ceases entirely after Act 3. Non-Egyptian venues are the setting for one of Act 1's five scenes, for six of Act 2's seven scenes, and for three of Act 3's thirteen scenes. Act 3 also features scenes set in Actium, the military midpoint as well as watershed between Rome and Egypt; these scenes presage the shift to entirely Egyptian action in Acts 4 and 5.

29. Sir Thomas North, *Plutarch's Lives of the Noble Grecians and Romans*, 6:10. North's Plutarch details how, after Antony and Cleopatra joined forces, they dallied together in Greece: "So that, where in manner all the world in every place was full of lamentations, sighes and teares: onely in this Ile of Samos there was nothing for many dayes space, but singing and pyping, and all the Theater full of these common players, minstrells, and singing men. . . . [Next, Antony] went unto the citie of Athens, and there gave him selfe againe to see playes and pastimes, and to keepe the Theaters" (6:59). Earlier, Plutarch remarks on a certain Roman actress, Cytheride, "whom [Antony] loved derely: he caried her up and downe in a litter unto all the townes he went, and had as many men waiting apon her litter, she being but a player, as were attending upon his owne mother" (6:10). Most telling of all, perhaps, is Plutarch's description of how before Antony's final defeat by Caesar, "the statue of Bacchus with a terrible winde was throwen downe in the Theater [in Athens]. It was sayd that Antonius came of the race of Hercules, as you have heard before, and in the manner of his life he followed Bacchus: and therefore he was called the new Bacchus" (6:63).

30. Laura Levine, *Men in Women's Clothing*, 44–72.

31. Levine, *Men in Women's Clothing*, 53.

32. See Jyotsna Singh, "Renaissance Antitheatricality, Antifeminism, and Shakespeare's *Antony and Cleopatra*," who argues, as I do, that Shakespeare "clearly

puts a more positive construction upon the conflation of the feminine and the the-atrical than was found in the cultural orthodoxies of the time" (113).

33. I am indebted to Janet Adelman's reading of "feeding" in this play, which corresponds in many respects to mine; Adelman, however, emphasizes feeding as a maternal attribute and hence its connection with abhorrent maternal flesh (*Suffo-cating Mothers*, 180–81).

34. For Cressida's transformation from character to disgusting spectacle, see Adelman, *Suffocating Mothers*, 42–63.

35. As Jonas Barish describes it, Protestant antipathy toward the Roman Catholic Mass combines a suspicion of popish spectacle with a distrust of the Eucharist's putative transformative powers: "The idea that so much supernatu-ral potency lay in an inert biscuit, or that anything so palpable and localized in space could wield such enormous leverage in the spiritual world, was one that the reformers could not easily accept" (*The Antitheatrical Prejudice*, 164). Cleopatra embodies exactly this combination of the spectacular, the sensual, and the sancti-fied—so much so that, as Enobarbus puts it, "the holy priests / Bless her, when she is riggish" (2.2.239–40).

36. Cf. Shakespeare's use of this sense of "from" elsewhere: "Your highness / Shall from this practice but make hard your heart" (*Cymbeline*, 1.6.23–24).

37. Stanley Cavell, *Disowning Knowledge in Six Plays of Shakespeare*, 20–37. See also David Willbern's analysis of the generativity of "nothing" ("Shakespeare's Nothing"). I do not invoke Lacanian terminology in my analysis of Antony's self as emerging from loss, because I see this as a phenomenon ascribed by this play to the theater alone. See Cynthia Marshall, "Man of Steel Done Got the Blues: Melan-cholic Subversion of Presence in *Antony and Cleopatra*," who argues that Antony's identity—and as a result, the audience's sense of him as a character—derives from "Antony's failure to be present to himself or to us as audience" (407). Marshall's argument seems to me stronger when it is specific to the theater than when it ex-tends to how human subject positions in general are constructed. In a valuable recent discussion of Antony and Cleopatra as "notorious" figures, Linda Charnes also analyzes Cleopatra as simultaneous creator and subject of theater (*Notorious Identity*, 125–47). Although my reading of the play coincides with hers at several points, Charnes emphasizes Cleopatra's mastery of spectacle, rather than (as my ensuing discussion does) her capacity for voiced imaginative projection.

38. Some of these pronouncements are deceptively explanatory. Many critics, for example, have read Enobarbus's barge description as a successful summing up of Cleopatra's capacity to combine self-display with erotic attraction (2.2.191–218). (The winds are "love-sick"; the water is "amorous" of the oar-stroke, etc.) This is a masterful account, but it also is insufficient in that Enobarbus attempts to dismiss Cleopatra as a purely aestheticized object, rather than a creative being. He also com-pares Cleopatra to a painting or statue: she "did lie . . . / O'er-picturing that Venus where we see / The fancy outwork nature" (2.2.198–201); the possessor of "the fancy" is ambiguous, but the metaphor of artwork implies that hers is not the cre-ative genius. Enobarbus is willing to grant Cleopatra histrionic cleverness, but he is incapable of grasping the extent to which she can herself make fancy emerge into nature. He is too eager to call her simply a "wonderful piece of work" (1.2.151–52).

39. Ridley is surely right not to join Capell and Dover Wilson in changing the Folio's period at the end of this sentence to a question mark, since Cleopatra is speaking to Antony in a way that does not call for uncertainty (*Antony and Cleopatra*, ed. Ridley, 39, note to 1.5.27–29). The third Arden edition restores the question mark (*Antony and Cleopatra*, ed. John Wilders, 121, note to 1.5.28–30).

40. The continued seventeenth-century credence granted in England to theories of spontaneous generation may be testified to by the popularity of Giambattista Porta's *Natural Magic*—published in Italy in 1558, but not until 1658 in England—which details, among other things, how "Frogs are wonderfully generated of rotten dust and rain," how "Red Toads are generated of dirt, and of womens flowers," and how "Serpents may be generated of mans marrow or the hairs of a menstrous woman, and of a horse-tail, or mane" (John Baptista Porta, *Natural Magick*, 28–29).

41. In "Horns of Dilemma: Jealousy, Gender, and Spectatorship in English Renaissance Drama," Katharine Eisaman Maus discusses the identification of voyeurism and sexual betrayal with theatrical delight as it occurs in plays like *Volpone* and *Othello*. None of these plays, however, explicitly puts the overt spin of pleasure on betrayal that Cleopatra does.

42. Adelman counts eight characters who are called simply "messenger" and at least eight others besides the protagonists who bear messages, news, and rumors (*The Common Liar*, 34).

43. Adelman, *Suffocating Mothers*, 191.

44. For Shakespeare's indebtedness to Plutarch's "Of Isis and Osiris," see Adelman, *Suffocating Mothers*, 183–85 and 337 n. 37. I follow Adelman in asserting that Plutarch's account suggests a Shakespearean play on how Cleopatra "remembers" Antony. At one point in his essay, as I discussed in Chapter 2, Plutarch describes Isis as recovering the dismembered pieces of her dead husband's body and fitting them together again; at another, however, Plutarch relates how she cannot find Osiris's penis, so she makes an artificial (and, one presumes, eternally erect) one for him ("Of Isis and Osiris," in *Plutarch's Moralia*, 5:131, 5:47). Cleopatra, as usual, has it both ways: her remembered Antony is both anatomically complete *and* monumentally phallic. Cavell's argument is congruent with mine in that he reads Cleopatra as presenting, through fulfilled sexual desire, Antony's self to himself: "he asks her satisfaction by him, the totality of it, and she, if she chooses, may convince him of it, endow him with it, show it, acknowledge it, consent. Here is the pertinence of Cleopatra's presentation of orgasm, staking the effect of her total theater, her transcendence, on that outcome ('Husband, I come' [5.2.286])" (*Disowning Knowledge*, 31).

45. As Edward Snow has pointed out to me, Cleopatra answers Antony's plea to the Cleopatra he had imagined dead, "Stay for me" (4.14.50), with her own last words, "What should I stay"—going on the word *stay*, contradictory to the end (5.2.312). I should give Antony credit in his suicide for colluding, as far as he is able and willing, with Cleopatra's project of re-membering. Although his language in many ways pulls apart from Cleopatra's—he seeks not multiplicity, but finality—he nevertheless joins her in granting truth to an impossible but courageous reformulation of Rome's founding myth. Antony rewrites Virgil so that Aeneas does

not pass a condemning Dido in Hades, but joins her in the Elysian fields; and then he rewrites the revision, making the nether world into a theater in which no ghost can keep eyes off Antony and Cleopatra: "Where souls do couch on flowers, we'll hand in hand, / And with our sprightly port make the ghosts gaze: / Dido, and her Aeneas, shall want troops, / And all the haunt be ours" (4.14.51–54). Nevertheless, Antony's use of the future tense casts this remade past only in terms of an indefinite afterlife; Cleopatra, in contrast, speaks of the dead Antony in the present tense, as she transfers her imagining of him once again from fantasy to certainty: "methinks I hear / Antony call. I see him rouse himself / To praise my noble act" (5.2.282–84). For *Antony and Cleopatra*'s Virgilian heritage see Barbara J. Bono, *Literary Transvaluation*. Also see Adelman, *The Common Liar*, 68–101, and Heather James, *Shakespeare's Troy*, 119–35, for the ways in which Shakespeare's play and particularly his portrayal of Antony resist Virgilian paradigms of Roman valor. Mihoko Suzuki concludes her book on Shakespeare's revisions of Homeric and Virgilian epic by briefly suggesting that Shakespeare's representation of Cleopatra indicates nostalgia for Queen Elizabeth, as well as an interest in diverging from epic tradition (*Metamorphoses of Helen*, 258–63).

46. "R. W." (perhaps Richard Wingfield), "Narration of the last days of the Queen of Scots," British Library Cotton Caligula Ms. C IX, fols. 589–99, in A. Francis Steuart, *Trial of Mary Queen of Scots*, 174.

47. Fraser, *Mary Queen of Scots*, 541.

48. Mary's inversion of power on the scaffold recollects, of course, Foucault's description of the public execution, in which the requirement of having witnesses risks disrupting the theatrical display of invincible sovereign power: "the people, drawn to the spectacle intended to terrorize it, could express its rejection of the punitive power and sometimes revolt" (*Discipline and Punish*, 59). The oscillatory tendency of power instigated by the taking and displaying of heads reached its logical conclusion with the English and French Revolutions' public guillotining of a king; see Regina Janes, "Beheadings."

49. "R. W.," in Steuart, *Trial of Mary Queen of Scots*, 183.

50. "R. W.," in Steuart, *Trial of Mary Queen of Scots*, 183.

51. Fraser, *Mary Queen of Scots*, 542–47. Mary died on February 8, 1587; the funeral took place at around 2:00 A.M. on July 31. In the interim, the corpse was housed in Fotheringay Castle, the last location of Mary's imprisonment; during this time her servants were not free to return to their homes in Scotland or France, but were imprisoned in the castle. They were not allowed to depart until October, two months after the funeral. Peterborough happened also to be the resting place of that other discarded and silenced queen, Catherine of Aragon (P. C. Headley, *The Life of Mary Queen of Scots*, 443).

52. For an extended consideration of the connections between Cleopatra and the Magdalen legend, see Laura Severt King's fascinating essay, "Blessed When They Were Riggish: Shakespeare's Cleopatra and Christianity's Penitent Prostitutes."

53. Phillips, *Images of a Queen*, 222–23. Phillips cites Thomas Parry to Cecil, February 13, 1604, Public Record Office State Papers, Foreign, France, 51. Montchrestien's fortunes were not finally so bleak, however. After James's accession to

the English throne, Montchrestien played his tragedy to the new king to great approval (Phillips, 223).

54. Paeans to Elizabeth had celebrated her undying youth and beauty ever since her middle age, but both the strength and the incongruity of such images seem to have grown as the queen grew older; see Roy Strong, *Gloriana: The Portraits of Queen Elizabeth I*. Characteristically, then, if Elizabeth staged anything about her death, it was her refusal to die. De Beaumont, the French ambassador, reported that even when she was gravely ill she shunned going to bed, to the point of lying for ten days on pillows on the floor of her bedchamber (Paul Johnson, *Elizabeth I*, 436).

55. See Joel Hurstfield, "The Succession Struggle in Late Elizabethan England"; also David Harris Willson, *King James VI and I*, 138–58.

56. Sir John Harington, *Nugae Antiquae*, 1:326, quoted in Hurstfield, "The Succession Struggle," 396.

57. From a contemporary note possibly by a secretary of Cecil's; quoted in Johnson, *Elizabeth I*, 436. Johnson reasons the story to be a posthumous fabrication because "[n]ot until eleven days [after Elizabeth's death] was it reported by the punctilious and accurate [French ambassador] De Beaumont" (436).

58. In a kind of grim joke, Elizabeth was posthumously forced to make room for James in a very literal sense: as Julia M. Walker has discussed, her body was moved from its original resting place next to Henry VII, the ancestor James wanted to claim as his own, so that James might himself eventually be buried there. See Walker, "Reading the Tombs of Elizabeth I." Walker compares James's changing Elizabeth's burial place to Caesar's changing Cleopatra's—she is buried not in the monument she built for herself, but rather next to Antony.

59. Woolf cites three instances of James using this phrase; see James I, *Political Works*, 75, 122, and 269.

60. Stephen Gosson, *The Schoole of Abuse*, B4r-v; see Levine, *Men in Women's Clothing*, 58–59.

61. For feminists who read this speech as enabling rather than canceling feminine being and desire, see Madelon Sprengnether, "The Boy Actor and Femininity in *Antony and Cleopatra*"; and Catherine Belsey, "Cleopatra's Seduction." For this speech's opposition between Cleopatran and Caesarian theater, see Levine, *Men in Women's Clothing*, 68–69.

62. For a cogent analysis of James's role in royal pageants—in which he, unlike Elizabeth, played at being apart from rather than an intrinsic part of the spectacle—see Jonathan Goldberg, *James I and the Politics of Literature*, 31–33. Leah Marcus studies *Cymbeline* as a manifestation of James's penchant to control rather than participate in theater (*Puzzling Shakespeare*, 106–59). The debate over the extensiveness and efficacy of Jacobean censorship of theater is summarized by Philip J. Finkelpearl, " 'The Comedians' Liberty': Censorship of the Jacobean Stage Reconsidered," who contends that Jacobean censorship was actually rather inefficient, considering the number of plays on record as mocking James himself; nevertheless, as Finkelpearl also admits, the apparatus to suppress theatrical expression was surely present, even if it occasionally lapsed. And James's personal interest in drama would have raised the symbolic, if not the material, stakes of flouting that apparatus. (See, though, Leeds Barroll, *Politics, Plague, and Shakespeare's Theater*,

23–69, for the view that James was not much interested in plays.) See also Annabel Patterson's *Censorship and Interpretation*, which describes "the strategies of indirection" by which "writers could communicate with readers or audiences . . . without producing a direct confrontation" with state censors (45). In a sophisticated exploration of who sought to profit by sponsoring and/or regulating theater, Richard Burt considers censorship as a practice not only of the court but also of all the agents involved in performing plays and publishing texts (*Licensed by Authority*, ix–xv). For a challenge to the "censorship model" of the relation between authors and the state, see M. Lindsay Kaplan, *The Culture of Slander in Early Modern England*.

63. Steven Mullaney, *The Place of the Stage*, 136–37.

64. For Duke Vincentio as dramaturge, see Mullaney, *The Place of the Stage*, 88–114; Tennenhouse, *Power on Display*, 154–71; and Goldberg, *James I*, 231–39. For Prospero as dramaturge, see Stephen Orgel's pioneering study, *The Illusion of Power*, 44–49. For the constrast between Theseus and Hippolyta's approval of theater and Duke Vincentio's restriction of theater I am indebted to an unpublished paper by Oliver Arnold.

65. David Lowenthal, *The Past Is a Foreign Country*, 10. Lowenthal's reference is to Johannes Hofer's *Medical Dissertation on Nostalgia* (1688).

66. See Jacques Le Goff, *The Birth of Purgatory*.

67. Renato Rosaldo, *Culture and Truth*, 69–70.

68. Friedrich Nietzsche, *The Gay Science*, 180–81, emphasis in original.

69. Valerie Traub, *Desire and Anxiety*, 44.

70. See David Schalkwyk's fine deconstructive analysis of how Hermione's words are repressed in favor of the imposed transcendental signifier of the sovereign man's word, "'A Lady's "Verily" Is as Potent as a Lord's': Women, Word and Witchcraft in *The Winter's Tale*." Howard Felperin connects Hermione's assumed "fallen" status to the fallen nature of language itself, the crisis in mimesis ("'Tongue-tied our queen?': The Deconstruction of Presence in *The Winter's Tale*"). For the play's interweavings of Ovidian issues of rape, female sexuality, and the female voice, see Lynn Enterline, "'You speak a language that I understand not': The Rhetoric of Animation in *The Winter's Tale*."

71. Adelman, *Suffocating Mothers*, 224.

72. Adelman, *Suffocating Mothers*, 226.

73. See Kaplan and Eggert, "'Good queen, my lord, good queen.'" For Hermione's reanimation as a desexualized creature isolated from her former self, see also Traub, *Desire and Anxiety*, 42–49; and Abbe Blum, "'Strike all that look upon with mar[b]le': Monumentalizing Women in Shakespeare's Plays." Richard Halpern notes, however, that the statue scene contains a hint of Hermione's former eroticism, in that the "rare Italian master, Julio Romano" who is said to have sculpted the statue (5.2.96) was best known in Shakespeare's time for a series of pornographic drawings involving the adulterous affairs of the gods (*Shakespeare Among the Moderns*, 152 n. 73).

74. For the statue scene as a commentary on theater, see Adelman, who believes the audience (Leontes and ourselves) accepts the theater's control over us (*Suffocating Mothers*, 234–35). Cavell sees Paulina's theater, with its echoes of St. Paul, of grace, and of faith, as a substitute for religion (*Disowning Knowledge*, 216–

19), whereas Jane Tylus sees in Paulina a stand-in for Shakespeare himself, who defends the efficacy of the public theater against that of the Stuart courtly masque (*Writing and Vulnerability in the Late Renaissance*, 144–73). While I agree with the equivalence between the statue's coming to life and the animating possibilities of theater, I must remark on the transitoriness of Leontes's open-minded, wondrous acceptance of what he sees. Nor do I agree with T. G. Bishop that Hermione's restored body reintroduces feminine eroticism into theatricality (*Shakespeare and the Theatre of Wonder*, 168, 173–75)—feminine physicality, yes, but eroticism, no. For a fascinating study of the statue scene as mourning (but also recreating) the irrevocable loss of Roman Catholic iconophilia, see Julia Reinhard Lupton, *Afterlives of the Saints*, 175–218.

75. See Adelman's persuasive and detailed account of how virginal daughters replace sexual mothers/wives in Shakespeare's romances (*Suffocating Mothers*, 193–238).

76. The ambiguity depends upon the pronoun *they* in *Pandosto*'s final sentence. The Leontes figure kills himself when he realizes he's been lusting after his own daughter. Thereafter the Florizel figure, Dorastus, "went with his wife and the dead corpse into Bohemia where, after *they* were sumptuously entombed, Dorastus ended his days in contented quiet" (Robert Greene, *Pandosto*, 204, my emphasis).

77. On Hermione's exclusion from the play's primary spatiotemporal organizational principles, see Michael D. Bristol, *Big-Time Shakespeare*, 147–74.

78. David M. Bergeron, "The Restoration of Hermione in *The Winter's Tale*."

79. Frances Yates, *Majesty and Magic in Shakespeare's Last Plays*, 32–33.

80. David M. Bergeron, *Shakespeare's Romances and the Royal Family*, 51.

81. Roy Strong, *The Cult of Elizabeth*, 187–91. For the "Elizabethan revival" that grew up around Prince Henry and then Princess Elizabeth, see also Yates, *Majesty and Magic*, 17–37. For Prince Henry's conscious adoption of Tudor opinions and symbology, see Strong, *Henry Prince of Wales and England's Lost Renaissance*, 8, 145–48.

82. Adelman, *Suffocating Mothers*, 193.

83. For the marginalization of queens in *Henry VIII*—Catherine of Aragon's replacement by the sketchily drawn and relatively silent Anne Boleyn—see Kim H. Noling, "Grubbing Up the Stock: Dramatizing Queens in *Henry VIII*."

84. Jodi Mikalachki makes a similar claim about *Cymbeline*'s romance form, which requires the substitution of the docile and sexually unthreatening Imogen for the Boadicea-like Queen (*The Legacy of Boadicea*, 96–114).

85. Of course, tragicomedy was a new form only for England, having been invented several decades before in Italy. See Robert Henke, *Pastoral Transformations*, for the avenues and results of this influence.

86. Philip Fisher, *Making and Effacing Art*, 6.

Chapter 6: Milton's Queenly Paradise

1. G. M. Trevelyan, *England Under the Stuarts*, 394.

2. Andrew Marvell, "A Dialogue between the Two Horses," in *The Poems and Letters of Andrew Marvell*, 212. There is some doubt over whether this poem

is really Marvell's, but it was attributed to him at its first appearance in the *Second Part of the Collection of Poems on Affairs of State . . . By A—M—l* (1689), and in all subsequent early editions of the *State Poems*.

3. Edward Norman, *Roman Catholicism in England*, 39. For a concise account of the relation between the Popish Plot and the Exclusion crisis see Mark Kishlansky, *A Monarchy Transformed*, 240–62.

4. J. E. Neale, *Elizabeth I and Her Parliaments, 1584–1601*, 74.

5. David Cressy, *Bonfires and Bells*, 136.

6. Cressy, *Bonfires and Bells*, 137. London churches in the 1620s and 1630s contained a significant number of memorials and inscriptions praising the late queen to the Stuart kings' detriment, which similarly spoke to the popular use of her memory against the current monarchy; see Julia M. Walker, "Bones of Contention: Posthumous Images of Elizabeth and Stuart Politics." For the ways in which nostalgia for Elizabeth intensified and became more critical of the monarchy during the reign of Charles I than it had been under James I, see also D. R. Woolf, "Two Elizabeths? James I and the Late Queen's Famous Memory"; Anne Barton, "Harking Back to Elizabeth: Jonson and Caroline Nostalgia," in *Ben Jonson, Dramatist*, 300–320; J. D. Alsop, "The Cult of Elizabeth—Astraea and the Anti-Catholic 'Jubilye' of 1624"; and Georgianna Ziegler, "England's Savior: Elizabeth I in the Writings of Thomas Heywood."

7. Stephen Marshall, *A Sermon Preached before the Honourable House of Commons . . . November 17. 1640*, 47, quoted in Cressy, *Bonfires and Bells*, 139. See also Cornelius Burges, *A Sermon Preached to the Honourable House of Commons . . . Novem. 17. 1640*, which urges Parliament to follow the example of Elizabeth, the English Deborah.

8. J. P. Kenyon, *The Stuart Constitution*, 19.

9. H. R. Trevor-Roper, "Oliver Cromwell and His Parliaments," in *The Crisis of the Seventeenth Century*, 345–91.

10. Trevor-Roper, *The Crisis of the Seventeenth Century*, 261.

11. Henry King, *A Sermon of Deliverance. Preached at the Spittle on Easter Monday, 1626*, 3, quoted in Cressy, *Bonfires and Bells*, 135.

12. Hence the (in my view) incorrect argument, that Elizabeth's masculine body politic was a successful fiction, actually proves true in terms of many posthumous representations of the queen. See my discussion of the king's two bodies in Chapter 1.

13. Milton's ultimate point is that if Queen Elizabeth herself was not to be trusted to set the proper religious course, "What liberty of conscience can we then expect of others . . . traind up and governd by *Popish* and *Spanish* counsels?" (*CPW* 7:457).

14. See James Grantham Turner, *One Flesh*, 215–18. In *Tetrachordon*, for example, Milton devotes considerable argumentation to disproving that Genesis 1:27's "in the image of God created he him; male and female created he them" implies equality between the sexes (*CPW* 2:589–90).

15. Janet E. Halley, "Female Autonomy in Milton's Sexual Poetics," 242–46.

16. For a comparison between Milton's views on female insubordination in marriage and those of other Renaissance thinkers, see John Halkett, *Milton and the Idea of Matrimony*, 83–90.

17. Turner, *One Flesh*, 22; see also 224. For the rabbinical history of the Lilith legend and its treatment by Renaissance authors, see James Nohrnberg, *The Analogy of "The Faerie Queene,"* 228–39.

18. M. Lindsay Kaplan points out the potential instability—one certainly not desired by Milton—of this analogy between family and state: if the wife, not the husband, is seen as the oppressed party in marriage, then she might assert her will and divorce her husband even as the oppressed subject of the monarch does when he dethrones the king ("Subjection and Subjectivity").

19. This statement from *The Judgement of Martin Bucer*, Milton's translation of excerpts from Bucer's *De Regno Christi*, appears not in the Bucer portions of the text, but in Milton's original preface.

20. For a summation of Milton's antigynecocratic remarks in the *History* and elsewhere, see Edward Le Comte, *Milton and Sex*, 54–67. The dating of the *History* is notoriously difficult, but Nicholas von Maltzahn makes a good case that Books 1–4, which include most of Milton's anti-gynecocratic remarks, were written in 1649, the same year as *Eikonoklastes* and *The Tenure of Kings and Magistrates* (*Milton's "History of Britain,"* 22–48).

21. Stevie Davies, *The Feminine Reclaimed*, 179–81.

22. Debora Keller Shuger describes Calvinists' discomfort with the Roman Catholic-derived portrait of the suffering Christ, and their preferring, instead, to dwell upon Christ's ultimate triumph over the forces of evil. The Calvinist narrative of Christ is of the suffering son's transition into his ultimate role as vengeful patriarch ("The Death of Christ," in *The Renaissance Bible*, 89–127).

23. For Milton's fear of men's thrall to women leading to their becoming women themselves, see Turner, *One Flesh*, 225–26. For the male fear of "descending" on the Aristotelian physiological continuum from masculinity to femininity, see also Stephen Greenblatt, "Fiction and Friction," in *Shakespearean Negotiations*, 66–93; and Laura Levine, *Men in Women's Clothing*, 10–25.

24. Milton's sources for *The Tenure of Kings and Magistrates*, for example, include the following antigynecocratic authors and texts: Christopher Goodman's *How Superior Powers Oght to Be Obeyd* (1558); Knox's 1660 debates with William Maitland of Lethington over whether Mary, Queen of Scots ought to be forbidden to marry the Catholic Henry, Lord Darnley; Anthony Gilby's *Admonition to England and Scotland* (1558); Knox's *John Knoxe to the Reader* (1558), bound in the same volume as Gilby's tract and promising a continuation of Knox's attack on queenship in *The First Blast of the Trumpet Against the Monstrous Regiment of Women* (1558); and George Buchanan's *History of Scotland* (1582), including the portions detailing Marie de Guise's autocratic regency, and Mary, Queen of Scots's "tyranny" after the murder of Darnley. In his commonplace book Milton also notes, in his entries on "The King of England &c.," that the French author Francis Hotman's "book entitled *Franco-Gallia* shows that ordinary women are excluded from all public administration of affairs" (*CPW* 1:459). For Milton's commonplace-book entries on female rule and female rulers see Ruth Mohl, *John Milton and His Commonplace Book*, 164–68.

25. William Whittingham [or Whitingham], preface to Christopher Goodman, *How Superior Powers Oght to Be Obeyd of Their Subjects*, A2r-v.

26. For an analysis of Milton's responses in his late poems to the way royal

spectacle had been used from Charles I's execution to the Restoration, see Laura Lunger Knoppers's fascinating *Historicizing Milton*.
27. Christopher Hill, *Milton and the English Revolution*, 23.
28. E. C. Wilson, *England's Eliza*, 182.
29. See *Speeches Delivered to Her Majestie this Last Progresse* (Oxford, 1592), in John Lyly, *The Complete Works*, 1:477–84. Louis Adrian Montrose analyzes the queen's mythos as portrayed in the Sudeley entertainments in "'Eliza, Queene of shepheardes,' and the Pastoral of Power."
30. See George Gascoigne, "The Princely Pleasures at Kenelworth Castle," in *The Complete Works of George Gascoigne*, 2:102–4. Milton could have been acquainted with the Kenilworth entertainments either through Gascoigne's text (first printed in 1576, then included in his *Whole Woorkes* [London, 1587]), or through Robert Langham's [or Laneham's] *A Letter*, a popular colloquial account of the festivities published in 1575. See Susan Frye's fascinating analysis of the Kenilworth entertainments in *Elizabeth I*, 56–96. Frye details how the Lady of the Lake device replaced another piece penned by Gascoigne, which was evidently censored by the queen, that argued for the queen's marriage—preferably to Dudley, of course. Though staged at a time at which Elizabeth was still engaged in marriage negotiations, the device that replaced Gascoigne's, as Frye notes, anticipated the cult of virginity that would mark Elizabeth's self-representation after she had passed marriageable age (Frye, *Elizabeth I*, 86–87). The multiplication of virginal doubles for Elizabeth, to the extent that one Elizabeth figure rescues another, becomes, of course, a favorite device for any Elizabethan writer who seeks to compliment the queen—Spenser's Britomart rescues Amoret, for example. It seems to me striking, however, that Milton should resurrect this device in *A Mask*, as Sabrina, "a Virgin pure" (826), is required to release the Lady from the curiously lust-laden "marble venom'd seat / Smear'd with gums of glutinous heat" (916–17).
31. Von Maltzahn, *Milton's "History of Britain,"* 101. Sabrina seems an appropriate shadow for Elizabeth for several other reasons: she is a descendent of the royal Trojan line ("Virgin, daughter of *Locrine* / Sprung of old *Anchises'* line" [922–23]); and, in one of Milton's sources, she is conceived out of wedlock—her father deserts his first wife and crowns the mother of Habren (Sabrina) his queen, just as Henry VIII deserted Catherine of Aragon for the pregnant Anne Boleyn (Geoffrey of Monmouth, *History of the Kings of Britain*, 31).
32. Maureen Quilligan elaborates on the way *A Mask*, via its echoes of *A Midsummer Night's Dream*, reworks the mystical Elizabethan conjunction of virginity and political power (*Milton's Spenser*, 212–18).
33. David Norbrook, *Poetry and Politics in the English Renaissance*, 240.
34. For a fascinating comparison between Milton's embattled sexual identity in the Sixth Prolusion and the Lady's embattled virginity in the *Mask*, see Michael Lieb, *Milton and the Culture of Violence*, 83–113.
35. John Rogers, "The Enclosure of Virginity," 238. Although I focus here on the *Mask*'s virginity as an outlet for republican individuality, I am cognizant of the way virginity in this context plays into ideologies of the control of women within the bourgeois marriage, and of the control of the undisciplined lower "sorts" or classes of England; see Richard Halpern, "Puritanism and Maenadism in *A Mask*"; and Christopher Kendrick, "Milton and Sexuality."

36. Rogers, "The Enclosure of Virginity," 239.

37. Stephen M. Fallon, "The Metaphysics of Milton's Divorce Tracts," 70.

38. Milton assails current marriage law for placing "the worthiest part of man which is his minde, . . . beneath the formalities and respects of the body, to make it a servant of its owne vassall" (*CPW* 2:598). For the divorce tracts' disgust with sexuality and the flesh, particularly female flesh, see Turner, *One Flesh*, 197–201.

39. For Dalila as wife and for the connections between *Samson Agonistes* and the divorce tracts, see John Guillory, "Dalila's House."

40. The title of a thoughtful essay by Susanne Woods epitomizes the tendency to segregate Milton's female characters as a special category for considering the limits of human liberty: "How Free Are Milton's Women?"

41. Samuel Daniel, *Poems and A Defence of Ryme*, 129, 134, emphasis in original.

42. Richard Helgerson, *Forms of Nationhood*, 60–61. It would be inaccurate, however, to characterize Daniel as a champion of monarchy. Helgerson argues that the "Gothic" chivalric romance revived by poets like Spenser and Daniel features "a shared resistance to the totalizing encroachment of a royal authority on which both nevertheless depend" and points out that Daniel's *Defence of Rime* was first printed in a volume that began with "A Panegyric Congratulatory to the King's Most Excellent Majesty" cautioning the new king James I not to impose any change—including, it is implied, an absolutist monarchy—on England (*Forms of Nationhood*, 59, 38–39).

43. Milton reportedly confessed to Dryden "that Spenser was his original"; see John Dryden, "Preface to the *Fables*," in *Essays*, 2:247. For Milton's fondness for poetry of the Spenserian school—his headmaster at St. Paul's, Alexander Gil, championed Spenser over "plain style" poets like Jonson—see Norbrook, *Poetry and Politics*, 240.

44. Quilligan, *Milton's Spenser*, 104.

45. Heather James argues, though, that Milton values romance in that it leads upward in the hierarchy of genres, and hence toward virtue ("Milton's Eve, the Romance Genre, and Ovid," 127–30).

46. David Quint, *Epic and Empire*, 282. Quint's argument is much more subtle and convincing than that of Gordon Teskey, who argues quite sweepingly that Milton views Spenserian romance, and indeed Spenserian allegory, as incompatible with revealing truth; see Teskey, "From Allegory to Dialectic." I discuss below how Milton might value the romance genre precisely for its wandering qualities. For Milton's use of romance see also Barbara K. Lewalski, "Milton: Revaluations of Romance"; and Annabel Patterson, "*Paradise Regained*: A Last Chance at True Romance," who gives a detailed and useful account of Milton's progressive disengagement from various kinds of chivalric and pastoral romance. For the relation between Satan and chivalric romance see also Lewalski, "*Paradise Lost*" and the *Rhetoric of Literary Forms*, 65–71.

47. Francis Bacon, "*In Felicem Memoriam Elizabethae Angliae Reginae*," trans. James Spedding, in *The Works of Francis Bacon*, 6:317.

48. Annabel Patterson, *Censorship and Interpretation*, 174–84. Patterson points out that romance was not necessarily an escapist genre during the Protectorate period, and describes a number of romances from the 1640s and beyond whose

topics were overtly historical and political (*Censorship and Interpretation*, 188–210).

49. The romances referred to here, Honoré d'Urfé's *Astraea* (published in parts in 1610, 1619, and 1627) and Jorge Montemayor's *Diana* (1559), are not, of course, about Elizabeth; but their titles would have been associated with the late queen by Milton's English readership.

50. For specific allusions to Charles in the portrayal of Satan, see Hill, *Milton and the English Revolution*, 371–73. For the collection of attributes that connects Satan to the king, see Stevie Davies, *Images of Kingship in "Paradise Lost,"* 3–50; and Richard F. Hardin, *Civil Idolatry*, 164–201.

51. For the connections between Error and Sin see Quilligan, who argues that Milton is squeamish about the Spenserian polysemy that suspends the reader in the state of Error and requires him/her to make a personal assay at discerning meaning (*Milton's Spenser*, 80–98).

52. Quilligan, *Milton's Spenser*, 69.

53. Retrospectively, this amalgamation of Shakespearean and Spenserian images of queenship sheds new light on Milton's granting to Shakespeare's verse the "astonying," Medusan power of Spenser's own unregulated verse: "thou our fancy of itself bereaving, / Dost make us Marble with too much conceiving" ("On Shakespeare," 64). John Guillory connects the paralysis experienced by the reader of Shakespeare with the paralyzing magic of Comus, and describes how Milton's later work takes care to dissociate his own poetry from this Shakespearean work of "fancy"; see *Poetic Authority*, 19–21. Regarding the connections between Shakespearean tragedy and queenship, we ought to remember that the Trinity Manuscript contains plans for an unwritten tragedy, "Salomon Gynaecratumenus," or "Solomon under the Sway of Women" (cited in Le Comte, *Milton and Sex*, 47).

54. Linda Gregerson, *The Reformation of the Subject*, 149; and Quilligan, *Milton's Spenser*, 39–40.

55. Albert C. Labriola, "Milton's Eve and the Cult of Elizabeth I," 42.

56. Quint, *Epic and Empire*, 290. See also Michael Schoenfeldt, "Gender and Conduct in *Paradise Lost*," who interestingly argues that Eve, along with being granted authority by Adam, takes on the qualities and the skills of the Renaissance courtier who gains ascendency precisely through claiming submission—in other words, through *sprezzatura*.

57. Patricia Parker, *Literary Fat Ladies*, 198–99. Turner finds in this passage evidence that Adam "is left suspended between two paradigms of the loving relationship, an embattled hierarchy of Reason and Passion, man and woman, and a vision of equality-in-difference" (*One Flesh*, 280). Like Parker, I fail to see that equality is a possibility in Adam's discourse here; he knows he ought to be superior, but feels that she is in control. Adam's own perception of things, then, contradicts Gregerson's view that Adam is, necessarily, marrying downward when he marries Eve (*The Reformation of the Subject*, 171–76).

58. Tasso, *Gerusalemme Liberata*, 16.21, quoted and translated in A. Bartlett Giamatti, *The Earthly Paradise and the Renaissance Epic*, 314.

59. St. John Chrystostom, "Homily 26," in *Homilies on First Corinthians*, 150–51.

60. Diane Kelsey McColley, *Milton's Eve*, 4. See also McColley, *A Gust for*

Paradise, 196–213; and Ilona Bell, "Milton's Dialogue with Petrarch," who argues that we should consider Eve's account of her creation in light of the fact that Milton significantly alters the Petrarchan tradition to make Eve not only a beloved object but also a loving subject.

61. Mary Nyquist, "The Genesis of Gendered Subjectivity." Similarly, Janet E. Halley argues that Eve's will consists only of a decision to enter into heterosexual marriage—a "bourgeois form of compulsory heterosexuality [that] 'interpellates' woman, as Althusser would say, [and] calls upon her to assume the subjectivity of a *fully assenting* heterosexual" ("Female Autonomy in Milton's Sexual Poetics," 235, emphasis in original).

62. Nyquist, "The Genesis of Gendered Subjectivity," 119. Julia M. Walker similarly believes Eve's creation narrative comes first so that Adam's may put hers in the shade; see *Medusa's Mirrors*, 171–77.

63. Gregerson, *The Reformation of the Subject*, 196, 155. Turner, in contrast, sees the conflict of Eve's equality versus her submission as an "irresolvable doubleness at the heart of Milton's apprehension of wedded love—a contradiction that lies dormant in Genesis and the Pauline tradition" (*One Flesh*, 286). David Aers and Bob Hodge attribute this contradiction to Milton's being unable to free himself from restrictive sexual attitudes that he nonetheless criticizes (" 'Rational Burning': Milton on Sex and Marriage"). John Guillory iconoclastically dismisses the question of Eve's psychology and her subjection as an incorrect perspective on what is actually an economic question: Eve, like other feminine entities in *Paradise Lost*, is associated both with the boundless superfluity of Eden, and with a new ethos of bourgeois domestic frugality ("From the Superfluous to the Supernumery"). I discuss Guillory's thesis further below. For a Lacanian reading of the relation between "subjection" and "subjectification" in Eve's portrayal, see Marshall Grossman, *The Story of All Things*, 218–52.

64. Schoenfeldt asserts Eve's creative accomplishments in even more concrete terms: "Throughout the epic, Eve's capacity to generate social behavior, to articulate marital desire, and to interrogate paradisal existence challenges the masculine hierarchy based on precedence and physiology that the work habitually reaffirms" ("Gender and Conduct," 319).

65. See Susanne Lindgren Wofford's discussion of God's rhetoric as enforcing epic's "figural compulsion" *(The Choice of Achilles*, 372–79). For Satan's action and rhetoric as both doomed to repetition, see Regina M. Schwartz, *Remembering and Repeating*, 94–103.

66. For the lack of figurative language in Books 11 and 12 of *Paradise Lost* see Quilligan, *Milton's Spenser*, 239–41. Stanley Fish notes the ease with which Adam now discerns Michael's (and hence God's) meaning; I would suggest that revelation indeed comes easier when rhetoric is so unadorned it leaves little to interpretation (*Surprised by Sin*, 319). For Michael's narrative as a brief biblical epic, see Lewalski, *"Paradise Lost" and the Rhetoric of Literary Forms*, 50–54.

67. Diane McColley, "Subsequent or Precedent?" 133. For a revised and expanded version of this essay that considers both Adam and Eve as artists, see McColley, "The Arts of Eden," in *A Gust for Paradise*, 106–51.

68. Of eleven uses in *Paradise Lost* of "wanton," "wantoned," "wantonly," or

"wantonness," seven apply to Eve, the Garden, or historical seductresses. One other instance (1.414) applies to the Egyptian gods in Hell that, as we have seen, are also associated with feminine authority; still another describes the "wanton mask" of the feminizing "court amours" that must be exorcized from the description of wedded love in Adam and Eve's marital bower (4.767–68). Last, Satan deploys the serpent's coils into a seductive "wanton wreath" to "lure" Eve's eye (9.517–18). Only one use of a form of "wanton," describing the unheeding populace that will be swept away by the Flood (11.795), applies generically to a misguided humanity and bears no connection to female authority or its seductions.

69. Guillory, "From the Superfluous to the Supernumerary."

70. For poetry's affiliations with ravishing, feminine Muses and Sirens throughout Milton's work, see Halley's fine discussion ("Female Autonomy," 236–38); and Noam Flinker, "Courting Urania." There is a large body of criticism that discusses the links among gender, sexual and asexual reproduction, and creation in *Paradise Lost*. See, for example, Davies, *The Feminine Reclaimed*, 186–247; Turner, *One Flesh*, 230–309; John P. Rumrich, *Milton Unbound*, 94–146; and John T. Shawcross, "The Metaphor of Inspiration in *Paradise Lost*."

71. James, "Milton's Eve, the Romance Genre, and Ovid," 125. James's point is that Eve's portrayal is bound up with references to Ovid's notoriously corrupting *Ars Amatoria*, and hence puts a test to the reader of *Paradise Lost* of how to read romance rightly.

72. Parker, *Inescapable Romance*, 123–24. See also Richard Corum, "In White Ink," who argues that "[w]hat is important about Eve . . . is that she can do what Milton and Adam cannot do: she can imagine alternatives . . . she can appropriate, however temporarily, the father's prerogative to author her own life and circumstances" (138). For a spirited refutation of Fish and other didactic readers of Milton, see John P. Rumrich's delightful *Milton Unbound*.

73. Parker, *Inescapable Romance*, 142. Gregerson similarly refutes Fish by distinguishing between the richness and multiplicity of language and its potential for hypocrisy (*The Reformation of the Subject*, 190–91); and Turner argues that, while a "fallen" perspective of reading dominates the poem, *Paradise Lost* also offers as models of response some that are not straightforwardly evil (*One Flesh*, 256–57).

74. Quint, *Epic and Empire*, 302–3. For the poem's commitment to creating a republican polity see also Mary Ann Radzinowicz, "The Politics of *Paradise Lost*," although Radzinowicz oddly does not even consider Eve as part of her analysis. For Milton's prose style as similarly putting republican liberty into action, see Susanne Woods, "Elective Poetics and Milton's Prose."

75. See Turner's description of Milton's treatment of poetry as a sensuous mode of apprehending truth (*One Flesh*, 184).

76. This point is made by Kevis Goodman, " 'Wasted Labor'?"

77. See, for example, James, "Milton's Eve, the Romance Genre, and Ovid." Quilligan renames this romance to which the end of *Paradise Lost* is committed a "marital epic" (*Milton's Spenser*, 238–39).

78. John Dryden, "Dedication of the *Aeneis*," in *Essays*, 2:165.

Afterword: Queenship and New Feminine Genres

1. Mary Sidney Herbert, the Countess of Pembroke, "A Dialogue between Two Shepherds, Thenot and Piers, in Praise of Astrea," in Francis Davison, ed., *A Poetical Rhapsody*, 40, 42.

2. Anne Bradstreet, "In Honour of that High and Mighty Princess Queen Elizabeth of Happy Memory," in *The Works of Anne Bradstreet*, 194; hereafter cited parenthetically in the text.

3. Catherine Gallagher, "Embracing the Absolute: The Politics of the Female Subject in Seventeenth-Century England."

4. Gallagher, "Embracing the Absolute," 28–29; and *Nobody's Story*, 49–56.

5. See Thomas Laqueur, *Making Sex*, 149–92.

6. For masculine appropriations of Cleopatra's directorial skills see Katherine Eggert, "Age Cannot Wither Him: Warren Beatty's Bugsy as Hollywood Cleopatra."

7. John Dryden, *All For Love*, in *The Works of John Dryden*, vol. 13, 1.1.183–84, 3.1.94–95, and 4.1.91–93.

8. Nancy Armstrong and Leonard Tennenhouse, *The Imaginary Puritan*, 89–113. See also Linda Gregerson, who argues that *Paradise Lost* invents the post-lapsarian subject as a *she*, but a *she* associated with domesticity as opposed to God's masculine monarchy (*The Reformation of the Subject*, 148–97).

9. Armstrong and Tennenhouse, *The Imaginary Puritan*, 196–216. For *Paradise Lost* as precursor of the novel see also Catherine Belsey, *John Milton*, 95–101. For Eve's subjectivity as formative of the subjectivity required for readers of the novel, see Mary Nyquist's argument that "the domestic sphere with which [Eve's] subjectivity associates itself will soon be in need of novels whose heroines are represented learning, in struggles whose conclusions are almost always implicit in the way they begin, the value of submitting desire to the paternal law" ("The Genesis of Gendered Subjectivity in the Divorce Tracts and *Paradise Lost*," 123).

10. For critical assessments of Milton as either a belated Puritan or a belated humanist, see Laura Lunger Knoppers, *Historicizing Milton*, 5–10. Richard Helgerson sees Milton as part of an entire generation of belated Elizabethan poets; see *Self-Crowned Laureates*, 185–282.

Bibliography

Adams, Simon. "Faction, Clientage and Party: English Politics, 1550–1603." *History Today* 32, no. 12 (December 1982): 33–39.

Adelman, Janet. *The Common Liar: An Essay on "Antony and Cleopatra."* New Haven: Yale University Press, 1973.

———. *Suffocating Mothers: Fantasies of Maternal Origin in Shakespeare's Plays, "Hamlet" to "The Tempest."* New York: Routledge, 1992.

Aers, David, and Bob Hodge. " 'Rational Burning': Milton on Sex and Marriage." In *Literature, Language and Society in England, 1580–1680*, by David Aers, Bob Hodge, and Gunther Kress, 122–51. Dublin: Gill and Macmillan; Totowa, N.J.: Barnes and Noble, 1981.

Akrigg, G. P. V., ed. *Letters of King James VI and I.* Berkeley and Los Angeles: University of California Press, 1984.

Allen, William. *An admonition to the Nobility and People of England and Ireland Concerninge the Present Warres.* Antwerp, 1588.

Alpers, Paul. *The Poetry of "The Faerie Queene."* Princeton: Princeton University Press, 1967.

———. "Spenser's Late Pastorals." *ELH* 56 (1989): 797–817.

Alsop, J. D. "The Cult of Elizabeth—Astraea and the Anti-Catholic 'Jubilye' of 1624." *Cahiers Elisabethains* 22 (1982): 93–94.

Altman, Joel. "Vile Participation: The Amplification of Violence in the Theater of *Henry V.*" *Shakespeare Quarterly* 42 (1991): 1–32.

Anderson, Judith H. "Arthur, Argante, and the Ideal Vision: An Exercise in Speculation and Parody." In *The Passing of Arthur: New Essays in Arthurian Tradition*, ed. Christopher Bagwell and William Sharpe, 193–206. New York: Garland, 1988.

Aptekar, Jane. *Icons of Justice: Iconography and Thematic Imagery in Book V of "The Faerie Queene."* New York: Columbia University Press, 1969.

Archer, John Michael. "Antiquity and Degeneration in *Antony and Cleopatra.*" In *Race, Ethnicity, and Power in the Renaissance*, ed. Joyce Green MacDonald, 145–64. Madison, N.J.: Fairleigh Dickinson University Press; London: Associated University Presses, 1997.

Ariosto, Ludovico. *Orlando Furioso*, trans. Sir John Harington, ed. Robert McNulty. Oxford: Clarendon, 1972.

Aristotle. *Poetics*, trans. S. H. Butcher. In *Critical Theory Since Plato*, ed. Hazard Adams, 48–66. New York: Harcourt Brace Jovanovich, 1971.

Armstrong, Nancy, and Leonard Tennenhouse. *The Imaginary Puritan: Literature, Intellectual Labor, and the Origins of Personal Life.* Berkeley and Los Angeles: University of California Press, 1992.

Axton, Marie. *The Queen's Two Bodies: Drama and the Elizabethan Succession.* London: Royal Historical Society, 1977.

Aylmer, John. *An Harborowe for Faithfull and Trewe Subjectes.* London, 1559.

Bacon, Francis. *The Works of Francis Bacon, with a Life of the Author,* ed. Basil Montagu. 3 vols. Philadelphia: Parry and McMillan, 1857.

————. *The Works of Francis Bacon,* ed. James Spedding, Robert Leslie Ellis, and Douglas Denon Heath. 9 vols. 1857; rev. ed. London: Longman, 1878.

Baldo, Jonathan. "Wars of Memory in *Henry V.*" *Shakespeare Quarterly* 47 (1996): 132–59.

Barber, C. L., and Richard Wheeler. *The Whole Journey: Shakespeare's Power of Development.* Berkeley and Los Angeles: University of California Press, 1986.

Barish, Jonas. *The Antitheatrical Prejudice.* Berkeley and Los Angeles: University of California Press, 1981.

Barker, Francis. *The Tremulous Private Body: Essays on Subjection.* 1984; 2d ed. Ann Arbor: University of Michigan Press, 1995.

Barroll, Leeds. "A New History for Shakespeare and His Time." *Shakespeare Quarterly* 39 (1988): 441–64.

————. *Politics, Plague, and Shakespeare's Theater: The Stuart Years.* Ithaca: Cornell University Press, 1991.

Barton, Anne. *Ben Jonson, Dramatist.* Cambridge: Cambridge University Press, 1984.

Bell, Ilona. "Milton's Dialogue with Petrarch." *Milton Studies* 28 (1992): 91–120.

Bellamy, Elizabeth J. *Translations of Power: Narcissism and the Unconscious in Epic History.* Ithaca: Cornell University Press, 1992.

————. "The Vocative and the Vocational: The Unreadability of Elizabeth in *The Faerie Queene.*" *ELH* 54 (1987): 1–30.

Belsey, Catherine. "Cleopatra's Seduction." In *Alternative Shakespeares Volume 2,* ed. Terence Hawkes, 38–62. London: Routledge, 1996.

————. *John Milton: Language, Gender, Power.* Oxford: Basil Blackwell, 1988.

————. *The Subject of Tragedy: Identity and Difference in Renaissance Drama.* London: Methuen, 1985.

Bentley, Gerald Eades. *The Professions of Dramatist and Player in Shakespeare's Time, 1590–1642.* 1971 and 1984; reprint in 1 vol., Princeton: Princeton University Press, 1986.

Berger, Harry, Jr. "Actaeon at the Hinder Gate: The Stag Party in Spenser's Gardens of Adonis." In *Desire in the Renaissance: Psychoanalysis and Literature,* ed. Valeria Finucci and Regina Schwartz, 91–119. Princeton: Princeton University Press, 1994.

————. *Imaginary Audition: Shakespeare on Stage and Page.* Berkeley and Los Angeles: University of California Press, 1989.

————. " 'Kidnapped Romance': Discourse in *The Faerie Queene.*" In *Unfolded Tales: Essays on Renaissance Romance,* ed. George M. Logan and Gordon Teskey, 208–56. Ithaca: Cornell University Press, 1989.

————. *Making Trifles of Terrors: Redistributing Complicities in Shakespeare,* ed. Peter Erickson. Stanford: Stanford University Press, 1997.

————. "Narrative as Rhetoric in *The Faerie Queene.*" *English Literary Renaissance* 21 (1991): 3–48.

————. *Revisionary Play: Studies in the Spenserian Dynamics.* Berkeley and Los Angeles: University of California Press, 1988.

Bergeron, David M. "The Restoration of Hermione in *The Winter's Tale.*" In *Shakespeare's Romances Reconsidered,* ed. Carol McGinnis Kay and Henry E. Jacobs, 125–33. Lincoln: University of Nebraska Press, 1978.

————. *Shakespeare's Romances and the Royal Family.* Lawrence: University Press of Kansas, 1985.

Berry, Edward I. "'True Things and Mock'ries': Epic and History in *Henry V.*" *Journal of English and Germanic Philology* 78 (1979): 1–16.

Berry, Philippa. *Of Chastity and Power: Elizabethan Literature and the Unmarried Queen.* London: Routledge, 1989.

Bertram, Paul, and Bernice W. Kliman, eds. *The Three-Text "Hamlet": Parallel Texts of the First and Second Quartos and First Folio.* New York: AMS, 1991.

Bishop, T. G. *Shakespeare and the Theatre of Wonder.* Cambridge: Cambridge University Press, 1996.

Blackwood, Adam. *Martyre de la Royne d'Escosse.* 1589; reprint, Ilkley, England: Scolar Press, 1978.

Blissett, William. "Spenser's Mutabilitie." In *Essential Articles for the Study of Edmund Spenser,* ed. A. C. Hamilton, 253–66. Hamden, Conn.: Archon Books, 1972.

Bloom, Harold. *The Anxiety of Influence: A Theory of Poetry.* New York: Oxford University Press, 1973.

Blum, Abbe. "'Strike all that look upon with mar[b]le': Monumentalizing Women in Shakespeare's Plays." In *The Renaissance Englishwoman in Print: Counterbalancing the Canon,* ed. Anne M. Haselkorn and Betty S. Travitsky, 99–118. Amherst: University of Massachusetts Press, 1990.

Boehrer, Bruce Thomas. *Monarchy and Incest in Renaissance England: Literature, Culture, Kinship, and Kingship.* Philadelphia: University of Pennsylvania Press, 1992.

Bono, Barbara J. *Literary Transvaluation: From Vergilian Epic to Shakespearean Tragicomedy.* Berkeley and Los Angeles: University of California Press, 1984.

Born, Hanspeter. "The Date of *2, 3 Henry VI.*" *Shakespeare Quarterly* 25 (1974): 323–34.

Borris, Kenneth. *Spenser's Poetics of Prophecy in "The Faerie Queene" 5.* English Literary Studies Monograph Series, no. 52. Victoria, B.C.: University of Victoria, 1991.

Bowers, Fredson Thayer. *Elizabethan Revenge Tragedy, 1587–1642.* 1940; reprint, Gloucester, Mass.: Peter Smith, 1959.

Bowman, Mary R. "'she there as Princess rained': Spenser's Figure of Elizabeth." *Renaissance Quarterly* 43 (1990): 509–28.

Bradstreet, Anne. *The Works of Anne Bradstreet,* ed. Jeannine Hensley. Cambridge, Mass.: Harvard University Press, 1967.

Bristol, Michael D. *Big-Time Shakespeare.* London: Routledge, 1996.

Buchanan, George. *Ane Detectioun of the Duinges of Marie Quene of Scottes.* London, 1571.

Burges, Cornelius. *A Sermon Preached to the Honourable House of Commons . . . Novem. 17. 1640.* London, 1641.

Burke, Peter. *The Renaissance Sense of the Past.* London: Edward Arnold, 1969.

Burt, Richard. *Licensed by Authority: Ben Jonson and the Discourses of Censorship.* Ithaca: Cornell University Press, 1993.

Cain, Thomas H. *Praise in "The Faerie Queene."* Lincoln: University of Nebraska Press, 1978.

Calderwood, James L. *Metadrama in Shakespeare's Henriad: "Richard II" to "Henry V."* Berkeley and Los Angeles: University of California Press, 1979.

Calendar of State Papers, Domestic Series, of the Reign of Elizabeth, 1598–1601. 1869; reprint, Nendeln, Liechtenstein: Kraus, 1967.

Calendar of State Papers, Domestic Series, of the Reign of Elizabeth, 1601–1603. 1870; reprint, Nendeln, Liechtenstein: Kraus, 1967.

Calendar of State Papers Relating to Scotland and Mary, Queen of Scots, 1547–1603. 13 vols. Edinburgh: H. M. General Register House, 1898–1952.

Campbell, Lily B., ed. *A Mirror for Magistrates.* 1938; reprint, New York: Barnes and Noble, 1960.

Carroll, Clare. "The Construction of Gender and the Cultural and Political Other in *The Faerie Queene* 5 and *A View of the Present State of Ireland*: The Critics, the Context, and the Case of Radigund." *Criticism* 32 (1990): 163–92.

———. "Representations of Women in Some Early Modern English Tracts on the Colonization of Ireland." *Albion* 25 (1993): 379–93.

Cary, Louise. "*Hamlet* Recycled, or the Tragical History of the Prince's Prints." *ELH* 61 (1994): 783–805.

Cavanagh, Sheila T. *Wanton Eyes and Chaste Desires: Female Sexuality in "The Faerie Queene."* Bloomington: Indiana University Press, 1994.

Cavell, Stanley. *Disowning Knowledge in Six Plays of Shakespeare.* Cambridge: Cambridge University Press, 1987.

Chambers, E. K. *The Elizabethan Stage,* 4 vols. 1923; reprint, Oxford: Clarendon, 1967.

Charnes, Linda. *Notorious Identity: Materializing the Subject in Shakespeare.* Cambridge, Mass.: Harvard University Press, 1993.

Chettle, Henry. *England's Mourning Garment; worn here by plain Shepherds, in memory of their sacred Mistres, Elisabeth.* In *The Harleian Miscellany,* ed. William Oldys, vol. 3, 500–18. London, 1745.

Chrystostom, St. John. *Homilies on First Corinthians.* A Select Library of the Nicene and Post-Nicene Fathers of the Christian Church, First Series, ed. Philip Schaff, vol. 12. Grand Rapids, Mich.: W. R. Eerdmans, 1956.

Coke, Edward. *The Second Part of the Institutes of the Laws of England.* London, 1662.

Colie, Rosalie. *The Resources of Kind: Genre-Theory in the Renaissance,* ed. Barbara K. Lewalski. Berkeley and Los Angeles: University of California Press, 1973.

———. *Shakespeare's Living Art.* Princeton: Princeton University Press, 1974.

Collection of Ancient Scottish Prophecies, in Alliterative Verse: Reprinted from Waldegrave's Edition, MDCIII. Edinburgh: Ballantyne, 1833.

Collections, Part III. Malone Society Collections, ed. W. W. Greg, vol. 1, no. 3. Oxford: Oxford University Press for the Malone Society, 1909.

Constable, Henry. *A Discoverye of a Conterfecte Conference.* English Recusant Literature, 1558–1640, vol. 6, ed. D. M. Rogers. 1600; reprint, Menston, England: Scolar Press, 1969.

Corum, Richard. "In White Ink: *Paradise Lost* and Milton's Ideas of Women." In *Milton and the Idea of Woman*, ed. Julia M. Walker, 120–47. Urbana: University of Illinois Press, 1988.

Cressy, David. *Bonfires and Bells: National Memory and the Protestant Calendar in Elizabethan and Stuart England*. Berkeley and Los Angeles: University of California Press, 1989.

Daniel, Samuel. *Poems and A Defence of Ryme*, ed. Arthur Colby Sprague. 1930; reprint, Chicago: University of Chicago Press, 1965.

Danson, Lawrence. "*Henry V*: King, Chorus, and Critics." *Shakespeare Quarterly* 34 (1983): 27–43.

Davies, Stevie. *The Feminine Reclaimed: The Idea of Woman in Spenser, Shakespeare, and Milton*. Lexington: University Press of Kentucky, 1986.

———. *Images of Kingship in "Paradise Lost": Milton's Politics and Christian Liberty*. Columbia: University of Missouri Press, 1983.

Davison, Francis, ed. *A Poetical Rhapsody*, ed. A. H. Bullen. 2 vols. London: George Bell, 1890.

The deceyte of women, to the instruction and ensample of all men, yonge and old. London, 1560.

de Grazia, Margreta. "Fin-de-Siècle Renaissance England." In *Fins de Siècle: English Poetry in 1590, 1690, 1790, 1890, 1990*, ed. Elaine Scarry, 37–63. Baltimore: Johns Hopkins University Press, 1995.

———. "Imprints: Shakespeare, Gutenberg and Descartes." In *Alternative Shakespeares Volume 2*, ed. Terence Hawkes, 63–94. London: Routledge, 1996.

Dekker, Thomas. *The Whore of Babylon by Thomas Dekker: A Critical Edition*, ed. Marianne Gateson Riely. New York: Garland, 1980.

Devereux, Walter B. *Lives and Letters of the Devereux, Earls of Essex in the Reigns of Elizabeth, James I, and Charles I, 1540–1646*. 2 vols. London: J. Murray, 1853.

D'Ewes, Sir Simonds. *The Diary of Sir Simonds D'Ewes, 1622–1624*, ed. Elisabeth Bourcier. Paris: Didier, 1974.

Dobin, Howard. *Merlin's Disciples: Prophecy, Poetry, and Power in Renaissance England*. Stanford, Calif.: Stanford University Press, 1990.

Dollimore, Jonathan, and Alan Sinfield. "History and Ideology: The Instance of *Henry V*." In *Alternative Shakespeares*, ed. John Drakakis, 206–27. London: Methuen, 1985.

———. "History and Ideology, Masculinity and Miscegenation." In *Faultlines: Cultural Materialism and the Politics of Dissident Reading*, by Alan Sinfield, 109–42. Berkeley and Los Angeles: University of California Press, 1992.

Dryden, John. *Essays of John Dryden*, ed. W. P. Ker. 2 vols. 1900; reprint, New York: Russell and Russell, 1961.

———. *The Works of John Dryden*, ed. Edward Niles Hooker, H.T. Swedenberg, Jr., and Alan Roper. 13 vols. to date. Berkeley: University of California Press, 1956- .

Dunseath, T. K. *Spenser's Allegory of Justice in Book Five of "The Faerie Queene."* Princeton: Princeton University Press, 1968.

Dutton, Richard. "Shakespeare and Lancaster." *Shakespeare Quarterly* 49 (1998): 1–21.

Eggert, Katherine. "Age Cannot Wither Him: Warren Beatty's Bugsy as Hollywood Cleopatra." In *Shakespeare, the Movie: Popularizing the Plays on Film, TV, and Video*, ed. Lynda E. Boose and Richard Burt, 198–214. London: Routledge, 1997.

Eliot, T. S. *Selected Prose of T. S. Eliot*, ed. Frank Kermode. San Diego: Harcourt Brace, 1975.

Enterline, Lynn. " 'You speak a language that I understand not': The Rhetoric of Animation in *The Winter's Tale*." *Shakespeare Quarterly* 48 (1997): 17–44.

Erickson, Amy Louise. *Women and Property in Early Modern England*. London: Routledge, 1993.

Erickson, Peter. *Patriarchal Structures in Shakespeare's Drama*. Berkeley and Los Angeles: University of California Press, 1985.

———. *Rewriting Shakespeare, Rewriting Ourselves*. Berkeley and Los Angeles: University of California Press, 1991.

Falco, Raphael. *Conceived Presences: Literary Genealogy in Renaissance England*. Amherst: University of Massachusetts Press, 1994.

Fallon, Stephen M. "The Metaphysics of Milton's Divorce Tracts." In *Politics, Poetics, and Hermeneutics in Milton's Prose*, ed. David Loewenstein and James Grantham Turner, 69–83. Cambridge: Cambridge University Press, 1990.

Farley-Hills, David. *Shakespeare and the Rival Playwrights, 1600–1606*. London: Routledge, 1990.

Felperin, Howard. " 'Tongue-tied our queen?': The Deconstruction of Presence in *The Winter's Tale*." In *Shakespeare and the Question of Theory*, ed. Patricia Parker and Geoffrey Hartman, 3–18. New York: Methuen, 1985.

Ferguson, Margaret W. "*Hamlet*: Letters and Spirits." In *Shakespeare and the Question of Theory*, ed. Patricia Parker and Geoffrey Hartman, 292–309. New York: Methuen, 1985.

Fiedler, Leslie. *The Stranger in Shakespeare*. New York: Stein and Day, 1972.

Finkelpearl, Philip J. " 'The Comedians' Liberty': Censorship of the Jacobean Stage Reconsidered." *English Literary Renaissance* 16 (1986): 123–38.

Firth, Katharine R. *The Apocalyptic Tradition in Reformation Britain, 1530–1645*. Oxford: Oxford University Press, 1979.

Fish, Stanley E. *Surprised by Sin: The Reader in "Paradise Lost."* 1967; 2d ed. Berkeley and Los Angeles: University of California Press, 1971.

Fisher, N. R. R. "The Queenes Courte in her Councell Chamber at Westminster." *English Historical Review* 108 (1993): 314–37.

Fisher, Philip. *Making and Effacing Art: Modern American Art in a Culture of Museums*. New York: Oxford University Press, 1991.

Fleay, Frederick Gard. *A Chronicle History of the London Stage, 1559–1642*. New York: G. E. Stechert, 1909.

Fleming, Juliet. "*The French Garden*: An Introduction to Women's French." *ELH* 56 (1989): 19–51.

Fletcher, Angus. *The Prophetic Moment: An Essay on Spenser*. Chicago: University of Chicago Press, 1971.

Flinker, Noam. "Courting Urania: The Narrator of *Paradise Lost* Invokes His Muse." In *Milton and the Idea of Woman*, ed. Julia M. Walker, 86–99. Urbana: University of Illinois Press, 1988.

Forse, James. *Art Imitates Business: Commercial and Political Influences in Elizabethan Theatre*. Bowling Green, Ohio: Bowling Green State University Popular Press, 1993.

Foucault, Michel. *Discipline and Punish: The Birth of the Prison*, trans. Alan Sheridan. New York: Vintage, 1977.

Fraser, Antonia. *Mary Queen of Scots*. New York: Delacorte, 1969.

Freud, Sigmund. *The Standard Edition of the Complete Psychological Works of Sigmund Freud*, trans. James Strachey. 24 vols. London: Hogarth, 1953–74.

Frye, Northrop. *Northrop Frye on Shakespeare*, ed. Robert Sandler. New Haven: Yale University Press, 1986.

———. *The Secular Scripture: A Study of the Structure of Romance*. Cambridge, Mass.: Harvard University Press, 1976.

Frye, Roland Mushat. *The Renaissance "Hamlet": Issues and Responses in 1600*. Princeton: Princeton University Press, 1984.

Frye, Susan. *Elizabeth I: The Competition for Representation*. Oxford: Oxford University Press, 1992.

———. "Of Chastity and Violence: Elizabeth I and Edmund Spenser in the House of Busirane." *Signs* 20 (1994): 49–78.

Gallagher, Catherine. "Embracing the Absolute: The Politics of the Female Subject in Seventeenth-Century England." *Genders* 1 (1988): 24–39.

———. *Nobody's Story: The Vanishing Acts of Women Writers in the Marketplace, 1670–1820*. Berkeley and Los Angeles: University of California Press, 1994.

Garber, Marjorie. *Shakespeare's Ghost Writers: Literature As Uncanny Causality*. New York: Methuen, 1987.

———. "'What's Past Is Prologue': Temporality and Prophecy in Shakespeare's History Plays." In *Renaissance Genres: Essays on Theory, History, and Interpretation*, ed. Barbara Kiefer Lewalski, 301–31. Cambridge, Mass.: Harvard University Press, 1986.

Gascoigne, George. *The Complete Works of George Gascoigne*, ed. John W. Cunliffe. 2 vols. Cambridge: Cambridge University Press, 1907–10.

Gawdy, Philip. *Letters of Philip Gawdy of West Harling, Norfolk, and of London to Various Members of His Family, 1579–1616*, ed. Isaac Herbert Jeayes. London: J. B. Nichols, 1906.

Geoffrey of Monmouth. *History of the Kings of Britain*, trans. Sebastian Evans, rev. ed. Charles W. Dunn. New York: E. P. Dutton, 1958.

Giamatti, A. Bartlett. *The Earthly Paradise and the Renaissance Epic*. Princeton: Princeton University Press, 1966.

Girard, René. "Hamlet's Dull Revenge." In *Literary Theory/Renaissance Texts*, ed. Patricia Parker and David Quint, 280–302. Baltimore: Johns Hopkins University Press, 1986.

Goldberg, Jonathan. *Endlesse Worke: Spenser and the Structures of Discourse*. Baltimore: Johns Hopkins University Press, 1981.

———. *James I and the Politics of Literature: Jonson, Shakespeare, Donne, and Their Contemporaries*. 1983; reprint, Stanford: Stanford University Press, 1989.

———. *Writing Matter: From the Hands of the English Renaissance*. Stanford: Stanford University Press, 1990.

Goldman, Michael. *Shakespeare and the Energies of Drama*. Princeton: Princeton University Press, 1972.

Goodman, Christopher. *How Superior Powers Oght to Be Obeyd of Their Subjects*. 1558; reprint, New York: Columbia University Press for the Facsimile Text Society, 1931.

Goodman, Godfrey. *The Court of King James I*, ed. John Sherren Brewer. 2 vols. London: R. Bentley, 1839.

Goodman, Kevis. "'Wasted Labor'? Milton's Eve, the Poet's Work, and the Challenge of Sympathy." *ELH* 74 (1997): 415–46.

Gosson, Stephen. *The Schoole of Abuse*. London, 1579.

Greenblatt, Stephen. *Learning to Curse: Essays in Early Modern Culture*. New York: Routledge, 1990.

———. *Renaissance Self-Fashioning from More to Shakespeare*. Chicago: University of Chicago Press, 1980.

———. *Shakespearean Negotiations: The Circulation of Social Energy in Renaissance England*. Berkeley and Los Angeles: University of California Press, 1988.

Greene, Robert. *Pandosto, the Triumph of Time*. In *An Anthology of Elizabethan Prose Fiction*, ed. Paul Salzman, 151–204. Oxford: Oxford University Press, 1987.

Greene, Thomas M. *The Light in Troy: Imitation and Discovery in Renaissance Poetry*. New Haven: Yale University Press, 1982.

Greengrass, M. "Mary, Dowager Queen of France." In *Mary Stewart: Queen in Three Kingdoms*, ed. Michael Lynch, 171–94. Oxford: Basil Blackwell, 1988.

Gregerson, Linda. *The Reformation of the Subject: Spenser, Milton, and the English Protestant Epic*. Cambridge: Cambridge University Press, 1995.

Grossman, Marshall. *The Story of All Things: Writing the Self in English Renaissance Narrative Poetry*. Durham: Duke University Press, 1998.

Guillory, John. "Dalila's House: *Samson Agonistes* and the Sexual Division of Labor." In *Rewriting the Renaissance: The Discourses of Sexual Difference in Early Modern Europe*, ed. Margaret W. Ferguson, Maureen Quilligan, and Nancy J. Vickers, 106–22. Chicago: University of Chicago Press, 1986.

———. "From the Superfluous to the Supernumerary: Reading Gender into *Paradise Lost*." In *Soliciting Interpretation: Literary Theory and Seventeenth-Century English Poetry*, ed. Elizabeth D. Harvey and Katharine Eisaman Maus, 68–88. Chicago: University of Chicago Press, 1990.

———. *Poetic Authority: Spenser, Milton, and Literary History*. New York: Columbia University Press, 1983.

Gurr, Andrew. *Playgoing in Shakespeare's London*. Cambridge: Cambridge University Press, 1987.

———. *The Shakespearian Playing Companies*. Oxford: Clarendon, 1996.

Guy, John. "The 1590s: The Second Reign of Elizabeth I?" In *The Reign of Elizabeth I: Court and Culture in the Last Decade*, ed. John Guy, 1–19. Cambridge: Cambridge University Press, 1995.

Hackett, Helen. *Virgin Mother, Maiden Queen: Elizabeth I and the Cult of the Virgin Mary*. New York: St. Martin's, 1995.

Haigh, Christopher. *Elizabeth I*. New York: Longman, 1988.

Halkett, John. *Milton and the Idea of Matrimony: A Study of the Divorce Tracts and "Paradise Lost."* New Haven: Yale University Press, 1970.

Hall, Kim F. *Things of Darkness: Economies of Race and Gender in Early Modern England.* Ithaca: Cornell University Press, 1995.

Halley, Janet E. "Female Autonomy in Milton's Sexual Poetics." In *Milton and the Idea of Woman,* ed. Julia M. Walker, 230–53. Urbana: University of Illinois Press, 1988.

Halpern, Richard. *The Poetics of Primitive Accumulation: English Renaissance Culture and the Genealogy of Capital.* Ithaca: Cornell University Press, 1991.

———. "Puritanism and Maenadism in *A Mask.*" In *Rewriting the Renaissance: The Discourses of Sexual Difference in Early Modern Europe,* ed. Margaret W. Ferguson, Maureen Quilligan, and Nancy J. Vickers, 88–105. Chicago: University of Chicago Press, 1986.

———. *Shakespeare among the Moderns.* Ithaca: Cornell University Press, 1997.

Hamilton, A. C. *The Structure of Allegory in "The Faerie Queene."* Oxford: Clarendon, 1961.

Hampton, Timothy. *Writing from History: The Rhetoric of Exemplarity in Renaissance Literature.* Ithaca: Cornell University Press, 1990.

Hardin, Richard F. *Civil Idolatry: Desacralizing and Monarchy in Spenser, Shakespeare, and Milton.* Newark: University of Delaware Press; London: Associated University Presses, 1992.

Harington, Sir John. *Nugae Antiquae,* ed. Henry Harington. 2 vols. London, 1769.

———. *A Tract on the Succession to the Crown.* London: The Roxburghe Club, 1853.

Harris, Jonathan Gil. " 'Narcissus in thy face': Roman Desire and the Difference It Fakes in *Antony and Cleopatra.*" *Shakespeare Quarterly* 45 (1994): 408–25.

Harris, Victor. *All Coherence Gone.* Chicago: University of Chicago Press, 1949.

Hayward, John. *An answer to the first part of a certaine conference, concerning succession, published not long since under the name of R. Dolman.* London, 1603.

Hazlitt, William. *Characters of Shakespeare's Plays,* ed. Arthur Quiller-Couch. Oxford: Oxford University Press, 1916.

Headley, P. C. *The Life of Mary Queen of Scots.* Boston: Lee and Shepard, 1853.

Heisch, Allison. "Queen Elizabeth I: Parliamentary Rhetoric and the Exercise of Power." *Signs* 1 (1975): 31–56.

Helgerson, Richard. *Forms of Nationhood: The Elizabethan Writing of England.* Chicago: University of Chicago Press, 1992.

———. *Self-Crowned Laureates: Spenser, Jonson, Milton, and the Literary System.* Berkeley and Los Angeles: University of California Press, 1983.

Henderson, Diana. *Passion Made Public: Elizabethan Lyric, Gender, and Performance.* Urbana: University of Illinois Press, 1995.

Henke, Robert. *Pastoral Transformations: Italian Tragicomedy and Shakespeare's Late Plays.* Newark: University of Delaware Press; London: Associated University Presses, 1997.

Herman, Peter C. " 'O, 'tis a gallant king': Shakespeare's *Henry V* and the Crisis of the 1590s." In *Tudor Political Culture,* ed. Dale Hoak, 204–25. Cambridge: Cambridge University Press, 1995.

Heywood, Thomas. *An Apology for Actors*. London, 1612.

Hibbard, G. R. "The Chronology of the Three Substantive Texts of Shakespeare's *Hamlet*." In *The Hamlet First Published (Q1, 1603): Origins, Form, Intertextualities*, ed. Thomas Clayton, 79–89. Newark: University of Delaware Press; London: Associated University Presses, 1992.

Highley, Christopher. *Shakespeare, Spenser, and the Crisis in Ireland*. Cambridge: Cambridge University Press, 1997.

Hill, Christopher. *Milton and the English Revolution*. Harmondsworth, England: Penguin, 1977.

Hillebrand, Harold Newcomb. *The Child Actors: A Chapter in Elizabethan Stage History*. University of Illinois Studies in Language and Literature, vol. 11, nos. 1–2. Urbana: University of Illinois Press, 1926.

Holinshed, Raphael. *The Chronicles of England, Scotland, and Ireland*. 3 vols. London, 1587.

Honigmann, E. A. J. "The Politics in *Hamlet* and 'The World of the Play.'" In *Hamlet*, Stratford-upon-Avon Studies, vol. 5, 129–47. New York: St. Martin's, 1964.

Hooke, Henry. *Of the succession to the Crowne of England*. British Library Royal Ms. 17 B XI, fols. 1–19. Dated "Anno regni Elizabethae 43."

———. *Sermon preached before the King at White-hall, the eight of May. 1604*. London, 1604.

Howard, Henry, Earl of Northampton. *A Defensative against the Poyson of Supposed Prophecies*. 1583; reprint, London, 1620.

Howard, Jean E. "The New Historicism in Renaissance Studies." *English Literary Renaissance* 16 (1986): 13–43.

———. *The Stage and Social Struggle in Early Modern England*. London: Routledge, 1994.

Howard, Jean E., and Phyllis Rackin. *Engendering a Nation: A Feminist Account of Shakespeare's English Histories*. London: Routledge, 1997.

Hurault, André, Sieur de Maisse. *De Maisse: A Journal*, trans. and ed. G. B. Harrison and R. A. Jones. London: Nonesuch, 1931.

Hurstfield, Joel. "The Succession Struggle in Late Elizabethan England." In *Elizabethan Government and Society: Essays Presented to Sir John Neale*, ed. S. T. Bindoff, J. Hurstfield, and C. H. Williams, 369–96. London: Athlone, 1961.

Jackson, Gabrielle Bernhard. "Topical Ideology: Witches, Amazons, and Shakespeare's Joan of Arc." *English Literary Renaissance* 18 (1988): 40–65.

James I, King of England. *The Political Works of James I*, ed. C. H. McIlwain. 1918; reprint, New York: Russell and Russell, 1965.

James, Heather. "Milton's Eve, the Romance Genre, and Ovid." *Comparative Literature* 45 (1993): 121–45.

———. *Shakespeare's Troy: Drama, Politics, and the Translation of Empire*. Cambridge: Cambridge University Press, 1997.

Jameson, Fredric. *The Political Unconscious: Narrative as a Socially Symbolic Act*. Ithaca: Cornell University Press, 1981.

Janes, Regina. "Beheadings." *Representations* 35 (Summer 1991): 21–51.

Jankowski, Theodora A. *Women in Power in the Early Modern Drama.* Urbana: University of Illinois Press, 1992.

Jardine, Lisa. *Reading Shakespeare Historically.* London: Routledge, 1996.

Johnson, Paul. *Elizabeth I: A Study in Power and Intellect.* 1974; reprint, London: Futura Publications, 1976.

Johnson, Samuel. *Selections from Johnson on Shakespeare,* ed. Bertrand H. Bronson. New Haven: Yale University Press, 1986.

Jordan, Constance. *Renaissance Feminism: Literary Texts and Political Models.* Ithaca: Cornell University Press, 1990.

———. "Woman's Rule in Sixteenth-Century British Political Thought." *Renaissance Quarterly* 40 (1987): 421–51.

Kahn, Coppélia. *Man's Estate: Masculine Identity in Shakespeare.* Berkeley and Los Angeles: University of California Press, 1981.

———. *Roman Shakespeare: Warriors, Wounds, and Women.* London: Routledge, 1997.

Kantorowicz, Ernst H. *The King's Two Bodies: A Study in Medieval Political Theology.* Princeton: Princeton University Press, 1957.

Kaplan, M. Lindsay. *The Culture of Slander in Early Modern England.* Cambridge: Cambridge University Press, 1997.

———. "Subjection and Subjectivity: Jewish Law and Female Autonomy in Reformation English Marriage." In *Feminist Readings of Early Modern Culture: Emerging Subjects,* ed. Valerie Traub, M. Lindsay Kaplan, and Dympna Callaghan, 229–52. Cambridge: Cambridge University Press, 1996.

Kaplan, M. Lindsay, and Katherine Eggert. "'Good queen, my lord, good queen': Sexual Slander and the Trials of Female Authority in *The Winter's Tale.*" *Renaissance Drama* n.s. 25 (1994): 89–118.

Kastan, David Scott. "'His semblable is his mirror': *Hamlet* and the Imitation of Revenge." *Shakespeare Studies* 19 (1987): 111–24.

———. "Proud Majesty Made a Subject: Shakespeare and the Spectacle of Rule." *Shakespeare Quarterly* 37 (1986): 459–75.

Kegl, Rosemary. *The Rhetoric of Concealment: Figuring Gender and Class in Renaissance Literature.* Ithaca: Cornell University Press, 1994.

Kendrick, Christopher. "Milton and Sexuality: A Symptomatic Reading of *Comus.*" In *Re-membering Milton: Essays on the Texts and Traditions,* ed. Mary Nyquist and Margaret W. Ferguson, 43–73. New York: Methuen, 1987.

Kenyon, J. P. *The Stuart Constitution, 1603–1688: Documents and Commentary.* 1966; reprint, Cambridge: Cambridge University Press, 1969.

Kernan, Alvin. *Shakespeare, the King's Playwright: Theater in the Stuart Court, 1603–1613.* New Haven: Yale University Press, 1995.

King, Henry. *A Sermon of Deliverance. Preached at the Spittle on Easter Monday, 1626.* London, 1626.

King, Laura Severt. "Blessed When They Were Riggish: Shakespeare's Cleopatra and Christianity's Penitent Prostitutes." *Journal of Medieval and Renaissance Studies* 22 (1992): 429–49.

Kinney, Clare Regan. "The Queen's Two Bodies and the Divided Emperor: Some

Problems of Identity in *Antony and Cleopatra.*" In *The Renaissance English-woman in Print: Counterbalancing the Canon*, ed. Anne M. Haselkorn and Betty S. Travitsky, 177–86. Amherst: University of Massachusetts Press, 1990.

———. *Strategies of Poetic Narrative: Chaucer, Spenser, Milton, Eliot.* Cambridge: Cambridge University Press, 1992.

Kishlansky, Mark. *A Monarchy Transformed: Britain 1603–1714.* London: Penguin, 1996.

Klein, Joan Larson, ed. *Daughters, Wives, and Widows: Writings by Men about Women and Marriage in England, 1500–1640.* Urbana: University of Illinois Press, 1992.

Knoppers, Laura Lunger. *Historicizing Milton: Spectacle, Power, and Poetry in Restoration England.* Athens: University of Georgia Press, 1994.

Knox, John. *The Political Writings of John Knox*, ed. Marvin A. Breslow. Washington, D.C.: Folger Shakespeare Library; London: Associated University Presses, 1985.

Kristeva, Julia. *The Kristeva Reader*, ed. Toril Moi. New York: Columbia University Press, 1986.

Labriola, Albert C. "Milton's Eve and the Cult of Elizabeth I." *Journal of English and Germanic Philology* 95 (1996): 38–51.

Lacan, Jacques. "Desire and the Interpretation of Desire in *Hamlet*," trans. James Hulbert. In *Literature and Psychoanalysis: The Question of Reading, Otherwise*, ed. Shoshana Felman, 11–52. Baltimore: Johns Hopkins University Press, 1982.

Langham [or Laneham], Robert. *A Letter*, ed. R. J. P. Kuin. Leiden: E. J. Brill, 1983.

Laqueur, Thomas. *Making Sex: Body and Gender from the Greeks to Freud.* Cambridge, Mass.: Harvard University Press, 1990.

Le Comte, Edward. *Milton and Sex.* New York: Columbia University Press, 1978.

Le Goff, Jacques. *The Birth of Purgatory*, trans. Arthur Goldhammer. Chicago: University of Chicago Press, 1984.

Leverenz, David. "The Woman in Hamlet: An Interpersonal View." In *Representing Shakespeare: New Psychoanalytic Essays*, ed. Murray M. Schwartz and Coppélia Kahn, 110–28. Baltimore: Johns Hopkins University Press, 1980.

Levin, Carole. *The Heart and Stomach of a King: Elizabeth I and the Politics of Sex and Power.* Philadelphia: University of Pennsylvania Press, 1994.

Levine, Laura. *Men in Women's Clothing: Anti-theatricality and Efffeminization, 1579–1642.* Cambridge: Cambridge University Press, 1994.

Levine, Mortimer. *The Early Elizabethan Succession Question, 1558–1568.* Stanford: Stanford University Press, 1966.

———. "The Place of Women in Tudor Government." In *Tudor Rule and Revolution: Essays for G. R. Elton from His American Friends*, ed. DeLloyd J. Guth and John W. McKenna, 109–23. Cambridge: Cambridge University Press, 1982.

Levine, Nina S. *Women's Matters: Politics, Gender, and Nation in Shakespeare's Early History Plays.* Newark: University of Delaware Press; London: Associated University Presses, 1998.

Lewalski, Barbara Kiefer. "Milton: Revaluations of Romance." In *Four Essays on*

Romance, ed. Herschel Baker, 57–70. Cambridge, Mass.: Harvard University Press, 1971.

———. *"Paradise Lost" and the Rhetoric of Literary Forms*. Princeton: Princeton University Press, 1985.

Lieb, Michael. *Milton and the Culture of Violence*. Ithaca: Cornell University Press, 1994.

Loades, David. *The Reign of Mary Tudor: Politics, Government and Religion in England, 1553–58*. 1979; 2d ed. London: Longman, 1981.

Lodge, Thomas. *Wit's Misery*. 1596; reprint, Menston, England: Scolar Press, 1971.

Loewenstein, Joseph. "Plays Agonistic and Competitive: The Textual Approach to Elsinore." *Renaissance Drama* n.s. 19 (1988): 63–96.

Loomba, Ania. *Gender, Race, Renaissance Drama*. 1989; reprint, Delhi: Oxford University Press, 1992.

Lowenthal, David. *The Past Is a Foreign Country*. Cambridge: Cambridge University Press, 1985.

Lupton, Julia Reinhard. *Afterlives of the Saints: Hagiography, Typology, and Renaissance Literature*. Stanford: Stanford University Press, 1996.

Lyly, John. *The Complete Works of John Lyly*, ed. R. Warwick Bond. 3 vols. Oxford: Clarendon, 1902.

MacCaffrey, Wallace T. *Elizabeth I: War and Politics, 1588–1603*. Princeton: Princeton University Press, 1992.

Maley, Willy. *Salvaging Spenser: Colonialism, Culture and Identity*. London: Macmillan, 1996.

———. "Spenser and Ireland: An Annotated Bibliography, 1986–96." *Irish University Review* 26 (1996): 342–53.

Mallarmé, Stéphane. *Oeuvres Complètes*, ed. Henri Mondor and G. Jean-Aubry. Paris: Editions Gallimard, 1945.

Mallin, Eric. *Inscribing the Time: Shakespeare and the End of Elizabethan England*. Berkeley and Los Angeles: University of California Press, 1995.

Marcus, Leah. *Puzzling Shakespeare: Local Reading and Its Discontents*. Berkeley and Los Angeles: University of California Press, 1988.

———. "Shakespeare's Comic Heroines, Elizabeth I, and the Political Uses of Androgyny." In *Women in the Middle Ages and the Renaissance: Literary and Historical Perspectives*, ed. Mary Beth Rose, 135–53. Syracuse, N.Y.: Syracuse University Press, 1986.

———. *Unediting the Renaissance: Shakespeare, Marlowe, Milton*. London: Routledge, 1996.

Marlowe, Christopher. *Tamburlaine*, ed. J. W. Harper. New York: W. W. Norton, 1984.

Marshall, Cynthia. "Man of Steel Done Got the Blues: Melancholic Subversion of Presence in *Antony and Cleopatra*." *Shakespeare Quarterly* 44 (1993): 385–408.

Marshall, Stephen. *A Sermon Preached before the Honourable House of Commons . . . November 17. 1640*. London, 1641.

Marston, John. *Antonio and Mellida*, ed. W. Reavley Gair. Manchester: Manchester University Press, 1991.

———. *Antonio's Revenge*, ed. W. Reavley Gair. Manchester: Manchester University Press, 1978.

———. *The Malcontent*, ed. Bernard Harris. London: A & C Black, 1967.

Marvell, Andrew. *The Poems and Letters of Andrew Marvell*. Ed. H. M. Margoliouth, rev. ed. Pierre Legouis. 3d ed. Oxford: Clarendon, 1971.

Maus, Katharine Eisaman. "Horns of Dilemma: Jealousy, Gender, and Spectatorship in English Renaissance Drama." *ELH* 54 (1987): 561–83.

———. *Inwardness and Theater in the English Renaissance*. Chicago: University of Chicago Press, 1995.

McCabe, Richard. "The Masks of Duessa: Spenser, Mary Queen of Scots, and James VI." *English Literary Renaissance* 17 (1987): 224–42.

McColley, Diane Kelsey. *A Gust for Paradise: Milton's Eden and the Visual Arts*. Urbana: University of Illinois Press, 1993.

———. *Milton's Eve*. Urbana: University of Illinois Press, 1983.

———. "Subsequent or Precedent? Eve as Milton's Defense of Poesie." *Milton Quarterly* 20 (1986): 132–36.

McCullough, Peter E. "Out of Egypt: Richard Fletcher's Sermon Before Elizabeth I After the Execution of Mary Queen of Scots." In *Dissing Elizabeth: Negative Representations of Gloriana*, ed. Julia M. Walker, 118–52. Durham: Duke University Press, 1998.

McEachern, Claire. *The Poetics of English Nationhood, 1590–1612*. Cambridge: Cambridge University Press, 1996.

McGrath, Patrick. *Papists and Puritans under Elizabeth I*. New York: Walker, 1967.

McIlwain, C. H. *The High Court of Parliament and Its Supremacy: An Historical Essay on the Boundaries Between Legislation and Adjudication in England*. 1910; rev. ed. New Haven: Yale University Press, 1934.

Melville, James. *Memoirs of Sir James Melville of Halhill, 1535–1617*, ed. A. Francis Steuart. London: George Routledge, 1929.

Mikalachki, Jodi. *The Legacy of Boadicea: Gender and Nation in Early Modern England*. London: Routledge, 1998.

Miller, David Lee. *The Poem's Two Bodies: The Poetics of the 1590 "Faerie Queene."* Princeton: Princeton University Press, 1988.

Milton, John. *Complete Poems and Major Prose*, ed. Merritt Y. Hughes. New York: Odyssey, 1957.

———. *Complete Prose Works of John Milton*, ed. Don M. Wolfe. 8 vols. New Haven: Yale University Press, 1953–82.

Mohl, Ruth. *John Milton and His Commonplace Book*. New York: Frederick Ungar, 1969.

Montrose, Louis Adrian. "'Eliza, Queene of shepheardes,' and the Pastoral of Power." *English Literary Renaissance* 10 (1980): 153–82.

———. "The Elizabethan Subject and the Spenserian Text." In *Literary Theory/Renaissance Texts*, ed. Patricia Parker and David Quint, 303–40. Baltimore: Johns Hopkins University Press, 1986.

———. "*A Midsummer Night's Dream* and the Shaping Fantasies of Elizabethan Culture: Gender, Power, Form." In *Rewriting the Renaissance: The Discourses of Sexual Difference in Early Modern Europe*, ed. Margaret W. Ferguson, Maureen

Quilligan, and Nancy J. Vickers, 65–87. Chicago: University of Chicago Press, 1986.

———. *The Purpose of Playing: Shakespeare and the Cultural Politics of the Elizabethan Theatre*. Chicago: University of Chicago Press, 1996.

———. "'Shaping Fantasies': Figurations of Gender and Power in Elizabethan Culture." *Representations* 2 (Spring 1983): 61–94.

Morris, Helen. "Queen Elizabeth I 'Shadowed' in Cleopatra." *Huntington Library Quarterly* 32 (1969): 271–78.

Mowat, Barbara. "The Form of *Hamlet*'s Fortunes." *Renaissance Drama* n. s. 19 (1988): 97–126.

Mullaney, Steven. "After the New Historicism." In *Alternative Shakespeares Volume 2*, ed. Terence Hawkes, 17–37. London: Routledge, 1996.

———. "Mourning and Misogyny: *Hamlet, The Revenger's Tragedy*, and the Final Progress of Elizabeth, 1600–1607." In *Centuries' Ends, Narrative Means*, ed. Robert Newman, 238–60. Stanford: Stanford University Press, 1996.

———. *The Place of the Stage: License, Play, and Power in Renaissance England*. Chicago: University of Chicago Press, 1988.

———. "Strange Things, Gross Terms, Curious Customs: The Rehearsal of Cultures in the Late Renaissance." *Representations* 3 (Summer 1983): 40–67.

Munday, Anthony. *A Second and Third Blast of Retrait from Plaies and Theaters*. London, 1580.

Nashe, Thomas. *The Works of Thomas Nashe*, ed. Ronald B. McKerrow, rev. ed. F. P. Wilson. 5 vols. Oxford: Basil Blackwell, 1958.

Neale, J. E. *Elizabeth I and Her Parliaments, 1559–1581*. New York: Jonathan Cape, 1952.

———. *Elizabeth I and Her Parliaments, 1584–1601*. New York: St. Martin's, 1957.

———. *Queen Elizabeth I*. 1934; reprint, New York: Doubleday, 1960.

Newman, Karen. *Fashioning Femininity and Renaissance Drama*. Chicago: University of Chicago Press, 1991.

Nichols, John. *The Progresses and Public Processions of Queen Elizabeth*. 3 vols. London: J. Nichols, 1823.

Nietzsche, Friedrich. *The Gay Science: With a Prelude in Rhymes and an Appendix of Songs*, trans. Walter Kaufmann. New York: Random House, 1974.

Nohrnberg, James. *The Analogy of "The Faerie Queene."* Princeton: Princeton University Press, 1976.

Noling, Kim H. "Grubbing Up the Stock: Dramatizing Queens in *Henry VIII*." *Shakespeare Quarterly* 39 (1988): 291–306.

Norbrook, David. "The Emperor's New Body? *Richard II*, Ernst Kantorowicz, and the Politics of Shakespeare Criticism." *Textual Practice* 10 (1996): 329–57.

———. *Poetry and Politics in the English Renaissance*. London: Routledge and Kegan Paul, 1984.

Norman, Edward. *Roman Catholicism in England from the Elizabethan Settlement to the Second Vatican Council*. Oxford: Oxford University Press, 1985.

North, Sir Thomas. *Plutarch's Lives of the Noble Grecians and Romans*. 6 vols. 1895; reprint, New York: AMS, 1967.

Nyquist, Mary. "The Genesis of Gendered Subjectivity in the Divorce Tracts and in

Paradise Lost." In *Re-membering Milton: Essays on the Texts and Traditions*, ed. Mary Nyquist and Margaret W. Ferguson, 99–127. New York: Methuen, 1987.

O'Connell, Michael. *Mirror and Veil: The Historical Dimension of Spenser's "Faerie Queene."* Chapel Hill: University of North Carolina Press, 1977.

Orgel, Stephen. "Gendering the Crown." In *Subject and Object in Renaissance Culture*, ed. Margreta de Grazia, Maureen Quilligan, and Peter Stallybrass, 133–65. Cambridge: Cambridge University Press, 1996.

———. *The Illusion of Power: Political Theater in the English Renaissance.* Berkeley and Los Angeles: University of California Press, 1975.

———. *Impersonations: The Performance of Gender in Shakespeare's England.* Cambridge: Cambridge University Press, 1996.

Ornstein, Robert. *A Kingdom for a Stage: The Achievement of Shakespeare's History Plays.* Cambridge, Mass.: Harvard University Press, 1972.

Parker, Patricia. *Inescapable Romance: Studies in the Poetics of a Mode.* Princeton: Princeton University Press, 1979.

———. *Literary Fat Ladies: Rhetoric, Gender, Property.* London: Methuen, 1987.

———. *Shakespeare from the Margins: Language, Culture, Context.* Chicago: University of Chicago Press, 1996.

Parsons, Robert [R. Doleman, pseud.]. *A Conference about the Next Succession to the Crowne of Ingland.* 1594; reprint, Menston, England: Scolar Press, 1972.

Paster, Gail Kern. *The Body Embarrassed: Drama and the Disciplines of Shame in Early Modern England.* Ithaca: Cornell University Press, 1993.

Patterson, Annabel. *Censorship and Interpretation: The Conditions of Writing and Reading in Early Modern England.* Madison: University of Wisconsin Press, 1984.

———. *"Paradise Regained*: A Last Chance at True Romance." *Milton Studies* 17 (1983): 187–208.

Peacham, Henry. *Minerva Britanna.* 1612; reprint, Leeds, England: Scolar Press, 1966.

Perry, Curtis. "The Citizen Politics of Nostalgia: Queen Elizabeth in Early Jacobean London." *Journal of Medieval and Renaissance Studies* 23 (1993): 89–111.

Phillips, James E. "The Background of Spenser's Attitude Toward Women Rulers." *Huntington Library Quarterly* 5 (1941–42): 5–32.

———. *Images of a Queen: Mary Stuart in Sixteenth-Century Literature.* Berkeley and Los Angeles: University of California Press, 1964.

———. "The Woman Ruler in Spenser's *Faerie Queene." Huntington Library Quarterly* 5 (1941–42): 211–34.

Plowden, Edmund. *The Commentaries, or Reports of Edmund Plowden.* London, 1816.

Plutarch. *Plutarch's Moralia*, trans. Frank Cole Babbitt. 16 vols. London: William Heinemann; Cambridge, Mass.: Harvard University Press, 1957.

Pont, Robert. *A Newe Treatise of the Right Reckoning of Yeares, and Ages of the World, and mens lives, and of the estate of the last decaying age thereof, this 1600 yeare of Christ.* Edinburgh, 1599.

Porta, John Baptista. *Natural Magick.* 1658; reprint, ed. Derek J. Price. New York: Basic Books, 1957.

Porter, Carolyn. "Are We Being Historical Yet?" *South Atlantic Quarterly* 87 (1988): 743–86.

———. "History and Literature: 'After the New Historicism.'" *New Literary History* 21 (1989–90): 253–72.

Prosser, Eleanor. *Hamlet and Revenge.* 1967; 2d ed. Stanford: Stanford University Press, 1971.

Prynne, William. *Histrio-Mastix. The Players Scourge or, Actors Tragedie.* London, 1633.

Pye, Christopher. *The Regal Phantasm: Shakespeare and the Politics of Spectacle.* London: Routledge, 1990.

Quilligan, Maureen. "The Comedy of Female Authority in *The Faerie Queene.*" *English Literary Renaissance* 17 (1987): 156–71.

———. *The Language of Allegory: Defining the Genre.* Ithaca: Cornell University Press, 1979.

———. *Milton's Spenser: The Politics of Reading.* Ithaca: Cornell University Press, 1983.

Quint, David. *Epic and Empire: Politics and Generic Form from Virgil to Milton.* Princeton: Princeton University Press, 1993.

Rabkin, Norman. *Shakespeare and the Problem of Meaning.* Chicago: University of Chicago Press, 1981.

Rackin, Phyllis. *Stages of History: Shakespeare's English Chronicles.* Ithaca: Cornell University Press, 1990.

Radzinowicz, Mary Ann. "The Politics of *Paradise Lost.*" In *Politics of Discourse: The Literature and History of Seventeenth-Century England,* ed. Kevin Sharpe and Steven N. Zwicker, 204–29. Berkeley and Los Angeles: University of California Press, 1987.

The Raigne of King Edward the Third: A Critical, Old-Spelling Edition, ed. Fred Lapides. New York: Garland, 1980.

Rainolds, John. *Th' Overthrow of Stage-Plays.* Middleburg, 1599.

Rambuss, Richard. "Pleasure and Devotion: The Body of Jesus and Seventeenth-Century Religious Lyric." In *Queering the Renaissance,* ed. Jonathan Goldberg, 253–79. Durham: Duke University Press, 1994.

———. *Spenser's Secret Career.* Cambridge: Cambridge University Press, 1993.

Reibetanz, J. "Hieronimo in Decimosexto: A Private-Theater Burlesque." *Renaissance Drama* n.s. 5 (1972): 89–121.

Rinehart, Keith. "Shakespeare's Cleopatra and England's Elizabeth." *Shakespeare Quarterly* 23 (1972): 81–86.

Rogers, John. "The Enclosure of Virginity: The Poetics of Sexual Abstinence in the English Revolution." In *Enclosure Acts: Sexuality, Property, and Culture in Early Modern England,* ed. Richard Burt and John Michael Archer, 229–50. Ithaca: Cornell University Press, 1994.

Rosaldo, Renato. *Culture and Truth: The Remaking of Social Analysis.* Boston: Beacon Press, 1989.

Rose, Jacqueline. "Hamlet—the *Mona Lisa* of Literature." In *Shakespeare and Gender: A History,* ed. Deborah E. Barker and Ivo Kamps, 104–19. London: Verso, 1995.

———. "Sexuality in the Reading of Shakespeare: *Hamlet* and *Measure for Measure.*" In *Alternative Shakespeares*, ed. John Drakakis, 95–118. London: Methuen, 1985.

Rose, Mark. "*Hamlet* and the Shape of Revenge." In *Shakespeare's Middle Tragedies: A Collection of Critical Essays*, ed. David Young, 7–17. Englewood Cliffs, N.J.: Prentice-Hall, 1993.

Rumrich, John P. *Milton Unbound: Controversy and Reinterpretation.* Cambridge: Cambridge University Press, 1996.

Sams, Eric. "Taboo or Not Taboo? The Text, Dating, and Authorship of *Hamlet*, 1589–1623." *Hamlet Studies* 10 (1988): 12–46.

Scalingi, Paula. "The Scepter or the Distaff: The Question of Female Sovereignty, 1516–1607." *Historian* 41 (1978): 59–75.

Schalkwyk, David. " 'A Lady's "Verily" Is as Potent as a Lord's': Women, Word and Witchcraft in *The Winter's Tale.*" *English Literary Renaissance* 22 (1992): 242–72.

Schleiner, Winfried. "*Divina Virago*: Queen Elizabeth as an Amazon." *Studies in Philology* 75 (1978): 163–80.

Schoenfeldt, Michael. "Gender and Conduct in *Paradise Lost.*" In *Sexuality and Gender in Early Modern Europe: Institutions, Texts, Images*, ed. James Grantham Turner, 310–38. Cambridge: Cambridge University Press, 1993.

Schwartz, Regina M. *Remembering and Repeating: On Milton's Theology and Poetics.* 1988; rev. ed. Chicago: University of Chicago Press, 1993.

Shakespeare, William. *Antony and Cleopatra*, ed. G. L. Kittredge, rev. ed. Irving Ribner. 1941; rev. ed. New York: John Wiley, 1966.

———. *Antony and Cleopatra*, ed. M. R. Ridley (New Arden edition). London: Methuen, 1954.

———. *Antony and Cleopatra*, ed. John Wilders (Third Arden edition). London: Routledge, 1995.

———. *Cymbeline*, ed. J. M. Nosworthy (New Arden edition). London: Methuen, 1955.

———. *Hamlet*, ed. Philip Edwards (New Cambridge edition). New York: Cambridge University Press, 1985.

———. *Hamlet*, ed. G. R. Hibbard. Oxford: The Clarendon Press, 1987.

———. *Hamlet*, ed. Harold Jenkins (New Arden edition). London: Methuen, 1982.

———. *Henry V*, ed. Gary Taylor. Oxford: Clarendon Press, 1982.

———. *King Henry IV Part 1*, ed. A. R. Humphreys (New Arden edition). London: Methuen, 1960.

———. *King Henry IV Part 2*, ed. A. R. Humphreys (New Arden edition). London: Methuen, 1966.

———. *King Henry V*, ed. J. H. Walter (New Arden edition). London: Methuen, 1954.

———. *King Henry VI Part 1*, ed. Andrew S. Cairncross (New Arden edition). London: Methuen, 1962.

———. *King Henry VI Part 2*, ed. Andrew S. Cairncross (New Arden edition). London: Methuen, 1957.

———. *King Henry VI Part 3*, ed. Andrew S. Cairncross (New Arden edition). London: Methuen, 1964.

———. *King Henry VIII*, ed. R. A. Foakes (New Arden edition). London: Methuen, 1957.

———. *King Richard III*, ed. Antony Hammond (New Arden edition). London: Methuen, 1981.

———. *A Midsummer Night's Dream*, ed. Harold F. Brooks (New Arden edition). London: Methuen, 1979.

———. *Romeo and Juliet*, ed. Brian Gibbons (New Arden edition). London: Methuen, 1980.

———. *The Taming of the Shrew*, ed. Brian Morris (New Arden edition). London: Methuen, 1981.

———. *Troilus and Cressida*, ed. Kenneth Palmer (New Arden edition). London: Methuen, 1982.

———. *The Winter's Tale*, ed. J. H. P. Pafford (New Arden edition). London: Methuen, 1963.

Shawcross, John T. "The Metaphor of Inspiration in *Paradise Lost.*" In *Th' Upright Heart and Pure: Essays on John Milton Commemorating the Tercentenary of the Publication of "Paradise Lost,"* ed. Amadeus P. Fiore, 75–85. Pittsburgh: Duquesne University Press, 1967.

Shuger, Debora Keller. *The Renaissance Bible: Scholarship, Sacrifice, and Subjectivity*. Berkeley and Los Angeles: University of California Press, 1994.

Sidney, Philip. *Miscellaneous Prose of Sir Philip Sidney*, ed. Katherine Duncan-Jones and Jan van Dorsten. Oxford: Clarendon, 1973.

Silber, Patricia. "The Unnatural Woman and the Disordered State in Shakespeare's Histories." *Proceedings of the PMR Conference* 2 (1977): 87–96.

Silberman, Lauren. "Singing Unsung Heroines: Androgynous Discourse in Book 3 of *The Faerie Queene.*" In *Rewriting the Renaissance: The Discourses of Sexual Difference in Early Modern Europe*, ed. Margaret W. Ferguson, Maureen Quilligan, and Nancy J. Vickers, 259–71. Chicago: University of Chicago Press, 1986.

———. *Transforming Desire: Erotic Knowledge in Books III and IV of "The Faerie Queene."* Berkeley and Los Angeles: University of California Press, 1995.

Singh, Jyotsna. "Renaissance Antitheatricality, Antifeminism, and Shakespeare's *Antony and Cleopatra.*" *Renaissance Drama* 20 (1989): 99–121.

Smith, Alan G. R., ed. *The Last Years of Mary, Queen of Scots: Documents from the Cecil Papers at Hatfield House*. London: The Roxburghe Club, 1990.

Spenser, Edmund. *The Faerie Queene*, ed. A. C. Hamilton. London: Longman, 1977.

Sprengnether, Madelon. "The Boy Actor and Femininity in *Antony and Cleopatra.*" In *Shakespeare's Personality*, ed. Norman N. Holland, Sidney Homan, and Bernard J. Paris, 191–205. Berkeley and Los Angeles: University of California Press, 1989.

Spring, Eileen. *Law, Land, and Family: Aristocratic Inheritance in England, 1300 to 1800*. Chapel Hill: University of North Carolina Press, 1993.

Stabler, A. P. "Elective Monarchy in the Sources of *Hamlet*." *Studies in Philology* 62 (1965): 654–61.

Stallybrass, Peter. "Patriarchal Territories: The Body Enclosed." In *Rewriting the Renaissance: The Discourses of Sexual Difference in Early Modern Europe*, ed. Margaret W. Ferguson, Maureen Quilligan, and Nancy J. Vickers, 123–42. Chicago: University of Chicago Press, 1986.

Stanley, Arthur Penrhyn. *Historical Memorials of Westminster Abbey*. 6th ed. London: John Murray, 1886.

Staves, Susan. *Married Women's Separate Property in England, 1660–1833*. Cambridge, Mass.: Harvard University Press, 1990.

Stephens, Dorothy. "Into Other Arms: Amoret's Evasion." In *Queering the Renaissance*, ed. Jonathan Goldberg, 190–217. Durham: Duke University Press, 1994.

———. " 'Newes of devils': Feminine Sprights in Masculine Minds in *The Faerie Queene*." *English Literary Renaissance* 23 (1993): 363–81.

Steuart, A. Francis. *Trial of Mary, Queen of Scots*. Edinburgh: W. Hodge, 1923.

Stillman, Robert E. "Spenserian Autonomy and the Trial of New Historicism: Book Six of *The Faerie Queene*." *English Literary Renaissance* 22 (1992): 299–314.

Strong, Roy. *The Cult of Elizabeth: Elizabethan Portraiture and Pageantry*. Berkeley and Los Angeles: University of California Press, 1977.

———. *Gloriana: The Portraits of Queen Elizabeth I*. London: Thames and Hudson, 1987.

———. *Henry Prince of Wales and England's Lost Renaissance*. London: Thames and Hudson, 1986.

Strype, John. *Annals of the Reformation and Establishment of Religion*. 4 vols. 1724–25; reprint, Oxford: Clarendon, 1824.

Stump, Donald V. "The Two Deaths of Mary Stuart: Historical Allegory in Spenser's Book of Justice." *Spenser Studies* 9 (1988): 81–105.

Suzuki, Mihoko. *Metamorphoses of Helen: Authority, Difference, and the Epic*. Ithaca: Cornell University Press, 1989.

Tennenhouse, Leonard. *Power on Display: The Politics of Shakespeare's Genres*. New York: Methuen, 1986.

Teskey, Gordon. *Allegory and Violence*. Ithaca: Cornell University Press, 1996.

———. "From Allegory to Dialectic: Imagining Error in Spenser and Milton." *PMLA* 101 (1986): 9–23.

Thomas, Keith. *Religion and the Decline of Magic: Studies in Popular Beliefs in Sixteenth and Seventeenth Century England*. London: Weidenfeld and Nicolson, 1971.

The Tragicall Historie of Hamlet. 1603; reprint, Menston, England: Scolar Press, 1969.

Traub, Valerie. *Desire and Anxiety: Circulations of Sexuality in Shakespearean Drama*. London: Routledge, 1992.

Trevelyan, G. M. *England Under the Stuarts*. 1904; reprint, London: Methuen, 1965.

Trevor-Roper, H. R. *The Crisis of the Seventeenth Century: Religion, the Reformation, and Social Change*. New York: Harper and Row, 1967.

Turner, James Grantham. *One Flesh: Paradisal Marriage and Sexual Relations in the Age of Milton*. Oxford: Clarendon, 1987.

Tylus, Jane. *Writing and Vulnerability in the Late Renaissance*. Stanford: Stanford University Press, 1993.

Underdown, David. "The Taming of the Scold: The Enforcement of Patriarchal Authority in Early Modern England." In *Order and Disorder in Early Modern England*, ed. Anthony Fletcher and John Stevenson, 116–36. Cambridge: Cambridge University Press, 1985.

Urkowitz, Steven. "Back to Basics: Thinking about the *Hamlet* First Quarto." In *The Hamlet First Published (Q1, 1603): Origins, Form, Intertextualities*, ed. Thomas Clayton, 257–91. Newark: University of Delaware Press, 1992.

———. "Good News about 'Bad' Quartos." In *"Bad" Shakespeare: Revaluations of the Shakespearean Canon*, ed. Maurice Charney, 189–206. Rutherford, N.J.: Fairleigh Dickinson University Press, 1988.

———. "'Well-sayd olde Mole': Burying Three *Hamlets* in Modern Editions." In *Shakespeare Study Today: The Horace Howard Furness Memorial Lectures*, ed. Georgianna Ziegler, 37–70. New York: AMS Press, 1986.

Van Laan, Thomas F. *Role-Playing in Shakespeare*. Toronto: University of Toronto Press, 1978.

Vickers, Nancy. "'The blazon of sweet beauty's best': Shakespeare's *Lucrece*." In *Shakespeare and the Question of Theory*, ed. Patricia Parker and Geoffrey Hartman, 95–115. New York: Methuen, 1985.

Villeponteaux, Mary. "'Not as women wonted be': Spenser's Amazon Queen." In *Dissing Elizabeth: Negative Representations of Gloriana*, ed. Julia M. Walker, 209–25. Durham: Duke University Press, 1998.

von Maltzahn, Nicholas. *Milton's "History of Britain": Republican Historiography in the English Revolution*. Oxford: Clarendon, 1991.

von Raumer, Friedrich. *History of the Sixteenth and Seventeenth Centuries, Illustrated by Original Documents*. 2 vols. London: J. Murray, 1835.

Walker, Julia M. "Bones of Contention: Posthumous Images of Elizabeth and Stuart Politics." In *Dissing Elizabeth: Negative Representations of Gloriana*, ed. Julia M. Walker, 252–76. Durham: Duke University Press, 1998.

———. *Medusa's Mirrors: Spenser, Shakespeare, Milton, and the Metamorphosis of the Female Self*. Newark: University of Delaware Press; London: Associated University Presses, 1998.

———. "Reading the Tombs of Elizabeth I." *English Literary Renaissance* 26 (1996): 510–30.

Wall, Wendy. *The Imprint of Gender: Authorship and Publication in the English Renaissance*. Ithaca: Cornell University Press, 1993.

Waller, Marguerite. "Usurpation, Seduction, and the Problematics of the Proper: A 'Deconstructive,' 'Feminist' Rereading of the Seductions of Richard and Anne in Shakespeare's *Richard III*." In *Rewriting the Renaissance: The Discourses of Sexual Difference in Early Modern Europe*, ed. Margaret W. Ferguson, Maureen Quilligan, and Nancy J. Vickers, 159–74. Chicago: University of Chicago Press, 1986.

Ward, David. "The King and *Hamlet.*" *Shakespeare Quarterly* 43 (1992): 280–302.

Watkins, John. *The Specter of Dido: Spenser and Virgilian Epic.* New Haven: Yale University Press, 1995.

Weimann, Robert. "Bifold Authority in Shakespeare's Theatre." *Shakespeare Quarterly* 39 (1988): 401–17.

———. "Mimesis in *Hamlet.*" In *Shakespeare and the Question of Theory*, ed. Patricia Parker and Geoffrey Hartman, 275–91. New York: Methuen, 1985.

Wells, Stanley, and Gary Taylor. *William Shakespeare: A Textual Companion.* 1987; reprint, New York: W.W. Norton, 1997.

Wentersdorf, Karl P. "The Conspiracy of Silence in *Henry V.*" *Shakespeare Quarterly* 27 (1976): 264–87.

Wentworth, Peter. *A Pithie exhortation to her majestie for establishing her successor to the crowne.* Edinburgh, 1598.

Wernham, R. B. *The Making of Elizabethan Foreign Policy, 1558–1603.* Berkeley and Los Angeles: University of California Press, 1980.

Werstine, Paul. "The Textual Mystery of *Hamlet.*" *Shakespeare Quarterly* 39 (1988): 1–26.

Wilcox, Lance. "Katherine of France as Victim and Bride." *Shakespeare Studies* 17 (1985): 61–76.

Willbern, David. "Shakespeare's Nothing." In *Representing Shakespeare: New Psychoanalytic Essays*, ed. Murray M. Schwartz and Coppélia Kahn, 255–56. Baltimore: Johns Hopkins University Press, 1980.

Williamson, Marilyn. "The Courtship of Katherine and the Second Tetralogy." *Criticism* 17 (1975): 326–34.

Willson, David Harris. *King James VI and I.* New York: Henry Holt, 1956.

Wilson, E. C. *England's Eliza.* 1939; reprint, New York: Octagon Books, 1966.

Wilson, J. Dover. *What Happens in "Hamlet."* 1935; 3d ed. Cambridge: Cambridge University Press, 1951.

Wilson, Thomas. *The State of England, Anno Dom. 1600*, ed. F. J. Fisher. Camden Miscellany, 3d series, vol. 52, no. 1, 1–43. London: Camden Society, 1936.

Winstanley, Lilian. *Hamlet and the Scottish Succession: Being an Examination of the Relations of the Play of "Hamlet" to the Scottish Succession and the Essex Conspiracy.* Cambridge: Cambridge University Press, 1921.

Wodrow, Robert. *Analecta, or Materials for a History of Remarkable Providences Mostly Relating to Scotch Ministers and Christians*, ed. Matthew Leishman. Maitland Club Series, no. 60. 4 vols. Edinburgh: Maitland Club, 1842–43.

Wofford, Susanne Lindgren. *The Choice of Achilles: The Ideology of Figure in the Epic.* Stanford: Stanford University Press, 1992.

Woodbridge, Linda. *Women and the English Renaissance: Literature and the Nature of Womankind, 1540–1620.* Urbana: University of Illinois Press, 1984.

Woods, Susanne. "Amazonian Tyranny: Spenser's Radigund and Diachronic Mimesis." In *Playing with Gender: A Renaissance Pursuit*, ed. Jean R. Brink, Maryanne C. Horowitz, and Allison P. Coudert, 52–61. Urbana: University of Illinois Press, 1991.

———. "Elective Poetics and Milton's Prose: *A Treatise of Civil Power* and *Considerations Touching the Likeliest Means to Remove Hirelings out of the Church.*" In

Politics, Poetics, and Hermeneutics in Milton's Prose, ed. David Loewenstein and James Grantham Turner, 193–212. Cambridge: Cambridge University Press, 1990.

———. "How Free Are Milton's Women?" In *Milton and the Idea of Woman*, ed. Julia M. Walker, 15–31. Urbana: University of Illinois Press, 1988.

———. "Spenser and the Problem of Women's Rule." *Huntington Library Quarterly* 48 (1985): 141–58.

Woolf, D. R. "Two Elizabeths? James I and the Late Queen's Famous Memory." *Canadian Journal of History* 20 (1985): 167–91.

Wormold, Jenny. *Mary Queen of Scots: A Study in Failure*. London: Collins and Brown, 1991.

Yates, Frances. *Majesty and Magic in Shakespeare's Last Plays: A New Approach to "Cymbeline," "Henry VIII," and "The Tempest."* Boulder, Colo.: Shambala Publications, 1975.

Ziegler, Georgianna. "England's Savior: Elizabeth I in the Writings of Thomas Heywood." *Renaissance Papers* (1980): 29–37.

Acknowledgments

Many colleagues, family members, and friends have helped me during the long process of writing this book, and it gives me great pleasure to acknowledge my debts to them here. I began to think about femininity in Renaissance art and literature in classes taught at Rice University by Edward Snow, who guided my first tentative explorations of Shakespeare and of Milton. He remains my model for how to read poetry, and I hope he will find something to like in this book. My ideas about queenship in Renaissance literature began to take shape under the guidance of Stephen Greenblatt and Janet Adelman, the best of readers and mentors. Along with my other teachers at Berkeley, Paul Alpers and Harry Berger, Jr., they are still —both in fact, and in my head—the audience for whom I write, and I am grateful for their ongoing help with my work. The astute advice of others at Berkeley, especially Oliver Arnold, Richmond Barbour, Teresa Faherty, Robert Henke, Dorothy Leman, Louis Montrose, Brian Myers, Randolph Starn, and Dorothy Stephens, has also made its way into the book. I owe special gratitude to the encouragement and critical acumen of Lindsay Kaplan, who has read more drafts of my work than anyone should have to, and of Sheridan Hough, who always helps me see the larger picture.

I have enjoyed and profited from the extraordinary combination of brilliance and kindness offered by friends and colleagues at the University of Colorado at Boulder, especially Richard Halpern, whose comments on several chapters were immeasurably helpful, and Charlotte Sussman and R L Widmann, who came to my aid on specific research questions. Special thanks go to Elizabeth Robertson and John Allen Stevenson, who both were instrumental to my getting this book into print. My graduate students at Colorado have listened to and improved the ideas in this book. Audiences at conferences where I presented portions of this work in progress—meetings of the Shakespeare Association of America, the Renaissance Society of America, the Modern Language Association, and the Washington, D.C., Colloquium for the Study of Women in the Renaissance—challenged and supplemented my arguments; comments from Richard Helgerson, Jeffrey Knapp, Phyllis Rackin, Valerie Traub, and

Susanne Wofford, in particular, helped me clarify my thinking. The members of the Folger Shakespeare Library seminar on "Shakespeare and the Arts of Memory," led by Stephen Greenblatt, gave me new ways to approach the material in Chapter 4. An anonymous reader for the University of Pennsylvania Press provided wonderful suggestions for revisions, particularly of Chapter 1. Sheila ffolliott and Rhonda Garelick helped me communicate with the Louvre Museum to acquire permission to reproduce the Rubens painting on the book's cover. Most of all, this book would not have seen the light of day without the advice and support of two people: Margaret Ferguson, who surely, and deservedly, must be the most-thanked scholar in Renaissance studies; and Jerry Singerman, Humanities Editor at the University of Pennsylvania Press, whose enthusiasm for the project encouraged me to complete it in good time.

Grants from the Folger Shakespeare Library and from the University of Colorado's Council on Research and Creative Work and Graduate Committee on the Arts and Humanities enabled me to undertake archival research; a grant from the National Endowment for the Humanities provided an uninterrupted year of writing. I am grateful to these institutions, as well as to those who wrote letters in support of my grant applications.

An earlier version of the second half of Chapter 3 appeared as "Nostalgia and the Not Yet Late Queen: Refusing Female Rule in *Henry V*," *ELH* 61 (1994): 523–50; and an earlier version of Chapter 2 appeared as "'Changing all that forme of common weale': Genre and the Repeal of Queenship in *The Faerie Queene*, Book 5," *English Literary Renaissance* 26 (1996): 259–90. My thanks to these journals and their presses for permission to reuse this material here.

I owe a lifetime's debt to my parents, Richard and Elizabeth Eggert, whose love of learning and unstinting support have always given me equal parts inspiration and comfort. For the gift of literature I am especially grateful to my mother, who even in her last weeks of life was looking for a good book to read, and to whom this book is dedicated. To me, she will always be Elizabeth the First.

No dedication could express what I owe to Mark Winokur, whose agile mind and brilliant critical insight improved every page of this book, and whose generosity, good humor, and confidence helped me both to begin and to finish it.

Index